Education and Psychology of the Gifted Series

JAMES H. BORLAND, EDITOR

Rethinking Gifted Education

Edited by

JAMES H. BORLAND

Teachers College
Columbia University
New York and London

Published by Teachers College Press, 1234 Amsterdam Avenue, New York, NY 10027

Library of Congress Cataloging-in-Publication Data

Rethinking gifted education / edited by James H. Borland.
     p. cm. — (Education and psychology of the gifted series)
   Includes bibliographical references and index.
   ISBN 0-8077-4304-6 (cloth : alk. paper)
    1. Gifted children—Education.   I. Borland, James H.   II. Series.
  LC3993.R48   2003
  371.95—dc21   2002042987

ISBN 0-8077-4304-6 (cloth)

Printed on acid-free paper

Manufactured in the United States of America

10 09 08 07 06 05 04 03   8 7 6 5 4 3 2 1

For Max and Nina

Contents

Acknowledgments

Many people were responsible for the production of this book. I will attempt to thank them here, with apologies to anyone inadvertently left out or embarrassed by association with this volume.

Dawn Horton is, at the time I am writing this, a doctoral candidate in the Program in the Education of Gifted Students in the Department of Curriculum and Teaching at Teachers College, my co-instructor in some of my courses, and the one person above all who helped me put this collection together. She handled much of the correspondence with the authors, coordinated the submission of manuscripts, and read each submission with a keen eye, impressive breadth of knowledge, and analytical intelligence. She kept after me when I put the book on the back burner. I only hope that when she is in a similar position in her academic career she has someone half as dependable, resourceful, and scholarly on whom she can rely, although I doubt she will need someone else's assistance as much as I needed hers.

Helen Krasnow assisted me in the initial stages of this enterprise, and her energy and good humor, as well as her suggestions as to whom I should approach to ask for manuscripts, are much appreciated.

Lisa Wright continues to be a wonderful friend and valuable colleague at Teachers College. Our work as co-directors of Project Synergy informed much of what I write these days, and our continued work together with schools and other educational agencies is an important source of growth and learning.

Numerous colleagues and students at Teachers College encouraged the production of this book and read and commented on my chapter. John Broughton, Bahar Eris, Cathy Freeman, and Juliana Lasta-Irasarri did the latter, and their comments were perceptive and helpful. I also want to thank the students in the Department of Curriculum and Teaching at Teachers College, Columbia University, who attended the department's "Chat and Chill" seminar, at which I presented a paper based on my chapter, for their percipient comments and their ability to maintain the appearance of consciousness as I spoke.

Brian Ellerbeck and Carole Saltz at Teachers College Press have been patient with and encouraging to me for quite a while, which is how long it takes me to deliver a manuscript. They are savvy professionals, perceptive critics, and good people, and it is a pleasure to be associated with them.

This book is dedicated to my son, Max, and my daughter, Nina, whom I love beyond my power to express. I hope this and a few other things I do make them proud.

Introduction

A great deal has changed in, and in relation to, the field of gifted education since 1989, when the first book in this series was published. True, there has been no single watershed event, no *Genetic Studies of Genius*, no Sputnik, no Marland Report. However, there has been a series of events and movements, primarily outside the field, that have been the catalysts for over a decade of change and that collectively have the potential to transform the field.

Education has acquired a position of prominence in our national discourse unparalleled since the post-Sputnik period, and a number of the issues that have constituted the substance of that discourse—equity, assessment, standards, school reform—have direct implications for gifted education. This has brought an unusual intensity of focus to bear on the field, much of it highly critical. Writers such as Leslie Margolin, Jeannie Oakes, and Mara Sapon-Shevin, the last of whom has a chapter in this volume, have criticized the field for perpetuating inequality, promoting tracking, disrupting classroom communities, and in general constituting an obstacle to reforming and restructuring an educational system that as most observers would admit badly needs a major overhaul.

Initial responses to these criticisms from writers in the field of gifted education, this one included, were defensive. A circle-the-wagons mentality prevailed, and justifications of gifted programs soon issued forth in a variety of media, perhaps as a conditioned response to decades of resistance to the idea that students of high ability or achievement had special educational needs that were not being met in most classrooms.

However, this time, things were different. Our critics were no longer blithely dismissing the idea that capable students required an adequate education. Instead, an argument grounded in notions of equity, predicated on the idea that all children are entitled to an appropriate education, an argument we were accustomed to making on behalf of gifted children, was being used against us. This time, our critics were draped in the same mantle of equity we had found so comfortable for so many years, and we were cast as the apologists for, and the advocates of, inequitable educational provisions.

What was being criticized—the tendency for gifted programs to over-enroll White middle-class and upper-middle-class students; the educationally and ethically questionable nature of reserving such things as technology, instruction in higher-level thinking, and field trips exclusively for students in gifted programs; the use of gifted programs in some localities to reinstitute the upper level of a tracking system or to create a mostly White enclave in a diverse educational system—added up to an indictment of the field that was considerably more difficult to dismiss out of hand than the old, crude gifted-kids-do-fine-on-their-own-and-don't-need-anything-special arguments with which we were used to dealing. These were serious charges, and they were backed by hard data that could not easily be dismissed.

It soon became clear, to some of us at least, that defending gifted programs missed the point. The point was to defend not the means (gifted programs as they existed at that time) but the end (appropriate education for all students, including highly able ones). In a 1996 article, I asked whether we might have gifted education without gifted programs. That idea was initially unpopular within the field, but I was not alone in suggesting it, and it soon became a commonplace notion, as the welcome proliferation of schoolwide enrichment models and books and articles on curricular and instructional differentiation for all students, many of them by scholars identified with the gifted education movement, has demonstrated. Furthermore, looking critically at the theory and practice of gifted education began to be seen as something that rightly belonged to scholars within the field as well as to those without, as is the case in any healthy field. In short, writers and practitioners within the field began to rethink gifted education. And thus this book.

My goal in putting together this collection was to encourage some of the writers whose work I most admire to rethink aspects of the field of gifted education that most interest them and to look at where we have been, where we are, and where we ought to go. Not everyone I asked was able to participate, and I have realized since this project began that there are many others whose voices ought to be heard. However, I am very pleased by what has resulted from the hard work of the scholars who were kind enough to accept my invitation to participate. Let me briefly describe each of the chapters contained herein.

Section I, *Reconceptualizations of Giftedness*, contains papers concerned with the construct of giftedness itself. In the first chapter, David Henry Feldman reviews the history of gifted education, locating it within the psychometric tradition established by Terman, and proposes a developmental framework, incorporating his concept of nonuniversal development, that he believes would serve the field better. He outlines a research agenda grounded in this framework that serves as a challenge for the century ahead and also serves as an appropriate beginning of the dialogue this book represents.

The next chapter is by one of the leaders in the field of gifted education who brought the field back to life and to renewed prominence in the last quarter of the 20th century, John F. Feldhusen. His reflections on the field he helped create, or recreate, are both retrospective and prospective and illustrate the degree to which what we call *gifted education* really *is* being rethought. Feldhusen explicates the concept of talent development, as opposed to general giftedness, showing how this conception is consistent with developmental research and is reshaping practice in the field. Inherent in this discussion, although not sharply foregrounded, is the question whether the notion of *gifted children*, the bedrock construct of our field, is valid or useful.

Mary Anne Heng, drawing on examples from her native Singapore, approaches the issue of the meaning of giftedness from another perspective, one frequently ignored. She problematizes typical conceptions of success and asks whether helping gifted students make meaning out of and see meaning in their lives ought not to be our highest priority. Drawing on both theory and her inquiries with gifted students in Singapore, she raises important issues that are often given short shrift in our discussions of intellectual giftedness and talent development.

Laurence J. Coleman, arguing that theory ought to play a more prominent role in the scholarship of the field, asserts, seemingly paradoxically but ultimately persuasively, that the field is both "atheoretical, yet theory-laden." Toward his goal of greater reliance on theoretically oriented practice, Coleman describes theory use in the field of gifted education in terms of a series of sometimes fanciful, but always illuminating, metaphors and suggests more appropriate ways in which theories can undergird our work.

Phenomenological and other interpretivist inquiries are relatively rare in this field, not surprisingly in light of our origins in the differential psychology tradition, but disappointing in light of the promise such *emic* approaches hold for our field. In his chapter, Tracy L. Cross discusses phenomenological inquiry and develops an argument for its appropriateness in the field of gifted education. He lucidly explicates the axioms of phenomenology and discusses the methodological implications for inquiry in our field.

Aimee Howley, Craig B. Howley, and Edwina D. Pendarvis have, separately and together, contributed some of the most lucid and trenchant critiques of the field of gifted education in recent years. Their chapter on the possibilities of gifted programs in rural communities is consistent with their previous writings with respect to the breadth of its scholarship and the depth of its analysis. Their assertion of the particular worth of the rural, and their insistence that education ought to draw on and reflect local knowledge and local values, is based on a principled rejection of what they see as the empty and deracinated (not to mention cosmopolitan and modernist) pan- (or *a-* or *supra-*) national capitalist society and the schools that serve it. Although they advocate meeting the special educational needs of high-achieving students through multi-age grouping and acceleration, they subordinate this good to that of social justice, should they conflict (see, in this vein, the brief discussion of Isaiah Berlin in the chapter following theirs) and argue that "most gifted programming could easily be terminated without ill effect."

Finally in Section I, my own chapter, with its intentionally provocative title, asks whether we might not be better off without the construct of giftedness altogether.

The second section, *Gifted Education and Equity*, contains three essays that, in various ways, try to come to grips with our most vexing conundrum, reconciling the competing demands of equity and excellence, as well as the most conspicuous failure in our field, our historical inability to reconcile our commitment to equity with practice in which it is conspicuously absent and dishonored.

In her chapter, Mara Sapon-Shevin both offers a critique of gifted education and seeks, as her title suggests, common ground with advocates for gifted children. Sapon-Shevin's 1994 book, *Playing Favorites: Gifted Education and the Disruption of Community*, was, for the most part, an indictment of the field to which many writers, myself included, reacted defensively. However, especially in light of her calls in this chapter (see also her 1996 *Journal for the Education of the Gifted* article) for developing a common agenda that will benefit all children—and her belief that one-size-fits-all, whole-class teaching will be neither effective nor equitable in heterogeneous, diverse, inclusive classrooms, it has become clearer to many of us that she and we have many concerns in common and that finding common ground may be a less daunting proposition than she fears.

In "Desegregating Gifted Education," Donna Y. Ford argues that "the poor participation of minority students in gifted education will continue unless the principle of equity becomes central to policies, practices, and procedures in: (1) educational philosophy; (2) student assessment; and (3) curriculum and instruction design." She identifies a number of barriers to a more inclusive and equitable practice of gifted education and, perhaps more important, offers suggestions for improving our sorry collective record in this respect. This is one more important contribution to our literature from one of the most impressive writers in a new generation of scholars.

Margie K. Kitano draws on a broad range of research literature, especially the sociocultural literature, including her own work, to identify "What's Missing in Gifted Education Reform." She identifies the sources and manifestations of discrimination that low-income gifted students from diverse backgrounds experience and asks, "Can efforts to provide challenging curriculum for all students, including the gifted, succeed if we fail to address issues of what happens to culturally and linguistically diverse students in the class-room?"

Joyce VanTassel-Baska is probably our best-known writer on issues relating to curriculum for gifted students, and her chapter leads off the third section, *The Practice of Gifted Education—Identification, Curriculum, and Programming*. VanTassel-Baska rightly asserts that "curriculum is at the heart of what matters in gifted education" and provides solid guidance as to how we can keep that heart beating. She delineates five policy issues relating to curriculum for gifted students that, in her opinion, must be addressed by educators in this field, and her recommendations concerning how to address them are worthy of close attention by teachers, administrators, and policymakers.

Sally M. Reis, drawing on a phrase made famous by former Secretary of Education Terrel H. Bell, argues that the curriculum and textbooks in American schools have been "dumbed-down" to the significant detriment of students in general and gifted students in particular. Drawing on her own school experience and her work and that of others at the National Research Center on the Gifted and Talented, Reis looks at how gifted students fare in regular classrooms. The picture, unfortunately, is not very rosy. She concludes by offering three recommendations in the form of propositions for remaking the field.

Susan K. Johnsen discusses one of our most central and controversial issues, the assessment of gifted learners. Our field was born at the beginning of the testing movement—as a direct consequence of it, in fact—and ever since, issues related to testing and identification have provided no end of problems, issues, and controversies. Johnsen explores the question of authentic assessment in depth and closes with a discussion of significant issues that must be addressed "before the promise of developing talents is realized."

Jonathan A. Plucker and Ronald A. Beghetto bring a fresh perspective to creativity, a topic that while generating a great deal of innovative and exciting work outside the field of gifted education has been mired in tired ideas within the field that gave it legitimacy in the 1960s and 1970s. Their distinction between "Big C" creativity (genius-level creativity; think Mozart, Picasso, et al.) and "little c" creativity (something we all have to varying degrees that can be enhanced through various interventions; think you and me) is extremely useful in sorting out the sometimes contradictory claims of researchers and developers of methods for enhancing creativity. And, *mirabile dictu*, they even have interesting things to say about the tired topic of divergent production.

Rena F. Subotnik, Paula Olszewski-Kubilius, and Karen D. Arnold close the book with a discussion of the factors and dilemmas related to the development of high-level talent. Drawing on their own substantial body of research and that of others, they examine how talent develops—or does not develop—

using, among other lenses, Bronfenbrenner's theory of ecological development and Bourdieu's notion of cultural capital. Case studies of extremely talented young people illustrate the trade-offs and often intensely difficult decisions parents and children alike must confront when evidence of unusual ability is present in those too young to make life decisions on their own.

One of the joys of editing this volume derived from the happy necessity of reading successive versions of each of these chapters. Each reading was rewarding and, unfailingly, a pleasure. I am proud to have been in part responsible for the work of my valued colleagues that appears between these covers. I envy anyone with an interest in the field of gifted education—where it's been, where it is, where it's going—who approaches these essays for the first time.

Reconceptualizations of Giftedness

CHAPTER 1

A Developmental, Evolutionary Perspective on Giftedness

David Henry Feldman

INTRODUCTION

The purpose of this chapter is to discuss two issues that are central to the meaning of giftedness. The issues pertain to the extent to which the term *developmental* and the term *evolutionary* have a role to play in how our field views giftedness. The premise of this chapter is that these two concepts, woven together into a framework through which to interpret giftedness, can be a fruitful and productive perspective for the field. This is not to say that the proposed framework is the only way to look at giftedness, or even necessarily the best way for all purposes. Rather, the proposed framework is offered in the hope that it will help the field integrate its considerable achievements from the first century of effort into a vision for the future that ensures its continued vitality.

Giftedness was first systematically defined for practical purposes by its relationship to IQ. Although not always consistent in practice, an IQ of two standard deviation units above the population mean (usually 130) has been the most commonly used mark of gifted intelligence. A score of at least three standard deviations above the mean (usually above 145) has been the most common definition of genius, while a score of 180 or above has been sometimes used as a mark for prodigy (Hollingworth, 1942). While subject to criticism virtually from their inception, these definitions, especially that of giftedness, have endured and become deeply ingrained in scholarship and research as well as in policy and practice.

In many ways the traditional definition of giftedness has served the field well. Whatever its other limitations, an IQ-based notion of giftedness is admirably clear and can be precisely assessed. The technology of assessment has been refined and extended greatly since the early years of the century and is now part of the fabric of society in this country and in most other Western countries. At this point commercially available tests are required to meet high standards of technical quality; they must be reliable and must show that they assess intelligence adequately (almost always in reference to a criterion test such as the Stanford-Binet).

From the beginnings of the field, there have been those who have criticized both the definition of giftedness as IQ and the tendency of practice to focus on those who score well on the tests (Morelock, 1996; Witty, 1951). These critics were themselves influenced by critics within the field of scholarship and research in intelligence. Ever since the advent of IQ tests, there have been lively (and sometimes bitter) arguments that intelligence is not simply IQ but consists of several independent qualities of mind that are at best loosely related to general intelligence, or g. Many models of intelligence have been proposed over the decades, some with IQ at the top of a hierarchy (e.g., Spearman, 1927; Carroll, 1993), others with no general intelligence at all (e.g., Thurstone, 1938; Guilford, 1967; Gardner, 1983), others more complex in their arrangement (e.g., Cattell, 1963; Sternberg, 1985a). The reign of IQ has been challenged many times, but it has always emerged intact as the central and most important single measure of intellectual potential (see, e.g., Hunt, 1997).

The last major assault on IQ occurred at mid-century in the wake of the Second World War (Guilford, 1950). While that effort did not ultimately succeed in displacing IQ as the field's one best measure, it did bring the new field of creativity research into existence, a field that has endured if not triumphed (Feldman, Csikszentmihalyi, & Gardner, 1994). Originally proposed as a challenge to IQ, creativity has become more of an adjunct to IQ giftedness, a quality that must be attended to but that does not challenge the field's fundamental commitments to IQ-based giftedness (Gallagher, 1996; Morelock, 1996).

For most of its history, gifted education has been tied to special education, an uneasy alliance at times but one that has served the field well (Gallagher, 1996). There is, for example, a division of the largest and most powerful organization for handicapped children (Council for Exceptional Children) devoted to gifted education. The style of advocacy and political structure of the organized field of gifted education is similar to that of advocacy groups for mentally retarded and blind and deaf children, and, more recently, those with attention deficit disorder (ADD). By keeping its focus on a relatively small group of children with demonstrable special needs, the field of gifted education has carved out a modest niche for itself in many budgets in many localities at all levels, including a national center for gifted education at the University of Connecticut established in the 1990s.

The gifted education movement has shown that, given the limitations and constraints of public school systems in most parts of this country (and in a number of other countries as well), there are students whose academic potential will go unchallenged or worse unless special resources are provided to assist in their educational development (Borland, 1989; O'Connell-Ross, 1993; V. S. Ward, 1961/1980). The field has also been able to document a range of services that, when done well, make a real and substantial difference to their clientele (Borland, 1989; Renzulli, 1978, 1992; Renzulli & Reis, 1985).

THE PROBLEM

So what is the problem? As the field enters a new century it would seem that all is well. As summarized in the previous paragraphs, there is a great deal that is healthy and good about what is now in place. The efforts of many devoted advocates—Barbara Clark, John Feldhusen, Jim Gallagher, Joe Renzulli, Nancy Robinson, Abe Tannenbaum, and the late Harry Passow perhaps foremost among them—have established a legacy that is substantial and worthwhile. Therefore it is not surprising that there is deep suspicion of and determined resistance to efforts to move the field away from its traditional commitments and beliefs. To reprise the opening paragraph of this chapter, any proposal to change the field's direction will have to integrate (indeed celebrate) its traditions and accomplishments into whatever vision of the future it might propose. Otherwise, it has no chance to succeed.

There appear to be several problems facing the field. Perhaps no one of these would be sufficient to reach threshold in terms of leading to a need for a change in direction, but the joint import of the problems points to the conclusion that there is a compelling need to reach for a new paradigm under which to rally the forces and move the field forward (Feldman, 1992; Treffinger, 1991). The most vexing problems seem to be the following:

1. The scholarly field on which gifted education has depended for its concept of giftedness (and the technology to measure it) has recently been challenged in fundamental ways.
2. The resources dedicated to the field's work are a diminishing proportion of the education dollar and likely to diminish further.
3. The population of this country is changing dramatically and moving toward a "majority minority."
4. Research and theory in the field of gifted education have become somewhat stagnant, generating few exciting ideas and major breakthroughs. There are indications that the paradigm that has guided the field may have exhausted its most valuable resources.
5. The leadership of the field is aging and the field does not seem to be drawing as many exceptional young scholars into its fold as was

the case in earlier decades. Many meetings seem to be doing the same things year in and year out.

6. The social/political climate is such that there are growing resentments among those outside the field toward those who are passionate advocates within it. Mostly this resentment takes the form of an anti-elitism stance.

7. There are ideas and theories that have been developed in fields not traditionally associated with gifted education that pose some serious challenges to its central assumptions.

8. The traditional alliance with special education is increasingly less satisfactory. That field has moved from primarily behavioral/educational intervention toward medical/drug intervention, thus shifting its main concerns away from those of gifted education. While the notion of "special needs" might still make sense, the nature of those needs is so different from group to group that academically talented children's needs often seem to pale when compared with those of their disabled peers (see Number 2 above).

9. The landscape of jobs and careers is dramatically changing. It has become increasingly clear that the aptitudes and abilities that were crucial for success in the last century may not be as important in the next one.

10. The internationalization of society has shown us that in other cultures the concept of giftedness often varies sharply from our own. This contextualization of the field makes it harder and harder to defend IQ-based giftedness.

The problems have been presented here in highly condensed form and without supporting evidence. They should therefore be interpreted as efforts to capture some of the most pressing issues facing the field rather than as strong claims about the accuracy of each, intended to provoke discussion and response rather than to compel belief. Given the need to limit the present chapter to reasonable length, only two of the above problems will be delved into in more detail; they are the first and seventh statements, which propose that the field of scholarship and research on intelligence is undergoing important changes, and that fields not generally linked to gifted education have also changed in important ways that are likely to have impact on the field of gifted education.

Changing Conceptions of Intelligence

Since the field of gifted education has traditionally drawn directly from the scholarly field of intelligence theory and research, changes in that scholarly field are likely to impact the applied field. And there have been some striking changes in the scholarly field, changes that are already reflected in many of the articles that have come out in recent years in journals from the gifted education field (e.g., *Gifted Child Quarterly, Journal of the Education of the Gifted, Roeper Review*). If our understanding of the nature of intelligence is altered our notion of giftedness is likely to be altered as well.

Although there have been a number of new perspectives on intelligence, two of these have had particularly great impact. Sternberg's (1985a) triarchic theory and Gardner's (1993) theory of multiple intelligences have proven to be highly influential challenges to traditional notions of intelligence. Each theory has its distinctive qualities, but both make strong claims that IQ is not a viable definition of intelligence—that it is too limited a conception of intelligence to capture the most significant dimensions of human capability, and both claim that intelligence is a more plastic set of capabilities than has been the case with traditional, hereditarily fixed IQ (Herrnstein & Murray, 1994; Jensen, 1997).

Sternberg's (1998) theory proposes three distinct forms of intelligence: academic, practical, and creative (here the legacy of the creativity-research movement is turned to a new purpose). Each is given equal status within Sternberg's triarchy, and each may vary in strength in any person. Academic intelligence is similar to traditional IQ, but practical intelligence and creative intelligence are almost never represented in IQ measures. Practical intelligence refers to those abilities that relate a person to his or her surroundings; help the person interpret what is called for in social, personal, and professional situations; and help the person form successful strategies for succeeding in real situations in the real world.

Creative intelligence has to do with changing things about the world so that they might be better suited to solve certain problems, alleviate difficulties, enrich experience, transform environments, and the like. This kind of intelligence represents the novel and divergent forms of thinking and acting that are involved in many important activities: composing music, designing buildings, marketing a new product, generating support for a political or social cause, generating new knowledge and interpretations of knowledge, and of course making new images through photography, visual arts, or other media.

For Sternberg (1998), a theory of intelligence that does not include at least the three components just described is impoverished and restricted in ways that can no longer be defended. Within Sternberg's framework, giftedness can be manifested in any of the three broad dimensions as well as in how the dimensions interact. (In a version of the theory that focuses more on how the child learns, giftedness has more to do with the use of executive control processes than the broad dimensions of academic, practical, and creative. But even the executive control mechanisms are not, strictly speaking, the same as

IQ (see Sternberg, 1984). In all instances, the kinds of abilities that triarchic theory proposes are subject to improvement through strategic intervention, including self-improvement (Sternberg, 1986). Implications for the field of gifted education from such a theory are not hard to find. Both the nature of giftedness and the kinds of responses to giftedness that might be put into effect differ markedly from those derived from traditional IQ notions of intelligence.

For the traditional field, IQ is not subject to improvement; rather, programming is intended to respond to the existence of high IQ, not to improve it. Providing challenges for children who possess more than average g or general intelligence is the main purpose of most programs in gifted education, whereas enhancement of each of the dimensions of intelligence or matching strengths to challenges in school would be the central purpose of programs inspired by triarchic theory (see Sternberg, 1986).

Although there have also been some efforts from within the traditional field of gifted education to differentiate levels of giftedness, with the goal of differentiating the kinds of educational interventions called for (often using a medical diagnosis metaphor), these efforts have not challenged the underlying assumption that giftedness of all sorts, from moderate to profound, is best captured by an IQ test (see, e.g., Gross, 1998). What is perhaps more significant than the specific nature of the responses to external pressure from outside the field is the very fact that such responses are occurring. There is a palpable sense that all interested parties recognize that change is in the air, the only issue being the kinds of changes and how deeply they will affect traditional beliefs and practices in the field.

Perhaps more influential than any other force from outside the field has been Howard Gardner's theory of multiple intelligences (Gardner, 1993, 1995). This theory, with roots going back to the beginnings of the psychometric movement early in the 20th century, proposes seven (or in more recent versions, eight) distinct, independent intelligences, no one of which has inherent value beyond the others. Which among the intelligences is important tends to vary from society to society (although most Western societies favor linguistic and mathematical/logical intelligences). Cultures can be found, nonetheless, in which each one of the intelligences holds a central place: Musical, spatial, bodily-kinesthetic, inter- and intrapersonal intelligences (even the more recent naturalist intelligence) are valued and promoted as gifts to be treasured somewhere (Gardner, 1993, 1995).

The remarkable acceptance in educational circles of the idea of multiple intelligences has meant that the field of gifted education has little choice but to deal with it in some form or fashion. As has been true for more than a century, the challenge to g has usually come in the form of a proposal for a set of s intelligences to displace it. In each previous challenge (there have been several), IQ or g has eventually prevailed, and the field of gifted education has been able to continue to pursue its goals without distraction for a number of years until the next rival theory appears.

Much else has changed, of course, both in the wider society and in the field of psychometrics. Even within the field of gifted education, some of its most prominent leaders (e.g., Borland, Callahan, Cohen, Feldhusen, Gagne, Piirto, Passow, Piechowski, Renzulli, Treffinger) have called for fundamental changes in the field. The call for a "paradigm shift" has begun to be heard from within as well as from outside the field (Feldman, with Goldsmith, 1986/1991; Treffinger & Feldhusen, 1996). Recognition that the field of gifted education is holding an increasingly untenable position appears to be growing, perhaps to the critical point at which real change becomes possible, even necessary. Multiple intelligences theory has had great impact on this trend.

It is therefore unlikely that a determined adherence to traditional notions of giftedness as g or IQ will be sufficient to sustain the vitality of the field through the 21st century. A more productive strategy might be to integrate the field's traditional commitment to IQ into a framework that is able to organize future efforts. In this respect, we may view the previous 20 years or so of activity in the field of gifted education as a *thesis-antithesis* period, with theories like multiple intelligences and triarchic views challenging the hegemony of the "one intelligence as central" view that has dominated the field for so long (Morelock, 1996).

If it is reasonable to characterize the most recent period in the field of gifted education in thesis-antithesis terms and not distort or trivialize the many subtleties and complexities that characterized that time, the obvious next step is to try to envision what a *synthesis* of different perspectives might look like. It is to that challenging task that we now turn.

The view of giftedness that guides the field into the new century must preserve and represent the best of the traditional focus of the field even as it honors the kinds of diverse gifts that have become ever more apparent. What sort of framework should be constructed? For these purposes, a view of giftedness that is, at its core, a *developmental* one may help move beyond the dichotomy of one versus many gifts. That view may be informed by processes of *evolution* of the human mind, which may have produced two systems for adapting to environmental challenges. One system is keyed to the specific features of a particular habitat, the other equipped with general strategies and problem-solving techniques that can be used in a wide variety of habitats (Feldman, with Goldsmith, 1986/1991). The view I will be proposing focuses on the interplay between the two systems of thinking as they encounter and engage the various possibilities available to them in human cultures.

The proposed framework is not the first to draw on the disciplines of developmental science, nor even the first to use the twin pillars of developmental theory and evolutionary theory as central architectural supports (see Simonton, 1999a). What is perhaps distinctive about this proposal is its explicit goal of providing a framework to guide and sustain the work of the field of gifted education, using concepts of development and evolution to transcend the either/or, one-versus-many-intelligences dichotomy that currently characterizes the debate. From research on extreme cases of prodigies and savants, with recognition of the risks in generalizing from extreme cases, a view of human intellectual capabilities has emerged that has the potential to help the field transcend its current unproductive controversies and move forward productively.

The lessons from developmental and evolutionary theories for our understanding of giftedness arose from research done with child-prodigy and savant-syndrome cases (Feldman, 1993a; Feldman, with Goldsmith, 1986/1991; Morelock, 1995; Morelock & Feldman, 1991, 1993, 1997; Treffert, 1989). In trying to comprehend, for example, the nature of the prodigy and how a prodigy might differ from someone exhibiting savant syndrome, an apparent role for more general as well as more specific forms of intellectual ability presented itself. These roles turned on the level of general and specific abilities available in the prodigy versus the savant, and on the relationships between and among the abilities.

Briefly, it appeared that the prodigy and the savant differed primarily in the level of general intellectual ability they could draw on in support of their more specific talents. Prodigies tended to demonstrate above-average general intelligence (IQ) in addition to their remarkable specific talents for music, chess, mathematics, art, dance, and the like. Savants were dramatically less able than prodigies when required to demonstrate the kinds of reasoning required on IQ tests (abstract, symbolic, and logical reasoning). Their specific talents, however, seemed equal to or in some instances exceeded those of prodigies (Goldsmith & Feldman, 1988).

Evolutionary Theory. The study of evolution—physical and cultural—is of course a major field in itself. For our purposes, there are three aspects of evolution that are particularly useful in interpreting prodigies and savants. The first of these is the assumption that through processes of genetic recombination that occur in reproduction, *variations* in traits and features occur both randomly and systematically. An example of variation is the range of heights found in human populations, as well as occasional deviations that go beyond current ranges of variation (e.g., a nine-foot person whose height exceeds that of all known persons). The second aspect of interest is the tendency of evolution to *select* redundant and/or complementary traits or systems of qualities that are of special importance to survival. An example of this tendency is that birds use sight, sound, and weather conditions to help them determine when it is time to migrate south, as well as to find their way en route. The three sources of information are used by systems that coevolved to support an activity crucial for bird survival. The third feature of evolution of special interest for the present discussion is a tendency for traits or systems not selected for survival purposes nonetheless to *endure and evolve*. Each of these tendencies of evolution was used to help interpret the appearance and importance of child prodigies, savants, and other extreme cases documented in the research literature (Feldman, with Goldsmith, 1986/1991).

In addition to physical evolutionary tendencies such as those just described, there are also sets of cultural evolutionary tendencies that have proven helpful in efforts to comprehend and interpret extreme instances of abilities and talents. Perhaps most helpful of all has been the *joint* consideration of physical and cultural variations. The existence of bodies of knowledge and skill, constructed within cultures that seem designed to engage and facilitate the development of specific abilities and talents, is one such tendency found in cultural evolution. An example of such a domain is music. A related phenomenon is a tendency in some societies to select certain of the available bodies of knowledge and skill for support and recognition and to discourage others. For example, in U.S. society there are substantial resources available to develop mathematical ability, but few such resources to develop appreciation of rock music. Presumably, the decision to allocate public resources is based on a set of beliefs about the importance of mathematics as well as beliefs about the negative effects of rock music.

A final tendency of cultural evolution that proved relevant to work with extreme cases is the process of integration of outlying cases into cultural belief systems, practices, and institutions. For example, Tibetan Buddhist culture revolved around finding prodigy children, children believed to be reincarnated religious leaders from previous generations (Feldman, with Goldsmith, 1986/1991; Feldman, 1993a, 1993b). These observations of extreme cases of ability led to the speculation that nature may have hedged its bets on human evolution in several ways. One of these ways was to produce as part of natural variation a small number of individuals with extremely specific talents for doing extremely specific things. The other major way to hedge was to give human minds access to *both* general adaptive symbolic and problem-solving processes and specific abilities that tend to be yoked to particular domains such as music, art, mathematics, dance, chess, and perhaps others (Feldman, with Goldsmith, 1986/1991).

As Jerome Bruner (1972) observed many years ago, certain monkey species seem to possess one or the other of the two castes of mind (general adaptiveness across habitats versus specific match to a single habitat), but no primate species has a combination of both tendencies to the degree that humans do. Some species are exquisitely evolved to thrive in a certain place under certain specific conditions, but have little ability to transform themselves or their environments if the need arises. Other species seem to have remarkable abilities to change to respond to changing habitat (Weiner, 1997). What may be the key to human evolution's success to date is the *combination* of the two ways to survive that have appeared in our progenitors and our predecessors in the primate chain.

The prodigy and the savant both appear to be specialists, with highly specific talents that can be expressed only in sharply constrained ways. The savant, however, may have received only the specific gifts in areas like arithmetic calculation, music, drawing, calendar calculation, or memory of arbitrary facts. These narrowly constrained gifts, however profound, can be used in only narrowly defined ways since they do not seem attached to more general adaptive qualities of mind such as is found in the normal transactions between a person with greater access to IQ-related abilities and his or her environment, including other human beings.

Thus the savant seems to be severely limited to function only in a constrained realm and only in certain ways. For example, a savant may not be able to stop in the middle of a song and begin again, or may have to perform in a fixed sequence a set of songs, or play only in a single key (Miller, 1989; Treffert, 1989). The particular constraints and limitations of a given person's talents are varied, but what seems to hold true across most cases is an inability to manage the rest of life (or even to engage other parts of the domain in which one's talents lie), making it unlikely that a savant can function successfully in society even with massive, protracted intervention.

The prodigy, in contrast, has access to broader abilities and is able to connect specific gifts and talents with the demands and opportunities of a field at a given moment in time (Csikszentmihalyi, 1988, 1997). The prodigy thus connects with a field as it exists in a highly productive manner, leading to the impression that performance is effortless. What gives the prodigy the ability to connect so well appears to be the combination of general abilities that keep the child tuned to the demands of the real world and specific abilities tuned to the challenges of a domain (e.g., playing a piece from the currently accepted repertoire for a solo violinist on a concert tour). The person's more specific domain abilities can then be harnessed to a set of goals and purposes that, in principle, could lead to a successful career in music (or another field in which prodigies are found).

Like savants, prodigies also often have limitations in their more general adaptive abilities, but less severe ones. Their tendency to specialize and require specific conditions for successful expression of their best potential typically means that others will have to provide some of the general support needed for survival. Ervin Nyiregyhazi, the remarkable piano prodigy from the early part of the 20th century, never learned to cut his own meat (Revesz, 1925). Mozart's father constantly was called on to arrange, rearrange, rectify, apologize, and otherwise try to keep Mozart's career from careening out of control. In some ways, Wolfgang didn't "get it" (Morris, 1994). But that is just the point: Prodigies, while they certainly have greater general ability than savants, often show similar lacunae in their adaptive resources, making it necessary to marshal a support system to sustain their trajectory of talent development.

In the savant, the response of the community tends to be to try to shelter, protect, and often isolate the child from the rest of society (with occasional exceptions such as Leslie Lemke, the gregarious singer/piano player; see Treffert, 1989). Most savants are institutionalized and cared for by the medical/nursing community. For the prodigy, the promise of fulfillment of potential through a rewarding career often leads to a very different response from adults; gaps or even gaffes in adaptability are forgiven, covered up, compensated for, or turned into charming eccentricities, all in the service of sustaining the development of the specific talent of the child into a successful career (Feldman, with Goldsmith, 1986/1991). It should not be surprising that one of the most fragile periods for the growing prodigy is the transition from child performer (with attendant adult support and fail-safe measures) to young-adult independent professional (Bamberger, 1991). If the child cannot call on g-related capabilities to make this transition and construct a viable independent existence, the chances of a successful adult career are greatly diminished.

The key point to be emphasized is that our best hope of understanding extreme cases such as savants and prodigies is by considering both the specific talents and the more general abilities characteristic of each, in the context of the social and cultural realities that confront them. Granted that it is risky to generalize from extreme cases such as prodigies and savants to less sharply etched situations (see, e.g., Case's comments on Feldman, 1993b), it nonetheless seems plausible to suppose that the mix of more general and more specific capabilities revealed in the study of extreme cases may appear in more muted form in others (Feldman, 2000). The arguments about general versus specific intelligence, about one versus many abilities, about gifts versus talents (Morelock, 1996), might be more productive if directed toward relationships between more general and more specific capabilities (but see Gagné, 1999, for a different view). As with a number of recent intelligence theorists in the psychometric tradition (e.g., Carroll, Vernon, Cattell), the view here is that determining the ways in which broader forms of intellectual functioning interact with specific forms is the key to better understanding of human potential in human cultures (H. Gardner, Kornhaber & Wake, 1996).

In most theories of intelligence, g has been placed at the top of a hierarchy, with dominion over and superiority to more specific talents (including, perhaps surprisingly, some versions of Sternberg's [1984] triarchic theory). While a case can certainly be made for this sort of higher/lower, top/down relationship, research with prodigies and savants suggests a more reciprocal, horizontal, complex, and varying set of relationships. A clear structure does not emerge from research on prodigies and savants, nor does the kind of stable structure that might come from factor analysis or path analysis using psychometric instruments. It appears that the days of simple hierarchies and linear relationships may be over when it comes to intellectual abilities.

Psychometric approaches are less promising as frameworks for future theory, policy, and practice if what we have seen with prodigies and savants is typical of other forms and degrees of gifts and talents. More likely to bear productive fruit in future discussions will be a focus on the kinds of general capabilities relevant to specific ones, and the way in which and the purposes for which they are relevant (Feldman, 1995). It may be that an excess of one or another g like ability (e.g., deductive reasoning) might be irrelevant to the development of a particular s ability (e.g., ballet) and absolutely crucial to the development of another one (e.g., chess).

The trend in the field of gifted studies to differentiate degrees of giftedness with varying IQ levels (e.g., Gross, 1998) is a step toward recognizing greater diversity in giftedness, but it needs to be supplemented with more subtle analyses of both general and specific abilities, differentiating among them and refining their distinctive qualities. When this kind of work is done, we will be able to put in play an array of potentially important abilities that may well extend, to be sure, beyond strictly cognitive ones (Feldman, 1993a, 1993b, 1994a, 2000; Goleman, 1995).

How combinations of general and specific abilities and talents play themselves out in various cultural contexts should be the central issue for a field that professes to study giftedness. How to best use what is known about combinations of gifts and talents as they interact to constrain, influence, transform, sustain, or distort the optimal expression of potential in unique human beings should be the focus of a field that professes to support the development of gifted children.

Human Development. The second concept proposed as a pillar to support a transformed vision for gifted education, the idea of human development, would seem to be the more straightforward of the two. Evolution is, after all, a complex and subtle biological issue, dealing as it does with the largest questions of the origins and history of all life forms. Development, on the other hand, is used primarily to try to describe and explain major positive changes in the organization of capabilities and how they come into being. My use of the term *development* will be a refinement of this notion that emphasizes transformation not only in each individual, but in domains of expertise and even cultures as well. There are traditional aspects of the meaning of development that are indeed straightforward and that will play an important role in any framework that successfully guides the field of gifted education (see, e.g., Gagné, 1999), but these are not the aspects that need to be introduced into the framework. They are already there, and their being there has not helped bring about needed changes in the field.

For example, in Francoys Gagné's (1999) important exegesis aimed to achieve consensus in the field on the meaning of terms like *gifts* and *talents*, the main distinction between the two terms is that talents are developed, while gifts are natural, unchangeable potentials. The fact that some qualities are subject to influence through development and others are not is at the heart of Gagné's attempt to clarify and define the two key terms in current debates about the nature of gifts and talents (see Morelock, 1996, for an alternative view).

The nature of the proposed influence on talent or how it works is not an important part of that discussion; Gagné's (1999) key claim is that a quality that is subject to influence is a [mere] talent, while a quality that is not subject to influence is a [truly important] gift. (The bracketed terms in the previous sentence are intended to reveal the real intent behind the distinction between gifts and talents, as defined by Gagne, i.e., to diminish the significance of one and raise the significance of the other; see Feldman, 1999).

As the discussion up to this point has tried to suggest, it may no longer be productive to try to place one set of abilities above another. More productive, it seems, is to define key terms in relation to the dimensions of broad/general/adaptive abilities versus more narrow, specific abilities limited to certain situations. For this purpose, the term *gift* refers to the set of more general abilities and the term *talent* to the more specific set; this usage serves the purposes of clarification and placement of the terms into an appropriate overall framework.

This way of using the terms *gifts* and *talents* places both as natural events that can be detected early in life, does not prejudge their responsiveness to influence (development in the usual psychological sense), and encourages consideration of relationships between and among various gifts and talents over time (Feldman, 1999). For the field of gifted education to fulfill its potential, however, processes of development in person, domain, and culture will have to move to center stage, organize the conversation, and become the most important criteria for assessment of the strength of talents and gifts (see, e.g., Vygotsky, 1978). The meaning of development and its role in the transformed framework that will guide the field must therefore be explicated. It is toward that end that the remainder of the present chapter is aimed.

Universal Versus Nonuniversal Development

One reason for confusion in the field has been a failure to distinguish between two forms of development: universal and nonuniversal (Feldman, 1994a). Efforts to describe this distinction and its implications for developmental theory have become an increasingly important part of the work of developmental science (Cairns, Elder, & Costello, 1996; Lerner, 1998).

Essentially, the difference between universal and nonuniversal development turns on the difference between spontaneous, natural change and change that requires sustained, systematic effort on the part of others to help the process along. Universal development tends to occur in most normal children under a wide range of environmental circumstances, while nonuniversal development occurs only when appropriate intervention occurs and is sustained for a sufficient period of time. Learning how to walk is a spontaneous, universal developmental milestone, whereas learning to play chess is a nonuniversal achievement dependent on the availability of a specific set of environmental conditions (e.g., availability of a chess board and chess pieces, a set of rules to play by). Virtually every domain within which gifts and talents express themselves is a nonuniversal domain. A key assumption about nonuniversal domains is that development proceeds through a sequence of levels of increasing mastery.

Why the universal/nonuniversal distinction is so important in the field of gifted education goes back to the place of IQ and how IQ has defined conceptions of giftedness. IQ is seen as a natural, unchanging (and largely unchangeable) trait (see Feldman, 1974; Gould, 1981). Theoretically, it does not develop in any meaningful sense. Given this notion of intelligence (and, relatedly, of giftedness), the possibility of significant development is minimal. Development in the context of IQ refers not to the trait of IQ or the ability underlying giftedness; it refers instead to how a child uses the gifts with which he or she has been biologically blessed (Gallagher, 1996; Tolan, 1994).

Ironically, IQ was originally measured in terms of mental age (MA), a construct entirely based on a sequence of orderly changes in capability among children of various chronological ages. Mental age was estimated by determining the deviation of a given child's capabilities from those of the typical child of the same chronological age (CA). Thus, a trait presumed to be unchanging and unchangeable was measured in terms of a set of changes that were calibrated by testing changed capabilities in children of different ages. Little wonder that Piaget found the approach of Binet and Simon problematic when he first encountered it as an assistant in Simon's laboratory in Paris in the 1920s (see Bringuier, 1980).

The idea of trying to significantly change the underlying trait or traits of giftedness is therefore precluded, virtually by definition, in the traditional definition of giftedness. Not surprisingly, the field's resources have tended to be directed largely toward identification of giftedness and less effort has been invested in its development. Finding the gift and assaying its size were consistent with the assumption of a biologically determined trait (like blue eyes or foot speed). Finding ways to enhance or transform a gift would not follow from the basic assumption of a fixed trait of giftedness.

For most of their histories, then, the two fields of gifted education and developmental psychology were, each in its own way, focused on a different kind of universal. For gifted education, IQ was conceived to be a universal trait, varying to be sure, but varying only as a function of natural biological causes and (later, when the field of genetics came into being) genetic recombination. Developmental psychology focused on universal milestones, common across virtually all members of the species, with little attention to individual variation. Both fields assumed a determining role for biology; the roles were different but concerns about modifiability, plasticity, changeability, control, and transformation were largely alien to both fields. The field of gifted education took natural variation in intelligence as a bedrock assumption, while developmental psychology took universal sequences of changes as a bedrock assumption.

Given the pervasiveness of these constraining assumptions in both fields, it is not surprising that they have had little to say to one another for nearly a century. Nonuniversal (or nonspontaneous) developmental theory offers the opportunity for the concerns of the two fields to be more productively linked, to the potential benefit of both. I have discussed elsewhere the role that the study of giftedness, especially extreme giftedness, can play in the field of developmental psychology (Feldman, with Goldsmith, 1986/1991). The role that contemporary developmental theory can play in the field of gifted education merits further discussion.

Nonuniversal Development and Gifted Education

The field of gifted education will have little need for a concept of development if it continues to hold to its traditional assumption that giftedness is natural, unchanging, and unchangeable. A focus on development will become an important goal for the field only when it encompasses a wider range of talents and abilities than it has traditionally embraced, national reports like the well-known Marland one (1972) notwithstanding. Previous efforts to broaden the definition of giftedness have had little effect on policy and practice at the local level (Passow, 1993).

The present discussion, therefore, assumes that there will be increasing pressure from within and from outside the field of gifted education to extend its reach to gifts and talents beyond IQ, even beyond different levels of IQ such as "moderate," "profound," and "extreme" (see Gross, 1998). Recognizing that different levels of IQ almost certainly require different sorts of response is, to be sure, a step toward the kind of broadening of the field that the present discussion proposes (Gross, 1998). The basic assumption of unchanging and unchangeable IQ, however, remains the same in modifications to policy and practice that might follow from a more differentiated set of IQ-based categories.

My argument is not that traditional IQ-based conceptions of giftedness should be abandoned altogether. After a century of research (and often controversy; see Jensen, 1997), the reality of a set of natural gifts that involve abstract reasoning and logical thinking, symbolic manipulation and linguistic sophistication, is well established (Sternberg & Grigorenko, 1997). Differentiation of IQ into more useful subcategories of the sort that Gross (1998) has proposed (moderate, high, profound, extreme) and into more accurate subtypes (practical, academic, creative) such as Sternberg (1986, 1988) has proposed will certainly help keep viable the more traditional areas of interest in the field of gifted education, but these innovations, however welcome, are insufficient.

The field of gifted education has used a notion of development consistent with its traditional emphasis, and extending general intelligence to several levels will not solve the problem. Development within gifted education has tended to mean assuring that the natural gifts of a child are nurtured, supported, and responded to in ways that guarantee that they will be fully expressed in the child's experiences and accomplishments (see Renzulli, 1978, 1992). The idea that development could actually transform a person's gifts has not had much currency in the field to date, and the failure to embrace a more profound concept of development is at the heart of the current tension in the field as well as the key to its future.

The sequences of universal changes established in the traditional field of developmental psychology have often been perceived (accurately) as not relevant to gifted education, which, by definition, concerns itself with exceptional cases. Traditional developmental milestones and stages are perceived as more of a backdrop to gifted education than they are central to its mission and purposes.

While it is true that the field of gifted education has had reasonable consensus around a concept of development, it should be noted that different strands of the field have seen the purpose of development differently. Morelock (1996) reviewed the history of the "gifted-child" versus the "talent-development" strands within the field and found that they emphasize different purposes for development. The gifted-child advocates (who see IQ as the most appropriate marker for giftedness) emphasize the importance of protecting the internal sensitivities and special qualities of their charges, whereas the talent-development group, which embraces a more diverse set of markers for giftedness, sees achievement and tangible results as more important than test performance. Aside from the fact that the two groups are often interested in different children, they differ in their views of the main purpose of "nurture" or support for expression of a child's gifts. Much of the (often heated) debate between these two groups turns on their differing ideas about the purposes of development, while at the same time sharing the view that development is intended to foster the expression of existing, unchanging traits.

Fortunately, progress is being made on both fronts and in gifted education and developmental psychology. Influenced by newer theories of intelligence such as Howard Gardner's (1993) multiple intelligences and Robert Sternberg's (1988) triarchic theory, and by increasing pressures to respond to diversity in North American populations, the field of gifted education has begun to respond. Although differentiated notions of giftedness are not often fully integrated into the field's core values, it is increasingly apparent that they are seen as increasingly necessary if the field is to remain viable (see Feldhusen, 1992a: Gagné, 1998, 1999; Morelock, 1996; Renzulli, 1978, 1992). Although it is difficult to predict the precise form that the more diverse concept of giftedness will take, it seems reasonable to predict that a concept incorporating greater diversity is almost certain to emerge from the current conversations.

On the developmental psychology side, the field has become increasingly involved in individual variability as well as in efforts to intervene in the course of developmental change (Feldman, 1994a; Horowitz, 1989; Siegler, 1996). As in gifted education, it is difficult to predict the precise form that the emerging consensus will take, but it seems reasonable to predict that, at the least, it will be no longer possible to ignore developmental changes of the nonuniversal sort, and consequently, such a consensus will require systematic attention to the best ways to ensure optimal development in these areas (Feldman, 1994a). Almost certainly, the value of a distinction between the terms *gifts* and *talents* is likely to animate the discussion about what range and variety of capabilities should be encompassed within the field of gifted education (Feldman & Fowler, 1998; Gagné, 1998, 1999; Morelock, 1996).

When one refers to nonuniversal developmental changes, many of the domains within which such changes take place would be seen as areas of talent development by most people in gifted education. For example, learning to play the flute, studying landscape design, working on a cure for a pernicious disease, leading a government, and many other domains are clearly not universal. Nor, however, are they likely to be explained (in terms of which people do well in them) by reference to IQ or general giftedness alone (Simonton, 1994, 1999a, 1999b).

My recommendation about how to incorporate a meaning for gifts and talents into the field of gifted education in a way that meets the needs of the field but places development of gifts and talents more centrally is this: *Gift* should be used to refer to more general, adaptive, broader, and domain-independent kinds of abilities (e.g., hypothetico-deductive reasoning), while *talent* should be used to refer to abilities more specific to a given domain (e.g., finger dexterity). Forming a strategic plan to carry out a scientific experiment would be an example of the former type of ability; rapidly mastering the fingering and hand placements necessary to play a complex piece of music on the piano would be an example of the latter type.

For a person to accomplish a high degree of mastery and/or to find satisfaction and fulfillment within a given area of nonuniversal development, both gifts and talents are almost always involved (see Morelock, 1995). In extreme cases such as those we have studied, we saw that even the most powerful gift or the most exceptional talent is unlikely to lead to successful real-world accomplishment without at least a modicum of support from the other kinds of abilities (Feldman with Goldsmith, 1986/1991; Morelock, 1995; Morelock & Feldman, 1993, 1997). That is, unless one's general abilities are somehow focused toward fulfillment of one's unique potential in a specific domain, whatever that might be, the gift is likely to go unfulfilled.

Similarly, an exceptional talent for numbers, drawing, playing an instrument, or throwing a ball is unlikely to be sufficient to guarantee successful mastery of a complex domain such as mathematics, visual art, concert-quality musical performance, or competitive athletics. Indeed, the phenomenon that is now called "savant syndrome" (Treffert, 1989) is best explained as extreme specific talent in the relative absence of more general symbolic, abstract, logical, linguistic, and interpersonal abilities (Goldsmith & Feldman, 1988; Miller, 1989; Morelock & Feldman, 1997; Treffert, 1989).

There are savant cases with astonishing specific abilities ("talents" in the terminology we recommend) who are severely constrained in what they can do with them. A savant like Leslie Lemke, for example, seems to be able to play on the piano almost any song he has heard, as well as to sing his own accompaniment without delay and to be able to do so permanently (Treffert, 1989). On the other hand, no one who has heard a concert by Leslie Lemke would claim that he is an accomplished musician or a highly trained vocal talent. A case like David Helfgot, featured in the film *Shine*, seems to be more complicated: An extreme talent for piano, substantial general intellectual ability, a disturbed family that impacted his development profoundly, all seem to have influenced his musical performances. For example, critics of Mr. Helfgot's concerts have generally rated his performances as remarkable but not of the highest caliber. What makes his concerts so worthwhile to so many people, apparently, is the widely shared sense among audience members that a person with such enormous personal and psychological challenges has transcended them sufficiently to be able to perform exceptionally well in a highly demanding field, that of the solo concert pianist.

Developmental Domains. To help organize a developmental framework capable of incorporating the great diversity of realms within which gifts and talents may express themselves, nonuniversal theory has proposed a continuum of "domains" from *universal*, through *cultural, discipline-based*, and *idiosyncratic*, to *unique* (Feldman, 1994a, 1995; Feldman & Fowler, 1998). This continuum is intended to show how much of development is not universal and to suggest the kinds of developmental changes that should be of interest to the field of developmental science (Cairns et al., 1996; Feldman, 1986). Although not designed specifically with gifted education in mind, the continuum may nevertheless be of use to the field.

As gifted education expands its horizons to encompass a wider range of capabilities, there is risk that the coherence, communicability, and clarity of the field's traditional theoretical paradigm will be lost. Universal to unique offers a relatively straightforward framework within which to reconceptualize what giftedness means for the field, and it does so in a manner that integrates traditional preoccupations with general ability with more contemporary preoccupations with specific talents for specific domains (Feldman, in press). As touched on earlier, nonuniversal theory assumes that mastery of any challenging domain requires both general and specific abilities.

It should be noted that I am focusing the discussion on mastery and achievement of expertise. If one chose to place happiness and life satisfaction at the center of the discussion, many of the savant cases and possibly David Helfgot too might be among the most fulfilled in the sense that they appear to be content with what they are able to do in the domains in which they are active. My purpose in the discussion of fulfillment of potential is to highlight the need for differentiation and expansion in conceptions of giftedness and talent and their development. The relationship between these purposes and the more general issues about how a person should live his or her life and toward what ends are beyond the scope of the present discussion, although I have touched on them elsewhere (e.g., Feldman, with Goldstein, 1986/1991; Feldman, 1993a, 1993b, 1994b).

Moving from left (universal) to right (unique) on the continuum implicates ever greater roles for certain domain-specific talents and abilities associated with a given field at a given point in time. Learning to speak, for example, requires both a general ability to understand that one thing can stand for another and a more specific ability to grasp that a given set of aural inputs represents a specific set of meanings. The spoken sound of the word *chair* represents (in English) a set of objects on which it is possible for a person to sit. Language-specific abilities, apparently natural to every child, are necessary for speech to be acquired (Keil, 1984, 1989). The number of domains associated with the different regions of the universal-to-unique continuum is large (perhaps thousands), but only a subset of those will be of value within a given society during a given period of time.

Each domain can be described in terms of its distinctive qualities as well as the qualities that it shares with other domains within (and sometimes across) boundaries. For example, law and medicine may both be categorized as representing "discipline-based" domains on the universal-to-unique continuum, and in this respect would be expected to share certain features (e.g., that they are chosen professions, that a relatively small number of people pursue them, etc.). Yet the same abilities are not called for in both domains: Medicine demands extensive understanding of biology, anatomy, pharmacology, and other relevant disciplines, law demands extensive understanding of torts, contracts' jurisprudence, and other relevant topics. General intellectual abilities are relevant to both fields, of course (traditional giftedness), but certain specific talents, unique to each field, are required for successful practice of either profession.

The key common qualities of all domains within the theoretical reach of the universal-to-unique continuum is that they are *developmental* in nature, which implies that progress through them can be assessed using a sequence of broad, qualitative shifts such as stages or levels. Domains are developmental also in the sense there are sets of environmental conditions that catalyze movement from one level to the next. Other than in universal and perhaps some pancultural domains, all other domains require increasingly specific sets of abilities for successful mastery, along with increasingly specific sets of sustained interventions, institutions, technologies, pedagogies, and practices applied in appropriate ways for sufficient periods of time. These domains are engaged by fewer and fewer individuals within a society as one moves toward the unique end of the continuum, but they are nonetheless developmental in the sense that a sequence (or sequences) of levels or stages must be achieved in each domain (Feldman, 1994a, 1995).

How a given person with a unique blend of general and specific abilities within a unique cultural context moves toward more advanced levels of domains in various regions of the universal-to-unique continuum is the main problem for the field of developmental psychology to solve. How people with extraordinary general and specific abilities move toward mastery of unusually challenging developmental domains and occasionally transform them is the prime concern of the field of gifted education.

Both fields require a vital and viable concept of development at the core of their efforts. Development as the natural unfolding of inherent potentials will continue to be of value as part of an overall concept of development in both fields. But the meaning of development needs to be expanded to include movement through levels of increasing mastery and understanding in nonuniversal domains, including domains that have been marked for special recognition in a particular society.

The main differences between more talented and less talented individuals are the *rate* at which they move toward the more advanced levels of a domain and the *number* of such levels they eventually achieve. Understanding these sorts of developmental changes requires much more than knowing what natural gifts and talents an individual has been given. It requires an understanding as well of the environmental conditions under which positive movement takes place; the kinds of interventions that serve the purposes of development in nonuniversal domains; the kinds of technologies, institutions, resources, support systems, and the like that are crucial to optimal development; and the kinds of broader contextual, cultural, and historical conditions that favor one sort or another of domain over others (Feldman, 1993a, 1994c; Simonton, 1992, 1994, 1999b, 1999c).

The Development of Expertise and the Experience of Creative Transformation

Although it is not the only goal possible for the field, understanding the development of greater and greater mastery in valued domains is a reasonable place to start as a goal for gifted education. To be sure, there have been concerns that the field has gone too far in the direction of performance, achievement, products, and outcomes to the detriment of quality of experience, satisfaction with one's efforts whether or not they aim to master anything, and satisfaction with the simple joy of being gifted (see, e.g., Morelock, 1996; Piechowski, 1997; Roeper, 1990; Tolan, 1994).

Without denigrating these very real concerns, it is the premise of this discussion that the most promising route to satisfaction and joy in experience is through productive, sustained, effective efforts toward deep mastery of a domain that has value, both to the individual and to those who share the environment with that individual. This is not to say that mastery of a valued domain is the only route to happiness and fulfillment, and in this respect the critics of mastery or achievement have a point. But it is hard to imagine how the expression of one's potential in a deeply satisfying way would not involve doing so through one or more cherished domains.

There should always be a place for the individual, however gifted and in whatever ways, to be free of the need to prove the reality of his or her giftedness by performing at levels deemed to be remarkable, and the community should be careful in imposing achievement and mastery standards where they are inappropriate. It is nonetheless true that for most people in most communities, satisfaction and fulfillment of potential will involve finding something to do well and striving to do it better (Feldman, 1976; with Goldsmith, 1986/1991).

With the premise that achieving ever more satisfying levels of expertise in valued domains represents a reasonable central image for the field of gifted education (although, again, not the only image), a number of implications for research follow. Indeed, a research agenda presents itself that is sufficiently broad, challenging, and diverse to occupy the sustained efforts of the best scholars in the field well into the next millennium. Consider the following research questions as guides and goads to action:

1. What combinations of general and specific abilities are involved in mastery of the developmental domains valued in a given culture?
2. What levels of strength in general and specific abilities are necessary for moving to higher levels in valued developmental domains?
3. What qualities of temperament and character are associated with involvement in various developmental domains? Do these qualities differ from one domain to another?
4. Are there social/cultural constraints that channel ability and talent into or away from various domains? For example, are there religious practices that proscribe certain activities? Are there gender roles that proscribe certain activities?
5. What are the conditions necessary for a given individual, with a given set of abilities and talents, including qualities of character and temperament, to move to the most challenging levels of a valued domain?
6. How have domains developed over time, through what processes and by what mechanisms?
7. Are domains subject to extension, elaboration, and transformation through the efforts of individuals who are involved with them? How, in other words, does creative transformation come about?
8. How do we account for the fact that some contributions to a domain are not recognized immediately? What are the sources of such recognition or the lack of it?
9. Do the most extreme cases of mastery in valued domains have lessons to teach us about giftedness and creativity within domains?
10. Is mastery of a domain to its most challenging levels necessary as a prerequisite to transformation of that domain?
11. Is it necessary for an individual to want to transform a domain before being called creative? Can unintended transformations also be considered creative, and if so, in what sense?
12. What mechanisms or processes of change and transformation account for movement from level to level within developmental domains? Are they the same processes in all domains? At all levels?
13. Can general abilities be used as a substitute for specific talents in certain domains? For example, can someone gifted with very high IQ master the more challenging levels of musical performance even in

the relative absence of the specific musical talents presumably required for mastery at that level?

14. What do the dramatic advances in knowledge of the brain and central nervous system have to tell us about the issues raised thus far? What constraints does physical development put on the development of expertise? What opportunities are dependent on certain features of brain and body?

15. Are the dimensions of development emphasized appropriately in the proposed framework? For example, are qualities of personality, of historical context, of spirituality, of gender, of ethnicity, given appropriate attention in appropriate ways?

16. Do the "traditional" gifted children get lost in the shuffle? Is there still a place for the gifted education movement served so well by children during its first century? Is their place still a valued one?

17. Will the proposed framework help us sort out the confusing terminology in the field? For example, the terms *gifted, talented, creative, prodigy,* and *genius* (and no doubt others) seem to be up for grabs. Will the field be helped to find consensus on the meaning of these central terms?

18. Is the field ready for the challenge of an approach like the one proposed here? Does the field really need to change that much? Can it continue to survive (or even thrive) without a paradigm shift of the sort proposed here?

Perhaps needless to say, the questions just posed do not exhaust the possibilities. They are intended to show the heuristic value of an evolutionary/developmental framework for sharpening and clarifying issues in gifted education. Would questions such as the ones just listed have occurred anyway? Have they already been posed and answered within the traditional paradigm? The premise of the present discussion is that, while many of the same issues would have been raised anyway, and perhaps some of them are being addressed within the field now, systematically organizing the effort along the lines briefly summarized here will help assure the continued vitality of the field of gifted education.

CONCLUSION

Recall that at the outset of this discussion it was recognized that the framework presented in this chapter to guide the field may turn out not to be the best one. Others may be able to better articulate a sense of direction for the field and to better express their ideas for doing so. Such efforts are welcome. The difficulties and challenges in trying to formulate, then communicate, a clear vision for a field as complex and diverse as that of gifted education is likely to require the yoked efforts of many scholars. More important than the fate of this or any other individual effort to guide the field is that the call for discussion on the need for a new framework be heeded. How acute that need is and how to best prepare to meet the challenges that the new century will most assuredly present will animate our discussions for the foreseeable future. The field will judge the success of this or any other effort, as it appropriately should (see Csikszentmihalyi, 1988; Feldman, Csikzentmihalyi, & Gardner, 1994).

Whatever form the emerging framework eventually takes, it will, I believe, need to have central roles for the two themes that have been the focus of the present discussion: evolution and development. While the field of gifted education has sometimes utilized concepts of both sorts, the importance of the evolutionary process and (especially nonuniversal) developmental processes has not been fully realized.

From the evolutionary record, it appears that one of the unique features of the human species is that it endows each of its members with an array of abilities of at least two sorts: a general set that assists the individual member in finding ways to survive (and thrive) in a wide variety of habitats (or environments) and a specific set that both enables and constrains the range of domains a given person might choose to pursue. It is almost as if nature has hedged its bets in human evolution by not having the species depend too greatly on general adaptability, on the one hand, or on always having available a specific set of environmental conditions and opportunities on the other (Feldman, 1986/1991, 1994a; Feldman et al. 1994).

For our primate relatives, evolution has equipped species with one or the other set of abilities, but rarely both; an exception seems to be a species of finches in the very Galapagos Islands where Darwin observed the complexity of adaptation on his journey around the world (Weiner, 1997). While more generally adaptable species have an overall better chance to survive because they can find ways to sustain life across a range of habitats, they are limited in specific abilities that might greatly enhance their viability in certain habitats. And species that have highly specialized adaptations to a particular habitat are less likely to survive if there are changes in that environment.

As for the concept of development, the term has had too restricted a meaning in gifted education. Traditionally, development has meant the successful use of stable natural abilities. It was assumed that these natural abilities were unchangeable and unchanging, but that with proper support and the right set of opportunities, each gifted child would be able to derive full benefit from the natural gifts with which he or she is endowed. While this meaning of development is certainly legitimate, it is far from the only one. Nor is it the most appropriate one for the field's next century.

The more appropriate meaning of development, as proposed in this chapter, is of a sequence or sequences of levels of expertise from engagement and early learning (a "novice") to the most challenging levels known for that domain (a "master"). Development within the context of expertise focuses on the capabilities, general and specific, that are involved in movement through a domain's levels, including abilities that are not necessarily cognitive in nature. It also focuses on the conditions that foster, encourage, challenge, crystallize, and recognize expertise in each valued developmental domain. Fulfillment of potential through engagement and mastery of valued developmental domains is the central image that should guide the field of gifted education as it begins its second century.

CHAPTER 2

Beyond General Giftedness: New Ways to Identify and Educate Gifted, Talented, and Precocious Youth

John F. Feldhusen

How do we help youth who are gifted, talented, or academically precocious recognize, understand, and commit themselves to the optimum development of their abilities and become creative achievers or expert professionals in adulthood? Is their ability genetically determined, or can parents, schools, peers, and the broad environment surrounding them as they grow up make a substantial contribution to their eventual successes and achievements in life? How do motivation and other personality factors influence their long-term development? Are career planning and goal setting vital aspects of such long-range development? How much do models, mentors, physical examples of creative achievement or productivity, the artistic or professional fields, or the leaders in the field in which youth talents are manifest influence the long-range development of their talents? How does creativity relate to all these issues of youth talent development? These are critical questions that we face in our efforts to understand and assist in the education and development of gifted and talented youth.

Through observations of youngsters as well as my own experience as a teacher and my observations of other teachers, I have become convinced that we must change direction in our approach to children and teaching. The task, I believe, is not simply to engage in the great inclusionary effort to teach all children so that they uniformly achieve some basic levels or standards of performance but rather to help each youngster utilize his or her emerging talents, aptitudes, and capabilities to the fullest extent in order to achieve career success and personal fulfillment at the highest level possible.

All students have talents, strength, gifts, aptitudes, or abilities that represent potentials to be developed. While the level of potential may vary from child to child and the types of talent may be diverse, all or most children come to school with a variety of strengths that can be developed. We recognize, however, that whatever the talent strength in a child, it must be developed and made to grow and that "gifts" are not full-blown, mature capabilities. With encouragement from parents, teachers, and peers as well as other agencies in the community and with a lot of commitment and effort from the child, potential can become mature expertise, creative performance, or very high level achievement.

While gifted programs strive to help "gifted children" develop their general capabilities, good programs help youth identify and develop their special talents. Several major research efforts (Achter, Lubinski, & Benbow, 1996; Bloom, 1985; Csikszentmihalyi, Rathunde, & Whalen, 1993) have shown us clearly that the high-level development of talent into creative careers depends not only on early recognition of a child as "gifted" but much more so on recognition and nurturance of special talents, aptitudes, and emerging capabilities. This may mean testing to identify talent strengths, but it equally, or more likely, means astute parents and teachers helping children and youth discover and understand their own specific talents.

The field of gifted education has depended almost entirely on intelligence and achievement tests along with nonstandardized rating scales and checklists to identify the all-purpose gifted child, assuming that that was all we really needed to know before proceeding to provide appropriate educational services (Richert, 1991). Identification procedures also were based on the assumption of a dichotomy in which some children are truly gifted and others are not. The typical identification process also yielded youth whose high abilities were only in academic areas such as mathematics, science, social studies, and language arts.

Although newer research suggested that identification, categorization, and labeling children might create some problems (Colangelo & Brower, 1987a, 1987b; Robinson, 1986), the evidence was ignored and the field continued to use outdated practices in both identification and programming for able youth. Research by Bloom (1985), Gagné (1993), Feldhusen (1997), Achter et al. (1996), and Csikszentmihalyi et al. (1993) shows that specific aptitudes or talents should be identified and used as guides in developing programs and curricula. Talented youth must come to recognize and understand their own abilities and set personal and career goals for their development (Feldhusen & Wood, 1997).

In their intensive study of 120 high-level creative achievers in young adulthood, Bloom and his associates (1985) reported that students who had come to know and understand their own talents well, who had strong parental support and encouragement, and who had excellent teachers at each stage of their development had the necessary ingredients to go on to high-level creative achievements in such field as the arts, psychomotoric activity, and academic-cognitive pursuits. Contrary to the one-shot-one-time identification systems often used in gifted education programs, the process was really continuous throughout childhood and adolescence and required many types of informational input to youth, their parents, and teachers from tests, school successes and failures, mentors, and experiences in the broader environment around them.

Gagné (1993, 1995a) is now well known for his extensive efforts to help us understand better the nature and development of human talents. Human abilities are more general in early childhood and may be characterized as gifts or aptitudes that are intellectual, creative, sensorimotoric, and so forth. From these general abilities specific talents grow as a result of environmental and interpersonal catalysts that may be either positive or negative in their impact. The environmental influences include persons, undertakings or activities in which youth are involved, impactful events, and the general physical surroundings. During childhood and adolescence, inter- and intrapersonal conditions influence motivation and personality development in ways that are closely linked to talent development. Out of this long-range process of talent development, specific talents emerge. Gagné has also pursued a continuous program of research to clarify still further the general and specific areas of the emerging human talents. The Gagné model of talent development (1993) is the most comprehensive view so far presented in the fields of gifted education and talent development.

Research by Csikszentmihalyi et al. (1993) is particularly relevant to the issues addressed here because, like the Bloom study (1985), it focused on trying to understand the nature and the course of development of talents. Unlike the Bloom study, however, in which the researchers interviewed creative achievers in young adulthood (around age 35), it looked directly at the emergence and development of talent during adolescence using both interviews and behavioral observations. The results of the study indicate quite clearly that youth whose talent development is progressing in positive ways are characterized by increasing awareness and understanding of their own talents and by commitment to the development of their talents. They can withstand the drudgery of working and studying alone, are less likely to work long hours on part-time jobs, and often experience "flow," or deep motivational involvement in activities related to their specific talents.

A statement of philosophy and policy regarding human abilities that had a profound influence on the development of systems for identifying highly able youth and programs for their education was the Marland report (1972) from the U.S. Office of Education. It proposed not one general form of giftedness but rather six distinct categories of talent: general intellectual ability, specific academic aptitudes, creative or productive thinking, leadership ability, visual and performing art talent, and psychomotoric ability. Some of the early developers of programs for the gifted actually sought to find all of those abilities in a child before declaring him or her gifted. However, more often than not, early program developers sought only youth who fell in the first two categories and only youth who could be labeled "generally gifted."

The Marland report (1972) was, in a sense, updated in 1993 with the publication of the report *National Excellence: A Case for Developing America's Talent* (U.S. Department of Education [USDE]), the report of a committee that had studied the status and extent of education of gifted and talented youth in the United States. In defining the term *gifted*, they declared that it should be used only to designate mature achievement, not childhood potential. Furthermore, the very title of the report reflected a new "talent" orientation. Most important, the report stated the new definition as follows:

> Children and youth with outstanding talent perform or show the potential for performance at remarkably high levels of accomplishment when compared with others of their age, experience, or environment.
>
> These children and youth exhibit high performance capability in intellectual, creative, and/or artistic areas, possess unusual leadership capacity, or excel in specific academic fields. They require services or activities not ordinarily provided by the schools.
>
> Outstanding talents are present in children and youth from all cultural groups, across all economic strata, and in all areas of human endeavor. (p. 26)

Thus, the stage was set for a substantial rethinking of the direction of gifted education. Talent identification and development is now the right direction.

THE NEW DIRECTIONS

There are now research, theory, and practical experience to guide us for future development of programs, curricula, and services in the realm of talent development. The task can be viewed as addressing four major areas of human talents: cognitive-academic, artistic, personal-social, and vocational-technical. It seems to be abundantly clear that human gifts or talents are not limited to the cognitive-academic realm and that for the long-range benefit of both our society and the young people growing up in it, we must recognize the full range of human talents that we need to function well and prosper as a society. It will not be argued that all youth are highly gifted or talented, for that patently is not the case. Youth and adults exhibit an extensive range of individual differences in their talents and abilities. However, it probably is true that, given a broader view of the range of human talents, a much larger percentage of the population has talent potentials than the severely limited percentages identified for gifted programs. Since we also recognize that talents are products of both genetic endowment and unfolding, as well as the quality, range, intensity, and diversity of experiences to which youth are exposed, it follows that our efforts to identify talents in youth must recognize the cultural inequality and unfairness that many youth face because of neglectful parents, impoverished homes, poor schools, and barren communities without inspiring mentors and peers.

ASSESSMENT OF TALENTS

While the field of gifted education often uses the term *gifted and talented*, common practice in the field continues to be to combine scores from tests and rating scales into a general index of giftedness and to offer programs and services of a general nature, supposedly appropriate for the gifted and most often in the form of the ubiquitous pull-out enrichment program. Specific talents are rarely identified, and talent, if identified, is often seen as a lower level of giftedness. Recognition and identification of specific talents, however, was used in a few early programs, such as DeHaan and Kough's (1956) in Quincy, Illinois. They developed checklists and procedures for the following talents: (1) intellectual, (2) scientific, (3) leadership, (4) creative, (5) artistic, (6) literary, (7) dramatic, (8) musical, (9) mechanical, and (10) physical. In their suggested program services, DeHaan and Kough included specific and differentiated education activities and curricula for each of the specific talents.

Perhaps the most widely known of talent models, Talents Unlimited, was developed by Taylor (1968, 1985) and promoted more recently by Schlicter (1986). Here the major categories of talent identified and nurtured differentially in the program are the following: (1) decision making, (2) communication, (3) forecasting, (4) planning, (5) creative thinking, and (6) academic.

The models developed by DeHaan and Kough (1956) and by Taylor (1968, 1985) undoubtedly influenced the ten categories of the widely known and used Scales for Rating the Behavioral Characteristics of Superior Students developed by Renzulli, Smith, White, Callahan, and Hartman (1998): (1) learning, (2) motivation, (3) creativity, (4) leadership, (5) art, (6) music, (7) drama, (8) communication—precision, (9) communication—expression, and (10) planning. Although these scales came to be widely used in identification, Treffinger (1991) noted that school practice was to sum the scores, identify the all-purpose gifted child, and disregard specific talents.

In his effort to define talents less categorically, Tannenbaum (1983) noted the lack of consensus and the confusion prevalent in educators' use of the terms *ability*, *aptitude*, *gift*, *talent*, and *factors*. Recognizing that we can approach the field of gifted education from different perspectives—those of educators, psychologists, and utilitarians—he proposed the use of the framework of (1) scarcity talents, (2) surplus talents, (3) quota talents, and (4) anomalous talents. Scarcity talents are those of world-class inventors, discoverers, writers, or philosophers. Surplus talents are those possessed by writers, artists, and dramatists, who make our lives better aesthetically or give new meanings to the human experience. Quota talents are those of the experts and specialists who provide goods and service for our daily lives, such as physicians, surgeons, teachers, social workers, clinical psychologists, managers, and CEOs. Finally there are anomalous talents such as gourmet cooking, trapeze artistry, game show winners, and so forth, for which there is no need as such in our daily lives but which may be amusing, pleasing, or sought after.

Our own research focused on a sample of 305 students, ages 9 to 17, all of whom showed very high level academic talent (Feldhusen, Wood, & Dai, 1997), and revealed the following 10 talent categories through self-reports from the students: (1) academic, (2) artistic, (3) cognition, (4) creative, (5) communication, (6) athletic-physical, (7) games, (8) language, (9) personal-social, and (10) technical. The number of talents reported by individuals ranged from 1 to 9, with a mean of 3.2.

Gagné (1995a) has developed a major model of the talent-development process. He delineated four types of giftedness (intellective, creative, socio-affective, and sensorimotor) as well as nine specific talent domains that emerge developmentally as a result of interpersonal and environmental catalysts in children's lives (arts, athletic, business, communications, crafts-trades, education, health services, science and technology, and transportation). He has also published recently a kit of rating scales for the assessment of talents. Gagné's work is the most promising new approach to the identification of giftedness and talents. Kay (1999) has also developed a talent-profile system that provides a graphic view of youth's specific talents.

The move toward the conception and identification of talents was strengthened tremendously by the appearance in 1983 of Gardner's *Frames of Mind*, which introduced the seven intelligences. His model is now widely used to identify and nurture talents, and in a publication in 1992, Gardner, Walters, and Hatch use the terms *talent* and *talent development* to denote their focus of concern.

As noted earlier, most recent influences moving away from the general giftedness conception and toward the realization of specific human talents came in 1993 in a report from the U.S. Office of Education, *National Excellence: A Case for Developing America's Talent*. That report called for an end to the use of the term *gifted*.

CURRICULUM AND INSTRUCTION FOR TALENTED YOUTH

Piirto (1994), more than any other current educational specialist, addresses the full range of human talents in her book *Talented Children and Adults: Their Development and Education*. She presents instruments and procedures for identification and education of talents in the visual and performing arts, business, and leadership, in addition to the usual academic talents. She also provides extensive guidance for curriculum development across the K–12 grade span, counseling of talented youth, and procedures for organizing and conducting educational activities, based on a sound review of the development of talents from birth through adolescence.

In *TIDE: Identification and Educating of the Gifted and Talented at the Secondary Level*, Feldhusen, Hoover, and Sayler (1990) suggest a wide variety of educational programs and activities that can be adapted to individual student talents. Feldhusen has also set forth curricular and instructional models, programs, and activities to facilitate the development of specific talents and interests in *Talent Identification and Development in Education (TIDE)* (1995).

There have been a number of efforts to provide guidance to program developers in the arts, notably in the work of Clark and Zimmerman and Haroutounian. In a series of articles and books, Clark and Zimmerman have delineated techniques for the identification of art talent (1992, 1995) and have presented a wealth of ideas and guides for curricula, instructional programs, and teaching techniques (1994, 1998). Haroutounian (1995) has also addressed issues of teaching music and other arts to artistically talented students. She stresses the absolute need for assessment of performances and products in the identification of artistic talent, the need for the identification process to be seen as long-term and cumulative in judgment, and the need for art specialists as evaluators in the identification process. Haroutounian also recognizes that well-constructed rating scales and checklists can be useful in early stages of the identification process.

Feldhusen, Hoover, and Sayler (1990) carried out an extensive study among teachers of academic, art, vocational, and social studies courses to identify the behavioral characteristics of students in each domain. They then constructed rating scales for each of the four areas, including four scales for the vocational areas of agriculture, home economics, business and office, and trade and industrial occupations. They found the scales to be reliable measures of talent in the four domains. In *Talent Identification and Development in Education* (1995), Feldhusen also presented guidelines for the identification and nurturing of talents in the vocational areas.

Major efforts to recognize and educate gifted and talented youth have been spearheaded by Renzulli and Reis at the University of Connecticut and in recent years at the National Center for Research on the Gifted and Talented at the same location. The publication in 1976 of the *Scales for Rating the Behavioral Characteristics of Superior Students* and the publication in 1978 of "What makes giftedness? Reexamining a definition" in *Phi Delta Kappan* propelled gifted education into the forefront of educational development in the United States and later around the world. Renzulli (1978) proposed that there are three major components to giftedness: high ability, task commitment or motivation, and creativity. This model of the components of giftedness was used to identify youth for his School-wide Enrichment Model (Renzulli & Reis, 1997). Renzulli extended the concepts of talent development in the 1994 book *Schools for Talent Development* and in the 1998 publication of the revised *Scales for Rating the Behavioral Characteristics of Superior Students*. Renzulli's orientation is clearly reflected (1994) in his statement that "talent development is the business of our field." Our field was once gifted education. Now it is talent identification and development. We have ample theoretical and practical guidance to establish programs for the identification and nurturance of youth talents.

TEACHERS

Teachers of classes for the gifted, regular classroom teachers, special education teachers, and counselors all need training in the identification and nurturance of youth talents. Much of the training in special classes on gifted education is relevant to the talent domain, especially as it relates to highly talented youth, and it is very important for teachers of the gifted to learn how to assess specific talents, aptitudes, and interests and how to modify curriculum and instruction to address specific talents. However, there are also relative degrees of talent and aptitude as well as specific interests in all children at all levels of ability, and they should be identified and nurtured in school. Teacher training for work with highly talented youth is chiefly an extension of what applies to the talents of all children and an extension of traditional gifted education concepts.

Children begin to show talent potential as early as the preschool years. Identification of talents at the preschool level (ages 3–6) is predominately informal and based on either rating-scale results or direct observation of children's behavior. Karnes and Johnson (1987) pioneered rating scales for talent identification in early childhood, the Renzulli Scales (Renzulli et al., 1976) are widely used at the elementary and middle-school levels, and the Purdue Academic Rating Scales (Feldhusen, Hoover, & Sayler, 1990) are used at the high school level. Teachers need training in the use of these rating scales and the many other tests and rating scales available for assessment in gifted education (Feldhusen, Jarwan, & Holt, 1993) as well as in how to assess talent through observation of student performance and products in school.

Selecting and using appropriate curricula and instructional methods are also areas in which teachers need special training. For teaching highly talented youth that means curriculum and instruction at a challenging level commensurate with their levels of talent; for those who have lower levels of talent that means curriculum and instruction that is in the areas of students' specific talent strengths. While all students need basic instruction in all of the core subject areas, special opportunities to study in cognate areas such as drama, art, leadership, computers, business, and so forth, should also be organized and delivered by teachers in regular or special classes and in extra-school sessions at the end of the school day or on weekends.

Clearly, training and special assistance are necessary to help teachers understand how to provide specialized instruction. Many states now offer special training, which often leads to special certification or endorsements on teachers' licenses, at colleges and universities or through in-service workshops. Hansen and Feldhusen (1994) conducted a comprehensive study of trained and untrained teachers of gifted and talented students and found that trained teachers were far superior in the range and quality of instructional services delivered to students.

PARENTS AS NURTURERS OF YOUTH TALENTS

The emergence, recognition, and development of talents depend to a very great extent on the nature and impact of family in the early lives of young people. Parents provide all the resources and parents and siblings all the formative social interactions in early childhood, when intellectual abilities and social and emotional processes are developing in the child. Of course, the child is not simply a passive receiver of the formative experiences but also very much an interactive influence on the nature of the interactions and the allotment of resources. Out of all this experience, intelligence, special aptitudes, nascent talents, and social and emotional dispositions emerge as unique configurations in each child. For some, a combination of superior genetic endowment and nurturing leads to precocity, early prowess in one of the arts, extraordinary mathematical talent, or advanced physical skills. Fowler (1992) has documented the development of verbal abilities in precocious children and has provided abundant examples of the nurturing activities that parents use to stimulate verbal development. His research demonstrated that early and abundant verbal stimulation in the home leads to both higher verbal competency in adolescence and adulthood and to higher levels of motivation to learn.

Robinson and Noble (1991) presented a comprehensive overview of the social and emotional development of gifted and talented children and concluded that they tend to grow up in advantaged families and show advanced levels of social and emotional maturity, high levels of perseverance and commitment, positive self-concepts and self-esteem, and fewer behavior problems than children in general. However, they also noted that family influences may lead to competitiveness, perfectionism, depression, and perceptions of talents as social handicaps.

Moon, Jurich, and Feldhusen (1998), in a comprehensive review of the literature on the role of families in the cognitive, social, and emotional development of highly able children, concluded that, when viewed from a social-systemic point of view, family plays the major role in the development of children's talents. The family is an interactive emotional system, with all members reacting and proacting to one another. The family can best be understood as a functioning whole, not as a set or jumble of separate people and influences. The family also operates within the context of many other social systems, and understanding the child in the family calls for recognition of the other interacting subsystems such as schools, peers, the neighborhood, and community social groups. Moon, Jurich, and Feldhusen note also that families have value systems that have profound influences on the development of children's talents.

Silverman (1997a) and Rimm (1994) have led the field in offering guidance and direction to parents in their efforts to rear talented children. Silverman is a strong advocate of the use of individual intelligence tests in the early assessment of children's intelligence to help understand their intellectual, social, and emotional development. Rimm (1995) traces the impact of child-parent interactions on the highly talented child. She stresses that the pattern of interactions influences powerfully children's achievements in their areas of special talent, their self perceptions and self-esteem, and their long-range career achievements.

Smutny (1998), in her edited volume *The Young Gifted Child*, suggests that parenting a gifted child presents all the challenges of child rearing in general and an additional set of problems that grow out of the interplay between the child's superior talents and precocity, on the one hand, and his or her emerging personality and social development on the other. Six specialists in parenting and family organization offer guidance and advice on how to cope with these challenges and optimize the development of both the talents and the whole child. Recurrent themes are assertions of independence and capacity for self-direction by precocious children, their strong sense of curiosity and

desire to explore the world around them, the critical role of reading and literature in the home, and the value of adults who model good intellectual characteristics. It seems clear that home and family are the predominant force in
the early years, determining the nature and direction of talent development
for young gifted children, and the role of family probably continues to be
strong throughout the adolescent years.

TALENT, EXPERTISE, AND CREATIVE ACHIEVEMENT

Talent development is a lifelong and systematic process (Ericsson, 1996), but
with fortuitous circumstances also playing a role along the way as a child
moves toward expertise and creative achievement or mediocrity in adulthood.
The family is the first in a number of a systems in which the child lives and
functions as an integral member; later systems include school, one or more
professional domains, and various other organized fields of activity. We can
identify some major resources, influences, and individuals that interact with
youth along the way and become a part of the development system, always
recognizing that the child is not only acted on but is also interactive and
influences the people, resources, and environments that are a part of his or
her developing system.

We expect that many highly talented and precocious youth will become
experts in their fields of endeavor or careers (Ericsson, 1996). Bereiter and
Scardamalia (1993) argued that true high-level expertise is characterized by
creative adaptivity, that is, the ability to address new and unique problems in
one's field and come up with original solutions. Indeed, what might be called
"creative problem solving" characterizes the talented expert. Whereas expertise has often been viewed as repetitive and precise skilled performance, it
may more appropriately be seen as high-level creative professionalism.

SUMMARY

In the early years of childhood, talents and aptitudes are quite undifferentiated, and we may be aware simply that the child has one or more very general
areas of talent strength, such as verbal precocity, appreciation of natural
beauty, or psychomotor agility. However, with good experiences at home, in
the neighborhood, and at school, more and more specific talent strengths begin to emerge. Enriched and accelerated learning experiences in school can
play major roles in this process of talent development.

It is imperative that youth come to know and understand their own talents and take an active part in their development. We can offer classes,

courses, resources, books, counseling, and encouragement, but ultimately youth must assume responsibility for their own talent development and set their own educational, career, personal, and social goals.

A diversity of experiences in school, at home, and in the community can provide the opportunities for youth to test their capabilities, discover areas of strength, and begin to integrate all their self-knowledge with a composite picture of the adult artist, professional, expert, or high achiever they hope to become. There is no single route to high-level achievement in life, but successful achievers do seek out and take advantage of the best opportunities around them.

Highly talented youth profit from interaction with other talented youth. Talented youth working together in the classroom affirm one another's capabilities and the value of their shared talents. While some peer pressure is negative, youth who share talents, interests, and enthusiasms reinforce positive perceptions of their talents. They also motivate one another to greater interest and activity in the shared talent area. Talented youth need models of high-level achievement, artistry, accomplishment, excellence, or expertise in their own areas of strength. Models provide integrated pictures of careers for youth with similar talents. Models can be parents, teachers, or accessible individuals in the community. It is particularly useful for talented youth to meet eminent or famous adults who can serve as symbols of very high level achievement.

Talents grow best in youth who have energy, openness, perseverance, responsiveness, thoughtfulness, and so forth. Talented youth respond to both details and patterns or relationships and thereby master and take into long-term memory more aspects of the world around them than the average student does. They are also likely to be more excitable, enthusiastic, or dynamic in learning situations. They experience "flow" or deep immersion in what they are studying (Csikszentmihalyi et al., 1993) and may lose all sense of time. Finally, they are risk takers who are not bothered by ambiguity and often seek ill-defined goals.

Schools should devote more time and attention to identifying and nurturing talents. The ideal gifted program touches all or nearly all youth in a school, as it focuses on helping youth find and develop their special talents.

CHAPTER 3

Beyond School: In Search of Meaning

Mary Anne Heng

> *If we possess our why of life we can put up with almost any how.*
> —*Nietzsche*

San Ng, a 30-year-old Singaporean, had a lucrative law career and was considering a marriage proposal when she turned her back on the good life to find her life's mission as a volunteer helping the economically less privileged ("Learning About Real Life," 2000). "I have led the perfect Singaporean life for so long—going to the best schools, scoring straight A's in my 'O' levels and a string of A's in my 'A' levels, [and] doing law to please my parents. . . . I needed more from life, out of life," San says. A volunteer in Thailand with the French-based charity Medecins Sans Frontieres (Doctors Without Borders), and tasked with setting up a framework of indicators to help the Gates Foundation—the biggest philanthropic foundation in the United States—spend $17 billion, San is happy to have turned her back on her "perfect life" and empty routine in exchange for what she sees as a life of meaning and greater fulfillment.

The dawn of the third millennium has arrived. This is the era of futurist Alvin Toffler's emerging Third Wave civilization (Toffler & Toffler, 1995). Factory-style, bureaucratic, Second Wave models of operation of 20th-century industrialization have become obsolete. With the emergence of de-massified societies aimed at variation, customization, and individualization, paralleling Third Wave economic change, Toffler (1970) has called for a revolutionary transformation in the fundamental concepts of schooling in modern society. To "learn, unlearn, and relearn" (p. 367), Toffler argues, individuals need to be able to envision a better tomorrow, to think, probe, question, ask, innovate, and take risks in the new knowledge-based agenda of the Third Wave.

What is success? Are gifted children able to think, in the way San Ng is able to—long, hard, and deeply—about what matters to them? How many gifted children find themselves, really live life and become what they want to become? Turning to the field of gifted education, one might ask if as educators, we are really true to ourselves and to the children we reach out to. Do we help children in their search for the deeper meaning behind the "why school" question?

"If we possess our *why* of life we can put up with almost any *how*," Nietzsche (1889/1990, p. 33) so eloquently reminds us. Indeed, in the field of gifted education, the threat of irrelevance is real, Borland (1996a) cautions, unless we go to the root of things to ask big philosophical questions fundamental to educational research and practice. Thus, revisiting some of the fundamental issues that are the heart and pulse of contemporary conceptions of giftedness and speak to the philosophical issues of meaning, purpose, and direction, I will examine children's perceptions of the larger meaning of school beyond traditional notions of school and school success. Before attempting to understand giftedness through the more expansive lenses of meaning and purpose, however, there is a need to reexamine the limitations of traditional conceptions of success that underlie traditional conceptions of giftedness.

THE LIMITS OF EDUCATING FOR ACADEMIC SUCCESS

In the United States, educators in the field of gifted education (e.g., Roeper, 1996; Silverman, 1997b) have, for some time now, argued for the importance of going back to the "psychological roots" and of not losing sight of the needs of the gifted child. For too long, the dominant emphasis in education has been on achievement, on what the child is able to do rather than on who the child really is. Roeper (1995) cautions, "education has become a one-sided instrument. It relates to academic learning but does not stress the development and the growth of the self. Yet it is this inner self, the unique self of each human being, that is the central point of their lives" (p. 142). Roeper distinguishes between two philosophies of education: educating for success and educating for life. For the most part, she argues, schools have been guided by the philosophy of educating for success. In this model of education, the emphasis is on academic achievement and on perceiving education as a factory-style enterprise operating within the existing norms and expectations of society. The philosophy of educating for life, in contrast, is grounded in the concept of self-actualization and individualization; children are valued for their uniqueness, and the emphasis is on the "inner agenda" and passions of the child, within the larger context of the growth of the self.

"Do schools educate for life?" is a question that bears asking. Is there meaning to school beyond the academic A? Conceivably not, at least in a number of instances typified by individuals such as San Ng in her recounting of her existential void despite her academic achievements and "perfect life" in Singapore. In fact, Singapore caricatures well a country in which intense academic competition is pervasive and in which school is often perceived as instrumental to pragmatic ends, and it is perhaps germane to unfold a little of the Singapore story and, therein, an awakening of the need to educate beyond academic success.

But, you may ask, of what relevance is the Singapore experience to the field of gifted education in the United States? The idea that the experiences of a city-state with a population of 4 million people (out of which 1 in 5 individuals is a non-resident, see "Singapore Population," 2000) crowded onto a small island of 648 square kilometers (about one-sixth the size of Rhode Island) can bear relevance to the United States, a leading first-world economy with a population of 270 million people (*Europa World Year Book*, 1999) and described as a country where the "future usually happens first" (Toffler & Toffler, 1995, p. 87) may, at first glance, seem manifestly absurd. However, comparisons of scale aside, from its humble origins as an obscure fishing village with no hinterland to the economic miracle that it is today, the Singapore story (see Lee, 2000)—with its dependence on human capital, high premium on education, and preoccupation with academic excellence—is a story worth telling, at least in the brief.

THE SINGAPORE STORY

First, it is perhaps apt to point out that although there are clear differences between the United States and Singapore, striking commonalties nonetheless exist. For the most part, both countries share a common ideology in that they celebrate ethnic and cultural diversity, subscribe to a democratic ideology, and generally prize academic success as a means to real-world accomplishment. Additionally, as a competitive global economy second only to the United States ("Global Competitiveness Ranking," 2000), Singapore has, in recent years, been thrust into the academic spotlight with the impressive performance of its students at the Third International Maths and Science competition (e.g., Keys, Harris, & Fernandes, 1996). U.S. Education Secretary Richard Riley, in his visit to Singapore schools during the 2nd Education Ministerial Meeting of the Asia-Pacific Economic Cooperation economies, commended the rigorous academic curriculum and the focus on basic concepts and foundational skills in mathematics and science ("U.S. Education Chief Praises Singapore Way," 2000).

In the wake of its academic success, however, Singapore is awakening to the rude realization that the A students and venture capitalists of its new,

Third Wave economy may not be asking the right questions—the fundamental and systemic questions that transcend possibly utilitarian ends and look, instead, toward meaning and purposeful direction. "Will Straight A's Matter in Tomorrow's World?" a headline in the *Singapore Straits Times* (2000) asks. A study by the Singapore National Youth Council ("Wake-up Call for Singapore Youths," 2000) indicates a worrying trend of complacency among Singaporean young people. The study reports that, increasingly, Singaporean teenagers exhibit narrow-mindedness. In the age of globalization and borderless economies, youth find it difficult to break out of their comfort zones as they see no need to understand the implications of globalization, tend to be smug and egocentric, and see the paper chase as the all-important pragmatic means to a good job and a good life.

In recent years, therefore, educational reform in Singapore has taken on the proportions of a paradigm shift. Rethinking and lively debate have gained momentum in the last few years, as scholars and policymakers reexamine the field of education and its *raison d'être*. The theme of the Education Work Plan Seminar 2000, "Ability-Driven Education: Making It Happen," heralds the paradigm shift from an efficiency-driven to an ability-driven vision of education in Singapore. These days, the *Zeitgeist* reflects both conceptual transformation and educational reform. The emerging paradigm emphasizes broader definitions of success and more expansive notions of ability. In comparison with the efficiency-driven orientation, which perceives education as largely knowledge assimilation in pursuit of academic ends, the ability-driven orientation celebrates the many abilities and talents in every individual and values the holistic development of the individual (Nothing Like a Teacher's Eye, 1999). Signaling fundamental changes in mindsets, the thrust of the ability-driven vision of education is toward character and motivation, with intellectual capacity, understanding, and knowledge regarded as important constants in a quality education.

No longer content with merely educating for academic excellence, Singapore is moving toward more holistic educational approaches that aim to develop the character as well as nurture the intellect of children. The ability-driven vision of education in Singapore is about rethinking, reenvisioning, and reappraising, critically and without prejudice, fundamental issues and concerns that underlie assumptions and practices. Among educators, is there a genuine quest to examine the deeper meaning of school? Do children, particularly those regarded as academically able, have a sense of mission and purposeful direction beyond the relentless paper chase?

As a crucible of change and as a recipe for a crowded planet (Mahbubani, 1998), the Singapore voice, as a voice for the new Asia, bears some relevance to new thinking about the fundamental perspectives and philosophies of academic excellence. Nevertheless, in an age of rapid change and uncertainty, a more fundamental question begs to be asked. What do we make of, and where do we turn for, meaning, purpose, and direction in the modern world?

THE HUNGRY SPIRIT

World-renowned management guru, founder of the London Business School in the 1960s, and professor of business with theological affinities, Charles Handy emphasizes the importance of living a genuine life, of being true to oneself. In his book *The Hungry Spirit* (1998), Handy uses the hungry spirit as a metaphor for the modern condition, for the emptiness people feel after the quest for material success (and in the field of gifted education and in competitive societies, academic success to the exclusion of everything else) leaves them dissatisfied. He writes:

> I am angered by the waste of so many people's lives, dragged down by poverty in the midst of riches. I am concerned by the absence of a more transcendent view of life and the purposes of life, and by the prevalence of the economic myth which colours all that we do. Money [and traditional conceptions of success] is the means of life and not the point of it. There must be something that we can do to restore the balance. (p. 3)

I have chosen Handy's philosophical views to illuminate some of the thoughts and ideas put forth in this chapter for several reasons. First, Handy's philosophical views revolve around the timeless value of being true to oneself so as to make a difference beyond the bounds of duty, and in this respect, makes refreshing and important links between the realities of the school-as-instrumental-end perspective and the school-as-ruthless-academic-competition perspective (perspectives rife in countries such as Singapore), on the one hand, and the bigger perspective of education as a search for meaning, on the other. Second, his many books (e.g., 1994, 1995, 1998) force us to take a long hard look at the consequences of capitalism and its attendant implications with respect to traditional notions of success, to go beyond the quest for material and pragmatic success to the quest for purpose. *Waiting for the Mountain to Move* (1995), for example, is a collection based on his daily three-minute religious "Thoughts for the Day" on BBC radio some years ago. Provocative and inspirational, Handy's philosophical ideas resonate with the concerns of the modern world, the restlessness and discontent that plague seemingly successful individuals such as San Ng, the bright, straight-A student we met earlier, and several others whom we shall meet in a later section.

Central to Handy's thesis of self-knowledge and self-discovery is the need to maintain a balance between core responsibilities, on the one hand, and broader responsibilities and values that transcend the core, on the other. Handy's notion of core responsibilities refers to the largely definable roles and duties of closed societies—roles that, more often than not, are bounded by traditional conceptions of success and absolute truths. Beyond primary responsibilities, however, Handy calls attention to the opportunity to contribute to a cause bigger than oneself, to live up to a vision larger than one's life. It is ironic, he argues, that in the age of economic progress and external manifestations of success, individuals remain increasingly dissatisfied with themselves. Transcending definable roles and duties, therefore, one encounters the realm of bigger causes and differing, pluralistic values that are allowed to coexist in more open societies, and it is this reach for bigger causes beyond one's grasp that may give greater meaning to one's life.

In school, students whose lives are driven by predetermined and definable roles would, quite naturally, tend to focus on doing well in the conventional (academic) sense, and generally expect to travel the path of economic success in later years. However, as Handy (e.g., 1994) argues, we need to look toward a broader and deeper understanding of school beyond academic achievement and pragmatic ends. This then leads one to question whether academically precocious children are able to appreciate the deeper meaning and larger goals of school, to live lives that go beyond core responsibilities, to be the best they can be and make a difference beyond the bounds of duty. Before we turn to more specific concerns that attempt to shed light on our understanding of gifted children and their fledgling search for meaning, it is important to pause for a moment to learn a lesson or two from those who have struggled in their search for meaning in the wider and more poignant embrace of life and death, suffering and dying.

The Quest for Meaning

A survivor of Nazi death camps, Viktor Frankl, in his seminal piece *Man's Search for Meaning* (1984), writes of his belief in man's search for meaning as the primary motivational force in life. Recounting the horrors of Nazi concentration camps—in which people, both "the swine and the saints," unmask themselves (p. 178)—Frankl offers valuable insights into the search for meaning in life:

> It is impossible to define the meaning of life in a general way. Questions about the meaning of life can never be answered by sweeping statements. "Life" does not mean something vague, but something very real and concrete, just as life's tasks are also very real and concrete. They form man's destiny, which is different and unique for each individual. (p. 98)

Inspired by the wisdom of Nietzsche, as given in this quote, Frankl witnessed the will to meaning in life as fortifying survivors with strength to overcome the worst of conditions.

Another survivor of the Holocaust, Samuel Oliner, as reported in *The Altruistic Personality* (Oliner & Oliner, 1988), researched the values and qualities behind the courageous stories of ordinary men and women who risked their lives on behalf of others. In comparison with nonrescuers (bystanders), rescuers tended to exhibit virtues of connectedness and commitment, and a deep understanding of the meaningfulness of life above and beyond the needs of the self. Rescuers pointed out, importantly, that the way in which one interprets events very often shapes the way in which one responds to events. Pendarvis and Howley (1996) offer similar insights: "Intellect is a process of discerning. An education that works to cultivate discernment will, by virtue of its substance and method, prepare students to evaluate ethical and political questions thoughtfully. Intellect supports the quest for meaning, so intellectual work clearly entails contemplation of the human condition" (pp. 228–229).

In other words, can there be real individual fulfillment without a real quest for meaning? "Is it possible for a people to achieve excellence if they don't believe in anything?" John Gardner asks in *Excellence* (1961/1984, p. xiv). Can bright children truly achieve excellence if they do not have a real sense of purpose, if they lack the ability to discern that, with purpose, the vision of the whole is far more powerful than the sum of well-reasoned parts? Gardner does not seem to think so. He argues that "talent in itself isn't enough. . . . We find ourselves asking 'Talent in the service of what values?' Talent in the service of truth or beauty or justice is one thing; talent in the service of greed or tyranny is quite another" (p. 144). One's intellect and one's talent, therefore, are twinned to the notion of responsibility.

Thus far, it appears that the existential angst evident in the lives of many seemingly successful students today may mean that these individuals should begin to think about meaning, purpose, and direction in school and in later life—not in a generic and vacuous sense, but rather through intellectual discernment, "answer to life by *answering for*. . . [one's] own life . . . [and] by being responsible" (Frankl, 1984, p. 131). To paraphrase J. Gardner (1961/1984, p. 173): A gifted child who does not believe in anything will never achieve excellence. What do gifted children believe in? How do they see school as preparing them for the future? What do they perceive an intelligent person to be? What is life success? These are timely questions. These are also some of the more fundamental questions that may shed some light on children's attempts to read reality, to think at a meta-level, and to search for meaning. In a larger sense, these questions may serve to create an awareness and understanding of self beyond defined roles and responsibilities, an awareness wherein may lie the seeds of meaningful and fulfilling life goals.

VOICES FROM WITHIN, BUT DO WE LISTEN?

Meaning, purpose, and direction—what do Singaporean teenagers make of these? Is the hungry spirit—Handy's (1998) metaphor for the absence of a transcendent view of life and the ensuing emptiness and dissatisfaction felt as a result of the frenetic, single-minded, narrow pursuit of traditional forms of success—a palpable presence, even among school-going children? As a microcosm of change in the modern world, the Singapore voice provides an emic (within-culture) perspective that, at the same time, has ramifications for etic (culture-free or universal) interpretations (Berry, 1969). As noted earlier, the United States and Singapore share common ideologies in that, for the most part, both countries are ethnically and culturally diverse and, as modern democracies, see academic achievement as important to real-world accomplishment.

So, what is success? How does school prepare one for later life? Using clinical interviews (Ginsburg, 1997), I gathered the responses of 36 eighth-grade Singaporean adolescents (Heng, 1998, 2000) to the phenomenological realities of school, intelligence, and later life experiences. Of these students, 18 were in self-contained classes for the gifted that were housed in the same schools as the remaining 18 students, who attended regular classes for mainstream children (and who were not identified for the Gifted Education Programme in Singapore).

Regardless of academic ability, adolescents who displayed a heightened sense of self as learner tended to be introspective, mature in thought, and deeply reflective. Their responses evidenced a keen awareness of some of the larger and long-term goals of school, of its hidden curriculum, and of how the individual, working in tandem with various aspects of school, is able to achieve success, both in school and out. With purpose and direction, these individuals advocated the need to move beyond the pursuit of "superficial success" in school, the need to extend their mental horizons beyond the bounds of a grade-centered approach to academic learning, and the need to develop a sensitivity to and an understanding of the complex interplay of abilities and factors central to life success.

When asked the question "How does school prepare you for later life?" a gifted female student responded:

> School is a small society. In school, you learn to live and work with different people. This helps because when you leave school, you should be less introverted and less self-oriented. I think being self-oriented is bad because you only want a kind of *superficial success*. In some ways, school encourages superficial success, because society encourages this in the first place. . . . People only work for superficial success. Money is impor-

tant because without money, our economy will just die. But I mean, come on, let people develop themselves!

Contemplating the larger long-term goals of school and learning, this student appears to be cognizant not only of the more tangible and immediate aims of school but, more important, of the hidden curriculum of school that may have indelible influences on later life. Her views of school as a mini-society and of self-oriented thought as a precursor to superficial success find resonance in Roeper's (1995) interdependent model of thinking. Within the framework of interdependence, Roeper envisions "shared success," achieved in the spirit of cooperation rather than competition. In contrast, the individual in competition with others is driven by an ego orientation in the quest for personal, possibly superficial, success. Another gifted female student echoed: "School is like a pre-sampling of society, you get to interact with people from all over." Yet another mainstream student had this to add: "School gives you a rough idea of what society is like so that you won't be too surprised when you meet up with unexpected things later in life, for instance, unreasonable or overly critical people."

On the issue of what it means to be intelligent, students with a greater understanding of self tended to embrace a multidimensional approach to intelligence. A gifted learner, for example, alluded briefly to IQ as the "most basic measure" of one's intelligence but then added that "intelligence really isn't about your actual mental capacity, it is about how you harness your mental capacity." She added that insight, an individual's general philosophy toward life, and sensitivity to other people are equally important aspects of an intelligent individual. A mainstream learner remarked, quite perceptively, "Intelligence or smartness does not imply wisdom or integrity or leadership. The former may sometimes be a test of one's memory."

It appears, therefore, that some adolescents have a fairly good understanding of the more implicit and expansive notions of intelligence held by older people (e.g., Sternberg, 1985b; Sternberg, Conway, Ketron, & Bernstein, 1981). This understanding is important, Cain and Dweck (1989) point out, as it casts some light on the achievement motives that drive the goals children formulate for themselves, and this in turn plays a pivotal role in helping educators guide children toward discovering authentic life goals.

What all this indicates, in essence, is that among bright adolescents, individuals like San Ng, whom we met earlier, appear to show a heightened understanding of the dialectical tension between school, with the pursuit of academic excellence that may, ironically, hold little meaning for the high academic achiever, and life achievements, with the pursuit of broader forms of success that may hold more meaning and fulfillment for the individual. In

H. Gardner's (1983) words, these individuals struggle to find a balance between the "promptings of 'inner feelings' and the pressures of 'other persons'"
(p. 242). On the one hand, these learners are empathic to societal demands
for academic excellence; on the other, they are able to examine inner feelings,
listen to inner voices, and ultimately reach for a gestalt in making meaning of
their lives.

Among other bright learners, however, it is disconcerting to note that
some lack a tacit understanding of self in relation to the external world beyond
school and tend to be engulfed by societal expectations and more immediate
academic concerns. These individuals generally subscribe to more conventional and narrow aims of school, perceive school as synonymous with academic success, and are less keen to contemplate broader and less tangible
facets of learning. For the most part, intelligence is viewed as a unidimen-
sional, absolute entity—one either is in possession of it or is not—with academic achievement, via school grades, hailed as the single valid measure of
one's intelligence.

On the issue of what it means to be intelligent, for example, one gifted
student announced, "Being smart; basically, remembering facts and academic stuff. The dictionary definition." On the issue of how success in school
relates to success in later life, another gifted student dwelt on the need to
do well in school so as to be able to clinch a good job later in life. The
question, then, is: Should there not be more to school success than good
academic grades? To be sure, all students know that getting good grades
matters a lot. Students with a more mature and enhanced understanding of
self and their environment, however, know that grades are not the only
things that should matter.

It seems, therefore, that the specter of the hungry spirit looms larger in
the lives of those individuals who are unable to subscribe to more transcendent perspectives—individuals whose lives tend to be empty, unsatisfying, and
devoid of meaning, save for the transient fulfillment of the roles and responsibilities of the here-and-now. These are individuals whose sense of self as
learner is shaped less by personal aspirations, feelings, needs and the big-
picture vantage of the call of duty than by the more powerful utilitarian and
pragmatic forces of the sociocultural milieu they live in. In other words, these
are individuals who lack an inner compass—a guiding light that emanates
from a tacit understanding of self as learner as well as of self in relation to
society at large and that provides some sense of purposeful direction for the
way ahead. Several important questions remain in to be asked: What should
the driving philosophical vision for education be? How can educators bring
vision into focus, to nurture the intellect of all children so as to educate for
academic success and beyond? These are the issues I turn to next.

RETHINKING WHAT MATTERS IN GIFTED EDUCATION

Reenvisioning a Pluralistic View of Excellence

Let us re-visit J. Gardner's (1961/1984) seminal work, *Excellence*, in which he embraces a pluralistic approach to conceiving of excellence and to celebrating the many facets of human abilities. As with Handy (1998), who believes that everyone is good at something, J. Gardner puts forth a way of assessing excellence that does not involve comparing individuals. Rather, the comparison is between oneself at one's best and oneself at one's worst. It is important to note, therefore, that it is this comparison from within that determines whether one is true to the best one is capable of.

In schools, the focus has long been on the core curriculum, on academic excellence, and on the exaggerated academic pursuit of instrumental ends. In fact, we overdo the core, Handy (1994) points out, and we foster a form of academic impotence. To engage in "perpetual self-discovery, perpetual re-shaping to realize one's best self, to be the person one could be" (J. Gardner, 1961/1984, p. 162), gifted children need space to grow, to develop both mind and spirit, to delight not only in the opportunity to fulfill given responsibilities, but also to envision the challenge of making a difference.

As educators, we need to think seriously about ways in which we could move away from traditional conceptions of giftedness based on traditional conceptions of success. The British philosopher Isaiah Berlin was cautious of "positive" views of freedom, that is, the "freedom of self-mastery, of rational control of one's life" (Gray, 1996, p. 16). This is, in other words, the freedom to shape, by rational choice and experience, one's life goals, and the freedom to lead a self-determined life, usually somewhat scripted by society (through traditional or conventional, but not necessarily coherent, ways of knowing and doing). Berlin favored, instead, a more nuanced basic, "negative" notion of freedom, "the choice among alternatives or options that is unimpeded by others" (p. 15). This is the freedom of the self to create and act on, in the most fundamental, value-driven (and therefore somewhat diverse but real) sense possible, one's life themes and life goals. Are academic grades all that matter? What is life success? According to Berlin, Borland (1999) argues, the notion of *the* good life loses meaning as it stifles choice, giving way to a kind of pseudo-freedom. In other words, Borland reminds us, Berlin believes that choice, driven by values, supersedes reason and anything else—and it is this choice that makes us truly human.

To reiterate, I would like to underscore the existence of multiple notions of good and pluralistic views of excellence in open, mature societies. In these societies, tensions between multiple truths and multiple goods provide vigor and stimulate fertile growth. If we are indeed to move from atomistic conceptions of success toward more molar and expansive conceptions of reality and excellence, the greatest challenge must be to help gifted children discover themselves. If school is to be about meaningful rather than merely instrumental ends, educators must help children engage in the constant reexamination and reshaping of self. To be true to the best one is capable of, children must engage in a continual search for self and meaning. The process of soul-searching has never been easy. On the contrary, the process is long and uncertain, and very often fraught with tension, as one contemplates and arrays the value of one good against that of an equally compelling, valuable good. In the greater scheme of things that looks toward helping children discover and create their life themes as opposed to living life scripted by society, however, it is perhaps timely to consider it a moral responsibility, on our part, to guide children in their first steps as they journey pluralistic paths of excellence that begin and emanate not so much from without, but from within the individual.

Educating for Success and Life Through a Curriculum of Conscience

Contemporary thinkers, for example, Howard Gardner (1999) in *The Disciplined Mind*, underscore the central importance of the *paideia*, the purpose of education, as one in which an educated community has a deep understanding of truth, beauty, and good. In other words, truly educated individuals must have a sense of connection between self and the larger community, between the lessons of the past and the challenges of the future, between the individual as a thinker and creator and as a human being, between intellect and character. These days, it is heartening to note that many are no longer content with merely educating for academic excellence. One sees emerging efforts to help children understand the larger and more fundamental purpose of school. Indeed, enlightened educators are beginning to respond to the call for more holistic educational approaches that will provide children with a glimpse of something bigger than themselves, of the vision of a calling as a sublimation of the intellect.

   Roeper (1995), you may recall, subscribes to a philosophy of educating for life as opposed to educating for success (the latter conceived of in the conventional and narrow sense whereby success is regarded as a metric of academic grades). She writes, "true success in teaching gifted children can only be achieved when the passions of the child—her soul and mind—are accepted as the foundations upon which we bridge society's expectations as well as our own" (1997, p. 166). Elsewhere, Roeper (1996) strongly urges educators to nurture the psyche of the child in the direction of self-actualization. At the same time, she emphasizes the importance of building "bridges to the expectations of the world. Indeed, the Self cannot grow in isolation. . . . The Self must find a place in the world" (p. 19).

Roeper (1996) therefore calls attention to the important need for educators to build bridges—to listen to the inner agenda of the child—and at the same time to be able to read the realities of the external environment to keep an open mind to societal needs and expectations. Paralleling Roeper's thoughts, and as noted earlier, H. Gardner (1983) also stresses the importance of maintaining a healthy equilibrium between the "promptings of 'inner feelings' and the pressures of 'other persons'" (p. 242). Roeper, however, makes it clear that the spotlight is now on the self of the child even though, for a long while, the dominant emphasis in education has been on achievement, on what the child is able to do rather than on who the child really is.

As does Roeper (1996), I strongly subscribe to the philosophy of educating for life. In the era of the knowledge-based Third Wave economy, I firmly believe in the need to help children move beyond one-dimensional, parochial thinking and toward a more holistic understanding of problems and an expansive awareness of the realities around them. At the same time, perhaps somewhat in part as a voice from Singapore—where competition tends to create a closed society in which only one thing matters, namely, academic success to the exclusion of everything else—I also view the pursuit of academic excellence as a good in itself. I say this because I envisage academic competencies to be as important in tomorrow's world as they are in today's and it would be a shame if we decry academic excellence and throw out the proverbial baby with the bathwater. However, it is important to remember that academic grades are not all that should matter. In other words, I do not think that Roeper's philosophy of educating for success (in the traditional academic sense) is entirely at odds with her philosophy of educating for life. On the one hand, I view the pursuit of academic success as a good in itself, and healthy competition in which one assesses excellence from within rather than from without as important; on the other, I fully embrace Roeper's philosophy of educating for life as it helps situate the purpose of school within the context of bigger life issues.

Ultimately, educating for success and for life requires the nurture of the intellect, the force that drives the "life of the mind" (Howley, Howley, & Pendarvis, 1995) as well as the "life of the spirit," a life that is driven by the desire of self-realization and that culminates in a vocation (Grant, 1995). Indeed, Ginzburg (1989) regards a person's vocation as the "highest expression of his love of life. . . . A vocation is man's one true wealth and salvation" (pp. 107–108). In a powerful sense, if educators are to nurture both mind and spirit, there is a need to give some thought to a "curriculum of conscience" (Cooper, 1998). To bring one into being, there is a need for passion, commitment, and an honest awareness of the goals and motives that may shed some light on why children learn or fail to learn. For a start, as educators, perhaps our views of school, excellence, and success can serve as *memes*—"commonly shared values [that] provide the bonds that keep people working together who otherwise might compete to maximize their genetic progeny at each others' expense" (Burhoe, 1976, cited in Csikszentmihalyi & Rathunde, 1997, p. 27)—that can act as catalysts to help children achieve a clearer view of reality.

Moreover, central to a curriculum of conscience is a cogent need to think about a truly *learner-centered vision* for education. In learner-centered schools, Darling-Hammond (1997) argues, there are genuine attempts to understand children from the *inside*—their thoughts, feelings, and beliefs about self and about school. Specifically, Darling-Hammond identifies nine key features of learner-centered schools: "active in-depth learning organized around common goals, a focus on authentic performance, attention to student development, appreciation for diversity, collaborative learning, a collective perspective within the school, structures for caring, support for democratic learning, and connections to family and community" (p. 32). In essence, a curriculum of conscience assumes a child-centered emphasis. Children are regarded as ends, not means, and there is a pervasive consciousness to help children flourish, both in mind and spirit, in school and in the years ahead.

Rediscovering Connection and Purposeful Direction

In closing, let me return to Frankl (1984), who, in his search for meaning after years in Nazi death camps, wrote, "man should not ask what the meaning of his life is, but rather he must recognize that it is *he* who is asked. In a word, each man is questioned by life; and he can only answer to life by *answering for* his own life; to life he can only respond by being responsible" (p. 131). What is the real purpose of school? Should not educational integrity be about helping children develop a sense of connection—between head and heart, mind and spirit, reason and conscience—and, in a broader sense, "individual fulfillment within a framework of moral purpose" (J. Gardner, 1961/1984, p. 169)? Gifted education must take on a new level of meaning. To quote Jung in Handy (1998): "'I' needs 'We' to be truly 'I'" (p. 130). Moreover, Frankl (1984) reminds us that if success in school is to be meaningful and fulfilling, true success, like happiness, cannot be pursued. In fact, true success can ensue only when individuals lose themselves in causes that may surpass school itself. In other words, the fulfillment that comes with true success, meaning, and purposeful direction in life is possible only with self-transcendence, when the individual reaches beyond the closed system of the self to the discovery of the self within the larger purpose of the world.

If, indeed, school is to be beyond grades and is to transcend instrumental ends, we must ask the big questions. Do our children have an inner compass? Do they have a sense of purposeful direction and mission that stems from a deep understanding of self as learner as well as self in relation to society at large? Answers to these questions may begin to unfold if educators are encouraged to listen to the inner voices of academically able learners and of all learners, to help them bring to consciousness the tacit and to guide them in their search for a gestalt in making meaning of their lives. Only then, perhaps, as Csikszentmihalyi (1993) envisions, can we liberate our children from mindless competition, narrowly utilitarian pursuits, impoverished lives, and opportunities missed and guide them toward the freedom to discover life themes, to shape, by rational choice and experience, meaningful and authentic life goals.

Kingsolver (1992) in *Animal Dreams* shows us a hope-inspired way forward in our attempts to help gifted children understand themselves and in our own attempts to further our understanding of giftedness: " The very least you can do in your life is to figure out what you hope for. And the most you can do is live inside that hope. Not admire it from a distance but live right in it, under its roof" (p. 299). Do we care to live inside the hope that our children will someday find individual fulfillment within the larger vision of a shared moral purpose.

CHAPTER 4

An Essay on Rethinking Theory as a Tool for Disciplined Inquiry

Laurence J. Coleman

INTRODUCTION

The subject of this chapter is the role of theory in scholarly inquiry in our field. I define theory as an organized set of statements that explain a phenomenon in a manner that increases our understanding of that phenomenon. I believe that the creation of theory is essential to the development of a program of scholarly inquiry and, ultimately, the advancement of our understanding of giftedness (Cohen, 1988). Advocating theory-based inquiry and practice may be judged as too little, too late, or, in this postmodern world, as an irrelevant attempt to reinvent an outmoded grand narrative about rationality (Thomas, 1997) . However, I hold the modern, perhaps naïve, conviction that credible, disciplined inquiry in a field cannot be purely atheoretical, and I believe that our underuse of theory has hindered the pursuit of knowledge about the development of giftedness and slowed the development of the field.

In this chapter I will attempt to make that case by analyzing the field and putting forth a broader notion of theory than appears to be common in our part of the social sciences. I begin with an orientation to theory, noting that theory is both dangerous and liberating. I examine the literature to illustrate the state of theoretical inquiry in our field and offer several metaphors to describe the present state of theory in the field. Acknowledging the place of past theoretically based scholarship, I go on to argue that there are other ways to develop theories or models that promise to be useful, proposing that we move away from common theoretical postures toward the creation and elaboration of substantive theory based on study of development and practice in the natural world.

Before continuing, I want to acknowledge some beliefs that shape this chapter. I believe that by illustrating our disciplinary differences we can fashion a dialogue that leads to change. I confess that at heart I am an ameliorist who believes that in the long run we can increase our understanding of giftedness and improve the education of gifted persons. I define myself as a special education teacher who does research, so the way I think of our field is from that perspective. Many of my colleagues in the field of gifted education are psychologists and start instead from that base.

DEFINITION AND PURPOSE OF THEORY
IN SCHOLARLY INQUIRY

A theory orders ideas so that the relationships among events, persons, and context can be understood with more clarity than is possible without a theory. Theories may be formal or informal. A formal theory implies a system of some sort that explicitly and publicly states a relationship about what is happening in a person or a group. Implicit personal beliefs one holds about some idea or phenomenon constitute an informal theory. Such informal theories may fuel the creation of formal theories, but I am not concerned with them here because they are not available for critique.

A theory states carefully crafted propositions about a phenomenon. Theories in the natural sciences move toward an axiomatic form, such as A causes B, where the axioms describe highly predictable events. Theories in such social sciences as education, psychology, and sociology are unlikely, in my view, to reach that kind of form, although one can conclude that axiomatic theory is the goal of some social scientists (Snow, 1973). Social theories are unlikely to reach that point because their subject matter—human social action, which derives from intention and creativity—lacks the predictability of physical matter and forces in nature.

Researchers are often faced with two situations: contradictory findings and uncertainty about what step to take next in one's research program. Theory can be liberating in that, by stating relationships among constructs or variables, it enables one to see more clearly what is happening among the data, to construct alternate explanations for what has been observed, and to direct attention to inconsistencies or discrepancies that need explanation.

Theory is neither *the* truth nor the final word. It is not static, not an end point, but a place along the road toward greater understanding. Even a sound theory cannot prove everything, including propositions that seem true, nor can it fit all circumstances of a phenomenon (Hofstadter, 1979; Kuhn, 1962/ 1996). And, the canon wars aside, theory cannot be the exclusive property of either quantitative or qualitative researchers.

Theories that fire our imagination and push us to think deeply and clearly are good theories, as are theories that generate new questions that are a basis for long-range inquiry (in my opinion, the highest form of theory is one that has heuristic value and leads to increased understanding about a phenomenon). Moreover, good theory in the social sciences leads to good practice. Or as Lewin remarked, "There is nothing so practical as a good theory" (http://www.top-psychology.com/9059-Kurt%20Lewin/quotations1.htm).

The Relationship Between Paradigm and Theory

Theory is developed to explain a phenomenon or a series of phenomena. What defines an adequate explanation? What makes a theory good or valid or useful? There is no universal answer. Rather, it depends on the paradigm within which one works. A paradigm is a system of beliefs about, among other things, the nature of reality, the ways knowledge is produced and understood, how inquiry should take place, and what problems are worth studying. Thus, a good theory is "one that is consistent with and satisfies the requirements of the paradigm to which I hold allegiance."

My colleagues and I have described three distinct paradigms that incline social scientists to define the meaning of adequate explanation and good theory differently (L. J. Coleman, Sanders, & Cross, 1997). Those who work within the *empirical-analytical paradigm* (positivists) look for lawful, objective relationships. Those who work within the *constructivist paradigm* look for regularities and rules in social symbols and relationships. Those who work within the *transformationalist paradigm* (critical theorists) look for an understanding of power, gender, and value inherent in relationships.

Each paradigmatic system has its own goals, what Habermas referred to as "knowledge-constitutive interests" (e.g., Young, 1990), and the extent to which a theory furthers the goals is a primary criterion in determining the goodness of a theory. The goal of inquiry in the empirical-analytical paradigm is prediction and control. In the constructivist paradigm, inquiry should lead to interpretation and understanding. In the transformationalist paradigm, the goal of inquiry is to change the social world. Thus, a theory that leads to inquiry that allows us to understand and interpret peoples' actions from their phenomenological perspective would be sound within the constructivist paradigm. However, if it did not further our ability to predict and control behavior, it would lack validity and utility for those working within the empirical-analytical paradigm, and if it did not provide a basis for social change, it would similarly be found lacking by those working within the transformationalist paradigm.

Thus, we cannot judge theories according to a single standard. Most theory that has been referenced in the literature on gifted education has been grounded in the empirical-analytical paradigm, and one could argue that our neglect of other paradigmatic stances has, until recently, limited our reach, theoretically and with respect to practice. However, one can question the extent to which our field has been theory-driven at all, and it is to that topic that I will now turn.

THE STATE OF THEORY IN OUR FIELD

In order to gauge the extent to which theory plays a role in the field of gifted education, I used a search engine, WebSPIRE 4, a program that enables one to search various data bases, and searched the PsychINFO data base. I started with the descriptor "gifted and talented" and then added the descriptor "theory." I was unsure what I would find, but my experiences as an editor and field reviewer suggested that relatively few manuscripts would appear with a theoretical framework. I also knew that a "call for papers about theory" by the *Journal of the Education of the Gifted* produced relatively few submissions (Ambrose, Cohen, & Coleman, 1999).

Thousands of citations were reported for gifted and talented since 1976. However, adding the descriptor "theory" reduced the list to 188. Perusing these, I found 160 in which theory was a major topic. As I read through the annotations, I categorized them by name of theory. My hunch that little theoretically based scholarship was being produced was confirmed, although I found a range of papers that supposedly had a theoretical bent. In addition, it became clear that no unanimity exists about what a theory is.

There were frequent instances in which a single theory was the foundation for a study. Typically, a scholar would advance a theory or theoretical construct and produce associated research. In those cases in which the scholar (and his or her students) was highly productive, the theoretical perspective acquired some prominence and was cited in the work of others. Sternberg's (1985a) triarchic theory is an example. However, these theories did not seem to inspire others to do further independent work under that theory.

In other cases, theories were referenced, even mentioned as foundational for the author's work, but there was no evidence that the work in question was actually driven by the theory. Frequent mentions in the gifted education literature of Guilford's structure of intellect model (e.g., 1967) are an example of this.

From this analysis and from my professional experience, I conclude, admittedly, somewhat paradoxically, that our field is both atheoretical and theory-laden. By this I mean that there are big ideas floating around that are linked to theories, yet research in the field is not linked to those theories. In fact, the theories tend to be isolated. This is evident in how theories are treated within the field. In the next section I have some fun with this situation.

METAPHORICAL USES OF THEORY IN OUR FIELD

In this section I present four metaphors to describe the state of our theory-laden yet atheoretical field, and I suggest a fifth metaphor as a promising alternative to the four that precede it. The first four metaphors typify the ways theory is used, exists, and operates in our field. Like all metaphors, what they stand for has fuzzy boundaries, and I am hard pressed to maintain clean distinctions. The metaphors are not descriptive of the work of any one person or school of thought. One could argue that the situation they describe is not a negative one because, in a number of demonstrable ways, our field has advanced. However, each has some problematic aspects that can interfere with the emergence of new ideas and the expansion of knowledge.

Theory as Feudalism

Theories and models in the field of gifted education can, and often do, function like a feudal system. In feudalism there is a monarch under whom there are vassals who owe allegiance to and derive power from the lord. The nobility and clergy provide protection and control the serfs and the few freemen. Applying this metaphor to theory in gifted education, the role of the monarch is taken by the federal or state government, which provides resources and establishes policy and, in concert with academics (the nobility and clergy), sets the scholarly agenda of the field. The ruler provides the resources, academics provide the ideas that are proclaimed as truth, and serfs (graduate students and practitioners) work the fields, applying the ideas generated by the nobility in the service of the monarch.

   An overriding goal of feudalism is the maintenance of the system itself, a system that is viewed as the divinely sanctioned natural order, a notion foreign neither to the halls of government nor to the groves of academe. The occasional freeman attempting to work outside the system has a difficult time finding sustenance in the face of pressure to adhere to the received truths that support the system. Although the feudalism metaphor works to some extent, it does not wholly describe theory use in gifted education. Other metaphors are needed if we are to have a fuller picture of the current state of affairs.

Theory as Solipsistic Cult of the Personality

A second metaphor draws its title from solipsism, a branch of philosophy, long discredited, in which the self is the sole source of knowledge. What is known, what can be known, and what happens are created and understood by the individual alone. Thus, anything I call a theory must be one because I propose it. Or, any theory is as good as any other because I say so. Better ideas are unlikely, even impossible, without my acknowledgement because all flows from my wisdom and perspective. Speakers at conferences can be seen adopting this posture. Fortunately, such theory is rarely seen in the journals of our field, but it is found in psychology and education programs across the country.

Theory as Patriarchal Nuclear Family

My third metaphor is based on the perhaps exaggerated notion of the prototypical 1950s' patriarchal nuclear family with its father-knows-best mentality. This is, I think, an apt metaphor for capturing the tenor of the present time. In the patriarchal nuclear family, the father controls the resources and access to the resources, and he determines how the resources will be used. The rest of the family, certainly the children, exists to carry out his ideas and to maintain at least the facade of an ideal family. Mothers are expected to act as intermediaries between sometimes rebellious children and the male parent.

Applying this metaphorically to our field, patriarchs (professors) generate theories to which children (graduate students and teachers) adhere and on which they base their behavior, thus gaining access to resources and earning the blessing of the patriarch. The notion of equality of ideas is paid lip service, but questioning of ideas is inhibited because of the threat of loss of resources, approval, and access to the father.

Theory as Eclectic Practice

My fourth metaphor is implicit in the belief "If it works, it is a sound theory." This stance is taken by those oriented toward direct action as practitioners in gifted education and who take bits and pieces of various theories as the basis for their practice. Striving for effective practice is laudable, but, in our field at least, what results is usually atheoretical on several levels. One cannot be eclectic and maintain a theoretical stance. A theory, by definition, comprises elements that are linked, logically and operationally, which argues against eclecticism as theoretical. Additionally, a theory must be testable or falsifiable (Popper, 1968). A theory is not a theory unless there is some way to test its validity or its viability.

Theory as eclecticism is closely allied with "theory as fad' and its sibling "theory as voodoo." An idea emerges, to uncritical acclaim, it becomes a bandwagon, and many jump on it. Brain-compatible learning is one example. Some good practices may emerge in this manner. However, in the absence of a theoretical underpinning with logically derived propositions and practical implications, it is difficult to determine whether a promising practice will live up to the hype. Furthermore, and maybe more significantly, apparently effective practices may work against desirable outcomes (for example, Ausubel & Robinson's 1969 explanation of rote discovery learning). Theory can provide a context for the examination of the implications of such practices.

I have presented four metaphors to capture the way theory tends to be used in our field. My wish is to move us to a fifth theoretical metaphor, "theory as tool," which advances the idea that theory should function as a tool, not as a goal, for organizing disciplined inquiry (Marx, 1963), a tool that may come in different forms. In the next section I advance that proposition.

DIFFERENT APPROACHES TO THEORY AS TOOL

Theory may be developed and can function in various ways (Marx, 1963; Slife & Williams, 1997). In the next section, I describe some of those. All are ways in which theory can function as a tool to promote inquiry, although some approaches fit certain paradigms better than other approaches.

Model Building

A priori assumptions about relationships among variables, persons, or events underlie theories I call "model-building theories." I use this term because, in our field, such theories tend to be the basis for programs or curriculum. In this approach, one puts forth a model of service delivery or development that is based on ideas about how the world should or might be. Such models can derive from a mixture of experience and armchair theorizing and, in that sense, are good examples of "atheoretical theories."

The model is the basis for a deductive process that generates statements connecting actions of people and organizations. Data are gathered to test these statements and, thus, substantiate the model, although disconfirming data are generally viewed as the result of mistaken implementation or improper measurement. The standards for judging such models tend to be grounded in the empirical-analytical paradigm. An example of a model-building theory is the Schoolwide Enrichment Model (Renzulli & Reis, 1985, 1997).

Borrowing from Theories from Other Places and Incorporating Them into Practice

Importing ideas from other disciplines is a time-honored way in which theories from other disciplines enter our field. The danger is that the interpreter may be going beyond the theory or misinterpreting it, a problem I noted earlier. To borrow a theory properly requires careful analysis so that the relationships among the elements of the theory and between the theory and inquiry and practice are made explicit. Three examples of this approach in the field of gifted education come to mind. In Porath's (1997) neo-Piagetian theory of the development of artistic talent and L. J. Coleman and Cross's (1988) neo-Goffmanian theory of the stigma of giftedness, the relationships are made explicit. In applications of Dabrowski's theory to the study of the development of gifted individuals (Miller & Silverman, 1987; Schiever, 1985), the relationships are somewhat murkier. I am not arguing that this is a result of poor theory or poor interpretation of theory, although that is one possibility, but that it is the result of the difficulty inherent in explaining the relationships between the terms of a theory and the practice it is supposed to inform.

Theory Knitting

This approach is a reaction to the way psychologists advancing different theories about the same phenomenon vie for superiority or acceptance by showing the predictability of their theory and the lack of same in those of others. Several problems arise from this "segregative approach," which "masks an underlying theoretical indistinquishability of theoretical predictions . . . cause[s] psychologists to focus unknowingly on different aspects of the same phenomenon . . . [and] locks the theorist into a particular way of looking at a phenomenon" (Kalman & Sternberg, 1988, pp. 1153–1154). In contrast, theory knitting is an "integrative approach" in which a theorist combines the best of a group of theories with his or her own. Competing theories are pulled together to create a unified explanation. This approach values prediction, yet sees explanation as a better criterion for a good theory. Two examples would be Sternberg's (1985a) triarchic theory of intelligence and Gagné's (1999) notion of abilities.

Grounded Theory

As the name implies, grounded theory, which is frequently used by inquirers working within the constructivist paradigm, starts from the ground or soil of experience (Glaser & Strauss, 1967), not from propositions deduced from an a priori abstract theory. Thus, instead of starting with a theory, empirical observations are used in a systematic inductive process to construct a theory; data come from the field and point upward toward the theory. Care is taken to root the theory in actual phenomena grounded in actual substantive experience. Two examples in the field of gifted education are Peine's dissertation on waiting (1999) and Hébert's study of African-American youth (1998).

Participatory Inquiry

This type of theory differs markedly from the others in that the source of the theory is the participants in an inquiry in a social setting. Knowledge is viewed as neither objective nor separate from the participants, that is, not as the sole property of the researcher, but as co-created by all who are engaged in the inquiry, all of whom are engaged in trying to understand their situation and to make changes that seem appropriate to them. The process is better described as "dialogic" than "inductive" because the participants negotiate the theory as they build a network of propositions describing their world and their world as they want it to be. Participatory inquiry is typically in flux as the situation and the participants change. This form of theory has been linked to action research, participatory action research, and action inquiry (Reason, 1994). The standards for judging such theory would be consistent with the transformative or critical paradigm.

I can think of no clear-cut examples in our field, although I believe more action research could be in participatory in nature. Several pieces have appeared that are suggestive of the parameters of this kind of research (see, for example, Frey, 1998; Jatko, 1995). The work of Pendarvis and Howley (1996) moves in that direction, as does Armenta's (1999) paper on the formation of one's identity as a gifted person.

These five models of theory development fit my notion of theory as tool. Each is a way to organize and provide an opening for systematic exploration of a phenomenon of interest to the field. By purposeful effort, these approaches could become a standard part of scholarly activity and help advance our knowledge of gifted and talented persons.

CONCLUSION AND RECOMMENDATIONS

How can my analysis help our field? When theory is used to generate as well as to test ideas, the theory illuminates predicted interactions and outcomes. The actual theory may be thought of as a template of statements suggesting relationships among people, organizations, and variables in various situations. Armed with the propositions of a theory, one can analyze or create situations in order to test whether the theory applies. The key is to go out into the world of practice and development to see if those relationships are evident while keeping in mind the basic question: Do those propositions actually help us to understand the phenomenon of interest? Additional concerns about prediction and control, understanding and interpretation, or transformation can be judged in a manner consistent with the appropriate paradigm. If the theory does not help us understand more about phenomena in our field, then the theory should be reconfigured, recreated, destroyed, or put on hold until a later time.

I have argued that theory can be used to organize and reinterpret the domain of gifted and talented education, but few have actually done research to validate specific theoretical positions. When a theory is used simply to assimilate information, not as a vehicle for research, it becomes a theory in repose and can become a repository of received knowledge. With no activity directed toward establishing its usefulness, such a theory should be recognized as dangerous. However, when one employs a theory to conduct inquiry, that kind of action can increase one's understanding of a phenomenon by making clear what is known, unknown, or pending and can provide one with an opportunity to escape the bounds of the known.

Some Recommendations

Given that my purpose is to increase the incidence of theoretically based inquiry in gifted education, I make the following recommendations on how to advance that goal.

1. Change the way we educate future researchers. Doctoral programs should teach graduate students to do theoretical analysis and theory construction. Professors should teach different approaches to using theory as a tool as outlined in this chapter. I recommend that advanced graduate students become knowledgeable about a single theory of their choice by analyzing what a theorist actually has said about the phenomenon. My own students report that much of what is said about a theory or theorist in classes across colleges does not match what they learn the person actually wrote, a realization they experience as an empowering moment. They discover that they can think about and come to understand sophisticated ideas that seemed to be solely the province of professors. The students also tend to become more careful about using terms from different theories interchangeably. Last, I recommend that graduate students be asked to construct an inchoate theory on some phenomenon of personal interest that is based on their observations, readings, and practices. This serves as an effective means for helping them unpack their underlying beliefs about a phenomenon.
2. Change the editorial policy in scholarly journals and consistently ask writers, where appropriate, to embed their study or paper in a theory or to comment on the theoretical significance of the piece. This may help remedy the problem of disconnected studies.
3. Build bridges more deliberately between theory and practice. The fact

that our theories are incomprehensible or largely irrelevant to practitioners, including parents, is an indictment of the present state of our knowledge and theory. In my own research I am moving from studying the gifted individuals to studying settings (persons and environments) that seem to be pivotal in the development of those special individuals (L. J. Coleman, 1997, 2001). I urge more careful study of practice and development in natural settings as the basis for building theory.

CHAPTER 5

Rethinking Gifted Education: A Phenomenological Critique of the Politics and Assumptions of the Empirical-Analytic Mode of Inquiry

Tracy L. Cross

In this chapter, I explore giftedness by drawing on a phenomenological approach to lived experiences. Because it is rooted in a paradigm (Kuhn, 1970) that differs significantly from most accepted theories and research in gifted education, this conception sheds new light on the nature of giftedness and the needs of gifted individuals.

Since the beginning of the field, the positivistic, mechanistic world view has underpinned many aspects of our understanding, decision making, and approaches to problem solving, as it has in the social sciences in general (Tarnas, 1991). According to Ambrose (2000) "the mechanistic world view, based on the root metaphor of machine, encourages us to perceive reality as stable and fixed, predisposing researchers to reductive analysis and the simplest search for cause-effect explanations" (p. 161). Patterned on inquiry in the physical sciences, social science research has rendered cause-and-effect relationships the primary focus of research, and any other approaches are treated as pseudoscience (Cross, 1994).

How did this paradigm emerge and come to dominate thinking and inquiry in education? Mainly because of the influence of the public school system and military in the early part of the 20th century. First, immigrants from Eastern and Southern Europe who were culturally and linguistically different were seen as outsiders whose children needed to be "Americanized" through public education. Second, with this country's entry into World War I there was a need for efficient ways to make decisions about who would serve as officers and foot soldiers in the armed services, complicated by the large numbers of non–English speaking individuals who were part of the military pool. There emerged at this time a new, highly mechanistic behavioral psychology, which hastened the fall of Freud's dominant psychoanalytic approach. The rise of behaviorism led to the development of educational technologies, such as objective testing practices, that were seen as scientific, equitable, and consistent with the country's growing industrial and technological might.

Thus, by the time of Terman's (e.g., 1925–1959) seminal studies of gifted children, the mechanistic paradigm was the basis for research in psychology and education. Its underlying ontological and epistemological assumptions—along with its primary tool, the IQ test—shaped our conceptions of giftedness and the needs of gifted students. It also wedded gifted education to the emerging dominant mode of inquiry in behavioristic psychology that pursued cause-and-effect relationships: the empirical-analytic mode (L. J. Coleman, Sanders, & Cross, 1997). Understanding this mode of inquiry, as well as the alternatives, will help in developing the argument for a phenomenological approach to giftedness.

BASIC MODES OF INQUIRY

Modes or paradigms of inquiry represent the philosophical assumptions, goals, and methods of research used by scholars in their approaches to problems and issues. Although there are numerous ways to categorize research, there are three basic modes of inquiry: the empirical-analytic, the interpretive, and the transformative (L. J. Coleman, Sanders, & Cross, 1997). Examining each highlights some of the different perspectives one can take when pursuing topics of research and illuminates some of the reasons for the findings that result.

Scholars who adhere to the *empirical-analytic* mode of inquiry, a term coined by Popkewitz (1984), see the universe as comprised of pre-existing universal natural laws that scientists can discover through the application of empirical methods. Empirical methods and logical deductive reasoning enable scientists to determine the validity of ideas, uncover causal relationships, and make predictions about events. By using objective methods, researchers strive to minimize bias and be neutral observers. This mode of inquiry is grounded in positivism, which is based on empiricism and has been the predominant paradigm in Western science for the past two centuries (L. J. Coleman, Sanders & Cross, 1997, p. 106).

Scholars working guided by interpretive inquiry see knowledge as mediated by the signs and symbols people use to interpret their world. Knowledge is therefore subjective, and what is of the greatest importance and use is how others understand the world. Interpretivist researchers work to uncover the patterns or rules in social relationships as seen by individuals and groups. They do not expect to find a single, most appropriate explanation for all phenomena (see Guba, 1990; Popkewitz, 1984). Phenomenological inquiry is closest in nature to the interpretivist mode of inquiry.

Scholars who ascribe to the *transformative* mode see knowledge as embedded in a cultural matrix of values. All inquiry and human behavior are locked into a web of power relationships grounded in struggles around gender, race, social class, and other culturally and economically determined variables, understand which enables understanding of the world and the ability to transform it. Proponents of this view believe that values are a vital focus of inquiry and that values define the ideal relationships among individuals (L. J. Coleman, Sanders, & Cross, 1997, p. 107).

Clearly, these three inquiry paradigms reflect radically different views of reality, knowledge, and values. One's orientation determines whether one believes that reality is external and preexisting or constructed by the individuals to varying degrees; whether one believes that objective, absolute knowledge is possible or that knowledge is contingent and situational; whether one believes that inquiry can be value-free or that it cannot, and should not, aspire or pretend to objectivity (Guba, 1990). It should be obvious that one's paradigmatic stance or mode of inquiry profoundly shapes what one deems worthy of study, how one studies that which is deemed worthy, and, to a considerable extent, the results of one's inquiry.

Some have claimed that since the tenets of these paradigms are irreconcilable, that communication across paradigms is not possible. Because the dominance of one mode of inquiry over the others is tied to power relations and the maintenance of the status quo communication becomes a means of wielding power, akin to what Foucault (1995) called "technologies of power." Sampson (1993) describes the way in which communication is limited by those who dominate in a society:

> Insofar as the speaking parts that are available to the cast of humanity have already been scripted in ways that implicitly represent the standpoint of dominant societal groups, merely to have a speaking part is still not to have one's own groups' interests, point of view, or specificity represented in a genuine dialogue. If, in order to be heard, I must speak in ways that you have proposed, then I can be heard only if I speak like you, not like me. Rather than being an equal contributor, I remain enclosed in a discursive game that ensures your continuing advantage. The clear message is that current forms of cultural and psychological practice deny certain groups any possibility of being heard in their own way, on their own terms, reflecting their own interests and specificities, and that this condition does not reflect mere chance but rather reflects the operation of the power of those in charge to dictate the terms by which psychological and social reality will be encountered. (p. 1220)

The connections between the dominant culture and politics, research approach, and knowledge construction are subtle but omnipresent. These factors come together to yield the intellectual climate in which research on gifted children takes place, and their confluence within the mechanistic, empirical-analytic mode has painted researchers into a corner in terms of the conceptions of giftedness as well as the tools with which it is studied. For years, researchers in education have attempted to emulate the research methods used by psychologists. The expectation placed on educational researchers to follow psychology is analogous to a train. The caboose is the field of education, trailing in the rear. The car leading the caboose (psychology) is not the locomotive, but rather a freight car, carrying the baggage of the natural sciences. The true locomotive pulling the caboose of educational research is the natural sciences (Cross, 1990, p. 98). Education is not a natural science, it is a social science, or perhaps more accurately should be called a human science.

PHENOMENOLOGICAL INQUIRY

The assumptions adopted by behavioral psychologists that have become codified in the empirical-analytic mode include the notion that "a phenomenon must be 1) observable, 2) measurable, and 3) appear such that its essence can be agreed upon by more than one observer" (Valle & King, 1978, p. 4), assumptions that equate phenomena, people, and objects. This reflects the dominance of *etic* perspectives in research accounts, in which the interpretation of an outside observer is of primary importance, irrespective of the views, beliefs, perceptions, or experiences of those being observed. The empirical-analytic mode of inquiry, which is based on the idea that methods employed in the physical sciences can be used to study human beings and their institutions, makes little distinction between objects and people as the subject of research.

However, there is another way to think about people as the foci of inquiry. In his description of the primary difference between an object and a person, Franz Kafka once said that "to understand why a stone rolls down a hill, we must look to see what force loosened it from its place at the top, but to see why a person climbs the hill, we must discover what that person seeks at the top" (quoted in Bugental, 1989, p. x). This echoes the *emic*, or inside, perspective that is the goal of much qualitative inquiry, including phenomenological inquiry. Phenomenologists argue that to understand people we must study the most essential element of their makeup—consciousness. A research model based on mechanistic assumptions objectifies people in ways that, phenomenologists suggest, undermine the results and meaning of the research.

Phenomenology was developed by Edmund Husserl (1859–1938) with the goal of enabling a clear and unbiased study of human consciousness and experience by describing the structures of experience as they present themselves to consciousness, without recourse to theory, deduction, or assumptions from other disciplines such as the natural sciences. Phenomenology is based on the premise that reality consists of objects and events as they are perceived or understood in human consciousness. Hence, phenomenology has the potential to remove the outside observers' respective world views, values, and personal biases.

Perhaps the most potent criticism levied by phenomenologists at the research of behavioral psychologists is the same argument that Husserl (1962) made against all "ologies"—that every "scientific" field is built on a priori assumptions about what is being studied that render the findings meaningless. The meaninglessness is due to the phenomena being studied "being told" what they can be in advance by how data are gathered. Giorgi (1970) stated that traditional science decided on "specific criteria [that] are known and announced beforehand" (p. 26). However, phenomena exist in their own right. The various scientific fields are nothing more than lenses to view the world through.

Despite that Husserl was well known among his peers around the world, his ideas did not have a big impact in the United States until Martin Heidegger succeeded him at the University of Gottingen and built on his work. In his classic book, *Being and Time* (1927), Heidegger claimed that phenomenology is concerned with the "being" (experience and behavior) and with human experience and behavior is either "authentic" or "inauthentic." After *Being and Time* was published, American intellectuals revisited Husserl's writings. Of particular interest was Husserl's rigorous approach to obtaining the essence of human experience through research approaches aimed at consciousness. In Husserl's phenomenological reduction,

> we are to "bracket," or abstain from positing the existence of, the natural world around us. That is, we put out of action the general thesis of the everyday "natural" standpoint, our background presupposition that there exists a world independent of our experience. We will then, Husserl holds, be in a position to describe "pure" consciousness, abstracting from its embeddedness in the world of nature. By carrying out the reduction we abandon the "natural" or "naturalistic" attitude which takes the world for granted and come to adopt instead the phenomenological or what is called the "transcendental" attitude. (Heidegger, 1927, p. 11)

There are two important concepts underpinning phenomenology: *Lebenswelt* and *epoche*. *Lebenswelt*, or lived experience, was Husserl's (1962) term for a person's pre-reflective experience. According to Husserl, this most basic type of experience was free from interpretation of second-order analysis. Uncovering and describing the *Lebenswelt* of human experience became the primary goal of phenomenology because it is believed to be the most rigorous approach to research. Husserl believed that through phenomenological research, the essence of human experience could emerge.

Epoche is the process of bracketing presuppositions prior to conducting a study, a suspension of judgment, a way to let the phenomena speak while holding at bay the usual presuppositions that are in force in any given situation. Husserl believed that this process reduces the unintended influences that prevent a phenomenon from appearing on its own terms.

EPISTEMIC COGNITION AND KNOWLEDGE FORMATION

If the concepts of giftedness utilized by various practitioners are in some ways flawed, will the problem be solved by developing a different or better conception of giftedness? The answer, from a phenomenological point of view, is no. What is needed is not the "correct" conception of giftedness, a notion that is perhaps counterintuitive, but rather an understanding of the various ways people think about inquiry or research and how this relates to the aforementioned issues. This awareness is called "epistemic cognition" (Kitchener & Brenner, 1990).

By accepting a single mode of inquiry, a lens is created through which one judges various practices and issues (L. J. Coleman, Sanders, & Cross, 1997). Like an optical lens, this philosophical lens is transparent, and one might not even be aware of its existence. A person may view the world through this lens, which determines what and how one sees, and believe that he or she is viewing the world "as it is," unmediated by a philosophical framework. Educating researchers to understand the tenets and consequences of multiple modes of inquiry is the only assurance that they will be aware of the lens through which they see the world through and that they understand there are other ways of seeing. Without this knowledge, researchers tend to reify their own findings and not explore other possibilities. According to Ambrose (1998),

> those without well developed epistemic cognition may understand clearly defined issues that are amenable to logical or formal reasoning. But when faced with ambiguous issues, they tend to ignore multiple perspectives while using only the decision rules that apply to their own preferred perspective. A lack of epistemic cognition reinforces dogmatic insularity in scientific work when scholars fail to appreciate the value in the tenets, procedures, and initiatives of different investigative paradigms. Scholars with strong epistemic cognition are able to recognize the strengths *and weaknesses* of their own research paradigms and world views, the weaknesses *and strengths* of competing paradigms and world views, and the barriers that inhibit the development of their own epistemic cognition. (p. 80)

ONGOING PROBLEMS IN GIFTED EDUCATION

Although there are numerous lenses through which professionals in the field consider gifted education, there seems to be an intellectual bottom line in the minds of many: the belief that gifted education opportunities should be made available to the greatest number of students possible. Beyond this agreement, however, there are competing trends, two of which are noteworthy. The first is evidenced by the evolution of a group of professionals who propose a taxonomy of giftedness that parallels the disability categories of mild, moderate, severe, and profound mental retardation. This is clearly an extension of an IQ-based definition and gives new life to and extends the properties of the conceptual underpinnings of the IQ notion of giftedness, with all of the implications for practice inherent in that notion.

A second and conflicting stream of thought is prompted by the underrepresentation of minority gifted students, which many see as a consequence of the use of IQ as the measure of giftedness. The primary focus of this diverse group of professionals is the creation of an alternative method for assessing giftedness. One criticism of these new approaches is that they create a second-class citizenry among those identified by opening the door to those who do not show their giftedness on an IQ test. This criticism, however, is rooted in a particular IQ-based conception of giftedness and reflects the fact that the dominant paradigm creates the language in which conversations are held (see Frasier, 1997, for a good explanation of the belief system commonly held in the field). Only within the paradigm that I identified earlier as the empirical-analytic mode is identification of students with less-than-stratospheric IQs a problem. Within alternative conceptual systems in which IQ is not privileged as it is in the traditional one, the absence of an extremely high IQ is hardly a barrier to being identified as gifted.

The point is that the enshrinement of IQ is not a fact of nature but a historical event tied to particular circumstances and the belief in the inevitability of the use of IQ as a, or the, defining attribute of giftedness reflects a pronounced lack of epistemic awareness. Many researchers are struggling because of their tendencies to be wedded to a concept of giftedness that limits to what can be done. Success in identifying unrecognized gifted students requires a decoupling of our mechanistic view of the world and understanding that giftedness is a function of our country's dominant culture and modes of inquiry.

THE UNIQUE CONTRIBUTION OF PHENOMENOLOGICAL RESEARCH TO GIFTED EDUCATION

The epistemological and ontological assumptions of empirical-analytic modes of inquiry can be juxtaposed with phenomenology to illustrate the inherent limitations of the former. The greatest detriment to the study of gifted education has been defaulting to high-ability indicators such as IQ and thereby studying the same people through the same lens. How would gifted education be different if researchers conducted phenomenological studies of different subgroups of gifted students? For example, children who believe themselves to be gifted, passionate about, or excited by *art* would be studied as a subgroup of gifted children. Others who represent any domain—music, sports, science, English, mathematics—with a belief in their competence in or passion for the subject would become subjects of phenomenological studies. Formal identification processes would follow and, in a way, validate these descriptions rooted in the lived experiences of the gifted children rather than being the starting point of the inquiry.

Although empirical-analytic, interpretivist, and transformative modes of inquiry vary significantly in epistemological and ontological assumptions as well as goals, they are similar in that they have not resolved many of the problems in the field of gifted education. The shortcomings of the empirical-analytic mode have been noted previously. A primary limitation of the interpretivist mode is its limitation of findings to the specific groups studied, i.e., no generalizations are made across groups or settings. The transformative mode explicitly aims first and foremost to counter the dominance of the privileged elite, and the production of knowledge or interpretative insights is secondary to this goal.

Phenomenology incorporates qualities of all three modes of inquiry while contributing unique features of its own. For example, phenomenology can be used as a means to create valid interview protocols or surveys that allow the data to reveal themselves as they exist, not as researchers suppose they must (Giorgi, 1970). It is interpretivistic by revealing characteristics of lived experience that encourage dramatic rethinking on the part of those involved in the dominant culture. Its unique contribution is that it is perhaps the most radical of human science research types—radical in the original sense of going to the root of things—because it aims to uncover the prereflective experience of subjects, unmediated by researchers' a priori assumptions, thereby illustrating the invariant structures of human experience, which may be generalizable across groups. Phenomenologists also believe that engaging in the bracketing process enables researchers to leave behind many if not all of their preconceived notions of the phenomenon being studied. This can allow researchers to break the intellectual bondage of accepted notions of giftedness and how to measure it, while incorporating the benefits of all three modes of inquiry.

By beginning studies through a phenomenological lens, a priori assumptions are replaced with actual characteristics of the phenomenon being studied, using the language of the subject rather than that of the dominant culture. What is likely to emerge in the field of gifted education is a more human-centered, diverse understanding of giftedness, one less obscured by old metaphors and limiting assumptions.

CHAPTER 6

Talent Development for Rural Communities

Aimee Howley, Craig B. Howley, and Edwina D. Pendarvis

The treatment in this chapter takes the view, which will be strange to most educators, that schooling has actively contributed to the demise of rural communities.[1] We present arguments to support this perspective, but we acknowledge at the outset that the thesis rests on a sensibility beyond warrant—a feeling that the rural world is richly meaningful in spite of its troubled existence. It seems to us that these meanings should inform a pro-rural sort of schooling and that they just might inform a "ruralized" form of schooling for academically talented youngsters.

The chapter consists of four parts. The first traces the history of rural education, shows how national purposes have decided the direction taken by rural schooling in the 20th century, explains how rural schools have arrived at the dilemmas and contradictions they now confront, articulates the distinction between cosmopolitan and rural purposes, and details meanings inherent in the rural life-world. The second part considers academic talent and miseducation in the rural circumstance. It considers and critiques the conventional cosmopolitan purposes of rural programs for gifted students and explains why few regard antirural education as a recognizable issue. The third part considers issues and dynamics related to restoring properly rural purposes to rural schools. The final part derives insights from the first three in charting options for "ruralizing" gifted programs in rural schools and also contains confessions relevant to our own rural life experiences that make it possible for us to propose such options.

THE COUNTRY AND THE CITY

Many accounts of the history of education in the United States (e.g., Butts & Cremin, 1953; Spring, 1997) begin in rural places and end in urban ones. Conventional histories tend to overlook the institution of rural schooling, often portraying it as sheltered from reform movements and, hence, inhospitable to improvement. Rural education, however, had its own history, which was, in general, characterized by traditional pedagogical practices and resistance to state control (Theobald, 1995). Despite these common features, rural schools and districts showed considerable variation—in attendance level, length of school terms, requirements for teachers, condition of buildings, forms of governance, and ideological commitments (Gilmore, 1982; Kaestle, 1983; Link, 1986; Theobald, 1995).

Rural schools traditionally served as a focus of community identity as well as providing serviceable instruction in basic reading, writing, and arithmetic (DeYoung & Lawrence, 1995). Well into the 20th century, many rural schools were taught by one or two teachers. Most such schools actually comprised their own districts and were governed by their own boards of education. This arrangement meant that the ratio of board members to citizens was *much* higher than it is today. In 1929, 127,000 districts operated schools, but in 1989 there were just 15,400 school districts—a drastic reduction of nearly 90% (Howley, 1996).

The extreme variability of these small schools and districts was thought to contribute to important deficiencies, and rural schools became an early target for educational reform. Progressives of the early 1900s sought to connect school improvements to a broader program of rural reform. They blamed rural schools for the depopulation of rural areas and for other purported defects of rural life (Fuller, 1982; Maxcy, 1981). The strategies for reforming rural schools adopted by progressives in the early 1900s characterized those used throughout the remainder of the century: consolidation of schools and districts, the deployment of state-level standards, the cultivation of infrastructure, and the introduction of various technologies (see, e.g., Fuller, 1982; Superintendent of Public Instruction, 1920).

The history of rural education typifies the history of rural places more generally—a series of events rooted in the conflict between local identities and the rural life-world, on the one hand, and regional and national priorities, on the other. Place by place, with greater and less alacrity and with more or less ardor, rural places sacrificed their traditions, land, people, and values to an increasingly uniform and unfailingly urban version of the "good life" (Berry, 1990a).

This cultural movement slowly but steadily denuded rural places of meaningfulness, which has had the general effect of muting rural variability.

Of course, such variability was what early 20th century reformers construed as the real deficiency of rural schools. Rural locales themselves were viewed as "lagging behind" cities and the emerging suburbs. Reformers sought to improve such places from the perspective of modernization.

In the United States and Canada, subsequent technological and economic changes were also responsible for removing large numbers of people from rural places. In 1880, the United States was about 75% rural, and about 42% of the population lived on farms; in 1920, it was 50% and about 30%; in 1960, 30% and 10% (Dacquel & Dahmann, 1993).

For the small percentage of the population still living in the country, life has changed drastically during the 20th century. Their socioeconomic status has been reduced, and their way of life devalued. These changes have a significant impact on the likelihood that gifted students in rural areas will be educated equitably and effectively.

Stereotypical, polarized views of the country have grown out of centuries of economic and cultural tension between the rural and the urban. In his historical analysis of literary representations of city and country, Williams (1973) says: "On the country has gathered the idea of a natural way of life, of peace, innocence, and simple virtue. Powerful hostile associations have also developed . . . on the country as a place of backwardness, ignorance, and limitation" (p. 1). Both of these characterizations distort country life, representing it and its inhabitants as lacking in complexity. Life there is seen as neither demanding nor developing intellect. Whether the terms are flattering or— more typically—insulting, rural people are relegated to the categories of simple and quaint, often to the point of comedy. Herzog and Pittman (1995) cite *bumpkin, hillbilly*, and *hick* as illustrative of the tendency. *Yokel* and *hayseed* also come to mind. The etymology of the word *clown* (which means "rustic" or "boor") indicates the long history of the negative stereotype of rural intelligence.

Bright students in rural areas are aware of the stigma attached to their way of life, though they are probably less aware of the romance of it. Some are resentful and defensively proud; some accept their supposed inferiority as real. Neither response serves their interests. Teachers often reinforce these responses instead of countering them by honoring the rich complexity of rural life, the value of local knowledge, and the importance of developing intellect.

What's Rural

Our account follows our own participation in rural life, but also builds on the importance Habermas (1987) accords the life-world. We therefore locate what is rural in the meaningfulness of the rural life-world. What *is* the rural life-world? What are these meanings? What *is* rural, properly speaking? This final question is critical because, in imagining decent rural futures, those who care for the *rural* quality of such futures must give some account of the distinguishing features of the rural life-world, lest these decent futures be conceived as extensions of the cosmopolitan agenda (e.g., the capitalist project of global economic dominion).

The life-world is necessarily a situated experience. No one actually lives a totally unsituated existence, though we are clearly arguing that globalization and the cosmopolitan perspective cultivate an existence that is not situated in particular (geographic) *places*. Raymond Williams (1973), for instance, describes the world-city as uniquely placeless.

The rural life-world for the time being still presents an antithesis to cosmopolitan culture. The parameters of this life-world entail a "sensibility of place," the struggle to do good work locally, physical and emotional proximity to relatives, accessibility to neighbors, care for and struggle with the natural world, and love of home. This antithesis to the cosmopolitan life-world is described eloquently and in detail by such writers as Wendell Berry, Gene Logsdon, and Wes Jackson. David Orr (1995), the renowned environmentalist, argues that "re-ruralizing" education is necessary both to help preserve the natural world and to prepare rising generations to deal better with the otherwise inevitable dislocations.

To contrast cosmopolitan and local rural communities as they apply to schooling, we provide two illustrative lists. First, we give cosmopolitan concerns as they apply to rural schooling:

- insulating the school from patronage politics,
- overcoming the disadvantages of students' backgrounds,
- implementing state and national reforms,
- increasing the level of students' aspirations,
- providing world-class buildings for students and teachers,
- offering a broad high school curriculum,
- teaching to developmental norms,
- infusing "cutting-edge" technology,
- overcoming resistance to consolidation and school closure, and
- keeping the school distant from local culture.

Corresponding commitments that characterize the rural life-world of schooling might include the following:

- caring for rural places,
- sustaining school and community,
- grounding education in local knowledge,
- illuminating pathways to decent rural adulthoods,

- serving communities in practical ways,
- celebrating community identity (in rituals like athletic competitions),
- developing curricula to sustain rural places,
- keeping the small local school open,
- using technology in locally appropriate ways, and
- grounding moral critique in local values.

What is properly rural? This question probably cannot be answered with a simple or even a complex operational definition. We, indeed, have a personal view of the matter. Many readers will not be persuaded by it, and we do not insist that our view is best. It is, however, the ground of our experience and commitment.

We distinguish between wilderness, industrial outposts, and "properly rural" places—where we understand "place" as composed equally of commitment, community, and an inhabited local terrain, and not just a political jurisdiction that encloses a population to be characterized demographically. To call wilderness "rural" seems to us an oxymoron. Rural is a populated countryside. Calling industrial outposts, such as mining districts located within the countryside, rural is also problematic. The work of mining sustains the very machinery that threatens the rural life-world. People who live there are not, of course, to blame. Indeed, many of us carry out jobs that contribute to the global project of placelessness and deracination—certainly this is true of those who work in colleges, universities, most schools, and related enterprises.

So what is "properly" rural? For us, farming best epitomizes what is properly rural. The judgment, however, is not a simple or definite one. Not all farming, for example, is properly rural: Large-scale agriculture and corporate agriculture resemble mining outposts by degrading the land. So do timbering and fishing outposts run in similar ways. None is sustainably rural, and none can sustain a properly rural life-world. The properly rural is something rare in the here-and-now, but its vestiges and the sources of its remaking exist in many communities. The nature of that remaking mostly resides in imagination, but those imaginings embody hope (Woodhouse, 1999).

Sustenance of functional communities and of the planet's resources is not, after all, a trivial concern. What we imagine are rural communities that thrive by growing and caring for plants and animals in a sustainable plan that maximizes the common good on local ground, and not as a distant abstraction. In truth, imagination of this sort could encompass mining, timbering, and fishing enterprises (and other economic ventures) that *would* sustain rural communities. An example of appropriately rural technology, and its concomitantly appropriate social organization, appears in *Gaviotas: A Village to Reinvent the World* (Weisman, 1998).

Style as Local Knowledge

Local knowledge constitutes ways of being in the world as well as perceptions and understandings about a particular place. Teachers who do not respect a style of living born of local knowledge are likely to evoke resentment and disengagement among students rooted in such knowledge. As with many bright students, rural gifted students may question teachers' authority when it is not bolstered by a rationale that conforms to the students' way of understanding the world. A long history of being misunderstood by local elites representing distant money and power has created cynicism among rural populations. Teachers may find they need to justify instructional practices in terms that make sense to some rural gifted students and their families.

Language is also a common representation of style associated with local knowledge, but students who speak any of a number of rural dialects (e.g., East Kentucky, Cajun Louisiana, Downeast Maine, East Texas) are likely to be regarded as deficient in language skills (e.g., Christian & Wolfram, 1979). Grammar standards, however, are the result not of logic, but of class and power distinctions (Fasold, 1990). According to Norman (1971) "urbanization makes itself most apparent in the 'correctness' of grammar" (p. 327).

Rural speech is often admired aesthetically by ethnological purists (Thomas, 1997); it is regarded neutrally by linguists; but it is seen as an intellectual shortcoming by many classroom teachers. In our experience, teachers who do not speak a rural dialect themselves find it difficult to see rural dialect as anything but incorrect. Many rural teachers have been told (in training programs) that their own speech is deficient, and they struggle to mask it.

Deriving personal identity from family ("familism") is another rural way of being in the world, another way of local understanding. Familism, a predominant rural value and economic resource in the past, has been weakened by industrial and postindustrial capitalism, but it continues to be an important element of contemporary rural life. Gifted rural students' loyalty to family and place may frustrate teachers who regard success as going to a prestigious college and pursuing a lucrative career. As Gaventa (1980) reports, entrepreneurs who came to rural areas in the late 1800s were surprised to see how little the inhabitants cared about money. The value system that prizes the extended family, autonomy, and the outdoors over affluence maintains some of its strength in rural communities.

Many teachers construe life goals in ways that inevitably represent local accomplishments as inadequate. Rural parents are right to take offense. As a consequence, bright rural children may regard school success with the same ambivalence that Harris (1993) attributes to high-achieving immigrant children. Like rural speech, rural students' values and behavior grow out of their knowledge of the world. Failure to respect and to appropriate that knowledge into classroom conversation justifiably elicits the resistance of students and parents.

ACADEMIC TALENT AND MISEDUCATION IN RURAL PLACES

Academic talent is widely misinterpreted as a national resource, and, under such terms, its cultivation often falls to the public schools. In part because of this misinterpretation and in part because of other dysfunctions of public education, schools often act unwisely when they provide or fail to provide special programs for talented youngsters (Howley et al., 1995). Schools' frequent failure to act wisely on behalf of talented students is by no means ubiquitous, however, and rural schools are certainly *not* the least wise in their decisions about how to handle students with high academic ability.

Our experiences with schools and our more systematic studies of them suggest that, by and large, schools take one of two approaches to dealing with highly talented students: They either ignore them or they privilege them. In our view the latter is by far the worse course of action because it tends to perpetuate political-economic relations that are damaging to human potential and ultimately to the life of the planet (Howley et al., 1995). When schools privilege children who, by and large, are *already* privileged, they cultivate selfishness among individuals. And they do so in the name of a larger selfishness—the global economic dominion of the United States.

The other course of action—ignoring the highly talented—is frequently the practice in rural schools. This approach sometimes functions to curtail opportunities for bright students. The deprivation of the individual, in these cases, is sometimes counterbalanced by benefits to the commons. When rural residents work to construct schooling as an enterprise dedicated to the cultivation of community, as in the case of the Amish, for example, their abridgement of individual liberty has strong warrant (Hostetler & Huntington, 1992). As our brief history of rural education suggests, however, many contemporary rural schools define their aims and base their practices on cosmopolitan visions of the way the world does or ought to work.

Conventional Rationale for Gifted Education in Rural Schools

At least since the passage of the GI bill and probably well before that, educators, policymakers, and parents have subscribed to the belief that a good education prepares students for good jobs (Levine, 1986). This belief is supported by functionalist theories of social stratification, which suggest that the most important of these "good" jobs ought to go to those individuals best suited for them by either native ability or training, or by some combination of the two. As a corollary to this conventional view, typical justifications for gifted education rely on the belief that students with the greatest academic (or creative or leadership) potential ought to be afforded training especially suited to their probable destinies as leaders in business, the professions, and government. The idea that talented students might prefer to slop hogs or teach in rural schools is almost unthinkable. For example, in a federally funded project in which one of us participated, rural girls were exhorted to "raise their aspirations" above those they expressed. The girls wanted to attend the local university and become teachers. Project staff directed them to consider distant urban universities and careers as pediatricians and engineers.

Attentiveness to economic motives for education encourages talented rural students to seek their fortunes—and thus fulfill their destinies—in cities and suburbs. From this vantage, residence in a rural place and upbringing by a rural family constitute disadvantages. Writers in the field of gifted education who concern themselves with bright students in rural schools usually construe residence in a rural community as an impediment:

> In some ways children from geographically remote areas resemble physically handicapped youngsters in that they experience reduced levels of contact with the stimulating experiences which are required to foster the acquisition of skills and the growth of knowledge. . . . In terms of social contacts, this isolation may result in the scarcity of appropriate role models. . . . At the socioeconomic level, family interests and values may place no great emphasis on academic achievement. (McLeod & Cropley, 1989, p. 128)

Viewing rural residence as a disadvantage and economic competitiveness as a goal, many educators imagine outmigration as the hopeful fate of talented country children. With this outcome in mind, they recommend programs designed to give rural gifted children "advantages" similar to those enjoyed by their urban and suburban peers. This approach typically brings the traditional academic curriculum to bear on the problem of offering bright rural students adequate preparation for admission to selective colleges and eventual participation in high-status careers. And it tends to consign students' aspirations to conventional paths—denying them opportunities to make connections between serious academic study and rural commitments.

Of course, many of the families that contribute children to rural gifted programs *do not* harbor rural commitments. Because of the durable association between social class and intelligence (measured conventionally), many—possibly most—students who are eligible for gifted programs come from local elites (Duncan, 1999). Often they are the children of professionals and businesspeople who live in the small towns that serve rural communities or in the open countryside surrounding somewhat larger cities. Some of their parents own large farms or manage mining operations. Rarely in our experience are the children of the poor—working or otherwise—identified for their unusual talents. The class interests of most parents of rural gifted children predispose them to support cosmopolitan purposes. For this reason, we are particularly suspicious of efforts exerted by such parents to divert school resources to support enrichment programs. Such programs tend, in general, to foist the cosmopolitan aspirations of the wealthy on all children found to have unusual talents. To the extent that gifted programs in rural locales support the entrenched interests of local elites, we find them morally objectionable. Moreover, we argue that unless properly rural values infuse gifted programs, they tend to do harm to rural places.

The Ideological Dynamics of Anti-rural Schooling for Rural Locales

Just as many rural places have sacrificed parts of their identities in response to the intrusions of urban interests and perspectives, so too have most rural schools embraced an "antirural" schooling (Berry, 1990b; Howley, 1991). Living in a rural area is often seen as an admission of deficiency; growing up rural is often considered an educational disadvantage. Rural educators who undertake reforms on behalf of the national economic interest do so with good intentions that are nonetheless based on misunderstandings about the relationship between rural areas and "the global economy": They believe they are preparing their students to *succeed* in a global economy. Antirural schooling, then, is by and large described by the all-too-familiar mainstream practices of schooling. Curriculum alignment, Goals 2000, School-to-Work, Comprehensive School Reform, proficiency testing, accountability, school consolidation—all come inscribed with antirural intentions. The originators of such programs would vehemently deny the antirural conception of their innovations. The rural life-world, however, is invisible to the originators of such programs, and consequently they dismiss appreciation of this life-world as merely "philosophical" and therefore impractical (DeYoung & Theobald, 1991; cf. Khattri, Riley & Kane, 1997, for an example of this dismissal).

Rural educators can sometimes deflect mainstream practices to support pro-rural schooling. Bruce Miller and Karen Hahn (1997), for instance, describe some rural-friendly school-to-work efforts in the Northwest. The Rural School and Community Trust has also been able to work toward pro-rural schooling without severely antagonizing the mainstream. Such efforts are nonetheless exceptions because teachers are socialized toward practices that reflect the cosmopolitan agenda. This socialization is not a conscious act of teacher educators or local administrators or colleagues. It is largely the result of the way meanings have been withdrawn from the life-world (cf. Habermas,

1984). The meanings most easily accessible to all individuals are those propagated by the state, large corporations, and the media (Sassen, 1996).

Simply because these meanings prevail, most individuals—rural, suburban, or urban—seldom question them. Teachers are not unlike other people in this respect. To question these meanings implicates intellectual capacities informed by wide reading, a disposition to ask unanswerable questions, outrage at injustice, and imagination of the requirements of the good life.

COUNTRIFYING RURAL EDUCATION

Educators—even many rural educators—argue that nostalgic romanticism underlies the claim that rural cultures offer special sets of virtues on which rural schooling might draw. This argument gains momentum when it is bolstered by empirical evidence of the breakdown of economic and social life in rural places. Even if destructive outside forces are blamed for this breakdown, its impact is typically construed as the impoverishment of rural life. The argument assumes that the domination of rural places by urban interests has either eradicated rural virtues or deformed them beyond usefulness. It does not admit a more complex reading of rural life that acknowledges a contradictory juxtaposition of traditional virtues, urban intrusions, ethnic vigor, and social dislocation.

Curiously, though, this argument, which might well be applied to any subjugated group in the United States, is believable only when it is applied to rural culture. In their attentiveness to multiculturalism, educators tend to emphasize (or at least to acknowledge) the positive contributions of other subcultural groups—even those that have durable connections to rural ways of life (e.g., Native Americans). Whereas this emphasis does not always ignore the damage done to these subcultures by capitalist imperatives (e.g., Manifest Destiny) and the social consequences of that damage, it typically seeks to resuscitate and build on the strengths of particular subcultures. Moreover, educators sensitive to pluralism often comprehend children's native cultures as the most appropriate starting point for their learning. This corresponds well with current thinking about child development and pedagogy, namely that learning is an active process of making sense of the world through the use of socially mediated conventions.

Multiculturalism, like many educational movements, offers a variety of sometimes conflicting perspectives (Sleeter & Grant, 1993). Our view of the possibilities of rural culture, therefore, conforms to certain versions of multiculturalism but argues against others. In particular, we reject versions of multiculturalism that unambiguously valorize folkways and artifacts, construing cultural formation as somehow immune to conflict, an approach characterized by Sleeter and Grant as the "human relations" approach to multicultural education. Instead, because we see cultural diversity as both a source and a product of conflict, we view all cultural formation as contradictory, embodying at one and the same time features that liberate and constrain individuals and groups (cf. Walzer, 1997).

This perspective does not, however, support a program of cultural fusion that draws the best from a variety of cultures into a rich conversation. Rather, we see cultures as far too situated and self-referential to engage in such conversations on a routine basis. Fusions do happen on their own, but their causes and outcomes tend to be unanticipated, and sometimes they are quite negative. By contrast, explicit efforts to engage subcultures in open exchanges of "best practice" are usually misguided, often tending to reinforce rather than to challenge prevailing dynamics of cultural domination, exploitation, and co-optation (Walzer, 1997).

Our approach to cultural pluralism comprehends every cultural location as both formative and problematic. Education rooted in this view seeks to enable children to draw meaning both from culture's clear imprint on identity and its ambiguous claim to authority over individual destiny. Education designed to address this complexity draws on the premises of the child's culture as the source of cultural affirmation as well as the basis for cultural critique (cf. Walzer, 1988). Its quarry is meaning; even when it encourages critique of the native culture, it does not necessarily, even usually, require renunciation. And even when rejection of native culture is the necessary outcome of the critique, it rests on moral and intellectual grounds, not on venal ones.

For example, in a deeply Christian rural community, the premises of Christianity may serve as the basis for critiquing racism. The critique may cause the child to renounce the racism of his or her community, but not necessarily to leave the community. This version of education does not try to convince the child that good lies outside of the community, but rather tries to show that both good and evil and the potential to pursue either lies *within* the purview of the community.

Given these general assumptions, it seems to us no more nostalgic or romantic to ground rural education in the traditions of rural life than it does to ground the education of inner-city Black children in the folk and literate traditions of African-American subculture (see e.g., Banks, 1992; Chevalier, 1995; Jeffries, 1994). Intellectual grounding, in fact, always depends on looking backward. Curiously, when mainstream education looks backward to Plato, Descartes, and Herman Melville, few critics brand it as nostalgic. Moreover, advocates of liberal education often tout the high-culture traditions of the West as especially educative because those traditions promote skepticism and critique (Guttmann, 1987; Hutchins, 1947; Mohrman, 1994). But high-culture

Western traditions also value commitment and faith (Bellah, Madsen, Sullivan, & Tipton, 1985). Indeed most traditions promote a rather incoherent mixture of skepticism, faith, critique, and commitment. In short, most offer a lot for educators and pupils to draw on. Rural cultures are no different from other cultures in this respect.

What Rural Traditions Offer

In an earlier part of this chapter, we defined "ruralness" in terms of the commitment to place. *Place*, in this construction, implies connectedness both to nature and to a human community. This way of looking at ruralness makes it possible to define the attachment of city-dwellers to ethnic or familiar neighborhoods as something other than "sense of place." Whereas city-dwellers can connect to place through involvement with a stable human community, the city-scape makes connection to nature almost impossible. In the rural context, connection to nature implicates work with and against nature; it is not simply the appreciation of natural beauty, which is something that city-dwellers can also enjoy (most often, of course, by leaving the city). Furthermore, the connection that a rural family has with nature is a relationship with a *particular niche in nature*, not with nature in general. Great Plains farmers do not understand and plan for boll weevil, but they understand and take heed of various types and intensities of wind. Frost prompts far different actions in the Great Plains and in Florida.

Sense of place founded on knowledge of and work with a particular place in nature produces rootedness that, under the best of circumstances, transcends generations. The human community that resides in a long-tended place nurtures the legacy of past events and practices. In doing so, it produces an accessible narrative that can assist members of the rising generation to establish identities that make sense. Anomie and "identity crises" are distinctly metropolitan conditions (Williams, 1973, 1989). By the same token, rigid expectations for conformity tend to prevail in rural places (Duncan, 1999).

Under the best of circumstances, the ethos of family and community that characterizes rural places supports cultural continuity. Such continuity does not require that generation after generation of the same families enact the same work in the same place. But it does require some legacy of family, some sustenance of interfamily relationships, and some consistency in the types of activities undertaken. The facts that there are always people in a place and always some type of enterprise going on do not assure that a community is striving to sustain a culture. For example, the in-migration of telecommuters to the hills of rural Colorado does not contribute directly to sustaining the rural culture there. Rural culture is sustained when traditional activities and traditional patterns of relationship are invoked on behalf of present needs and interests. Such invocations can be contradictory. In rural Appalachia, for example, the pattern of closeness between mothers and daughters is a long-standing and resistant cultural form. Daughters often abide poverty and single-parenthood in order to keep this important connection (Fiene, 1993). Although changes have degraded the economic base of the region, families struggle to preserve the cultural practices that sustain them.

Situated Schooling

Schooling that derives from and sustains rural cultures is rooted in the practices of particular places. And in most rural places, such practices involve intellectual work. A reading of the cultural terrain that locates intellect only within the purview of urban residents (or, more narrowly, only within the purview of an urban elite sanctified by cosmopolitan universities) misrepresents the daily life of most rural communities. Most rural communities, in fact, support social and economic practices, including narrative conventions, that connect with formal intellectual traditions. Furthermore, most rural places do not (or cannot) fully immunize themselves from the intrusions of popular culture.

Despite the many ways—intellectual ways among them—that rural people make sense of their world, educators often claim that rural families "do not value education." We believe these educators mis-speak. We know of no one at all who does not value education, although we know many people who do not value schooling. Our own lifework consists of various projects that question the value of schooling! When educators level the charge that rural people do not value education, they are making an accusation about local culture and the local life-world that says more about their own views than it does about the culture they thus, in fact, *devalue*. With this charge, these educators proclaim their ignorance of the devalued culture and life-world. The various rural life-worlds, as we have suggested, engage a wide variety of productive and cultural activities that absolutely require thoughtfulness, reflection, and problem-solving—the very kit of "higher-order skills" that state and national school reformers widely promote.

Certainly, the rural life-world is not the site of free-ranging intellectual critique, anymore than any place in urban or suburban America. And rural places experience varieties of racism, sexism, and class prejudice that are identifiable precisely because they are of a piece with all bigotry. The traditions of intellectual critique, so difficult for teachers *anywhere* to claim, are nonetheless as prospectively useful in rural schools as in any schools. Rural communities do not value education less than other communities on any terms, therefore, either in the conventional sense of devotion to "lower-order thinking" or in the more uncommon sense of the capacity to engage in critique. Where rural communities probably do often differ, according to our analysis, is in their continuing skepticism of credentialism, careerism, and official bureau-cracies that overturn local affections and commitments.

Intellectual critique, which we argue is an activity necessary to sustain any approximately democratic community, depends on capabilities that schools could indeed cultivate. Wide and deep reading, for example, has the advantage of helping rural students and community members articulate better their own commitments and affections. Raymond Williams (1973) realized that, without wide and deep reading, any appreciation of the rural circumstance would be limited. Writing about his own education, he observed:

> I came from a village to a city: to be taught, to learn: to submit personal facts, the incidents of a family, to a total record; to learn evidence and connection and altering perspectives. . . . It was only after I came that I heard, from townsmen, academics, an influential version of what country life, country literature, really meant: a prepared and persuasive cultural history. And I find I keep asking the same question, because of the history: where do I stand in relation to these writers: in another country or in this valuing city? (p. 6)

Recognizing that education in rural places can draw on traditional culture, the high-culture legacy, and popular culture, one cannot view rural places as only impoverished (the liberal deficit model) or only virtuous (the conservative sentimental model). Indeed, the interplay and tensions among the various threads that inform education in rural places can be particularly enriching. Such tensions, in particular, require students to make important moral choices, defining, for example, which parts of popular culture can coexist with and which parts impinge on traditional family teachings. Cosmopolitan education, by contrast, leads to a less critical engagement with both high and popular culture, viewing the two traditions as either coextensive or mutually exclusive. In either case, cosmopolitan education seeks to mine all cultural content for its contribution to salable skills and, as a consequence, fails to engage deeply or critically with any tradition. And the question that Williams (1973) poses to himself at the end of the passage above must be answered by rural students in one fashion or another (e.g., the city only, the country only, both or neither, sometimes one and sometimes the other).

ACADEMIC TALENT AND THE CONTRADICTORY LEGACY OF RURAL SCHOOLING

The one-room school is an organizational practice linked in popular imagination and in actual fact with rural places. The popular image is usually a sanitized and sentimental one, but very small schools (three or fewer teachers) continue to exist in many rural places. In such schools, children are often educated in multi-age groups, with each child progressing through the curriculum at whatever pace seems suitable. Indeed, the practice of grouping children by chronological age came about at the beginning of the 20th century in *urban* areas where schools struggled to handle large numbers of children. In rural districts, age-grade placement became prevalent in response to externally imposed reforms (e.g., consolidation). Advocates of consolidation, in fact, claimed that larger schools would enable educators to deploy the beneficial practice of grouping children by chronological age.

There is little evidence, however, to suggest that age-grade placement benefits children. Empirical studies tend to show just the opposite: Multi-age grouping appears to provide a small advantage both academically and socially (Lloyd, 1999). Moreover, as Lloyd notes in her comprehensive review of the literature on Multi-age grouping, the practice has particular benefit for academically talented students (cf. Christopherson, 1981, for a compatible view). It enables such students to move rapidly through the curriculum (i.e., "continuous progress," which will mean an accelerated pace for most gifted children) without the disruptions usually associated with grade skipping or cross-grade grouping. Furthermore, multi-age grouping, like other forms of acceleration, enables talented students to interact with students from a variety of backgrounds. Sequestering bright students in self-contained classrooms, by contrast, tends to place them with peers whose backgrounds are similar to their own. Multi-age classrooms, then, would seem to offer the more democratic option. Moreover, they do not require that special funds be diverted from general educational purposes to support the putative needs of a "special population."

School size is another critical issue. Rural schools and districts have been targets of consolidation and closure for over 100 years, and between 1903 and 1992, the total number of schools declined from about 238,000 to about 80,000 (Stephens & Perry, 1991). Many rural districts now have a single consolidated high school; two-hour bus rides are common.

In many districts where smaller schools are, however, retained, state and district aspirations for eventual consolidation find expression in the practice of starving small schools into submission. Innovation becomes difficult for these schools, particularly if they serve, as is often the case, as the dumping ground for the district's least competent teachers. In such cases—which are commonly reported in rural areas—the curriculum may be simultaneously chaotic, stagnant, and shallow as well as narrow. High schools of this sort (i.e., small schools explicitly underfunded in preparation for eventual closure) will probably not offer Advanced Placement classes or more than one foreign language. Gifted students who remain in such schools with their age-grade peers usually sacrifice academic challenge for the opportunity to maintain community and family connections.

The comments of bright students attending a small rural high school in West Virginia illustrate the dilemma:

> We hardly get anything. . . . [We're] not treated fairly. We get the left-overs. We got their pool table and juke box, their books—calculus books, Spanish books. . . . They got new ones; we got the old ones. . . . They think there is nothing but hicks and hillbillies here, rednecks. . . . It's like we're the trash. (Spatig, 1999)

Some students with intellectual interests may feel out of place in rural communities, in part because of a lack of resources for intellectual development, such as well-stocked libraries and well-equipped labs. Where school facilities are meager, where teachers and administrators devalue rural pursuits as undemanding of intellect, where families are distrustful of conventional intellectuals, students who are interested in ideas may find little companionship except in books. Howley, Harmon, and Leopold (1996) found evidence that gifted students in a rural state experienced a heightened level of cultural contradiction in comparison with nongifted rural students and expressed less satisfaction than the comparison group with their communities.

RURALIZING GIFTED EDUCATION

The subtitle of this section alludes to an essay by David Orr, "Re-Ruralizing Education" (1995), in which he suggests that *all* schooling be "re-ruralized." Writing from the perspective of concern for the fate of the earth, he believes that there is a limit to urbanization beyond which the earth becomes inhospitable to humans generally. Institutions that become too large not only become too impersonal; they crowd out care and attention with greed, personal ambition, and disregard of the common good. Orr—like us—views schooling as one of those institutions. Provisions for academically talented youngsters have *never been* a rural project. Gifted education originated in cities in support of some of the worst features of cosmopolitan purposes—racism and class bigotry in particular (e.g., Gould, 1981; Howley et al., 1995).

The Radical Character of Rural Purposes

The word *radical* means "rooted." It is often used to indicate critique "from the roots" or to indicate an approach that is thoroughly *grounded* in a particular perspective. Conservatives and socialists can be radicals. So can proponents

of just about any ideology. The rural world, in our experience, provides one
of the most solidly grounded perspectives available to humans. Standing and
understanding in a rural place bind one to meanings and relationships more
durable than many that now prevail in the contemporary world. The rural
world is inherently radical in this sense exactly because it is so much at odds
with 20th-century "modernism." The project of 20th-century modernism has
repudiated any rural grounding and has in fact insisted that millions of individuals and thousands of communities forgo this grounding.

Thus, some of the following proposals are wildly unusual in gifted education, and they are likely to be viewed as radical impossibilities, figments of a
dated romanticism. Nonetheless, since we know that some schools and districts *really do* center themselves more self-consciously than others on a rural
ground, we believe that ruralized gifted programs are possible, at least in those
places. Moreover, we think that many other rural schools and gifted programs
could easily *stop doing* the things that devalue the people and communities
in which they operate. Restraint in doing those harmful things would provide
a vacuum into which rural meanings would inevitably be pulled. Exercising
such restraint, however, is also a kind of active resistance, and either program—pro-rural action or pro-rural restraint—will probably elicit the opposi-
tion of local elites and others who benefit from the modernist project that
destroys rural communities.

The suggestions we make in the following discussion confront these difficulties indirectly. We imagine three alternatives that would, in effect, ruralize
provisions made *in rural schools* to assist academically talented youngsters:

- adopting rural purposes for gifted programs in rural schools,
- using acceleration in rural schools, and
- doing nothing in particular for gifted students in rural schools.

The last alternative may seem illogical. How can doing nothing assist academically talented youngsters? We think it makes sense in some cases.

True Confessions

Before outlining these options, however, we want to make a couple of confessions. The first concerns our somewhat changed views of schooling. The second concerns the identity of people who have or have not asked for our help
on a range of issues in rural education and gifted education. A report of these
experiences helps explain our approach in this part of the chapter.

Changing Our Perspectives on Schooling. Our views of schooling
have changed with our lengthening experience of schools, of child rearing, of

life in general, and of the rural life-world in particular. We continue our passionate approval of an idealized form of the intellectual project of the "liberal arts"—wide reading, writing, and the use of reason to explore and influence the world.

We are, however, less certain than ever that the path to understanding and wisdom has much to do with schooling. We have seen too many very able children come away from schooling with lousy grades but high test scores. Their school experiences leave them a measure of misery and an early distrust of others' motives, which they nonetheless usually overcome. We have also seen far too many middle- and upper-middle-class students set prestige, vanity, and convention above wide reading and a thoughtful consideration even of their own life purposes.

This experience with talented youngsters, their families, and their trials in school makes us doubt that the particular features of schooling are, in general, of much importance. Yes, we realize that a string of bad teachers can do real damage; yes, we realize that in an ideal world children would have wonderful teachers every year and in every class. But we do not think that the diversion of money and talent to expensive gifted programs has had much merit. Most gifted programming could easily be terminated without ill effect. There are numerous exceptions, of course.

We now believe that there is no ideal curricular content or sequence. Furthermore, we do not think that parents or educators can reliably predict which instructional experiences will be most meaningful for which children. Only in retrospect and with some regret can we intuit better choices than those that actually come to pass. This insight resonates with parents who have seen their children negotiate the sorts of institutions that have emerged under the current political-economic regime. Many of these schools are dysfunctional, and we insist that this charge applies to most middle-class suburban schools that smugly proclaim their "excellence." Happily, this critique elevates a good many rural schools *above* what is thought to be their *usual* deficient standing! These rural schools have some invisible advantages, which typically include smaller size, stronger sense of identity, closer ties to local people (most rural teachers were raised in the communities in which they teach), and, sometimes, a deeper skepticism toward modern and cosmopolitan values.

We have written extensively about how and why schools are hostile to intellect (Howley et al., 1995). Here, by contrast, we wish to emphasize the freedom that unpacking the foolishness and vanities of schooling bestows. Doing so offers insights into what might properly constitute a "true education." From our vantage, a true education has little to do with proficiency testing, trendy curricula, and systemic reform. Rather, a true education respects and engages students' minds by asking students to read difficult material, ponder apparently stupid questions, and regard their immediate life-world as the source of possibilities. To enable a true education, teachers must respect the thinking that goes on in students' families and communities. This stance of respect requires that teachers and administrators *appreciate the complaints those families have about schooling.* The secret of what schooling ought to be doing, we now think, lies in the respect for and appreciation of the dilemmas of community.

Who Asks for Help. Perhaps—here begins our second confession—our appreciation of the importance of parents and communities derives from the fact that we have found ourselves over the years giving information and counsel to parents and community groups. Intending to write for the profession, we have instead reached a concerned public eager for assistance. Coming to understand how the deep concerns of parents and community members are misapprehended by many school people, we are convinced that the starting point for a true education is the critique of schooling taking place in local communities. This insight fits in well with the more general observations of Michael Walzer (1988), who argues that the life-world and the complaints of ordinary citizens in the life-world are the proper ground for critique and philosophical debate. Justice, virtue, and the commonweal—the concerns of critique—inevitably play out on local ground. Therefore, argues Walzer, those issues are most effectively treated as they appear locally.

The approaches to ruralizing gifted education considered below encompass a range of contradictory recommendations that we formerly could not have articulated. None of these differing approaches, however, should be viewed by readers in terms that would square them with privilege, greed, or neglect of the common good.

Adopting Rural Purposes for Gifted Programs in Rural Schools

Our first, and most rooted, approach to ruralizing gifted programs concerns the aims of rural gifted programs. We have described the contrast between cosmopolitan and "properly rural" purposes in general terms. On those terms, the sorts of things that rural gifted programs ought to *stop* doing to make way for properly rural purposes are probably clear. The things to stop doing include disparaging rural livelihoods and the rural life-world; grooming gifted children for prestigious jobs accessible mostly in suburbs and cities; propagating the outmigration of rural youth; privileging gifted children with experiences valuable for all students; portraying the wider world as the touchstone of what is good; and mistaking cosmopolitan norms for universal norms (see, e.g., Williams, 1989).

What rural purposes might describe provisions for academically talented rural students? And, more radically still, for what "properly rural" purposes might some students demonstrate such unusual talent that special provisions might be advisable?

Ruralizing Purposes for Academically Talented Rural Students

Because of the importance we ascribe to liberal learning, we are most interested in imagining special arrangements that would help rural gifted students develop intellectual dispositions and commitments to the rural life-world. Such an enterprise would first require gifted programs to identify and nurture gifted rural children from those sections of the community attached to rural life-ways, those most likely to be overlooked when children are identified for gifted programs. Identifying such children would provide a basis for ongoing engagement with parents and communities. The program would strive to include the most academically able working-class rural youngsters in the school or district.

Such a program aims to cultivate intellectual development based on an appreciation and understanding of the rural circumstance. At the same time, it strives for academic substance, not mere enrichment. It differs from other programs by also using the rural life-world as a focus of attention and a site of work and thought. All rural places are connected to the wider world through economics, politics, and history; helping academically able children unravel these threads of connection and interpret them in light of local circumstances is the principal aim of such a program. Engagement with the rural life-world, undertaken in support of that world, would actually be risky business. The program would have to be so prepared as to defend itself against possible hostility from local elites. Nonetheless, designing and trying to place such a program into operation would be a remarkable adventure.

In establishing a program of this sort, teachers and administrators must be very clear that the general project of gifted education is a modernist one. A properly rural gifted program necessarily runs against the grain of the professional rhetoric of school reform. That is, the "official line" values math, science, and technology over arts and humanities. Arts and humanities, in turn, are reconstructed as class-based adornments, rather than as realms of moral insight and action. Indeed, ethics itself, in the modernist scheme, is made subservient to technique and technology. Further, the best math, science, technology, art, literature, and philosophy are reconstructed as urban enterprises, to be found almost exclusively in the cosmopolitan (or "world-class") universities. School subjects (or "academics") in this scheme constitute a realm from which rural understandings are monumentally excluded. Talent from this perspective, therefore, cannot properly be rural. And the properly rural—from this perspective—can hardly be permitted to have much connection with either school subjects or intellectual pursuits.

This misconstruction is really the way the cosmopolitan world views the rural life-world. We personally encounter it almost wherever we turn in the profession. Rural schooling has been reframed as an instance of this misconstruction, but because the reframing can never be complete, there is reason for hope.

Undertaking this hopeful project, teachers and administrators may find that they require some guidance. Although no handbook is available, *Local Schools of Thought* (Webb, Shumway, & Shute, 1996) offers a very accessible guide to mixing local and cosmopolitan knowledge to serve locally appropriate educational purposes. In addition, Howley and Eckman (1996) describe community-focused projects, which may give teachers and administrators a sense of what ruralized, academically based gifted programs might look like. The work of the Rural School and Community Trust (accessible via their Web site: http://www.ruralchallengepolicy.org/) is also germane. The decision to ruralize academic instruction for the gifted, however, probably depends more on disposition and ideological orientation than it does on "know-how."

Special Provisions for Hypothetically Rural Talents

American Indian educators have been working for some decades to establish gifted programs that respond to tribal needs for leadership (e.g., Barber, Bledsoe, Pequin, & Montgomery, 1999; Hartley, 1991; Montgomery, 1990; Navajo Tribe, 1984; Tonemah, 1991). Some of these programs, moreover, target identification of culturally valued talents rather than the academic talents that have been our long-standing personal concern. Our involvement with the dilemmas of rural schools, however, leads us to wonder if rural communities might not be advised to consider the American Indian example (see Swisher & Tippeconnic, 1999, for an excellent comprehensive view of school issues confronting American Indians). To write about such second thoughts is unusual for us, in view of our commitment to liberal learning.

Some features of liberal learning, however, render it problematic for the rural circumstance. First, as the postmodern interpretation shows, the technical rationality of two centuries—stemming from the Enlightenment—has led precisely to the practices that have subverted the rural life-world most viciously. Second, the association of liberal learning with the most elite schools and universities entails class interests that typically undermine the rural life-world of ordinary people. Third, liberal learning is founded on a secular view of the world that many rural communities have not and probably will not embrace. Our advocacy of liberal learning, of course, interprets these contingencies as negotiable detriments and not as fatal flaws. Since we might be wrong, it would seem necessary that some thought be given to alternatives to liberal learning as a foundation for gifted programs. From our perspective, local knowledge is the most likely candidate for replacing liberal learning as a foundation of gifted programs. Of course, very little work has been done suggesting what demonstrations would attest to unusual talent along these lines. We are not even very sure what the domains of properly rural knowledge might be, or how to relate them to schooling. American Indians, however, were not much more sure 50 years ago. Perhaps we can catch up to them.

We *do* believe that rural people encounter the world in ways that cosmopolitans and suburbanites cannot grasp. Some of these ways have to do with imagination, some with skill, and some with intimate knowledge of rural concerns. In the end, we personally believe that these ways of knowing are amplified and strengthened with the various skills of literacy.

For us, respect for local knowledge must inform instructional methods as well as curriculum, but the way to put this respect into action is not so straightforward. Some well-intentioned efforts to honor rural life may actually do a disservice to it. Sentimentalizing or sanitizing rural history, or the rural present, is positively harmful. Again, a key thrust of properly rural gifted education must be toward a pro-rural future.

Using Acceleration in Rural Schools

As our earlier discussion suggested, small rural schools (especially elementary schools) may find it relatively easy to use multi-age grouping. Where that arrangement is possible, it enables bright students to move rapidly through the curriculum. But in many rural districts, schools are already large, and multi-age grouping constitutes a change from the prevailing pattern of school organization. As an example of this change, in Kentucky, the Kentucky Educational Reform Act (KERA) re-inscribed nongraded primary education as a feature of reform, and the change did not sit well with many rural teachers (Kannapel, Aagaard, Coe, & Reeves, 2000). In many rural schools, therefore, establishing multi-age classrooms will be more intrusive than using other methods of acceleration. Early entry, grade-skipping, and cross-grade placement are options readily available to rural schools. Convincing teachers and principals that these arrangements will help, not harm, bright students is, however, no easier in rural schools than anywhere else.

Acceleration costs districts very little. Perhaps a district that introduces an acceleration program will have to employ someone to coordinate the effort; but the district will not have to employ special teachers, purchase extra materials, or provide separate spaces for "gifted classes." Furthermore, acceleration programs define giftedness narrowly—in terms of academic talent only. This approach vastly simplifies the process of establishing eligibility: Students who obtain *very high achievement-test scores* ought to be accelerated. By determining eligibility in this way, districts also greatly reduce the costs associated with psychological testing. In unusual cases, of course, individual tests of intelligence will be needed. And in most cases, individual achievement testing will be necessary: Grade-level group tests do not include items that are sufficiently difficult to discriminate between students who perform grade-level work competently and those who are functioning somewhere above grade level. There are many books that explain ways to implement acceleration, and, as far as we know, no special concerns associated with using it in rural schools. Acceleration, we think, might work well anywhere. So why do we discuss it in a chapter that attends specifically to the rural life-world?

From our perspective, acceleration is responsive to two circumstances in rural districts: citizens' desire to limit the costs of schooling and their tendency to value egalitarian arrangements over elitist ones. Because we regard these interests of rural citizens as rational and because we do not see them as evidence of a lack of support for education, we encourage educators to design school practices, such as acceleration options for the gifted, in ways that show proper respect for their legitimacy.

Doing Nothing in Particular for Rural Gifted Students

There was a time when we assumed that two important educational goods, rapid-paced academic instruction for the gifted and practices to advance social justice, could coexist. We are no longer so sanguine, as the discussion of the first of these three options indicated (ruralizing gifted programs). Whereas we do not see these "goods" as necessarily incompatible, we are now cognizant of the ways that practical circumstances often require educators to choose between the two. For us, when a choice is necessary, social justice ought to be accorded priority.

With regard to rural communities, local control of schooling is a central issue of social justice. If rural residents are thwarted in efforts to educate their children in ways consonant with the rural life-world, then, in our view, the state is intruding unfairly. Under most circumstances, in fact, state control over local schools tends to interfere with and discriminate against rural culture. The case is quite similar to requirements that Spanish-speaking children be educated in English only (e.g., California's infamous Proposition 227). In both cases, the practices of the state reify and institutionalize unfair prejudice. Our commitment to social justice compels us to oppose strictures that keep Spanish-speaking children from receiving instruction in their native language, and it compels us to oppose practices that exclude the members of rural communities from the arenas in which important decisions about their children's education are made. Therefore, if rural residents see gifted programs as elitist and if they determine that such programs are likely to prevent their children from seeing the possibilities available to them in local communities, then their resistance to such programs might constitute action on behalf of social justice. We endorse such action and can find no warrant for imposing gifted programs on schools in which parents take this stand.

We are also inclined to believe that small rural schools that base instruction on local knowledge and engagement with the local community—as proposed for place-based pedagogy (see, e.g., Nachtigal & Haas, 1998; Woodhouse, 1999)—will do more good for rural gifted students than the typical pedagogy of gifted education (see, e.g., Howley et al., 1995). At the same time, since dialogue is fundamental to social justice, concerned parents and teachers might invite community members to consider the possible merits of provisions like acceleration, which offer academic challenges to students ready to undertake them, cost so little to implement, and are consonant with once-common rural school practices.

Getting Started with Properly Rural Purposes

Properly rural purposes are difficult to identify and respect in face of the "cosmopolitan" agenda devised by professional associations, federal and state agencies, and the capitalist political economy itself. The weakening of nation states and the simultaneous rise in importance of "the local" (e.g., Heilbroner, 1993; Hobsbawm, 1990; Sassen, 1996; World Bank, 1999), of which the rural circumstance is one manifestation, however, may indicate the ultimate practicality of the effort.

Rural gifted students, so long socialized for life elsewhere, partly on account of their affinity with reading and theorizing (i.e., thinking), confront a tense role. On the one hand, their communities are likely to regard them in a hopeful frame of mind: a "better" future. On the other hand, such futures have usually been construed for them as unfolding elsewhere, in cities and suburbs and in the remote air of "professional life."

Many rural people believe that the departure of the "best and brightest" is practically inevitable. When it does happen, as it commonly does, rural communities are particular losers, but so is the idea of community generally. Rural places will survive in some fashion, of course. But they could thrive instead, if matters stood differently in the future. Schools could help.

NOTE

1. Readers should consider this chapter as addressing the rural circumstances only of white people, especially rural working-class whites. Many rural places are *mostly* white. However, ethnic segregation is very *common* in rural America. Other ethnic groups occupy rural circumstances so unique that we, as white people, are not

competent to articulate them. We urge readers, as well, to recognize that the histories of genocide, slavery, and dispossession directed by whites toward Indians, Blacks, and Mexican Americans are *rural* histories. Rank injustice is part of the complexity of the rural circumstance, and this fact is one of the reasons that sentimentalized or romantic views of the rural life-world are inadequate. The past was *not* better than the rural present, and decent rural futures had better differ from both past and present. The role of talented youngsters in realizing these futures is not more critical than that of other rural youngsters. People of color face unusual, sharp challenges in realizing such futures, challenges that we personally cannot articulate because our lives have not prepared us to do it.

CHAPTER 7

The Death of Giftedness: Gifted Education Without Gifted Children

James H. Borland

INTRODUCTION

In the 1960s, there briefly flourished among academic theologians a radical movement known as "Death of God Theology" (see Altizer, 1967; Gundry, n.d.; Vahanian, 1961). Drawing heavily on Friedrich Nietzsche's *The Gay Science* (1887/1974) and especially *Thus Spake Zarathustra* (1891/1967), from which the claim "God is dead" was taken, this movement "gave expression to an idea that had been incipient in Western philosophy and theology for some time, the suggestion that the reality of a transcendent God at best could not be known and at worst did not exist at all" (Gundry, n.d., p. 1).

This was one of a number of expressions of modernism that stemmed from a conviction that the traditional verities that had served as the axiomatic bedrock of Western society for centuries no longer held (one recalls Yeats's famous words, "Things fall apart; the centre cannot hold" [1967, p. 184]) and no longer allowed one to make sense of a world that had grown more murderous as it had grown more technologically competent. The task of reconciling the God that fit so nicely into the pre-modern world, the "Great Watchmaker" of the Enlightenment, with the grimmer realities of modern life became insuperable to a number of thinkers living in a century that produced, among other horrors, the mindless slaughter in the trenches of World War I, the genocide of the Nazi era, and a seemingly endless stream of violent expressions of racial and ethnic hatred. For some, the only explanation for the trauma of modern times was the belief that, literally or metaphorically, God was dead.

The ideas expressed by the theologians associated with this movement were troubling to a great many people, especially in this country, which should not be surprising in light of the widespread profession of traditional religious beliefs among the population at large and the sensational manner in which the work of these theologians was treated in the popular press. However, the ideas advanced even by such seeming radicals as Altizer (famous for saying, "God is dead, thank God") were much more subtle and less antagonistic to the fundamental essence of religious belief than was suspected by most people, few of whom ever took the time to read the original works and relied instead on the caricatures presented in the mass media.

For example, Gundry (n.d.) interprets Altizer's (1967) insistence that God has died as follows: "To say that God has died is to say that he has ceased to exist as a transcendent, supernatural being. Rather, he has become fully immanent in the world" (p. 2). Far from claiming that the death of God has resulted in a "Godless" world, such thinkers as Altizer believed that God is immanent, present in the world, not removed from it on some transcendental plane. This might not be mainstream theology, but, for those willing to approach it with an open mind and on its own terms, it is hardly the stuff of what the religious right is fond of calling "Godless atheism" (although I am not sure what other kind of atheism there is). If anything, it is an "atheism" in which God, or God's essence, so permeates the here and now as to make the label *atheist* more than a bit of a strain.

The point of this divagation is to draw what I think is a valid and, I hope, useful parallel between, on the one hand, a theological movement that at first glance seemed shockingly radical and, on the other, what I am proposing in this chapter, namely, that we could well do without the concept of the gifted child. As I suggest above, the Death of God Theology, when first proposed, appeared to be subversive of the very values, beliefs, and traditions that underlay the field in which its proponents were working. However, on closer examination, it became clear to those who read and impartially considered the ideas set forth by these thinkers that what was being proposed was a logical extension of and, the specifics of sectarian dogma aside, quite consistent with core Western theological beliefs and traditions. Similarly, the notion that, as a construct, the gifted child is, to borrow Gundry's (n.d.) words, an entity whose "reality . . . at best . . . [can] not be known and at worst . . . [does] not exist at all" will undoubtedly strike many readers as heresy or apostasy, although I am convinced that this idea not only can be reconciled with the traditions of the field of gifted education but is conducive to the realization of its (largely implicit) goals.

The thesis that I will attempt to develop in the following pages has four components. The first is an analytical argument in which I attempt to undermine the logical basis for the construct of giftedness and to advance the notion that the concept of the gifted child is a social construct of questionable validity. The second component of my argument, that educational practice predicated on the belief in the existence of the gifted child has been largely ineffective, is grounded in utilitarianism and pragmatism, and the third, that this practice has exacerbated the inequitable allocation of educational resources in this country (see, e.g., Kozol, 1991, 2000), has a moral as well as a pragmatic and utilitarian cast. The fourth component of my thesis, which is more speculative, is that the construct of the gifted child is not necessary for, and perhaps is a barrier to, achieving the goals that brought this field into existence in the first place. In other words, I will argue that we can, and should, have gifted education without gifted children.

THE QUESTIONABLE VALIDITY OF THE CONSTRUCT OF THE GIFTED CHILD

Giftedness is not a "thing." It has no physical reality, no weight, no mass. It is a social construct, not a fact of nature. It is something that was invented, not discovered. As I argue elsewhere, to state that giftedness is socially constructed is to state that it "gains its meaning, even its existence, from peoples' interactions, especially their discourse. Concepts and constructs that are socially constructed thus acquire their properties, and their influence, through the give-and-take of social interaction, not through the slow accretion of empirical facts about a pre-existing entity" (Borland, 1997b, p. 7).

This is not really all that radical a proposition. The late Stephen J. Gould, for example, made the same point about intelligence in *The Mismeasure of Man* (1981). It simply reflects the reality that we deal with in the social sciences and the professional fields informed by the social sciences: Since so much of what interests us is of an immaterial, intangible nature (e.g., intelligence, giftedness, disability), we must infer, even create, the constructs that guide our thinking and practice out of the messy raw material of human behavior and discourse.

Giftedness and gifted children are recent inventions in education that can be traced to the advent of psychometrics. It is no coincidence that the person universally regarded as being the "father" of gifted education in this country, Lewis M. Terman, was also the developer of the Stanford-Binet Intelligence Scale. Individual differences in test scores, as well as more apparent differences in academic achievement as compulsory education laws became more common and better enforced, can be seen as the direct progenitor of such constructs as those that later became giftedness and mental retardation.

How this came about can be understood in an illuminating and, I believe, useful manner (as one among many possible ways of understanding this historical phenomenon) by drawing on Foucault's thoughts about knowledge and power, discipline and control (see, e.g., Foucault, 1984, 1995; Gallagher, 1999;

Rabinow, 1984; Simon, 1995). Foucault believed that, in modern society, power takes a different form, operates in different ways, and has different representations from what was typical throughout most of human history. Power, Foucault argued, no longer takes the form of physical coercion, is no longer located with a particular individual or institution (e.g., the king or the state), and is no longer encoded in "majestic rituals of sovereignty." Instead, power is constituted and exercised within a network of discourse and social interaction (Foucault, 1995, p. 170).

This network is disciplinary in the sense of *discipline* as submission and control and also in the sense of *a discipline* as an organized body of knowledge and a professional field. At the core of this network of discourse is a particular knowledge system. This system has immense, if subtle, power, for it is through it that people are not only controlled but also constituted as individuals (illuminating in this context is Foucault's assertion that "humanism is a failed philosophical project because it takes Man to be its foundation for knowledge, whereas he is one of its effects" [Simon 1995, p. 25]).

Foucault (1995) believed that power and knowledge are inseparable. He wrote that "power and knowledge directly imply one another; . . . there is no power relation without the correlative constitution of a field of knowledge, nor any knowledge that does not presuppose and constitute at the same time power relations" (p. 27). For Foucault, power develops through a number of processes, "small acts of cunning endowed with a great power of diffusion," that satisfy the need for knowledge on which discipline depends. These processes are his well-known "technologies of power." He wrote that "the success of disciplinary power derives no doubt from the use of simple instruments; hierarchical observation, normalizing judgement and their combination in a procedure that is specific to it, the examination" (p. 170).

Foucault (1995) described the first of these technologies of power, *hierarchical observation*, by reference to the *panopticon*, Jeremy Bentham's ideal prison, in which each solitary inmate lives, and is aware that he lives, under the ceaseless gaze of an anonymous guard in order "to induce in the inmate a state of conscious and permanent visibility that assures the automatic functioning of power" (p. 201). In education, according to Susan Gallagher (1999), hierarchical observation is used as a technology of power when educators assume an "aloof and objective position from which they see students more clearly in both a figurative sense and a literal one" (p. 77).

One way of doing this is through psychometrics, using measurement as a way to control students not only by quantifying and ranking them, but also by reminding them that they are constantly being observed and measured. This technology of power has emerged in contemporary times in a particularly virulent form in the hands of educational bureaucrats and politicians who use the so-called standards movement—wholesale standardized testing—as a way of exercising control over both educators and students, especially marginalized students. Its effects are also apparent in the anxiety children experience over identification processes for gifted programs. Children who aspire to membership in such programs are aware that teacher judgment, grades, test results, and so forth play a determining role in whether they are selected for such programs, that is, whether they become "gifted," and this awareness functions as a technology of power. In this case, as Foucault (1995) held was the norm in modern life, one's internal knowledge of being observed and judged, not the external power of the state or its symbolic trappings, is the medium through which power and control are enacted.

In the early 20th century in this country, as children, hierarchically observed, began to be arrayed along the IQ continuum, a second technology of power, *normalizing judgment*, came into play. This is the process that "measures in quantitative terms and hierarchizes in terms of value the abilities, the level, the 'nature' of individuals . . . [and] traces the limit that will define difference in relation to all other differences, the external frontier of the abnormal" (Foucault, 1995, p. 183).

Educators, enacting the power relationships that had always obtained between school authorities and their charges—relationships whose importance was heightened by the perceived need to assimilate, to "civilize," the children of immigrants pouring into the country from outside the Western European nations from which most previous newcomers had hailed—embraced the new technology of testing (Foucault's hierarchical observation and normalizing judgment combine to create his third technology of power, "the examination"). The quantification of "ability" that resulted, which was reified in numerous—sometimes pernicious—ways (see Gould, 1981), was expressed as an array of IQ scores. Normalizing judgment was manifested, first, in the seemingly inevitable temptation to reduce the variegation of human diversity to a bipolar continuum and, second, in the demarcation of certain regions of this continuum as the province of the "normal" and the rest as the hinterlands of the "abnormal." Thus did students whose IQs fell below a certain score become designated "the subnormal" (Goddard's [1919] infamous "idiots," "imbeciles," and "morons"), whereas students whose IQs exceeded a certain threshold (e.g., 140 in Terman's [1925–1959] seminal study) became, in the original terminology, the "supernormal" and then, by the time of the publication of the *Nineteenth Yearbook of the National Society for the Study of Education* (Henry, 1920), the "gifted."

It is important to stress that the central concept in this process, that of the *normal*, is, as Foucault's (1995) "archaeology" demonstrates, an invention, not a discovery. It is imposed, as an exercise of disciplinary (in both senses) power, as a way to control, even—to employ the title of Foucault's most influential work—to discipline and punish. Foucault wrote of the examination that "with it are ritualized those disciplines that may be characterized in a word by saying that they are a modality of power for which individual difference is relevant" (1995, p. 192). In other words, the disciplines of psychometrics and education made students "normal," "subnormal," or "supernormal."

Thus, the process of defining "normal intelligence" was an enactment of the power of the educational system, as an instrument of society, to identify (1) children who fit, who were tractable, (2) children who could be marginalized and excluded from the benefits of a public education (and, in a number of cases, deprived of their freedom and human dignity), and (3) children—the "gifted"—who were to be especially nurtured because it was in the national interest or because it was believed that their exceptionality demanded it as a matter of justice or effective schooling.

It is useful to think about the genesis of the concept of giftedness and whether its advent in the field of education was inevitable or necessary (in an educational, psychological, or philosophical sense; a critical theorist might well argue that the creation of giftedness was a historical necessity arising from power relations playing out in an inequitable society). The concept did not arise *ex nihilo*. Clearly there was, and is, a situation in public education that could not be ignored. Children develop at different rates and in different ways, and this affects how and how well they deal with the traditional formal curriculum. To the extent that we are concerned with educational effectiveness and fairness, we need to make appropriate instructional and curricular modifications to respond to individual needs. The question is how to do this.

One possible response is to make curriculum and instruction flexible enough to accommodate the needs of all children, forgoing classification, labeling, and the examination in the Foucaultian sense that incorporates the normalizing gaze. This assumes that human variation is multifaceted, multidimensional—indeed "normal"—and that the "average child" is different in many ways, some of them educationally significant, from other "average" children. However, the social and political conditions that obtained at the time the field of gifted education was created—in which a Foucaultian analysis would locate a need to exercise power and control through discipline(s)—and the ascendant social efficiency movement in American public education (Kliebard, 1995) insured that technologies of power, rather than more democratic forces, would shape the field.

Thus, the profession's response to the fact that children differ in the ways in which they interact with the school curriculum (or curricula, including the informal curriculum) was to believe that at least some of this difference is the result of the existence of distinct groups of children, including gifted children, who possess characteristics that separate them from the average. Once one accepts that there exist separate qualitatively different groups, the inevitable next steps are to try to fashion a workable definition of the populations whose existence has been posited, to develop and implement identification procedures to locate these populations, and then to develop and implement separate educational provisions to meet their needs. This is the course of action that was adopted and, I would argue, the reason we have gifted children today.

There is an inescapable circularity in the reasoning here, especially with respect to giftedness. Sapon-Shevin (1994) writes, "Participants agree—sometimes explicitly and sometimes tacitly—to a common definition and then act as though that definition represents an objectifiably identifiable category. In this way, the category assumes a life of its own, and members of the school organization learn common definitions and rules" (p. 121). The category was created in advance of the identification of its members, and the identification of the members of the category both is predicated on the belief that the category exists and serves, tautologically, to confirm the category's existence.

This simplistic dichotomization of humanity into two distinct, mutually exclusive groups, the gifted and the rest (the average? the nongifted? the ungifted?) is so contrary to our experience of life in a variety of other spheres of human endeavor as to cause one to wonder how it has survived so long in this one. Is anything in human life that simple, that easily dichotomized? And are these two groups—the gifted and the rest—the discrete, discontinuous, structured wholes this crude taxonomy implies? That is, is giftedness really its own thing, qualitatively different and apart from averageness or normality, making those who possess it markedly different, different in kind, from the rest of humanity? Can such a notion, expressed in those terms at least, really ring true for many people?

However implausible, these beliefs are implicit in the manner in which the word *gifted* is employed in both professional and everyday discourse. We routinely talk about "identifying the gifted"; about so-and-so being "truly gifted"; about the "mildly gifted," "the moderately gifted," the "highly gifted." In other words, we treat giftedness as a thing, a reality, something people, especially children, either have or do not have, something with an existence of its own independent of our conceiving or naming of it.

Even a casual examination of the field of gifted education illustrates how difficult this dichotomy is to put into consistent and ultimately defensible practice. I frequently talk to my students about something I facetiously call "geographical giftedness," the not-uncommon phenomenon whereby a gifted child, so labeled by his or her school district, finds himself or herself no longer gifted after moving to another school system. Prior to a certain date, the student was a gifted child; after that date, he or she is "average." If we hold on to the notion of two discrete classes of humans, defined by measurable traits, into which children can be placed through correct educational assessment, we can explain this child's existential crisis only in terms of measurement error or one school system's adherence to an "incorrect" definition of giftedness.

But what is a "correct" definition of giftedness? Our failure, as a field, to answer that question is reflected in the multiplicity of definitions that have been proposed over the years. No one, to my knowledge, has as yet counted how many there are, but they are not few in number, nor are the differences between them insignificant. Take, for example, traditional psychometric definitions of academic giftedness that result in students with high IQs and reading and mathematics achievement test percentiles being identified as gifted. Contrast this with Renzulli's (e.g., 1978) highly influential three-ring definition, in which only "above-average" ability is required, combined with creativity and task commitment. Were a school district that had relied on a traditional IQ/achievement-test definition to change to Renzulli's definition, and if both old and new identification practices were based faithfully on the different definitions, there would be a pronounced change in the composition of the group of children labeled gifted. Some "gifted students" would stop being gifted, and some "nongifted students" would suddenly find themselves in the gifted category.

Not only do these two definitions of giftedness vary considerably from each other, but there is no empirical basis for choosing one over the other, or over any of the scores of others that have been proposed, since, I maintain, defining giftedness is a matter of values and policy, not empirical research. And in many, if not most, states, definitions are not mandated. The result is that local educators are free, and are of necessity required, to choose or write a definition of giftedness to serve as the basis for their program for gifted students, one that, to a large extent, determines who will and who will not be gifted. In other words, giftedness in the schools is something we confer, not something we discover. It is a matter of educational policy, not a matter of scientific diagnosis. It is a social construction, not a fact of nature. And it is neither an empirical nor a logical necessity.

All of this strongly suggests that "the gifted" and "the average," rather than being preexisting human genera, are labels for socially constructed groups that are constituted, in both theory and practice, in ways that are far from consistent and, in many cases, anything but logical, systematic, or scientific. Giftedness has become, probably always was, what Stuart Hall (e.g., 1997), writing about race, calls a "floating signifier," a semiotic term "variously defined as a signifier with a vague, highly variable, unspecifiable or non-existent signified. Such signifiers mean different things to different people: they may stand for many or even *any* signifieds; they may mean whatever their interpreters want them to mean" (Chandler, 2001, p. 33). Thinking about gifted children in the schools is, therefore, not a mirroring of nature but an invented way of categorizing children that must be judged on a utilitarian or pragmatic basis. The basic question to ask about giftedness is not whether giftedness exists but whether the outcomes of the application of the construct, especially in the field of education, are beneficial, innocuous, or harmful.

THE QUESTIONABLE VALUE AND EFFICACY OF GIFTED EDUCATION

Some have responded to the assertion that giftedness is a social construct by arguing that most things can be accurately so designated. Gallagher (1996) writes:

> We should admit that "gifted" is a constructed concept. . . . But "opera singer" is a constructed concept, "shortstop" is a constructed concept, "boss" is a constructed concept; every concept that we use to describe human beings is a constructed concept. Is giftedness an educationally useful construct? That is the important question. (p. 235)

I think Gallagher is right to argue that we should apply utilitarian or pragmatic criteria to the construct rather than ontological ones, but I would argue that the application of these criteria to the constructs he equates with giftedness reveals that, unlike giftedness, they are functional categories of demonstrable utilitarian and pragmatic necessity. Opera exists; without opera singers, there is no opera. Baseball, thankfully, exists as well, and without a shortstop, there is no baseball team. Schools also exist, but can one reasonably argue that without gifted children there would be no schools? "Gifted children" is a construct that, unlike "opera singer" and "shortstop," is not rooted in functional necessity.

And it is not merely a matter of labels. We could call opera singers "Chilean sea bass" and shortstops "guys with gloves who spit a lot," just as we sometimes substitute other terms, such as "talented" or "able," for "gifted." But whatever they are called, if we want to have operas, we need someone to give voice to the composers' and librettists' creations, and if we want to have baseball, we need someone to patrol the area between second base and third base and sign quarter-billion-dollar contracts. I am not convinced, however, that we need the distinct category of students usually labeled "gifted children" in order to have schools. Moreover, constructs such as opera singer and shortstop, denoting, as they do, roles in particular enterprises, are less value-laden than the construct "gifted child," which has built-in hierarchical connotations and raises the issue of whether the controversy surrounding the gifted label is compensated for by any educational benefits.

One central question regarding the utility of the construct of the gifted child concerns the efficacy of programs for gifted students. I would argue that there is little evidence that such programs are effective. Most programs for gifted students in this country take the form of part-time "pull-out" programs, in which students spend the majority of their time in a regular heterogeneous classroom from which they are removed ("pulled-out") for a period of time each week to meet with a special teacher and other students identified as gifted in order to receive some form of enrichment (Shore, Cornell, Robinson, & Ward, 1991). However, according to Slavin (1990), "well-designed studies of programs for the gifted generally find few effects of separate programs for high achievers unless the programs include acceleration" (p. 486). In other words, there is ample evidence that acceleration, as a means of differentiating the curriculum for high-ability students, does what it is intended to do: match content to the instructional needs of advanced students. Similar evidence that enrichment is an effective means of meeting goals, other than the goal of providing enrichment, is exiguous at best (Horowitz & O'Brien, 1986).

Over a decade ago, Shore et al. (1991), in their landmark *Recommended Practices in Gifted Education*, wrote that since "Passow remarked on the dearth of research on enrichment three decades ago, . . . the situation has changed little" (p. 82). In the absence of empirical data, they concluded that the frequently recommended practice "Enrichment should be a program component" was not among those supported, wholly or in part, by research but was instead among the practices "applicable to all children" (p. 286).

Not only is evidence supporting the efficacy of pull-out enrichment programs scanty, but what does exist is not very convincing. Two studies stand out as worthy of serious consideration. In a meta-analysis focusing on the effects of pull-out programs, Vaughn, Feldhusen, and Asher (1991) conclude that "pull-out models in gifted education have significant positive effects" (p. 92). However, this meta-analysis drew on only nine studies and examined outcomes related to four dependent variables. Since a maximum of three studies was used to supply effect sizes for any of the analyses, there is reason to question the validity, robustness, and replicability of this conclusion.

An admirable attempt to address the problem of lack of efficacy studies was the "Learning Outcomes Study" conducted by the National Research Center on the Gifted and Talented (Delcourt, Loyd, Cornell, & Goldberg, 1994). The subjects of this study were 1,010 students from 10 states who were either in various kinds of gifted programs, including pull-out enrichment programs, or in no program at all. Students in the latter group included students identified as gifted, formally and informally, and others nominated by teachers as comparison subjects. The authors concluded that the students in their sample who were in gifted programs academically outperformed both students given special provisions within heterogeneous classrooms and students receiving no provisions at all.

The problem with this conclusion is that the students whose academic performance was superior were formally identified as gifted and placed in special programs. The students with whom they were compared were either students identified, formally or informally, as gifted but not placed in programs or students not identified as gifted at all (and thus not in programs) who were nominated for the study by teachers. What Campbell and Stanley (1963) call "selection" is, unfortunately, as good an explanation for achievement differences as is program type or presence of a program. That is, there is reason to suspect that the groups were not really comparable, that students formally identified and placed in gifted programs were different in nontrivial ways from students who were not in programs and those who were not identified as gifted and that these differences, as much as anything else, might have affected the outcomes.

In short, there is remarkably little evidence that the most common type of programming for gifted students is effective. However, as Slavin (1990) argues, and as Shore et al. (1991) agree, the efficacy of one approach advocated for gifted students, acceleration, is supported in the research literature. Does this not suggest that some gifted programs are effective? I believe not. Few gifted programs specifically identified as gifted programs use acceleration as their primary means of meeting the needs of gifted students because, although it is strongly supported by research data, acceleration is controversial, misunderstood, and even feared (e.g., Coleman & Cross, 2001; George, Cohn, & Stanley, 1977; Southern & Jones, 1991).

Moreover, schools can, and do, employ acceleration without having gifted programs per se. Acceleration does not require identifying students as "gifted," special teachers, pull-outs, or any of the ordinary trappings of traditional gifted programs. If a student can work ahead of his or her age peers in, say, mathematics, he or she can simply be allowed to do so; there is no reason to identify the student as gifted. In New York State, for example, school districts are required to provide middle-school students with opportunities to accelerate in mathematics, and this is rarely done in the context of a gifted program. To sound a theme to which I will return later, acceleration is one example of how gifted education can be effected without either gifted programs or gifted students.

GIFTED EDUCATION AND SOCIAL
AND EDUCATIONAL INEQUITY

From the beginning, the practice of gifted education has been criticized on the grounds that it is at odds with education in a democracy and that it violates principles of equity that are, or ought to be, paramount in our society. Gifted programs and their proponents have been called "elitist" and worse, and advocates of gifted education have been seen as the last-ditch defenders of tracking and other damaging educational practices (Oakes, 1985). Educators in this field have vigorously countered these charges, denying both that their goals are anti-egalitarian and that gifted programs are necessarily antidemocratic.

These defenses of the field, in which I have participated (e.g., Borland, 1989), are, I believe, sincere in that educators in the field of gifted education see their advocacy of gifted programs as one a means of helping to realize the goal of an appropriate education for all children, regardless of exceptionality. They see gifted education as redressing a wrong, as a way of making the educational system meet the legitimate needs of an underserved minority. Moreover, professionals in gifted education believe that appropriate educational programs for students identified as gifted can be implemented without being elitist, racist, sexist, or blighted by socioeconomic inequities.

If, as I believe, the intentions of educators in the field of gifted education are unexceptionable, I also think it is the case that the results of our efforts far too often betray the purity of our intentions. Sufficient evidence exists to suggest that the practice of gifted education is rife with inequities that have proven to be extremely difficult to eliminate. Racial inequalities in the identification of gifted students have been a constant throughout our history (see, for example, Borland & Wright, 1994; Ford, 1996; Ford & Harris 1999; Passow, 1989; VanTassel-Baska, Patton, & Prillaman, 1989), and they persist today.

With regard to socioeconomic inequity, which, of course, in our society is not unrelated to racial and ethnic inequity, the National Educational Longitudinal Study of eighth-grade programs for gifted students by the U.S. Department of Education (1991) reveals the extent of the problem rather dramatically. Data from this study indicate that students whose families' socioeconomic status places them in the top quartile of the population are about five times more likely to be in programs for gifted students than are students from families in the bottom quartile. Despite decades of efforts to eliminate racial and socioeconomic imbalances in how gifted students are identified and educated, gifted programs have continued to serve White middle- and upper-middle-class children to a degree disproportionate to their numbers in the population while underserving poor children and children of color. It is worth repeating that this fact has nearly always been seen, within the professional field, as wrong and remediable. However, the persistence of the problem tempts one to question just how tractable the problem is within the field as it is currently established (see Borland & Wright, 2001, for a pessimistic speculation).

Moreover, there have been instances in which gifted programs have served purposes that few, if any, within the gifted education field could countenance. According to Sapon-Shevin (1994), within large urban districts, particularly those characterized by impoverished, struggling schools and large, ethnically diverse populations, gifted programs (including gifted magnet programs) have served (and sometimes been promoted) as a way of stemming *white flight*; by providing segregated programming for "gifted students," some white parents—whose children are in the gifted program—will remain within the district (and the tax assessment area). (p. 35)

I have experienced this firsthand in New York City (whose public school programs have come under the scrutiny of the press, advocacy groups [ACORN, 1996], and the office of the schools chancellor for discriminating against poor and minority families with respect to information about and access to gifted programs). My son attended a program for gifted students from across Manhattan that was housed, as an administratively distinct "school-within-a-school," in a school that primarily served neighborhood children. One rarely had any difficulty determining, even at a distance, whether a particular group of children from that school was in the gifted program or the "regular school." When one spied a group consisting primarily of White and Asian-American children, it was a class from the gifted program; a group of African-American and Latino children was invariably a class from the neighborhood school. As ACORN's *Secret Apartheid* (1996) report shows, this was not an isolated case in New York City.

I think that two things are indisputably true. The first is that professionals in the field of gifted education, no less than any other group of educators, are opposed to racial and other forms of inequity and are committed to fairness in access to education. Indeed, most would argue that educational equity is what brought them to the field in the first place. The second is that, despite the best of intentions, gifted education, as historically and currently practiced, mirrors, and perhaps perpetuates, vicious inequities in our society.

GIFTED EDUCATION WITHOUT GIFTED CHILDREN

My arguments thus far can be summarized as follows:

1. The construct of the gifted child, as it is widely understood in American education, is neither required nor supported empirically or logically. One could go further and claim that the construct is conceptually incoherent.
2. The acceptance of this construct has led to practice that fails to satisfy both utilitarian criteria (both in the broader sense, whereby the construct is judged on the basis of its usefulness, and in the Benthamite

sense (e.g., Bentham, 1843), in which the overriding goal is the greatest happiness for the greatest number) and pragmatic criteria (whereby
the construct is judged on the basis of its practical consequences).
3. The practice of gifted education, contrary to the goals and values of
the overwhelming majority of its advocates, has too often had social
and moral consequences that, especially in light of its other failings,
should force us to consider alternatives.

The alternative I propose is that we try, at least as a thought experiment,
to conceive of gifted education without gifted children. Obviously, I am not
suggesting that we carry on as always but do so without students. Rather, I
am advocating that we dispense with the concept of giftedness—and such
attendant things as definitions, identification procedures, and, for the most
part, pull-out programs—and focus instead on the goal of differentiating curriculum and instruction for all the diverse students in our schools.

Curriculum, I would argue, is what the field of gifted education is all
about. Differentiated curriculum is the field's *raison d'être*. The only justification for gifted programs is, in essence, a special educational one grounded in
a belief that the regular curriculum, which we believe, or pretend, meets the
needs of most students, is inappropriate for some students who, by virtue of
disability or giftedness, are exceptional and who will not receive the education
to which they are entitled unless the curriculum is modified. Unless one wants
to predicate gifted education on the desire to create an elite (or, perhaps more
benignly, but no more beside the point, to develop the talents of a special
few), the practice has as its goal, and major justification, curriculum differentiation as a means to educational effectiveness and the attainment of the right
to an appropriate education.

If differentiating the curriculum for students traditionally labeled "gifted"
is the justification and the goal of the field of gifted education, then such
things as defining giftedness, identifying "the gifted," preparing teachers to
work in gifted programs, and so forth, are merely means to this greater end.
As such, they are subject to questions as to whether they further the end they
serve, especially if my arguments concerning program effectiveness have any
validity.

So, how best to achieve our goal of providing not only a differentiated
curriculum, but a *defensible* differentiated curriculum, for the students whose
needs are our particular focus in this field? Does it make sense to start by
positing the existence of a class of individuals called "gifted children" and then
to wrestle with the problem of defining giftedness, something on which, as a
field, we have not agreed, and then to move to the process of identification,
whereby we endeavor to separate "the gifted" from the rest, and finally to
proceed to the development of differentiated curriculum, reserved exclusively

for those identified as gifted? Or does it make more sense to start with curriculum itself, which, after all, is the goal of our efforts?

In suggesting that we consider gifted education without gifted children, I am suggesting that we direct our efforts toward curriculum differentiation, bypassing the divisive, perhaps intractable, problems of defining and identifying giftedness, which is, as I argue above, a multifariously problematic construct. Were we to set as our goal the creation of schools in which curriculum and instruction mirrored the diversity that is found in the human race, and were we to achieve this goal, the only legitimate aim of gifted education would be achieved.

In such schools, the idea of "normal" and "exceptional" children would, for the most part, be abandoned, as would the idea of a Procrustean core curriculum into which students have to fit or be labeled "exceptional." Curriculum and instruction would be predicated on students' current educational needs. For example, our expectations for students' learning in, say, mathematics would be determined by what they now know and what instruction they demonstrably need in that subject, not on whether their ages mark them for the third-grade curriculum, the fourth-grade curriculum, or whatever. For students who are mathematically precocious, an area of interest in the field of gifted education, the differentiated curriculum would not be what Stanley (see Benbow, 1986) calls "busy work," "cultural enrichment," or "irrelevant academic enrichment," but a mathematics curriculum that is appropriate for these students with respect to its pace and its level of challenge.

Moreover, we would not be in the patently illogical position in which we now find ourselves, with an educational system predicated on the following beliefs: (1) the great majority of students in our schools are unexceptional or normal, and their curricular and instructional needs at any given time are determined by their year of birth; (2) some students have disabilities, and their curricular and instructional needs are determined by the nature of their disabilities; (3) some students are gifted, and their curricular and instructional needs are determined by any one of a number of diverse conceptual rationales (see, e.g., Sternberg & Davidson, 1986) and any one of a number of diverse educational models and schemes (see, e.g., Renzulli, 1986a); and (4) the existence and constitution of the groups mentioned above are determined, in no small part, by race, ethnicity, and socioeconomic status.

Thus, not only would making differentiated curriculum and instruction the norm for all students go a long way toward meeting the needs of students traditionally labeled "gifted," it would make schooling more effective and humane for many students labeled "disabled" as well as all of those students thrown together in that great agglomeration known as the "normal" or "average," a group that, in practice, is largely educationally undifferentiated but that, in reality, is remarkably diverse.

The idea of inclusive schools with heterogeneous classes, no labeling of students, and differentiated, responsive curriculum and instruction has been advanced before by, among others, advocates of inclusion in the field of special education (e.g., Stainback & Stainback, 1990) and critics of gifted education (e.g., Sapon-Shevin, 1994, 1996). However, among those within the field of gifted education, this notion has been met with either hostility and suspicion or assertions that it is too idealistic and impractical given the realities of contemporary American education.

Too many of us, myself included not very long ago (see, for example, Borland, 1996b), react to criticisms of gifted programs as if they were attacks on the idea that high-achieving students require appropriately differentiated curriculum. We end up defending the means, not the end, of gifted education and waste our energies trying to preserve gifted programs instead of considering whether there is a better way to achieve what we want to achieve (Borland, 1996a). Not only do I think we can remain true to our commitment to capable students by considering, and ultimately adopting, alternatives to gifted programs, but, especially in light of the exiguous evidence for the effectiveness of our traditional practice in this field, I think we can become even more effective advocates for these students by doing so.

With those who argue that it is easier to advocate than it is to create inclusive schools with curricula and instruction that are responsive to the diverse needs of individual students—schools in which the labels "normal," "disabled," and "gifted" not only are eschewed but make no sense—I can only agree. However, if one believes that such a state of affairs would make for a system of education that is not only more effective but more just, one is compelled at least to try to envision what would be required to make it a reality. At a minimum, the following conditions would have to obtain:

1. Teachers, administrators, students, and parents would have to expect differentiation of curriculum and instruction to take place as a matter of course; it would have to be viewed as the norm, not the exception.
2. Teacher education programs—in all branches of education, not just in special education and gifted education—would have to make the ability to differentiate curriculum and instruction a basic skill expected of their graduates. This skill would have to be taught and modeled in the college classroom and in student-teaching and practicum situations.
3. Continuing education for teachers now in service would have to be provided, both to maintain, reinforce, and strengthen the differentiation skills of new teachers and to assist experienced teachers, many of whom are neither used to nor comfortable with the idea of differentiation, in modifying the way they teach.

4. Our system of education would have to give up the notions of "the normal," "the disabled," and "the gifted" as they are typically applied in schools, especially for purposes of classification and grouping, and simply accept difference as the rule.

It is important to stress the direct and reciprocal linkage between heterogeneous classes in which diverse groups of children without labels learn together happily and effectively and the practice of differentiating curriculum and instruction. Educationally inclusive diversity demands differentiation. The alternative is not to respect difference and the uniqueness of each child and to force individual children to conform to a one-size-fits-all curriculum, which inevitably, I believe, leads us to such concepts as "the normal" and "the abnormal" and subjects the inescapable and delightful variegation that is humanity to Foucault's normalizing judgment.

A PARADIGM SHIFT IN GIFTED EDUCATION

Changing practice within a well-established field is difficult. Convincing the professionals in that field to abandon what most of them would view as its defining construct is more difficult yet, perhaps beyond the realm of possibility. Earlier I suggested we try conceiving of gifted education without gifted children as a thought experiment. I hope the foregoing pages have helped some readers see that—thinking about it—as a possibility, and perhaps this could be a prelude to real change. As Susan Gallagher (1999) writes, for change to take place, "we need to recognize how our taken-for-granted way of thinking from within the discipline's meaning-making system impacts the educational process in perhaps unintended ways" (p. 69).

Actually to abandon the construct of the gifted child and to proceed accordingly would truly constitute a paradigm shift, to borrow an overused and frequently misused term from Thomas Kuhn's *The Structure of Scientific Revolutions* (1962/1996). In this landmark work of intellectual history, Kuhn attempts to explain how "normal science," which he defines as "research firmly based upon one or more past scientific achievements, achievements that some particular scientific community acknowledges for a time as supplying the foundation for its further practice" (p. 10), changes over time. Why, Kuhn asks, do scientists working today believe different things, ask different questions, and proceed in methodologically differently ways from their colleagues in, say, the early 19th century, especially since these differences are not completely attributable to technological advances and the simple quantitative accretion of knowledge?

Kuhn's (1962/1996) explanation relies on the concept of the "paradigm," which Phillips (1987) defines as "a theoretical framework . . . that determines the problems that are regarded as crucial, the ways these problems are to be conceptualized, the appropriate methods of inquiry, the relevant standards of judgment, etc." (p. 205). A paradigm is the complex of theories and practices that constitutes the prevailing world view and the accepted *modus operandi* of scientists, and, as such, it is often what is distilled in textbooks as scientific truth and scientific method.

A paradigm allows normal science to proceed; indeed, Kuhn (1962/1996) argues, a paradigm is necessary for scientific inquiry. Inevitably, however, inquiry yields empirical data that are inconsistent with the prevailing paradigm. Often this leads to modifications of principles and theories that alter, but do not undermine, the paradigm. However, over the course of history, it has always been the case that sooner or later the reigning paradigm cannot accommodate the increasing accumulation of data unpredicted by and contrary to its fundamental bases. At that point, the paradigm has to give way to a new one that can account for and explain new knowledge.

These changes are anything but cosmetic, as the use of the word *revolutions* in Kuhn's (1962/1996) title suggests. He writes, "paradigm changes do cause scientists to see the world of their research-engagement differently. In so far as their only recourse to that world is through what they see and do, we may want to say that after a revolution scientists are responding to a different world" (p. 111). Moreover, as a result of the emergence of a new paradigm, a new version of "normal science" emerges.

If what I am proposing, conducting gifted education without gifted children, is ever to evolve beyond the level of a thought experiment, something equivalent to a paradigm shift in gifted education will be required. I do not underestimate either the difficulty that would entail or the resistance it would engender. Our equivalent to normal science, which one could call *normal practice*, is, to quote Kuhn (1962/1996) with multiple elisions, "firmly based upon . . . past . . . achievements . . . that . . . supply . . . the foundation for . . . further practice" (p. 10). These are the achievements of such pioneers as Terman and Hollingworth, who gave the field its start and its professional respectability in the first half of the 20th century, and those of a host of leaders who reestablished gifted education as an integral aspect of American education during the last quarter of that century.

Our normal practice derives from a paradigm that Hurn (1993) identifies as the "functional paradigm," a paradigm that, while not accepted as uncritically as it was in the past, governs much social and educational thought today. Under the terms of this paradigm, modern Western society is viewed as uniquely meritocratic (roles are achieved or earned rather than ascribed or inherited), as highly reliant on expertise and rational knowledge, and as making steady if imperfect progress toward the amelioration of social inequality.

Schools are defined within the functional paradigm as institutions that are responsible for "the production of cognitive skills, *the sorting and selection of talents*, the creation of an informed citizenry" (Hurn, 1993, p. 47; emphasis added), all of which are necessary for maintaining the qualities that characterize modern Western society and for continuing its progress toward a more democratic future. Essential to this paradigm is the belief that

> educational institutions sort and select talented people in a way, however imperfect, that is greatly superior to selection on the basis of such ascribed characteristics as parental social status, religion, or race. To tie occupational status closely to educational attainment . . . will maximize society's chances of discovering its most talented individuals and placing them in the most important occupations. (pp. 52–53)

It is not difficult to locate the traditional verities of the field of gifted education within this paradigm. Our field has at its heart a belief in the existence of a distinct population of schoolchildren, exceptional children with unusual merit, whose special educational needs must be addressed in the service of social justice and as a way of advancing the common good through the production of human capital, both of which are consistent with the functionalist paradigm.

The difficulty is that both the general paradigm and its specific realization in the field of gifted education are open to serious criticism. I made my arguments concerning the theory and practice of gifted education above. Hurn (1993; see especially pp. 50–55) exposes similar weaknesses in the functional paradigm as a general framework for understanding educational issues and for conducting educational practice. If his arguments are valid, there are data discrepant with the paradigm that cannot be accommodated within it, signaling, perhaps, the need for, or the inevitable advent of, a paradigm shift.

If something as radical as a paradigm shift in gifted education appears unlikely, the same might be said of maintaining the status quo. Normal practice in the field of gifted education—which consists of sorting students on the basis of being identified, or not identified, as gifted and then temporarily removing those identified as gifted from their heterogeneous classes so they can receive curricular (perhaps) enrichment and then return to join their non-identified peers—has held sway in this field since the publication of the landmark Marland report (Marland, 1972) over 30 years ago. The model has come under criticism from many from outside the field (e.g., Margolin, 1994, 1996; Oakes, 1985; Sapon-Shevin, 1994, 1996) and, increasingly, from some within. Moreover, as I argue above, it has produced very little with respect to demonstrable positive educational results.

There appear to be three possible courses of action for professionals in the field of gifted education with respect to the traditional model derived from the functional paradigm. One is to cling to it steadfastly, ignoring or deflecting criticism and hoping for a return of more congenial *Zeitgeist*. I think this is unrealistic and ignores substantive changes in how educators think about diversity, grouping, exceptionality, and related issues. For example, the notion of exceptionalities, including giftedness, being rooted in medical or psychometric necessity instead of reflecting historical and sociocultural forces is, along with other tenets of the functional paradigm, increasingly under attack (see, e.g, Franklin, 1987; Sleeter, 1987). It would require an unusually struthious stance on our part to believe that all of this will simply go away and we can return to the halcyon days of proliferating pull-out programs, even were that desirable.

A second possibility when a paradigm is threatened by discrepant findings is to modify, but not to abandon, the paradigm in order to accommodate the data that do not fit. This strategy can be seen in some recent writing in the field, including some of mine (e.g., Borland & Wright, 1994), in which proposals to remedy some of the field's more egregious failings, such as the chronic underrepresentation of poor children and children of color in gifted programs, have been advanced. However, the problems persist, and in a recent paper (Borland & Wright, 2001) we contemplate the possibility, rooted in Isaiah Berlin's notion of *value pluralism* (see Berlin, 1990; Gray, 1996), that there is no attainable reality in which we can effect the reconciliation of such indisputable goods as educational equity and such putative goods as differentiated programs for students labeled gifted. In other words, there may be no way to tinker with the paradigm, and its derivative normal practice, so that such things as effective education and equitable education can coexist with gifted education.

The third possibility is the fundamental change whose consideration I have been urging throughout this chapter. As radical as this may seem to some, it may be the only choice facing the field if, as I suspect, the prevailing paradigm comes to be seen either as something held on to by a progressively smaller band of retrograde gifted education stalwarts or as a framework in which indispensable educational, social, and moral goods cannot coexist. If that were to become the case, we might be faced with the paradox of viewing the death of giftedness as the only way to ensure the viability of gifted education.

Gifted Education and Equity

CHAPTER 8

Equity, Excellence, and School Reform: Why Is Finding Common Ground So Hard?

Mara Sapon-Shevin

Having written a controversial book in the field of gifted education, *Playing Favorites: Gifted Education and the Disruption of Community* (Sapon-Shevin, 1994), I have had the opportunity to observe the ways in which my ideas have been responded to and critiqued by others. A special issue of the *Journal for the Education of the Gifted* entitled "Critical Appraisals of Gifted Education" (1996) included an article by me (Sapon-Shevin, 1996) as well as several direct responses to my work (Borland, 1996a; J. J. Gallagher, 1996). I believe that unpacking the contested areas—the ways in which my thinking has been responded to by the "gifted establishment"—can teach us much about the nature of the debate in gifted education and the ways in which my position has challenged long-held beliefs and assumptions about education, democracy, and schooling. The way in which the debate becomes framed and battle lines drawn can give us a clearer picture of the scope of the controversy as well as areas of both possible reconciliation and intractable difference. While I have seen definite change and growth in the debate within the gifted education community (the special issue of the *Journal for the Education of the Gifted* cited above would be good evidence), understanding the ways in which people continue to talk past and misunderstand one another can illuminate deeper issues. In this chapter, I will briefly review my arguments about gifted education, analyze some of the challenges others have expressed in responding to my work, and discuss the ways gifted education can and must interface with the broader school reform movement in order to remain viable and useful.

A CRITICAL PERSPECTIVE ON GIFTED EDUCATION

Consider the following announcement made by a large urban school district in its monthly newsletter of district events:

> Students of Mr. B celebrated the end of the Fall semester with fantastic performances of shows they wrote. Starting with the brainstorming of subjects they were to write about, each of the six classes who has performed to date, developed 30+ ideas in cooperative groups of 5 to 8 students. From there, the 3 cooperative groups per class chose the 3 best ideas they wanted to write about. . . . Students chose the area of theatre they wanted to work in through a preference sheet, ranging from acting to stage managing to lights to handing out programs. All actors helped to devise and create their own costumes and all students helped make the sets.

Sounds like a wonderful project with good pedagogy, no? A theater production that involved all students in writing, performing, and technical aspects of theater? An inclusive, cooperative activity that engaged a range of student interests and skills? The opportunity for students to shine and be seen as engaged in an exciting endeavor?

It could be, but it isn't. It's a description of one of the projects of the Center for Inquiry, my local school district's gifted program. The article goes on to say that the CFI Theatre Fund began with an unsolicited donation from a parent and that, to date, a mailing to parents of theater students has produced an additional $200 in donations to offset some of the costs involved in producing a play: makeup, lights, costumes, microphones, sets, and programs. A side bar reads: "If you believe your child shows special talents and abilities, call us at CFI-555-1234."

The above scenario raises myriad questions, all of which frame an analysis of the politics of gifted education: Which children are in the gifted program and how are they chosen? What is there about putting on a play that makes it the exclusive domain of gifted students? What were the students in the regular program doing while the gifted students were working on the play? Why is this special opportunity being funded discretely and from the pockets of parents of gifted students? What are the effects of having a gifted program on the funding, educational programming, resources, and support for the general education program?

WHAT IS GIFTED EDUCATION AND WHY IS IT PROMOTED?

I argue that gifted education as it is currently defined and implemented in this country is elitist and meritocratic and constitutes a form of educational triage. Gifted programs are implemented for students for whom educational failure will not be tolerated (generally the children of White, privileged parents) and are enacted in ways that leave the general educational system untouched and immune to analysis and critique. Focusing our attention and energy on improving education for students identified as "gifted" removes our gaze from the need for more comprehensive, cohesive analysis, critique, and reform of the overall educational system.

Some students get certain educational benefits while others are denied them because a system has been constructed that reifies this differentiation in the guise of good, fair educational practice. I will examine here the reasons that gifted education systems are promoted and maintained, the implications of those constructions, and the ways in which the discourse about gifted education impedes a more critical stance.

The need and importance of providing discrete, specialized services for students identified as gifted are generally justified in three ways: educational need, social justice, and political and economic necessity. Those who argue from an educational perspective assert that providing different educational opportunities for students with accelerated skills is simply a way of meeting the individual (and different) needs of different students. In other words, it's just "good teaching" to treat different children differently. The social-justice perspective argues that it's only *fair* to treat different children differently; since schools already provide differentiated programming for students identified as "learning disabled," "bilingual," or "mentally retarded," a commitment to equity requires providing specialized programs for students identified as "gifted." Political and economic exigencies constitute the third major form of support for gifted programs: Our nation can ill afford not to develop the "best and the brightest" lest we lose our standing as a major world power or cease to be on the cutting edge of technology, medicine, and science.

Each of these arguments can be analyzed in terms of explicit and hidden agendas, intended and unintended outcomes, and how gifted education becomes linked to and embedded in broader political and economic ideologies. One way to explore this is to critically examine the assumptions that undergird the above justifications for gifted education:

- There is such a thing as "giftedness"; some children "have it"; we can test for it, and, once we have identified it, respond to it educationally.
- There is such a thing as a "gifted child" who can be objectively identified and confidently discriminated from a "nongifted" child;
- Gifted children represent a "class" of children, that is, we can speak of programming or education for the gifted in generic or group ways.
- What is good for gifted students would not be beneficial for everyone else (the Shakespeare in the park program, the young philosophers'

club, the Great Books programs, and community mentorships are not advisable or appropriate for other students).

- General educational reform can never be structured broadly enough to meet the needs of gifted students, that is, curricular and pedagogical reforms such as whole language, portfolio assessment, a focus on multiple intelligences, thematic instruction, or multilevel teaching are insufficient to address the discrete educational needs of students identified as gifted.
- Some curricular and pedagogical "best practices" are actually detrimental to students identified as gifted; cooperative learning, for example, with its focus on heterogeneous grouping, deprives gifted students of opportunities to match minds with others who work at their level and forces accelerated students into the inappropriate role of junior teacher or peer support (Johnson & Johnson, 1993; Sapon-Shevin & Schniedewind, 1993).

Challenging Assumptions

What are the consequences of the acceptance of the above arguments and assumptions, and how else might we talk about and respond to interindividual differences, educational goals, and social justice imperatives?

Assumptions about Giftedness. I argue that giftedness, rather than being an objective reality, is a social construct, a way of thinking and describing that exists in the eyes of the definer (Sapon-Shevin, 1987). It is not that children do not differ in many dimensions—clearly they do—but that decisions about how to define the category, where to make "cut-off" points, and how to discriminate between those in and outside the category are ethical and political decisions that are highly influenced by values; beliefs about children, intelligence, and education; and the cultural and economic context. Failing to acknowledge the socially constructed nature of the category makes it easier to ignore the political and economic consequences of its use.

It is also a mistake to issue blanket statements about "what gifted students need" as though they were, in fact, a coherent, homogeneous group with a unified set of educational needs. School districts that identify a segment of students as gifted and then provide a rigid, undifferentiated curriculum for those students as a block are as guilty of overgeneralization and lack of individualization as many of the regular classrooms from which those students are withdrawn. Designating funding and programs according to "categories" of students homogenizes some of the more blatant inequities in who gets what that would perhaps be more apparent if we compared specific students.

Assumptions About Differentiation. There is no research suggesting that the educational opportunities currently being provided for students identified as gifted would not also be positive for unidentified students or that specialized services cannot be provided within a broader context. Nor should one assume that the worksheets that dominate many classrooms are appropriate for "typical" children; changing conceptions of best educational practice would confirm that many of the tasks that frustrate and vex children with exceptionally high skills are also poor ways of teaching students with more typical skills. Consider, for example, the opening example of the gifted students who put on a play. This activity could easily have included all students in the school, involving them in different ways in a wide range of learning experiences: researching the background of the play, writing the play, designing scenery, organizing rehearsal schedules, designing and sewing costumes, helping others to learn their lines, composing and performing music. The list of many-layered tasks and opportunities is endless and could engage a whole range of student skills, interests, and performance levels. Arguing that differentiation is the key and that "one size doesn't fit all" (J. J. Gallagher, 1997, p. 281) implies that all children will be "fitted" with equal care and attention and masks the fact that most children will get baggy, unfitted rags while a few get personalized tailoring or designer clothes.

Assumptions about School Reform. Gifted education proponents argue that the regular classroom as currently organized and implemented is largely not amenable to change and that many teachers and students are hostile to gifted students, thus necessitating the removal of gifted students to a safe haven where they can be with other students like themselves. Generally, I would agree with the characterization of many (most?) classrooms as boring, uninspiring places filled with irrelevant curricula, unimaginative teaching, and a singular lack of community. I would also argue that those regular education classrooms—as they are currently organized—are not ideal (or even acceptable) for students identified as gifted. But neither are they the classrooms I would wish for any student. Deciding to remove some children from that setting to meet their putative educational needs elsewhere has significant implications. First, it communicates a sense of hopelessness and despair about the ability of teachers, classrooms, and schools to change and about the possibilities of ever structuring our classrooms as inclusive, stimulating, multilevel, diverse learning communities that meet the needs of a wide range of students within a unified setting. Second, removing those children whose needs are not being met in the typical classroom makes it painfully clear that some parents (because of wealth, information, connections, or power) *can* remove their children (whose scores are used to justify that removal) while others cannot (see

Kohn, 1998). Most significantly, however, the removal of gifted children to provide them with an "appropriate" education leaves untouched the nature and quality of the regular education classroom. Arguing that school reform is hopeless justifies an exodus from public school education and intensifies support for privatized and semi-privatized education (charter schools, magnets, voucher programs, and segregated gifted programs).

Assumptions about Fairness. By making a case for the ways in which gifted students are neglected, poorly served, often ridiculed and isolated, gifted education advocates argue that gifted programs are not inequitable at all, but simply a way of providing the differential education that different students need, and that to deny a specialized education to gifted students is no more just than denying such an education to students identified as "disabled" or "handicapped" (Marland, 1972). Justifying the validity of the educational needs of gifted students by referencing how schools have been willing or forced to meet the needs of students with disabilities (quite common among gifted educators) fails to take into account the fact that models of special education are changing dramatically in this country and that segregated special education classrooms, even pull-out programs, are increasingly being replaced by more inclusive, push-in models of service provision (Stainback & Stainback, 1990, 1996; Villa & Thousand, 2000). Declaring that "it's only fair" to provide services to gifted students doesn't tell us how those services should be provided, by whom, where, or with what relation to the services provided to other students. It is impossible to argue for justice for any particular group without discussing what constitutes justice for the majority. There are no absolute standards of justice; we must always know the context (political and economic) within which demands for justice are issued.

Justice arguments often fail to discriminate between the goals of equality of access, equality of services, and equality of outcome. The problem lies in determining which differences should be attended to and how. What is the difference between appropriate differentiation based on a valid difference and elitism or prejudicial treatment based on an assumed difference, a value-laden description of that difference, or assumptions about who can and cannot profit from such different treatment? Perhaps an argument for "equal treatment" should be recast as a need for "equally *good* treatment" or "equally responsive treatment." Perhaps arguing that gifted programs are fair is irrelevant and leads us away from a careful examination of the context in which such programs occur and the effects of gifted programs on children, teachers, parents, schools, and society.

Assumptions About Political and Economic Needs. Political and economic arguments for gifted programs are advanced at both local and national levels and are often coupled with justice arguments:

For several years now, the term elitism has been used to undercut efforts to support young musicians and scholars who are gifted. (Somehow, though, we are able to support, often royally, elite athletes.) Perhaps this common spirit goes back to a misreading of our nation's political credo, "All men are created equal." If so, it is not only a misreading of the intent of our Founders but a danger to the nation they brought into being. A nation that does not develop its gifted children is a nation that eats its seed corn. (Harris, 1995, p. 307)

Buttressing support for gifted programs in the name of democracy is an interesting twist; perhaps, as in Orwell's *Animal Farm*, some animals are simply "more equal than others." And while eating one's seed corn is admittedly foolhardy and short-sighted, what about noticing that the majority of the population is already going hungry and that the crop, even if planted and harvested, will not be distributed equally to all?

Within large urban districts, particularly those characterized by impoverished, struggling schools and large ethnically diverse populations, gifted programs (including gifted magnet programs) have served (and have sometimes been promoted) as a way of stemming White flight; when offered segregated gifted programming, some White parents whose children are in the gifted program will remain within the district and the tax-assessment area. Parental demand or an increased interest in gifted programming can be traced directly to the increasing racial integration of many schools and communities. Gifted programs often result in the resegregation of schools with White students in gifted programs and students of color in the "mainstream." The benefits provided by such programs—smaller classes, more enthusiastic teachers, a rich curriculum, more individualization—are changes that would help all students. How could we look, instead, at the problems of poor, urban schools and inadequate funding for education without resorting to resegregation in the name of quality education? What kinds of programs (schools within schools, multilevel curricula, mentorship programs) could be implemented that would meet the needs of a wide range of learners? What kind of nonexclusive quality educational programming would keep parents of privilege within city limits? (Ayers & Ford, 1996; Meier, 1995).

MAINTAINING INEQUALITY: CONSTRUCTING THE MODEL, CONTROLLING THE DISCOURSE

In order for an inequitable system to maintain itself over time, several conditions are necessary. First, the system must be designed so that it is self-sustaining, that is, that it self-perpetuates. The second requirement is that the discourse surrounding the system be controlled in such a way that people are socialized to accept the rightness or inevitability of the inequality. Gifted education meets both these criteria. First, "giftedness" is defined as a percentage of the population, often the top 3–5%, without standard criteria or external references. Inevitably, 95–97% of the population is "not gifted" and not entitled to the services provided to those who are—a tautological definition. Second, gifted education serves as part of the schools' general sorting and selection function in a capitalist society. Not everyone can go to college, so not everyone can be in Advanced Placement classes; if everyone did well in school and everyone were on the honor roll, how would we know who the really worthy and deserving students were, students who would reap the benefits of advanced educational opportunities and increased earning potential? Since, within this system, there isn't enough (time, money, resources) to go around, we must make a decision about who should receive these things, and identifying a small group of students as gifted allows us to do this without accusations of unfairness or elitism.

And, in order to maintain such a system of inequality, we must socialize the participants—students, teachers, parents, community members—to accept such differentiation as inevitable, desirable, or, at the minimum, not subject to discussion. Consider:

> A teacher is asked what she says to students who inquire, "When will I be going to that special program Michael goes to?" She responds, "Oh, they're good. They never ask." Another teacher, of sixth graders, responds, "Oh, by this age, they've stopped asking. They already know who's smart and who isn't."
>
> A new child in an elementary school stops the principal in the hall and says, "I heard about this thing some kids go to—how can I do that?" The principal confides to me, "I didn't know what to say. How could I tell him that he'll probably never go."
>
> A fourth-grade teacher who tries to honor multiple gifts and talents in her inclusive, highly diverse classroom shares with me: "I made the school psychologist come in and explain why only some children were going to the gifted program—I didn't want to be the one to have to explain it to them."
>
> Third graders are having a discussion. One girl makes a clever comment; her classmate turns on her, "You're not so smart. You don't go to [the gifted program]."

Gifted education constitutes an example of formalized meritocracy training; students are taught two things: (1) who is smart and worthy of exciting opportunities and who is not, and (2) when apparent unfairness or inconsistencies are noted, it is better *not to ask*. Not asking is "good"; making teachers uncomfortable with such questions is not good.

Because gifted education is "fair"—anyone who tests high enough can get in—the differential treatment must also be fair. It would be ungenerous and petty to find fault with one's exclusion from a game from which one was eliminated "fairly." The damage of meritocratic thinking—people who are worthy deserve what they get and get what they deserve—has the weight and power of educational objectivity and fairness to silence any protest or objection.

Borland (1996a) reacts to this critique by characterizing my argument as saying "the field of gifted education [is] a well-financed leviathan that has effectively silenced criticism of its tenets and practices" (p. 134) and then dismisses this as "implausible." In a recent review of my book, Schroeder-Davis (1994) says that there is a considerable debate and discussion about gifted education and there is no conspiracy of silence. I agree that it would be unfair to lay the silencing at the feet of those in gifted education; rather this is a co-constructed silence. But, unfortunately, much of the research and debate about gifted education takes place predominantly within a closely circumscribed community of "educators of the gifted" and this, by definition, cannot be the kind of discussion that links gifted education to broader issues of educational equity, school reform, and teacher education.

Broader societal notions about intelligence, worth, fairness, and merit also collude with existing school structures to deaden the dialogue. Alfie Kohn, in his article "Only for My Kid: How Privileged Parents Undermine School Reform" (1998), articulates the ways in which even those parents who would label themselves "progressive" and "liberal" respond negatively to school changes that would undercut their child's privileged or advantaged status or programs.

OPENING THE DISCUSSION: SITUATING GIFTED EDUCATION IN A BROADER CONTEXT

Gifted programs, however, have come under attack recently. Whenever a major urban school district explores the possibility of funding (or de-funding) a gifted program, the discourse community on gifted education becomes larger and more diverse. Within a two-month period, the *Washington Post* did a special issue on education with a feature called "The Best for the Brightest" (Kaufman, 1997); the *New York Daily News*'s front-page story was entitled "Gift Rap," and the *Congressional Quarterly* devoted an entire issue to "Educating Gifted Students" (*CQ Researcher*, 1997). No longer the province only of educational theorists, the discussion of gifted education and its fairness has taken to the streets. In the *New York Daily News*, a mother describes how one of her twins was admitted to the gifted program while another was denied, and her agonizing decision: "Should I hold Jordan back and not sacrifice his brother's feelings, or allow him to do the gifted program and get a much better education than Ari?" She laments, "They [the gifted class] get more money to spend and learn in classrooms with half as many students. Doesn't Ari deserve the same individual attention as his brother?" (Chang & Sugarman, 1997, p. 6).

The debate is impassioned, and intense, and some of the most basic questions of racial and social-class representation are raised: At the Johns Hopkins Center for Talented Youth, a study of its class of 1992 revealed that of the 3, 453 teenagers who completed summer camp sessions, only 1.4% were African Americans, and there were even fewer Hispanics. Yet the center refuses to change the rules of entry to the program: "Some have wanted us to use different or wider criteria for qualifications, but our experience with the SATs has been very good. That test has been an accurate predictor of which students can do the work and which cannot" says Talent Search director Linda Barnett (Kauffman, 1997, p. 35).

What Does the Criticism of My Work Tell Us about the Challenges We Face?

Some of my arguments about gifted education have been (begrudgingly) embraced by other leaders in the field; Borland (1996a), for example, says my challenges raise "embarrassing fundamental questions that relate to our very existence as a field" (p. 133) and devotes the majority of his article to buttressing, point by point, most of my key arguments (all the while lamenting that I, rather than a gifted-education insider, raised these crucial challenges). The number of people who have reacted with anger to my arguments is illustrative, I would argue, of more than their annoying quality. It would seem that I have struck a nerve, raw and exposed from years of external misunderstanding and critique and also relatively unused to critical internal debates (see Borland, 1996a; Callahan, 1996). There is, of course, the possibility that I have simply not made myself clear, and that the "failure" to connect are based on inadequacies in making my points. Another possibility, however, is that the antagonism and lack of communication are based on some fundamentally different assumptions about schools, change, and teaching that make consensus problematic if not impossible. We literally can't "hear" each other because what the other says is heard not as "intelligible speech" but as white noise. What are these areas of misunderstanding and how do they intensify the challenge of making gifted education an integrated part of broader school reform? What can we learn from the debate and how could understanding this "failure to communicate" help us to find common ground and move forward?

There are four major areas of debate surrounding my analysis of gifted education. I will explain and respond to each separately, although there is considerable overlap and relationship among them.

1. My arguments are viewed as idealistic, impossible, out-of-touch with reality, naive, or ridiculous. For example, in responding to my strong plea for classroom communities and my warnings about how segregated gifted programs can disrupt the sense of community important to classroom belonging and learning, Borland (1996a) accuses me of suggesting that "schools in this country were Edenic paradises in which children and teachers lived in prelapserian communitarian bliss before the advent of the serpent of gifted education" (p. 141).

This is evidence of a confusion between my expression of a desirable state and a visionary goal for schools and classrooms and a naive statement that schools once were this way and need only to have gifted programs removed to return to some pristine state of communitarian perfection. One does not create a responsive, educationally exciting school by removing the gifted class; if it were that simple, we could simply shut down all gifted programs and watch schools improve exponentially. We won't make schools better by removing the gifted program if that's all we do. Nor do I believe that schools were ever perfect, or that children with differences were, at some prior moment, fully accepted and included in general education classrooms. There is plenty of evidence to the contrary. I don't actually think we've ever had the schools that we need and children deserve. I do believe, however, that much can be done to make classrooms loving learning environments in which children across a wide range of differences learn to support and care about one another while maintaining and achieving high-level academic standards.

I perceive deep despair and deadening hopelessness within the gifted community about the possibility for widespread school reform. This is the essence of the triage mentality, an attitude that says "This can't possibly work for all kids—let's get what we can for ours." By holding another viewpoint, by believing in and working toward schools that value and honor all children because of (and not in spite of) their diversity, I am cast as a dreamer, an idealist, and an educator seriously out of touch with current reality or future possibility.

I am also indicted for being insensitive to the plight of gifted children who are made to feel strange, odd, excluded, and teased within typical classrooms. In truth, I care deeply about how children experience schooling and the ways that school communities can build acceptance and safety (Sapon-Shevin, 1999), and I am pained by the idea of *any* child who is rejected, unhappy, or unsupported in school. But focusing on the pain and difficulties of only one group of students limits our scope and sense of responsibility and agency. I do not believe that removing gifted children to a safe haven alters the classroom community in a long-term productive way. Unless our goal is to construct completely segregated schooling for gifted students (gifted classes, gifted lunch period, gifted little league, and gifted drama club), it is imperative that all students learn to accept, respect, and interact with a wide range of students. The goal of changing classroom climate and the culture of schools so that all students are accepted and valued is a long-term proposition, and I am not naïve about the complexity of the task. But neither will I abandon the goal of successful heterogeneous classrooms because it is difficult to achieve.

If gifted education is to be tied to broader school change and reform, then we *must* believe that change is possible and linked to our collective agency. Since much of the rhetoric of gifted education is premised on the unalterable nature of the boring, rigid traditional classroom (thus necessitating removal of gifted students), cynicism about changing regular classrooms works directly against the possibility that curricular, pedagogical, and structural school reforms can be organized for all children. Until those in gifted education join forces with those in general education to form successful coalitions and joint advocacy efforts, the divisive cynicism will impede widespread and long-lasting change. Callahan (1996) explains this well:

> In many school districts, the gifted program is seen as a "refuge" from a poor quality educational program. By failing to recognize and act on the tenet that the quality of services for gifted students is closely related to the overall quality of educational programs in the local school, state, or nation, we create an environment where gifted programs are considered special privilege and where we make programming for gifted students much more difficult. As long as the general education program remains in a state (real or imagined) where the client of the schools sees programming for the gifted as better or safer, or as taking needed resources from the general program, we are likely to see parents demanding that those resources be more equally distributed or to see parents seeking the alternate services or safer environment. It matters little that the meager resources that are allocated to providing services for gifted students are *highly* unlikely to significantly alter the whole school program; what matters to the individual who take those positions is the image and symbolism of the program. (pp. 159–160)

2. There is a continuing confusion about the difference between "fair" and "equal" treatment. Someone reviewing my book on Amazon.Com wrote:

> In a roomful of people, one person chokes on his food. "Fair" would be to give him the Heimlich Maneuver. "Equal" would be to give everyone the "Heimlich Maneuver." "Equal" would also be to give no one the Heimlich Maneuver, and that seems to be what the author is arguing in this sophomoric effort.

Not only do I not want anyone to choke on his or her food, I actually want everyone well nourished with a carefully planned, tasty, well-balanced meal, lovingly prepared and attractively presented. It's true that fair isn't the same as equal—feeding a 3-month-old and a 20-year-old the same diet would be patently absurd. But fair should mean that someone has thought carefully and responsibly about each person's menu and taken the same care in providing it. I share this commitment with those in gifted education who don't want to see "gifted" children in generic gifted programs in which every child receives the same Great Books, divergent-thinking, creative-problem-solving curriculum regardless of individual talents, interests, or challenges. Callahan (1996) warns that those in gifted education must stop talking about "a program" for which one finds students and talk instead about providing truly differentiated instruction. I also want every child to have a high-quality education, carefully constructed, individually tailored, and personally responsive— not just every gifted child, but every child. We need to distinguish between "equal" education meaning the same—the same curriculum, the same standards, the same teaching methods, the same evaluation—and an "equally good" education, one responsive to each child as an individual, an education planned by a group of people who know the child well and can envision exciting possibilities for his or her education. Furthermore, I believe and have seen evidence that this kind of multilevel, participatory, constructivist education can be provided within a common community, children working individually and collaboratively on tasks at their level, combining resources, supporting one another and sharing their learning and accomplishments in individually appropriate ways (Sapon-Shevin, 1999). No one need be "held back," and neither does any child need to be feel isolated, stigmatized, or marginalized by the high or low level of his or her learning and accomplishment.

3. It is hard for many to hold anything other than rigid conceptions of school and teaching. Although I believe I have been clear about my notions of a constructivist, highly participatory, multilevel, multiple-intelligence curriculum, I am still read by my critics as wanting everyone on the same page at the same time. J. J. Gallagher (1996), for example, accuses me of recommending that "no book should be used that cannot be read by the least prepared of their students" (p. 245) and claims that my thinking would lead to "educational mediocrity" (p. 244) in the name of social justice. Within this limited framework, in other words, there are only two options when confronted by high-achieving students: segregated gifted programs or boring/rigid curricula delivered through uninspired pedagogy with an emphasis on sameness and low standards. Some of my critics seem unable to imagine that education might be organized in any configuration other than one classroom with 30 children and an uninspired teacher who asks the children to do the same thing at the

same time in the same way. There is also a continuing confusion between "programs" and "services," a discussion that has been central to the move away from segregated special education classrooms and toward more inclusive teaching settings. Eliminating "programs" doesn't mean eliminating services. Children who have particular educational needs (speech therapy, physical therapy, emotional issues, reading challenges, etc.) may require and are entitled ethically and legally to such services. But many of these need not be delivered in some segregated setting, away from other children. Similarly, we could certainly envision ways to provide high-achieving students with individual services without removing them and providing generic gifted programs.

There are very real economic, political, and educational constraints on reinventing schools in this way. The new emphasis on high-stakes testing, for example, as well as a backlash against more "progressive" forms of pedagogy and curriculum, certainly makes envisioning alternative educational possibilities difficult. Funding is also often an obstacle; certain professionals are funded to work only with certain children, based on diagnosis and label rather than on individual need, common sense, or a commitment to maintaining community. But surely there are other possibilities! We must not equate "typical" with inevitable, or let a failure of imagination keep us from envisioning and actualizing other teaching and learning arrangements.

4. Linking educational change to broader political change is unrealistic, impossible, or somehow masks the real issue. Gallagher (1996), for example, writes:

> It is difficult to argue with Sapon-Shevin on educational grounds because what she argues for is not an educational solution for our schools, but a political or socioeconomic solution for our society. Excellence can only be considered once equity is reached. Let us all hope that we will be around to see that happy day! I am excited by this uncompromising approach to societal problem solving (not one cent for gifted as long as there is any injustice abroad for poor children) and declare that henceforth I will not pay one cent of taxes as long as there is inequity in the tax code. If you do not hear from me for a while, you will probably know where to reach me. (pp. 245–246)

Gallagher accuses me of wanting to deny good-quality education to the gifted as a way of improving the quality of education for everyone else. He calls my statement "To exclude any child from quality education is to fail all children" "world-class hyperbole" and states, "By implication, this means that unless all children receive a quality education then no one should receive a quality education." This argument confuses the symptom with the cure. Do I believe that there are gross (literally) inequities in the quality of education that children receive in schools? Yes. Do I believe that denying children identified as gifted high-quality education will automatically improve the quality of education available to the majority? No. But achieving quality for some cannot be taken as an indication of sufficiency, fairness, or justice for all.

Borland (1996a), acknowledging the political ramifications of gifted programs, presents two statements that he labels "true and empirically verifiable":

1. Programs for gifted students are at least in part effective; they provide advantages for the student they serve by advancing the academic and professional careers.
2. Services for gifted students are disproportionately allocated to students who are middle- or upper-middle-class and white.

He continues,

If these are valid premises, I submit that the following conclusion must logically follow:

3. Therefore, programs for gifted students are, without this being their advocates' intention, serving to widen the gulf between society's have and have-nots, between mainstream and minority cultures. (p. 139).

The pressing question is, once we acknowledge this, what do we do about it? As I have said earlier, simply eliminating gifted programs won't bring about social justice or educational equity. But—and this is a large *but*—raising that possibility can force the hands of those with privilege and power. I proudly embrace Gallagher's (1996) accusation that I am arguing for political and economic changes in society as much as, or as a basis for, educational change. To do otherwise is, to me, naive and self-defeating.

When we read Jonathan Kozol's *Savage Inequalities* (1991) or *Amazing Grace* (1995), for example, do we really believe that the problems or the solutions are educational ones, or is it clear that racism, poverty, and injustice are the bedrock on which our inadequate school systems are built and maintained? We can do nothing other than fight for political and economic justice if we want true school reform. This is not to say that immediate and specific changes cannot be made in how we organize schools and education, but that we must always keep one eye trained on the "big picture."

As I stated earlier, I believe that gifted education can be conceptualized as a form of educational triage—a decision about how different children will be treated that results in sacrificing and abandoning those considered less capable or less worthy of investment (Sapon-Shevin, 1994; 1996); Charles Derber (1995), in an article entitled "The Politics of Triage: The Contract with American's Surplus Populations," argues that the United States is currently engaged in economic, political, and cultural triage. Economic triage can be seen in the withdrawal of viable employment or livable wages from sectors of the labor force, creating surplus populations with no economic prospects. Cultural triage is manifest in intellectuals' embrace of ideologies that explicitly justify the abandonment or elimination of surplus populations. Political triage involves the explicit decision making by government leaders to stop assisting—with money, housing, or other services—the abandoned groups (p. 37).

Viewing the intersection among these other forms of triage makes it imperative that we not conceptualize excellence and equity as competing agendas. If we do, we will all lose. We cannot withdraw resources from the most needy. Trickle-down economics has not worked and neither has the belief that providing a good education to some children will somehow transform the education of all children. Rather, we have to explore excellence within the context of equity. How can we achieve success for all students? What must school communities look like? Derber (1995) warns: "Triage, like war, perversely offers the promise of solidarity based on mobilizing against a common enemy, in this case the enemy within. . . . Until we respond to our needs for both economic security and moral awakening with a positive vision of community, the politics of triage will loom as a barbaric surrogate" (p. 88).

How can we, as a nation, afford to engage in educational triage? Even from a strictly economic perspective, it makes little sense to abandon a majority of our children to mediocrity and leftovers. If we really believe in high-quality, democratic public schooling, we must guarantee first-class educational nutrition for all students, not haute cuisine for the chosen few.

CHAPTER 9

Desegregating Gifted Education: Seeking Equity for Culturally Diverse Students

Donna Y. Ford

INTRODUCTION

Any field that wishes to sustain itself must endure critical self-assessments, and gifted education is no exception. As Borland (1996a) suggested, gifted education must begin to question and examine its fundamental premises and practices to see if they remain (or ever were) valid. One of the most pressing and controversial topics is the underrepresentation of culturally and linguistically diverse students[1] in gifted education. Few topics have the power to spark debates, denial, and defensiveness. However, rather than addressing this topic aggressively, advocates of gifted education prefer the role of peripheral players in the examination of and debate over an issue so central to the education of gifted students in our nation's schools (see Borland, 1996a, p. 131).

The field of gifted education remains rife with inequities, particularly with regard to providing equitable educational opportunities for students of color. Since the 1954 *Brown v. Board of Education of Topeka, Kansas* decision, educators have wrestled—conscientiously or sometimes reluctantly—with issues of inequities and the lack of educational opportunity open to minority students.

This chapter addresses the participation of minority students in gifted education, and pays considerable attention to equity, a philosophical concept that embraces fairness, justice, inclusiveness, and excellence in schooling. It is argued here that the poor participation of minority students in gifted education will continue unless the principle of equity becomes central to policies, practices, and procedures in (1) educational philosophy, (2) student assessment, and (3) curriculum and instruction design.

The discussion here proceeds from five assumptions. First, compared with general education and special education, gifted education is the most segregated of our educational programs—it is disproportionately White and middle-class. Second, politics often intrude on efforts to increase the participation of minority students in gifted education. Third, because schools continue to define and identify giftedness, intelligence, and talent much as they did in the 20th century, schools remain ill-prepared to face the demands that increased cultural, linguistic, and economic diversity place on them. Fourth, even though they are socially abhorrent, biological theories of giftedness and intelligence persist. The very idea that genius is inherent rather than developmental supports racist (and classist and sexist) ideologies. Fifth, the burden to effect change often falls on minority students and their families to assimilate, to adapt, and to adopt mainstream norms. Essentially, rather than looking internally, educators frequently look beyond schools for changes and solutions to educational inequities.

The first section of this chapter discusses those "barriers to equity" that hinder the representation of minority students in gifted education. The discussion proceeds with recommendations for changes that promise to secure an excellent and equitable education for culturally and linguistically diverse gifted students. It concludes with a summary that rests, in part, on an observation by Sapon-Shevin (1996): "The ways in which gifted education is defined, constituted, and enacted lead directly to increased segregation, limited educational opportunities for the majority of students, and damage to children's social and political development" (p. 196).

PHILOSOPHIES AND ATTITUDES: THE DILEMMA OF DIFFERENCE AND BARRIERS TO EQUITY

Human difference remains an explosive theme, and perceptions about differences have taken many forms throughout history. Prior to the 1970s, cultural-deficit theories prevailed as the dominant explanation for substandard social and educational outcomes among minority groups. Racially and culturally diverse students did poorly in school, it was argued, because they were "culturally deprived" or "culturally disadvantaged" (Ford & Harris, 1999, 2000; Ford, Howard, & Harris, 1999). Thus, many social scientists, including educators, resorted to efforts aimed at changing children's cultures by way of assimilation. If students were willing to assimilate, to give up their culture—that is, to leave their beliefs, values, traditions, customs, and language at the schoolhouse door—they would increase their chances of becoming more advantaged and successful in mainstream America. In this respect, education became a sub-tractive process, taking what children brought to school out of them and re-placing it with cultural beliefs, values, and traditions the majority deemed more acceptable or practical.

The 1970s saw some changes in this deficit orientation. More publications and research focused on how "cultural differences" lead to cross-cultural mis-understandings or conflicts. The assumptions arose that people from different cultures lived in parallel (but not necessarily equal) subcultures in the United States and that their differences invited conflict in social and educational set-tings. With the notion of cultural deficit no longer in vogue (seen, in fact, as politically incorrect and even racist), schools were left with the question of how to handle diversity (a powerful treatise on this issue is Myrdal [1962], *An American Dilemma: The Negro Problem and Modern Democracy*). As we en-ter the 21st century, the question remains. The current answer appears to be the adoption of a colorblind philosophy.

One of the easiest or most convenient ways to avoid addressing differ-ences (including diversity) is to ignore them. A colorblind philosophy presents one way to abdicate our responsibility to respond to diversity. A colorblind philosophy gives educators the license to ignore differences under the pre-tense of fairness, that is, treating "all children the same." But this same treat-ment can be inherently inequitable, as we can easily see in gifted education where we abjure, from the start, the idea of treating all children the same. We believe gifted children learn at a faster rate than other children, so we use such curricular and instructional modifications as compacting and acceler-ation. We believe gifted students think in more sophisticated, complex ways than other students, so we expose them to high-level thinking skills, creative thinking, and problem-solving skills. As in gifted education, so in urban educa-tion and multicultural education, the idea of treating all children alike is re-ductive and educationally unsound.

Nonetheless, the recent history of American education reveals only mini-mal recognition of the profound differences that exist among children. Thus, the process of American education—whether one addresses the needs of gifted students or of minority students—resembles a one-size-fits-all Procrustean Bed (Ford, 1996). As Callahan (1996) remarked, we have a distressing history of uniformity in instructional planning, in spite of all the diversity among stu-dents we encounter ever day. Likewise, one or two ways to educate gifted students predominate, so that we speak of gifted education "programs" or "classrooms" as opposed to "services."[2] Stated differently, a strong sense of diver-sity among gifted students exists, yet we place most of those students in re-markably similar programs and rely on standard curriculum and instructional strategies to teach them (Callahan, 1996). All of this avoidance begs the ques-tion "What types of diversity do we value in gifted education, and how will we address individual and group differences when identifying and serving gifted and culturally diverse students?" Before addressing this question, one must move beyond one's own ethnocentrism or world view.

Ethnocentricity: Ignoring Multicultural Perspectives of Intelligence and Ability

Giftedness is a social construct. What one culture values as intelligence or giftedness may not be valued in another culture. For instance, Americans highly value cognitive and academic ability over spatial, musical, interpersonal, and other abilities (H. Gardner, 1993). We prize schoolhouse intelligence over tacit or practical intelligence (Sternberg, 1985a). Even within school subject areas, we appear to value reading, mathematics, and the sciences (the "core" subjects) above social studies, music, art, and physical education. One has only to examine programs or course offerings in the schools serving gifted students to readily reach this conclusion. Conversely, other cultures may value the arts and other "nonacademic" subjects as much as (or more than) the academic subjects.

Similarly, what is defined and labeled as giftedness in one school district may not necessarily be viewed and valued as gifted in another district. Evidence for this assertion appears in the number and diversity of definitions and conceptions of giftedness (and intelligence) in the field (e.g., H. Gardner, 1983; Sternberg, 1985a; Marland, 1972, USDE, 1993; Weschler, 1991). These multiple definitions suggest, as Borland (1996a) noted, that "giftedness is as much created as it is discovered. . . . We confer giftedness instead of discovering it" (pp. 133–134). Put another way, so many conceptions of ability, giftedness, and intelligence exist that one might conclude that giftedness, whatever it is, is shaped by social and cultural values and beliefs, as well as politics.

Just as definitions and conceptions of giftedness differ within the education profession and across school districts, other cultures hold different ideas and expectations about abilities and purposes of education. The biology-environment debate provides a case in point. While Americans have historically defined intelligence from a genetic perspective and continue to debate the relative contributions of the environment and genes to intelligence (and to any subsequent achievement), East Asians subscribe to Confucian beliefs, which stress an environmental view of human development. While acknowledging the role of heredity or innate factors in producing individual differences, East Asians focus more on environmental interventions, access to reading materials, tutoring, and so forth (Stevenson, Lee, Chen, Lummils, Fan, & Ge, 1990). Thus, Japanese and Chinese populations believe that performance rests heavily on the kinds and quality of learning experiences that schools provide. The teacher's skills and the student's diligence influence performance more than do genetics. As Waley (1989) observed, in these environmentalist and effort-oriented cultures, "human beings are by nature, near together; by practice, far apart" (p. 209). While it would be naïve to expect Americans to adopt outright the values and belief systems of another culture, the noted academic success of Asian Americans calls for some reconsideration of American values, belief systems, and practices. As the U.S. Department of Education (1993) noted, "Most American students are encouraged to finish high school and earn good grades. But students are not asked to work hard or to master a body of challenging knowledge or skills. The message society often sends to students is to aim for academic adequacy, not academic excellence" (p. 1).

Schools: Places of Inequity and Barriers to Talent Development

Every day, thousands of minority students enter the schoolhouse doors, but comparatively few of them enter challenging classrooms, and fewer still partic-ipate in activities designed for gifted students. Yet many of these culturally and linguistically diverse students are perfectly capable of high achievement. Many will miss an opportunity to realize their potential simply because of our current perceptions of diverse students and the appropriate ways to sort and reward (or penalize) them. As our schools become increasingly effective at pulling their complaisant students to the top, they become increasingly effec-tive at limiting the horizons of other students. In school settings, too many minority students discover their limitations rather than their potential. As Gardner (1961/1984) stated, educational systems have always had a great deal to do with the eventual roles of the students who pass through them. Are, then, gifted programs a form of social reproduction and, if so, in what ways do we reproduce the social order? As Sapon-Shevin (1994) observed, "Whether or not the intention of gifted programs is to reproduce existing economic and racial hierarchies or to produce cultural capital held by an elite group of stu-dents, these are in fact the consequences of such a system" (p. 192).

My consultations at schools reveal that some educators manage to devise elaborate institutional arrangements to avoid ensuring equity for gifted minor-ity students. In one urban public school district, students had to meet eight stipulations before they could be admitted to the gifted program, assuming they had already met the basic IQ and achievement criteria:

1. an admission fee ranging from $160 to $600, depending on the school building (no financial support given to families unable to pay the fee);
2. a history of perfect attendance or only excused medical absences;
3. no negative behavioral marks on report cards;

4. no grade below a C in any previous course;
5. official transcripts submitted by parents with an application (even if the student was already enrolled within the district);
6. application to be submitted to the school only on two specified dates and only during certain hours;
7. a contract signed by parent or guardian agreeing to participate in certain activities on predetermined dates and at predetermined times; and
8. all applications delivered in person.

These stipulations—hurdles, actually—contaminate perceptions of giftedness by emphasizing irrelevant behavioral responses. Gifted education, then, becomes based on privilege rather than need. Minority and economically disadvantaged students in this district suffered disproportionately from these stipulations: They represented 70% of the school district, but only 10% of its gifted program.

In a different urban school district, elaborate matrices were used to determine eligibility for gifted education opportunities. In total, nine test scores and subscale scores were entered into the matrix, along with scores from a teacher's checklist. IQ scores and achievement percentiles were weighted (e.g., 10 points were given to students with IQ scores over 145; 5 points for IQ scores of 130; 0 points for IQ scores below 130). Tests accounted for 90% of the information gathered. S. Johnson (1994) referred to such practices as "pseudo-scientific."

A third example involves test scores secondarily. In this urban school district, data indicated that minority students were under-referred for screening and identification. Yet teacher recommendation was the first step in the identification process. Once referred, students took a battery of tests. However, educators who hold low expectations and set low standards for culturally and linguistically diverse students are unlikely to refer them for gifted education opportunities, as was the case in this example.

How pervasive are examples like these? The Office for Civil Rights reviews approximately 5,000 cases annually, many involving gifted education, and we know that comparatively few parents prepare formal complaints challenging authority. Are the previous examples simply anomalies, or indices of the worst (that is to say, unethical and educationally unsound) practices in gifted education? The answer remains unclear; however, we do know that these gross inequities are avoidable and correctable. According to Edmonds, "We can, whenever, and wherever we choose, successfully teach all children whose schooling is of interest to us. We already know more than we need to teach all children successfully. Whether or not we do it must finally depend on how we feel about the fact that we haven't done it so far" (quoted in Boyer & Baptiste, 1996, p. xiv).

Edmonds's admonition raises the issue of expectations. Working insufficiently hard to redress inequities stems from low expectations. Ford (1996) reported that many of the gifted Black students she interviewed confessed to exerting low effort in school, yet few teachers encouraged them to put forth more effort. Low expectations also become evident when educators target instruction at the lowest levels: knowledge and comprehension. Students receive a steady diet of facts and seldom receive the opportunity to engage in critical and creative thinking. Ironically, Levin (1990) found that students designated low achievers, underachievers, or "at risk" profit from accelerated learning—that is, from a challenging curriculum and instruction.

Standardized Tests: Tools of Inequity and Barriers to Talent Development

American educators have much to be proud of, but much to be ashamed of as well. Testing and identification of gifted students fall on the negative side. We are so bound by tradition that the actual practice of identifying gifted students lags far behind the best research, knowledge, and theory that psychology, sociology, and education can provide (Callahan, 1996; Gould, 1981; Madaus, 1994). Standardized tests remain the primary instruments guiding decisions about students. Tests exert a lot of power as they carry out the unpopular job of sorting students while a presumption of objectivity protects them. But like curricula, tests are value-laden—developed by humans—from the items selected, to the test format, to the response format, to the "correct" answer.

Meanwhile, we forget that tests, like most instruments, are not perfect. Many parents whose children have had temperatures will recognize that a thermometer, a man-made instrument, is also imprecise. For example, there are different types of thermometers (digital, analog, battery-operated, manual), and temperatures (even with the same thermometer) will differ depending on where the temperature is taken (under the arm, under the tongue, in the rectum, on the forehead). The accuracy of the number (temperature) is also influenced by how recently one has had a cold or hot drink, whether one just been physically active, and the time of day. We also know that a high temperature in the elderly is often more serious than in a teenager. No credible doctor will make a diagnosis without taking these and other factors into consideration. Few parents would accept a diagnosis based on one number (a temperature).

Any school that treats tests as objective or infallible commits grave mistakes (Gardner, 1961/1984). Minority students often suffer misplacement and miseducation when tests extensively or exclusively control important educational decisions (see Gould, 1981). A single number, test, or label rarely captures existing or potential excellence (Friedman & Rogers, 1998). After all, traits that comprise a person's genetic endowment rarely operate in a straightforward, additive fashion. The available data offer no support for the view that racial or national origins set different limits on the potentialities of a child. The teacher has the right to assume that under similar conditions both the range of capacities and the average capacity of various groups will almost certainly be about the same. He or she has the duty, therefore, to treat each child as an individual (Klineberg, 1952).

The easiest and laziest course to take is to sort out youngsters by their test scores and forget any attendant complications. To the extent that we sort students on the basis of test scores that (roughly) measure or reify only one dimension of human performance, we constrict reality and deny the richness of human possibility (Gardner, 1961/1984, pp. 66–67). No reliable measures of innate capacity exist (Cleary, Humphreys, Kendrick, & Wesman, 1975, p. 17). We must relinquish the assumption that tests provide either all the answers or at least the most objective answers. More important, we must relinquish tests as an excuse to conduct "business as usual." Relative to desegregating gifted education, educators must ask themselves these questions: If minority students are not performing well on certain standardized tests of intelligence or achievement, why do we insist on using those tests? If the use of traditional tests and procedures has a disparate impact on minority students, why continue to use those measures and procedures? Ultimately, we must ask whether the culprit for low or differential performance on standardized tests is a fault of the student (someone with a "cultural deficit") or of the test (an instrument embodying "test bias") or of the curriculum (poor teaching, superficial design, or inadequate resources) or a combination of these variables.

How, in short, can we accurately assess the strengths of linguistically and culturally diverse students? The recommendations that follow reflect the goal of desegregating gifted education. They are not as much solutions as they are conditions that must be in place for the process of change to begin.

RECOMMENDATIONS FOR CHANGE

> There is a wealth of talent and intelligence in this field [of gifted education], but I worry that we are using it to defend yesterday, not to imagine and build tomorrow. (Borland, 1996a, p. 145)

As the foregoing makes clear, the underrepresentation of minority students in gifted education is a complex problem. The solutions can be equally complex. What follows are a few conditions that must precede positive change.

First is a sound philosophical orientation. What, we should ascertain, is the purpose of gifted education and how can our schools help all students to develop optimally? This question presumes schools to be places of talent development. It also presumes that schools continually examine their commitment to diversity and equity while they promise a mission to provide *all* students with equal opportunities to achieve. This implicit recommendation underlies equitable access to high-quality educational experiences. Further, schools must rethink the role tests play in forming educational (and social) decisions. If the data indicate that minority students are affected disparately by certain tests and procedures, schools must find other means of assessing the strengths and needs of diverse students. Similarly, if teacher referrals run low for minority students, schools must increase the defensibility of the referral process or reduce the impact of the teacher referral.

Equal Opportunity in Both Curriculum and Instruction

Cognitive ability, clearly inheritable, can still increase dramatically in an individual who undergoes intense training. Heritability amounts only to a probabilistic genetic influence in a population, not an immutable, predetermined outcome for an individual (Plomin & Thompson, 1993, p. 68). Simply put, genes are not destiny. For minority students to achieve their potential, schools must provide them with the appropriate kinds of educational opportunities and support. Our record in this regard is bleak (e.g., Kozol, 1991; Woodson, 1933).

Schools must expose *all* children to challenging instruction and academically rigorous curricula (Banks & Banks, 1995; Ford & Harris, 2000). Students have the right to learn critical thinking, problem solving, and creativity and to participate in academic investigations and independent study. All children must learn to analyze and evaluate. In view of how it is currently implemented (e.g., with enrichment activities and higher-level thinking), much of what we call "gifted education" is appropriate for all students. If the staple of a gifted education program is higher-level thinking skills, creative activities, problem solving, field trips, and games, all children should be identified as gifted, because all children should be exposed to such curriculum and instruction. Students don't need an IQ of 130 to go on a field trip or conduct a study.

Further, if we want minority students to rise to the challenge cognitively and academically, at least three opportunities must be in place: (1) the opportunity to gain essential metacognitive skills and strategies; (2) the opportunity to acquire essential study skills; and (3) the opportunity to acquire essential test-taking skills (see Ford, 1996). These opportunities assume that educators hold high expectations for culturally diverse students.

Pedagogical Responsiveness: Avoiding Instructional Discrimination

"Instructional discrimination" refers to any pedagogical act, practice, or behavior that results in unfair or inappropriate responses to the diverse or culturally influenced learning styles of students, and it usually hinders the academic achievement of minority students. Shade, Kelly, and Oberg (1997) and others (e.g., Stevenson et al., 1990; Saracho & Gerstl, 1992) report that, compared with other students, minority students tend to be concrete, inductive, field-dependent, spatial, tactile, and social learners. Thus, they require and deserve teaching strategies that match their patterns and opportunities to demonstrate their learning in diverse ways. When teachers understand these learning and thinking styles and their impact on student achievement, they can modify their instructional strategies so as to give their students greater access to knowledge and an opportunity to absorb and use it.

Multicultural Education: Being Culturally Responsive and Responsible

The traditional curriculum seldom validates or empowers culturally and racially diverse students. A monocultural or ethnocentric curriculum can be neither excellent nor equitable. If we expect minority students to accept the challenge cognitively and academically, they must *see* themselves in the curriculum, which is to say the curriculum must be affirming and responsive (Banks & Banks, 1995; Ford & Harris, 1999).

Multicultural education, according to Baptiste (1995), entails a comprehensive philosophical reform of the school environment, not just of the curriculum and instructional routines. It entails a curriculum responsive and responsible to its students. Multicultural education focuses on the principles of excellence, equity, and social justice so that students experience educational equality and cultural empowerment, principles best realized through judicious pedagogy and a commitment to high expectations. As a pedagogy of and for equity, multicultural education helps all students to appreciate and respect cultural diversity, overcome ethnocentric and prejudicial attitudes, and understand the sociopolitical and economical factors that have produced contemporary conditions of inequality (*Rethinking Schools*, 2000).

Defensible Assessment Practices

Historically, there has been an emphasis on finding the right number, the right test, and then the right student to participate in a predetermined gifted education class or program. However, the diagnosis or assessment of a student's ability to perform remains a haphazard undertaking. Mysteries in individual development still puzzle us, so no stone should go unturned to ensure that we base our decisions on a wide range of evidence, carefully gathered and evaluated. Experience teaches that the greatest enemy of sound and fair selection processes is the simple-minded and formula-ridden "efficiency" involved in assigning a single score to each student. Efficiency must never distort our diagnoses or narrow our conceptions of talent. Talent scouting is labor intensive (Gardner, 1961/1984, p. 67).

In sum, school personnel, especially those who administer and interpret assessment data, must adhere to ethical standards, use fair testing practices, choose tests for their technical merits (validity, reliability, norming procedures, and sampling), and apply them for the specific purposes and populations for which they were developed.

Self-Assessment and Evaluation

Borland (1996a) and Callahan (1996) persuasively urge prolonged reflection about our philosophies, practices, and purposes as educational professionals. A profession unable to be self-critical for the purpose of making positive changes leaves itself vulnerable to criticism from without. Such critical evaluations in the field of gifted education must center on: (1) improving identification and assessment measures, policies, and procedures; (2) ensuring and improving minority-student representation; and (3) improving curricula and instruction and must include an examination of the data aggregated by language background and ethnic background relative to students referred, assessed, and served. At the very least, such an evaluation must produce information about (1) the percentage of minority students referred versus screened versus placed by gender, grade level, and socioeconomic status (SES); (2) the percentage of minority students who persist with gifted education services and the reasons by gender, grade level, and SES; and (3) the most effective instruments and strategies for referral, assessment, and placement.

Schools as Places of Talent Development

Theoretically at least, all of education is about talent development. If schools fail to develop talent, they hardly deserve the name. Do we expect students to remain more or less the same after 12 years of schooling? Do we not expect students to change and grow affectively, cognitively, and academically? Too few gifted programs assume their share of responsibility for ensuring that talent receives encouragement, especially talent in children who come to school with limited opportunities.

In 1993, the U.S. Department of Education issued a report entitled *National Excellence: A Case for Developing America's Talent* and recommended that services for gifted students endorse a talent-development orientation. The report made this observation: "The term 'gifted' connotes a mature power rather than a developing ability and, therefore, is antithetic to recent research findings about children" (p. 26). The emphasis on talent development moves away from labeling students and placing them in prearranged classrooms and programs toward assessing individual strengths and needs and providing appropriate services. This requires reconsideration of the previous headlong efforts to find the "right test," the "right label," the "right program," and the "right gifted student" and a consideration, instead, of more effective ways to improve curriculum, instruction, and expectations so that minority students gain access to gifted education services. We must develop philosophies and services that rest on the notion of developing talent. Seizing the initiative, the Department of Education (1993) offered the following definition:

> Children and youth with outstanding talent perform or show the potential for performing at remarkably high levels of accomplishment when compared with others of their age, experience, or environment. These children and youth exhibit high performance capacity in intellectual, creative, and/or artistic areas, possess an unusual leadership capacity, or excel in specific academic fields. They require services or activities not ordinarily provided by the schools. Outstanding talents are present in children and youth from all cultural groups, across all economic strata, and in all areas of human endeavor. (p. 3)

Teacher Preparation: Increasing Cultural Competence

Today's teachers receive preparation to teach in classrooms that no longer exist. Few of them, including so-called specialists, receive formal coursework adequate to the needs of gifted students. This deficiency may explain why so few teachers can reliably identify gifted students (Ford, 1996). Just as troubling, teachers seldom encounter coursework and professional development targeting the developmental needs of culturally and linguistically diverse students in general. This lack of preparation places minority students in double jeopardy—enduring the usual prejudices while their academic strengths and needs go unmet in school.

Given that almost any teacher in any school can refer students for screening, all teachers need training in gifted education. At the most basic level, that preparation must include instruction in (1) identification and assessment; (2) characteristics of gifted students; (3) recognition of gifted underachieving students; (4) curriculum and instruction for gifted students; (5) multicultural education; (6) social-emotional needs and development; and (7) urban child development. Furthermore, administrators must make concerted efforts to recruit and retain minority teachers in gifted education (see Ford, Grantham, & Harris, 1997). In a national survey, Ford (1998) found that universities and schools neglected to recruit minority future teachers into the field of gifted education. Some minority teachers reported being actively discouraged from teaching in gifted classrooms. It is hardly surprising that students lack minority role models in their classrooms and have fewer cultural advocates than they could have (Ladson-Billings, 1994).

Beyond Educationally Unsound Debates

Even as debates about the relative contributions of genes and the environment continue, they have done little to improve the practice of education. Even if environment were a modest factor—and it is much more than that—in determining a student's ability to perform, educational policies could acknowledge and emphasize the importance of taking this factor into account. Even if only 2 children in 10 might gain some intellectual effectiveness thereby, we would still be obligated to make the effort. Whatever the scoring on the finer points of the abstract debate, our job is still to make the most of each child's potential (Gardner, 1961/1984). Accordingly, we must relegate idle bantering to the sidelines. After all, if the environment, which surely includes schools, does not matter, what is the purpose of education? Why do we need gifted education? Why do we need books? Why not base our entire society on genealogy? To attribute success or failure to genetics is to abdicate our roles and responsibilities as professionals. S. Johnson (1994) stated this position well: "These distractions, like flu and locusts, come with the potential not merely to annoy but to terrorize and cripple. They can influence national and local policy in dangerous ways" (p. 273).

In summary, to ensure the least discriminatory practices—that is to say, practices most likely to desegregate gifted education—the following requirements must inform and guide our assessments and services:

1. *Definitions*. Definitions of giftedness must embrace the notion of talent development and potential (e.g., Gardner, 1983; USDE, 1993). Definitions must be defensible (i.e., free of criteria featuring mainly behavior, attendance, previous grades, etc.).
2. *Assessments*. We must use multiple types of assessments (e.g., verbal and nonverbal intelligence tests, achievement tests, portfolios) and adopt valid and reliable instruments, particularly those least biased against culturally and linguistically diverse students.
3. *Policies*. We must determine the extent to which policies and practices hinder the participation of minority students in gifted education.
4. *Communication*. There must be early, consistent, and ongoing com-

munication with families about gifted education services, including the curriculum, identification and assessment instruments, policies, and procedures.

5. *Annual reviews and evaluations*. All aspects of education must be reviewed and evaluated—policies and procedures, assessment measures—in order to make data-based decisions.

6. *Personnel*. Personnel should be qualified to select, administer, and interpret assessment data. All personnel (teachers, counselors, psychologists, and administrators) must have formal preparation (e.g., coursework and professional development) in gifted and urban education.

7. *Talent development*. We need more efforts targeting early childhood students (from preschool to grade three) in an effort to develop and nurture talent in the early years. This recommendation is related to the "second-grade syndrome" in which many minority students, especially Black males, begin to show early, significant declines in achievement. It also relates to the talent-development philosophy discussed throughout the chapter.

8. *Multiple services or programming options*. Options for services are necessary to ensure a continuum of appropriate learning opportunities.

9. *Professional development*. Educators need ongoing opportunities for professional development in gifted education and urban education.

For these recommendations to be adopted, there must be a manifest desire among school personnel to educate all children, regardless of culture, socioeconomic status, and language.

SUMMARY AND CONCLUSIONS

It is not an exaggeration to claim that, when it comes to the honest examination of the fundamental questions that underlie the practice of our field, we [educators] lack conviction while others are full of passionate intensity. (Borland, 1996a, p. 145)

All of the conflicting and confusing ideas Americans have concerning equity, equality, excellence, and opportunity quickly surface in discussions of gifted education and minority students. We must rephrase the persistent question of minority student underrepresentation in gifted education from "How can we identify more minority students?" to "How can we provide opportunities and rewards for students of all degrees of ability from all backgrounds so that all will realize their full potentials?" We must deemphasize labeling in favor of providing enriched opportunities for students whose circumstances or abilities are less easily assessable and quantifiable by traditional means (Friedman & Rogers, 1998). The changes must be systemic; we cannot tolerate islands of excellence in a sea of inequity, intolerance, and injustice. All of education must examine the purpose and viability of its programs and services. For instance, we know that students whose educational experiences are fraught with poor instruction and inadequate resources have difficulty achieving at high levels when placed in more challenging programs, especially if they lack previous academic and social-emotional support.

Meanwhile, our field remains primarily responsible for minority student underrepresentation in gifted education to the extent that we have more or less chosen to ignore emerging conceptions of ability by focusing almost exclusively on a general unitary conception of giftedness (Feldhusen, 1998). This adherence to tradition has served mainstream children well, but we must aim for an educational system that serves each student in terms of his or her talents, stretching each, challenging each, demanding all the best that is in each. We must stop prematurely closing doors and limiting our students' futures because the predictive validity of our current measures of intelligence, creativity, and leadership for extraordinary adult achievement is dubious (Pendarvis & Howley, 1996, p. 217). Lemann (1999) reports that the SAT predicts only about 15% of the variance in freshman grades. What explains the remaining 85%? A. E. Housman said it well: "The house of delusions is cheap to build but drafty to live in" (cited in Gardner, 1961/1984, p. 138). It is past time for a renovation.

The potential for brilliance is spread evenly across all groups. While some social scientists and educators will resist this statement, every day students of color participate in segregated and substandard educational programs. How much longer must they wait for the promises of our Constitution, Bill of Rights, and Civil Rights Act to be fulfilled? As Martin Luther King (1963/1997) said so eloquently,

> When the architects of our republic wrote the magnificent words of the Constitution and the Declaration of Independence, they were signing a promissory note to which every American was to fall heir. This note was the promise that all men . . . would be guaranteed the unalienable rights of life, liberty, and the pursuit of happiness. . . . America has defaulted on the promissory note insofar as her citizens of color are concerned. . . . America has given the Negro people a bad check; a check which has come back marked "insufficient funds." (p. 13)

But Dr. King refused to believe that the bank of justice is bankrupt, and we too refuse to believe that the great vault of opportunity for every child in the United States contains insufficient funds. The obligation to cash this check of freedom and justice is long overdue.

NOTES

1. The terms *minority, culturally and linguistically diverse,* and *students of color* are used interchangeably in this chapter. These students include African Americans, Hispanics/Latinos, Native Americans, and Asian Americans. When addressing the topic of underrepresentation, however, Asian Americans as a group are not included, for much data indicate that they are overrepresented in gifted education.

2. Some scholars, such as Treffinger and Feldhusen (1996), prefer to speak of gifted education "programming" rather programs. Although we prefer "services," we agree that gifted education programming or services suggest a broad, rich array of services that might be provided in varying ways, places, and times, based on students' needs and profiles of strengths.

CHAPTER 10

What's Missing in Gifted Education Reform

Margie K. Kitano

Despite decades of national attention to underserved populations, low-income and culturally and linguistically diverse students continue to be underrepresented in programs for the gifted. Criticisms that gifted education perpetuates social inequities have prompted policymakers to call for schoolwide reform efforts that would provide challenging curriculum for *all* children. Such efforts to increase inclusion address otherwise problematic issues of biased identification practices, elitism, and withholding challenging curriculum from all but a few. Although schoolwide enrichment can coexist with special services for highly able students, some critics (e.g., Sapon-Shevin, 1996) favor elimination of gifted education programs.

That leaders in the field of gifted education have responded to underrepresentation is evidenced by the increase over time in professional conferences, publications, and policies focused on diversity issues. The annual Diversity Symposium of the Association for Gifted is one example. With such attention devoted to increased access to gifted programs, why have the data on underrepresentation remained essentially unchanged? This chapter suggests hypotheses and promising directions from a sociocultural perspective regarding what might be missing from current efforts to increase equity in representation and services.

A search for answers to issues of underrepresentation necessarily assumes that the potential for extraordinary performance exists in equal proportions in all groups (ethnic, cultural, gender, economic). This assumption does not have a moral or ethical premise, but derives from anthropological data suggesting that cultural groups differ not in cognitive processes, such as abstraction or inferential reasoning, but rather in the ways in which such processes are expressed (Cole & Bruner, 1971).

A SOCIOCULTURAL PERSPECTIVE

Sociocultural theorists describe children's cognitive development as inseparable from the cultural and historical aspects of their lives (García, 1999; Rogoff
& Chavajay, 1995; Tharp & Gallimore, 1988). Teaching and learning are recognized as social as well as cognitive processes that cannot be examined apart
from the cultural practices of teachers and schools. Thus, a child's cognitive
development can be understood only within the external social context within
which the child has lived. Schooling must be socially, culturally, linguistically,
and cognitively meaningful to students. García (1999) argues that schools have
failed to provide meaningful contexts to culturally and linguistically diverse
children and in fact may contribute to their educational vulnerability through
systematic exclusion from the curriculum of the histories, languages, experiences, and values of these children.

What may be missing from current approaches to identifying and serving
gifted students from diverse backgrounds is specific, sustained, systematic attention to the social and cultural contexts of the school and classroom. Maker
(1996) notes that promising identification procedures have been discontinued
because children identified were not successful when placed in existing programs designed for different types of children. Children may not succeed in
such programs because their behavior conflicts with teachers' beliefs about
the nature of giftedness or how gifted children behave. According to Maker,
many educators have inaccurate and negative perceptions about the abilities
of culturally and linguistically diverse children.

What goes on in classrooms is critical to student achievement. Based on
their research on programming arrangements and student outcomes, Delcourt
et al. (1994) concluded that program type (special school, separate class, pull-
out, within-class) does not differentially affect learning outcomes by race. However, they found lower performance on standardized achievement tests for
gifted African-American and Hispanic students compared with gifted White
students (Cornell, Delcourt, Goldberg, & Bland, 1995) across program types.
Cornell et al. suggest that test bias, differences in socioeconomic status, and
sociocultural factors may contribute to such differences. Indeed, Pollard
(1989) noted that comparisons across ethnic groups fail to "take into account
evidence that Black and White children receive quite different educational
experiences even when they are sitting in the same classroom. They also ignore the different historical and contemporary status positions that Whites
and different groups of minorities hold in this country" (p. 299).

Based on a sociocultural perspective, four specific aspects of the classroom context appear critical and may be missing from many classrooms serving gifted and talented students. These four elements have potential for increasing services to low-income and culturally and linguistically diverse gifted

students by (1) tailoring instruction to cultural and language diversity in the classroom; (2) reducing individual and institutional bias; (3) implementing multicultural curriculum; and (4) enhancing resilience through development of positive coping strategies.

TAILORING INSTRUCTION TO CULTURAL AND LANGUAGE DIVERSITY IN THE CLASSROOM

Contemporary instructional approaches for the gifted appear to be highly consistent with constructivist principles for teaching and learning (Feldhusen, 1998; Maker & Nielson, 1996). In fact, Tomlinson (1996) has argued that gifted education built its strategies over the last three decades on newer principles of cognitive psychology. She attributes general education's more recent adoption of constructivism as one reason for reformers' arguments that gifted education is no longer needed. Constructivist principles (see, e.g., the American Psychological Association's *Learner-centered Psychological Principles*, 1997) are intended to apply to *all* learners and appear supportive of the needs of diverse learners in their emphasis on linking new concepts with learner experiences, influence of culture and language on motivation and ways of thinking, application of higher-order thinking strategies, and active engagement of the learner in developing meaning through authentic tasks (García, 1999). Additionally, constructivist principles appear especially appropriate to gifted students' research-based characteristics, such as preference for complexity, ability to generalize and to learn from errors (Kanevsky, 1990), and use of prior knowledge to solve new problems (E. B. Coleman & Shore, 1991). However, as cogently argued by Reyes (1992), embracing any single approach does not take into consideration differences among learners. Is it possible that we fail some diverse (and mainstream) students through applications of constructivist methods not specifically designed for their needs?

Observing teacher interactions with Spanish-speaking and Hmong students, Reyes (1992) concluded that process approaches to literacy instruction, such as "whole language," can obstruct the success of students who have limited proficiency in English. Because constructivist approaches are intended to encourage learners' active participation and initiation, they can be "disconcerting for culturally and linguistically different students who expect teachers to provide direct and explicit instruction. . . . The high regard that Hispanics hold for teachers as authority figures . . . indicates that they rely on and expect direct instructional intervention from the teacher" (p. 439). Reyes urges educators to design programs that specifically address cultural and linguistic diversity as core issues rather than make peripheral (or no) adjustments to a program developed for mainstream students. To illustrate, she describes a program incorporating process instruction that resulted in successful second-language development for linguistically diverse students (i.e., English) and for some mainstream students (Spanish). The program emphasized literacy development rather than English, allowing students to write in whichever language they found more comfortable. Other elements included cooperative learning, explicit skills instruction within the context of learning activities, citing of errors, and high expectations.

Delpit (1988) offered similar cautions about the use of process approaches in educating African-American students. Based on children's behavior following progressive literacy instruction focused on higher-level critical thinking skills, she noted: "It merely provided an opportunity for those who already knew the content to exhibit that they knew it, or at most perhaps to build one new concept onto what was already known. This meant that the child who did not come to school already primed with what was to be presented would be labeled as needing 'remedial' instruction from day one" (p. 286). Delpit further argued that if teachers fail to provide explicit instruction to students, "what it feels like to people who are old enough to judge is that there are secrets being kept, that time is being wasted, that the teacher is abdicating his or her duty to teach. . . . This sense of being cheated can be so strong that the student may be completely turned off to the educational system" (p. 287).

Recently, Fradd and Lee (1999) added to this discussion the need to consider teachers' comfort level with direct instruction and inquiry approaches in teaching science to low-income English-language learners, as preferences appear to be related to their own cultural backgrounds and experiences. The authors cite evidence that student-centered instruction can be effective with culturally and linguistically diverse students and that direct and open-ended instruction should be considered complementary rather than opposing, especially for students with limited knowledge and experience in science.

Reyes (1992), Delpit (1988), and Fradd and Lee (1999) described interactions in nonselective classrooms. It is unclear whether their observations apply to gifted students from low-income, culturally and linguistically diverse backgrounds. Yet these authors' findings raise a question for educators of the gifted: Could emphasis on constructivist strategies interfere with the motivation and learning of some gifted students, particularly those from low-income, culturally and linguistically diverse backgrounds? None of these authors advocate a basic-skills approach for culturally and linguistically diverse children. Rather, they encourage educators to provide content that other children normally receive at home and incorporate strategies appropriate for all children. The fact that other experts on teaching culturally and linguistically diverse children (e.g., García, 1999) advocate constructivist approaches for this population strongly suggests the need to consider within-group differences and to balance teacher- and student-centered instruction to encourage development of basic knowledge and skills with independent inquiry and exploration.

REDUCING INDIVIDUAL AND INSTITUTIONAL BIAS

Most educators and psychologists agree that standardized intelligence instruments traditionally used to identify gifted individuals produce scores biased against individuals from diverse backgrounds. As a result, much of the work on increasing services to gifted students from diverse backgrounds has focused on using or developing nonbiased assessment instruments or procedures (e.g., Borland & Wright, 1994; Frasier, 1997; Maker, 1996), often derived from more inclusive definitions of intelligence or giftedness. Yet, as Borland (1986) sadly predicted some 15 years ago, "I believe that those who are so inclined will continue to hold some children down with or without the excuse of IQ tests" (p. 167).

Inherently biased instruments can be used in nonbiased ways, and nonbiased instruments can be used in biased ways. Bias—intentional or unintentional—does exist as a factor in underserving culturally and linguistically diverse students in programs for the gifted. Only recently has the field been willing to document its existence in national publications. Peterson and Margolin (1997) asked classroom teachers working with a sizable Latino minority in a midwestern community to nominate students for a gifted program. Results indicated that the teachers tended to select members of their own culture (White middle-class) and primary language. The researchers described the systematic selection bias as an unintentional outcome of teachers' failure to perceive the culturally determined nature of their criteria for excellence.

Critics of gifted education are less generous in their interpretations of the underrepresentation of low-income and diverse students in programs for the gifted. Wells and Serna (1996) found strong parent resistance to detracking reforms in their 3-year study of 10 racially mixed schools. The authors describe the parents' resistance as motivated by issues of both status and race. Elite parents wanted to maintain the "upper-track" label, and they valued diversity as long as the African-American or Latino students acted like White middle-class children or were not in the same classrooms as their own children. Wells and Serna also reported that students frequently were placed in tracks based on their parents' level of privilege rather than students' ability. "When children of the elite who were identified as 'highly able' in elementary school did not make the test score cutoffs for high school honors classes, the parents found ways to get their children placed in these classes anyway, as if the tests in that particular instance were not valid" (p. 105). In one school, a review of achievement test scores revealed that some "nongifted" students scored in the 90th percentile and above and while some gifted students ranked as low as the 58th percentile. Kohn (1998), in an article more explicitly directed at gifted education and parents of the gifted, noted that "we cannot discount, at least in some instances, the presence of more malign motives. One is racism (or its twin, classism)" (p. 575).

A number of studies of gifted individuals from diverse backgrounds (e.g., Arellano & Padilla, 1996; Arnold, Noble, & Subotnik, 1996; Kitano, 1994/1995; Richie et al., 1997) with respect to ethnicity, economic status, and gender indicate that many experienced racism and/or sexism at some point in their lives. Some encountered this during the K–12 years from teachers, counselors, principals, community members; others during adulthood in higher education or the world of work. While racially diverse individuals from lower economic backgrounds may report more experience with oppression than those from advantaged backgrounds (Arellano & Padilla, 1996), successful middle-class individuals of color are not immune (Feagin & Sikes, 1994).

The point is not to vilify anyone as biased or racist. Rather, the point is to acknowledge the existence of these powerful forces in identifying and serving gifted children and youth and in their achievement as adults. Without first acknowledging the problem, we cannot work toward resolution. What is missing in gifted education is open discussion and problem solving at all levels: K–12, higher education, parent organizations, and professional forums. Patton and Baytops (1995) and Frasier (1997) have admonished that attitudes about the potential of diverse students constitute the most pervasive reason for problems in their identification as gifted. Even if issues of access, assessment, and accommodation are resolved, "far more difficult problems related to attitudes about identifying gifted students need to be faced" (Frasier, 1997, p. 501).

McElroy-Johnson (1993) described the case of an African-American student, one of three in an Advanced Placement (AP) English class of 35. The student came to "hate" *Macbeth*; whenever she asked the teacher to explain something, the teacher suggested that she change to a less difficult class. The student expressed discomfort with small-group instruction in which she felt that the White students ignored the African-American students. The teacher never dealt with these problems. "When we ignore the issues facing our students, we contribute to their failures" (p. 103).

Why don't we openly address such issues with students? Several authors (e.g., Gersten, Brengelman, & Jiménez, 1994; Thompson, 1998) have observed that educators have a "fear of naming" that results in a failure to acknowledge and address issues of race and class in U.S. schools. The consequences can include demotivating students of color. Thompson (1998) noted that "many African American students, male and female, may regard the polite avoidance of colortalk as a betrayal of trust because it denies real conflict and real relationships" (p. 537). For African Americans and other racial groups—

including the gifted in these groups—discrimination is an obvious and common experience. Yet teachers seem to deny racial conflict.

> For African American students who are grounded in the Black community (and of course not all African American students are), or who face overt racism on a daily basis, the result is more likely to be loss of faith in teachers and loss of interest in school. Betrayed both by specific teachers and by White cultural norms concerning race, culture, and individualism, Black students my decide that their schools have little or nothing to offer them. (Thompson, 1998, p. 537)

In a recent article in the American Psychological Association newsletter, Burnette (1997) reported that open discussions about race can thwart racism in children: "The lack of dialogue about race in school and home fosters children's development of negative stereotypes" (p. 33).

IMPLEMENTING MULTICULTURAL CURRICULUM

Banks (1995b) traced the history of multicultural education to late 19th- and early 20th-century African-American scholarship and its more current form to the civil rights movement of the 1960s and 1970s. During the 1970s, mainstream professional organizations, such as the American Association of Colleges for Teacher Education and the Association for Supervision and Curriculum Development, issued position papers and publications encouraging K–12 curriculum integrating content about ethnic groups. Nonetheless, multicultural education remains on the margins of the curriculum in this country despite three decades of efforts to transform K–12 and higher education content (Winzer & Mazurek, 1998) and despite evidence that it can modify students' racial attitudes (Banks, 1995a). Multiculturally infused curriculum can significantly alter majority students' attitudes toward poverty and other racial groups, decrease ethnocentrism, and increase critical thinking skills (MacPhee, Kreutzer, & Fritz, 1994).

Banks (1995b) describes multicultural education as having several goals, including creating equal educational opportunities for students from diverse groups (including women) and helping all students acquire the knowledge, attitudes, and skills needed for effective functioning in a pluralistic democratic society. Integrating content about diverse groups, understanding how knowledge is created, reducing prejudice, facilitating the academic achievement of students of all groups, and creating an empowering school culture are dimensions of multicultural education that serve these goals. The goals of multicultural education clearly have application to students from all cultural and economic groups, including gifted and talented students.

In addition to these goals, Hilliard (1991/1992) and others (e.g., Morey &
Kitano, 1997) argue that multicultural education is central in presenting accurate, comprehensive knowledge about topics that must be understood through
several perspectives. For example, students can evaluate the activities of Columbus in the New World only when they consider his views, those of other
Europeans on his expedition, and those of the indigenous peoples he "discovered." Teachers and text present an incomplete version of truth when they
present only one perspective. Similarly, students of gifted education have incomplete knowledge about Terman's highly recognized contributions to the
field unless they learn about his initial views on the nature of intelligence and
race (Terman, 1916) within the context of Social Darwinism and the eugenics
movement.

While multicultural education goals of conceiving a broader truth, acquiring the skills needed for a diverse society, reducing prejudice, and understanding the contributions of diverse groups are critical for all learners, some authorities argue that learning about the contributions of one's own group is
critical to diverse students' identities, self-esteem, and motivation in school.
In a passionate essay, Thompson (1998) argued:

> African American students cannot trust teachers who (wittingly or unwittingly)
> lie to them about racism, ignore Black achievements, gloss over slavery and segre-
> gation, or confine the study of Black history and culture to Black History Month.
> . . . The curriculum is pivotal in part because defensible and desirable relation-
> ships must be predicated on knowledge rather than innocence, and in part be-
> cause teachers are responsible for helping students to develop and pursue ques-
> tions that matter to them. If African American students find that teachers are
> unwilling to provide them with that support, they have no reason to turn to them
> for an education. (p. 540)

The implications also pertain to gifted students. Ford's (1994/1995) study
of fifth- and sixth-grade gifted and average-achieving African-American girls
indicated that most found school more exciting and interesting when they
learned about Blacks. Patton and Baytops (1995) describe the unique needs
of gifted African Americans and call for a paradigm using African-American
culture as a mediator for curriculum and instruction for gifted African-American students.

In higher education, interviews of a sample of American Indian, Latino,
Black, Asian, White, and international college students (reported in Jones &
Young, 1997) suggested that most were pleased when instructors included
materials pertinent to their cultural group and were more likely to participate
when materials were culture-specific. Though some were embarrassed at feeling "singled out," others resented the absence in most classes of materials
relevant to their cultures. Students who had taken ethnic-studies classes

wanted to introduce this material in other classes, but were often afraid to do so because of perceived risks.

The commonly held assumption that multicultural education applies only to schools with diverse enrollments is grossly inaccurate. Multicultural education does seek to raise the achievement of culturally and linguistically diverse students as a way of supporting equity. However, the goals of preparing cross-culturally competent citizens to succeed in a global community, encouraging social change through prejudice reduction, and providing skills to create a more equitable society are critical for learners of all backgrounds. They are particularly relevant for gifted and talented students who have high potential to become leaders in their chosen fields. Ford and Harris (1999) provide guidelines and examples for multicultural gifted education that address these multiple aims. The Center for Gifted Education at the College of William and Mary also reports (Struck, 1999) the development of social studies curriculum units for gifted students based on Banks's (1995b) multicultural education. Kitano and Pederson (2002) share specific examples of elementary and secondary teachers' efforts to integrate multicultural content into curricula for gifted learners as well as teachers' perceptions of obstacles encountered and benefits derived.

ENHANCING RESILIENCE THROUGH DEVELOPMENT OF POSITIVE COPING STRATEGIES

The resilience or "invulnerability" literature seeks to identify factors contributing to the success of children and adults who thrive despite tremendous adversity. The last decade has seen increased interest in applications of this literature to the education of inner-city children in general (e.g., Benard, 1994; Pollard, 1989; Wang & Gordon, 1994; Wang, Haertel, & Walberg, 1998) and to gifted children in particular (Bland, Sowa, & Callahan, 1994; Ford, 1994; Hébert, 1996). Studies of gifted adults (Arellano & Padilla, 1996; Arnold et al., 1996; Kitano, 1994/1995, 1997, 1998a, 1998b; Kitano & Perkins, 1996, 2000) report tremendous perseverance and resilience as features of successful individuals across cultures and continents who experienced obstacles based on gender, race, religion, economic status, or political, social, or geographic conditions (e.g., war, family violence, famine). Some prestigious universities have used evidence of resilience in admissions criteria. Piirto (1999) includes resilience, persistence, and drive among the noncognitive variables in her model for identifying giftedness.

Most important to this discussion is evidence that resilience is not an immutable trait but an acquired response that can be encouraged by a supportive environment (Gonzalez & Padilla, 1997) and possibly by direct instruction in problem-solving skills (Cowen, Wyman, Work, & Iker, 1995). Conditions identified in the literature (Benard, 1994; Ford, 1994; Pollard, 1989; Wang, et al., 1998) as promoting resilience include caring teacher attitudes, high expectations, effective instructional practice, responsiveness to student diversity, and a multicultural, learner-centered curriculum with opportunities for solving complex, real-life problems.

Researchers investigating highly achieving adults from diverse backgrounds have identified factors similar to those described above, with the addition of culturally specific factors, such as a strong sense of ethnic identity or biculturalism. Socioeconomic status and level of ethnic homogeneity may contribute to within-group differences with respect to the contributions of ethnic identity to resilience. While supporters of school reform call for heterogeneous grouping by ability and cessation of labeling, there is some evidence that early identification and placement in programs for the gifted may contribute to academic resilience in students from economically, culturally, and linguistically diverse backgrounds. Studies also identify specific coping strategies perceived by gifted adults from diverse backgrounds as related to their success.

Arellano and Padilla (1996) worked with 30 undergraduate Latino students enrolled in a highly selective university to investigate conditions related to academic invulnerability. Within this group, the researchers compared "at-risk" students (from poverty to working-class backgrounds) with their more advantaged counterparts. Group membership was based on parent education level. An unexpected finding was that 73% of the total group were identified as gifted during their elementary school years; the others attended schools without academic tracking programs. Many attributed feelings of self-efficacy and competitiveness to identification as gifted. For the at-risk group, the researchers identified supportive families and teachers, biculturalism (ability to operate successfully in the mainstream without relinquishing one's cultural heritage and ethnic identity), and strong affiliation with their Latino ethnicity as contributing to resilience. The advantaged students reported different experiences in school and fewer barriers as well as a more neutral perspective on ethnicity issues.

Gonzalez and Padilla (1997) examined the academic resilience and achievement of a sample of mostly Spanish-speaking Mexican-American high school students. They identified a sense of belonging in school and a supportive academic environment as significant predictors of resilient status, with family and peer support enhancing the value that resilient students place on school. Findings also suggested that ethnicity and cultural pride may be more important for students attending ethnically diverse than ethnically homogeneous (i.e., 95% Latino enrollment) schools.

Kitano and Perkins (Kitano, 1994/1995, 1997, 1998a, 1998b; Kitano & Perkins, 1996, 2000) identified a number of positive coping strategies used across the life span by high-achieving women from African-American, Asian-American, Latina, White, and international backgrounds. These achievement strategies included active ignoring, reframing in a positive way, making the problem a tool to get things, confronting "head on," developing armor, thinking through problems, preventing by being prepared, becoming bicultural, acknowledging and moving on, affirming oneself, finding alternative paths, monitoring the environment, making good choices, seeking support from others, acting strategically, receiving discouragement as a challenge, assuming leadership for change, working harder, building skills, and planning. While some appeared to be related to culture-specific values, many appeared in all cultural groups and were similar to those reported in other studies (e.g., Arellano & Padilla, 1996; Richie et al., 1997).

These findings raise the possibility of supporting resilience in gifted students from low-income backgrounds through the teaching of positive coping strategies—a more specific approach to fostering resilience that can enhance the more general suggestions of having a caring attitude and high expectations. A focus group of high-achieving college freshman and sophomore women from low-income Latino, Asian, African-American, and White backgrounds reviewed a draft curriculum (Kitano, 1998c) integrating real-life dilemmas and coping strategies derived from studies of gifted women of color (Kitano, 1997, 1998a, 1998b; Kitano & Perkins, 1996, 2000) with problem-solving methods described by Cowen et al. (1995). As part of the process, students were given the opportunity to select a dilemma to problem solve faced by a gifted woman from any of the U.S. ethnic or international groups investigated. A student from Eritrea asked to discuss the problem of a Nigerian woman who as a 12-year-old was committed by her father to marry an older man. (The woman actually ran away and was disowned by her family.) She noted that this problem was an issue in her community in the United States. A Mexican-American student chose the dilemma of a gifted Latina whose father withdrew his support when she chose to attend a university away from home. An African-American student selected an example of blatant racial discrimination in the workplace. A student from Vietnam shared that the focus group was the first time she had ever discussed personal obstacles in a school setting; she did not feel comfortable discussing such problems with her parents. The students suggested providing this type of curriculum during middle school, when students often face major issues for which real-life problem solving would be helpful.

As these examples suggest, some of the dilemmas derived from actual gifted women's lives are controversial for inclusion in schools and would require careful collaboration with parents and families and highly sensitive implementation. The focus-group participants countered that such events happen in young people's lives, and to ignore their existence is not helpful. An alternative approach would be to integrate the study and practice of positive coping skills into a challenging standards-based academic curriculum, for example, through analysis of biographies and the survival of individuals during extreme hardship (e.g., war, forced relocation). Parents and families, who most frequently teach coping strategies to their children (including how to cope with racism), could benefit and contribute as well. Wang et al. (1998) caution that a set of activities or strategies will not create educational resilience and must be embedded within broader reforms that include schools, peers, families, and communities.

CONCLUSIONS

Schoolwide enrichment and other reforms designed to raise the achievement of all students, including the gifted, must confront underlying problems that contribute to inequity in educational outcomes. The literature indicates that, in many cases, gifted individuals from diverse backgrounds experience both overt and subtle discrimination in identification, instruction, and the world of work. Educators are often reluctant to recognize race-related problems that students face on a daily basis. Can efforts to provide challenging curriculum for all students, including the gifted, succeed if we fail to address issues of what happens to culturally and linguistically diverse students in the classroom?

The sociocultural literature points to the importance of naming these problems and to potential solutions. Efforts to combine constructivist approaches with scaffolding and direct instructional support, to eliminate individual and institutional bias, to transform the curriculum, and to enhance resilience through teaching of positive coping strategies merit investigation as possible contributors to educational equity. These strategies should not be interpreted as either creating separate structures for low-income and diverse gifted students or as advocating a more affective curriculum for these students. Rather, they should be investigated for their potential to improve the motivation and achievement of students from all cultural and linguistic backgrounds.

The Practice of Gifted Education— Identification, Curriculum, and Programming

Curriculum Policy Development for Gifted Programs: Converting Issues in the Field to Coherent Practice

Joyce VanTassel-Baska

Policy development in gifted education has been limited primarily to state and federal initiatives linked to funding priorities and has focused extensively on identification and general programming features (U.S. Department of Education, 1993; Council of State Directors, 1996). Some attention to teacher training has been addressed through selected state certification and endorsement programs. Curriculum has been less frequently addressed in policy at any level. This chapter advocates the institutionalization of curriculum policy initiatives for gifted learners at state and local levels that allow for compatibility with new state standards and assessment mechanisms yet retain essential flexibility based on the nature of the learner. School districts should initiate such policies in order to encourage curriculum access by underrepresented groups (Ford, 1996) and to retain the best students in public schools.

RATIONALE

The need for curriculum policy on behalf of gifted learners is based on three major assumptions about the role of curriculum in program development for the gifted. First of all, curriculum is at the heart of what matters in gifted education. Without challenging curriculum, well-delivered and appropriately assessed, there is no viable gifted program that is defensible. Cox, Daniel, and Boston (1985) delineated 7 out of 10 variables that represented exemplary gifted programs as curriculum-based, including a consensually derived philosophy and set of goals, clear expectations of learner outcomes, and challenge.

Moreover, recent lists of research-based best practices for schools (e.g. Wang, Haertel, & Walberg, 1996) also stress curriculum issues such as homework graded and returned, teaching to goals, direct teaching, and providing mastery learning for sequential skills. Therefore curriculum and school improvement are inextricably linked in both gifted and general education.

Second, we need a coherent strategy for curriculum development and program improvement. Due to lack of adequate resources, gifted education has always been a fragmented enterprise at the local level—a little pull-out program at grade levels 3–5, a little advanced math at grade levels 6–8, a smattering of Advanced Placement (AP) courses at high school level. In an age of general educational reform, such an approach has no chance of success. Instead, we must move through individualized sets of state standards, reorganizing, compressing, and adding as needed to keep a coherent framework for gifted student learning. Commensurate with this strategy, the field must have a systematic approach to improvement that takes into account planning, implementation, evaluation, and action formulated on studying what happens in implementation at the school level where proactive improvement can best be observed.

Last, the development of curriculum policy is a way to ensure long-term coherence as opposed to ad hoc action for each separate problem regarding gifted education in a school or district. It can serve to provide a kind of "standard notation" for research-based best practice because, in many respects, it provides the glue that holds gifted programs together across elementary and secondary levels, across subject areas, and across organizational models. Clune (1993) noted the importance of policy development in sustaining an educational reform agenda. In many respects, appropriate curriculum for the gifted, since it is typically an "innovation" in schools, should be treated in a similar vein, meaning that there is a need to identify policy goals, their components, the politics of implementation, and evidence of progress toward realizing the goals.

While curriculum policy has been absent in gifted education documents, curriculum issues have not been lacking. Ironically, it is usually the same issues that emerge again and again to plague program developers. How do we handle acceleration of learning? What is real differentiation? Does connection to regular education learning matter? What grouping model should we employ? How should teachers be prepared to work with the gifted? These issues have dominated the field for over 30 years. Perhaps the timing is right and the field sufficiently advanced to see the need for consensus on these issues and the need to convert them to policy initiatives that could serve as a template for program developers in the future. Reinventing the wheel has been one of the more worthless occupations in which practitioners have indulged, and no area is more susceptible to this process than curriculum-related issues for best learners. Thus, there are five important policy initiatives, if we convert these issues directly, that would support gifted learners in our schools. Three of these initiatives focus on curricular considerations specifically, and two on the support structures essential to carrying them out successfully. Each of these goals will be described, as will their relevant elements. It is hoped that such a template may offer a basis for cohesive practice in the field of gifted education.

THE POLITICS OF MAKING POLICY WORK

Various theories of change abound (Fullan & Stiegelbauer, 1991; Senge, 1990), yet most writers agree that it is a complex process, involving top-down and bottom-up movement. Schools are difficult contexts within which to enact change for several reasons, including resistance and entrenchment, chaotic operation that is more responsive than proactive, teachers' lack of content and related pedagogical expertise, and hierarchical models of administration that may inhibit positive change. Given these problems derived from general education reform, it is not surprising that institutionalizing gifted education curriculum practices is quite difficult.

Clearly the task of making innovation work is daunting. Recent studies of reform projects in mathematics and science have exploded many myths about what works (Cohen & Hill, 1998; Kennedy, 1999). Issues like contact hours, the model of implementation, and even broad-based involvement of educational staff appear to be relatively unimportant in the process. Primary, however, is the emphasis on what students need to learn in a specific subject area and the strategies that best help them learn it. If these findings continue to hold up across new studies, it would influence both how schools organize for instruction and how they prepare teachers to continue being effective. Borko, Mayfield, Marion, Flexer, & Cumbo (1997) found that large reform projects needed to work with the same teachers intensively for 2 years in order to effect classroom changes and to treat teachers as professionals without the "sword of tests" held over their heads. Such findings run counter to the current "take no prisoners" attitude of some school administrators bent on raising test scores at all costs. In many respects, however, successful policy implementation rests on a foundation of policy development.

Policy on Curriculum Flexibility

One of the most important curriculum policy initiatives that school districts might enact would be one that addresses curriculum flexibility. Curriculum flexibility assumes that different students of the same age are at different levels of learning within and across learning areas, thus necessitating diagnosis of learning level and prescription of curriculum at a level slightly above it. The government document *Prisoners of Time* (National Education Commission on Time and Learning, 1994) documented the importance of recognizing time as the crucial variable in learning, an understanding that Bloom (1985) had several decades ago: "If experience, research, and common sense teach nothing else, they confirm the truism that people learn at different rates in different ways with different subjects" (p. 4). That there are differences in learning rate for different subject areas at different stages of development is a crucial understanding for school patterning of curriculum and instruction. For gifted learners, the translation of this flexibility becomes several forms of acceleration. For disabled learners, extensions of time for curriculum tasks, tests, and even whole courses of study represent appropriate forms of flexibility. Flexibility in schooling, however, has been one of the most difficult tasks for public schools to enact in responding to students with special needs. Special education mandates have called attention to the need for the disabled but no similar spurs exist in state and federal law to accommodate the gifted learner, who is frequently in need of a speeded-up curriculum.

Various components must be considered in developing such a policy at the school district level. One such component should allow for early-entrance and early-exit procedures for students at various stages of development. Early entrance to kindergarten and first grade is one important stage for consideration, as is early entrance to high school and early entrance to college. Many gifted children are academically ready for school before they are at the "magic age," and others develop more rapidly than age peers once they are in a schooling environment. Early access to high school eliminates the holding pattern of the middle-school years so common in many schools around the country. Early college entrance can be accomplished by those already academically proficient in high school subject matter (Olszewski-Kubilius, 1995). One of the advantages of the new standards movement is a clear way to document mastery levels in each area of schooling, thus allowing students ready to move forward to do so.

Another component of curriculum flexibility involves offering content-based acceleration practices at all levels of schooling in all subject areas. Recently, schools have become more open to math acceleration but not to other subject area advancement. For gifted learners precocious in verbal, scientific, and artistic areas, such pathways are crucial to enhanced learning and development at their natural rate of progression. Not only is there a limit on subject areas to be considered for accelerative practices; there is also often a perception that the rate should be capped at six months or a year so as not to allow students to get too out of step with the school curriculum or other students their age. Both of these practices are faulty, as indicated by 80 years of research showing the positive outcomes of acceleration on enhanced learning, motivation, and extracurricular engagement of accelerated learners (Benbow, 1998; Swiatek & Benbow, 1991).

There are very acceptable forms of acceleration in operation at the high school level—the hallmark secondary programs of the College Board Advanced Placement Program (AP) and the International Baccalaureate (IB) Program. Both programs offer students the opportunity to engage in college-level work while still in high school and reward diligence with college placement or credit for work done in the high school years. Such models should be available to students at all ages, so that evidence of advanced work brings credit toward the next level of the educational experience. This is central to making learning more incentive-driven for bright students at all levels of the schooling process. Specific benefits to students from participating in AP programs include (1) flexible access to advanced coursework in high school, (2) credit or placement at the college level for high school work, (3) motivation for continuing challenging work, (4) provision of a model for college expectations, and (5) the garnering of student awards. Benefits to schools include (1) the provision of advanced-level curriculum syllabi rather than having teachers develop curriculum from scratch, (2) curriculum-based assessment data available for course and teacher evaluation, and (3) evidence of implementation of high standards. Similar advantages may be perceived to accrue from IB.

A third component of curriculum flexibility is simple grade acceleration for students advanced across the curriculum. This can be handled through early entrance policies, but it must be broadened to consider stages of schooling beyond the naturally occurring transition years. For students showing more than 2 years advancement in all school subjects, grade-level acceleration may be a good decision (Charlton, Marolf, & Stanley, 1994). Concern for individual social-emotional maturity levels should be considered in such decisions along with a student's desire to make such a move. Obviously, each case should be considered individually but more concern is voiced about this well-documented and researched practice than may be warranted. Grade acceleration at critical points of schooling can do much to counter boredom and disenchantment with school among our best learners.

For secondary schools, a component in the policy for dual-enrollment courses at local community and 4-year colleges would also be important. Many highly able students may wish to sample college early but not actually attend full-time. Dual enrollment offers a wonderful opportunity for this early academic and socialization process to occur. Students may take one or two classes away from campus, or dual-enrollment courses can be delivered on-site. Currently, 22 states have dual-enrollment policies, encouraging local districts to take advantage of the opportunity for students to gain access to higher education while still in high school. These courses are then banked for college and

will automatically be credited for a student attending a public college in the
same state. Often, the equivalent of freshman year in college may be credited.
For students and schools in rural areas of a state, dual enrollment provides a
strong alternative to AP and IB, which are often not possible to mount in small
schools due to lack of interested faculty or sufficient numbers of ready students.

A final component to consider in a school flexibility policy should be
in the realm of telecommunications. Advanced courses can now be provided
technologically in ways not possible a decade ago. School policy should reflect
these new alternatives to teaching and learning, especially for advanced students, who can profit greatly from them. Several universities offer on-line
courses, many tailored to younger students, such as the Stanford Education
Program for Gifted Youth (EPGY) computer-based program in mathematics.
Other universities, such as Ball State University, beam advanced courses to
rural schools through a telecommunications link. Independent-study opportunities with university faculty and research project work conducted globally can
now be a part of student learning beyond the classroom. We have the technology but lack the policy to regulate these newer forms of learning to the benefit
of students capable of breaking out of traditional models of learning.

Policy on Curriculum Differentiation

A second policy initiative in curriculum for the gifted requires a statement
on differentiation that recognizes the interrelated importance of curriculum,
instruction, and assessment. A differentiated curriculum is one that is tailored
to the needs of groups of gifted learners or individual students and provides
experiences sufficiently different from the norm to justify specialized intervention and is delivered by a trained educator of the gifted using appropriate
instructional and assessment processes to optimize learning.

Curriculum design is one major component of a differentiated curriculum policy for the gifted since it delineates key features that constitute any
worthwhile curriculum (Borland, 1989). A well-constructed curriculum for the
gifted has to identify appropriate goals and outcomes. What is important for
students to know and to be able to do at what stages of development? How
do planned learning experiences provide depth and complexity at a pace that
honors the learner's rate of advancement through material? Curriculum for
the gifted must also be exemplary for the subject matter under study, meaning
that it should be standards-based and current in the thinking of real-world
professionals who practice writing, mathematical problem solving, or science
for a living (VanTassel-Baska, 1998b). Moreover, it should be designed to
honor high-ability students' needs for advanced challenge, in-depth thinking
and doing, and abstract conceptualization.

Over the past 10 years, the Center for Gifted Education at the College of William and Mary has been involved in review, development, field-testing, dissemination, and follow-up studies of specially designed curriculum for gifted learners at the secondary level in language arts, science, and most recently social studies. Each of these projects has been carefully calibrated to the national standards in each respective domain of learning. Our research evidence to date suggests that differentiation policy for the gifted, given the new standards, requires more attention to helping educators develop advanced tasks that address the standards, organize the standards across grade levels to ensure an emphasis on higher-level skills and concepts, and provide opportunities for depth of exploration of concepts across sets of standards (VanTassel-Baska, Bass, Reis, Poland, & Avery, 1998; VanTassel-Baska, Johnson, Hughes, & Boyce, 1996). Of less help is creating whole new courses or units that are outside the intent of the standards.

Curriculum differentiation policy should also address the need for careful selection of materials for use in classrooms serving gifted and high-ability learners. These materials should go beyond a single text, provide advanced readings, present interesting and challenging ideas, treat knowledge as tentative and open-ended, and provide conceptual depth that allows students to make interdisciplinary connections. Ideally, each classroom will also have quality technology resources that would meet the same criteria (Johnson, Boyce, & VanTassel-Baska, 1995).

Instructional approaches that foster differentiated responses among diverse learners include those that are inquiry-based and open-ended, and employ flexible grouping practices. An example of an effective inquiry-based model would be problem-based learning (PBL), which has the learner encounter a real-world problem sculpted by the teacher out of key learnings in a given subject and proceed to inquire about the nature of the problem and effective avenues to research about it. It includes sources for acquiring relevant data. The instructional techniques needed by the teacher include high-level questioning skills, listening skills, conferencing skills, and tutorial abilities in order to guide the process to successful learning closure in a classroom. PBL also requires the use of flexible team grouping and whole-class discussion. Problem resolution requires student-initiated projects and presentations, guided by the teacher (Boyce, VanTassel-Baska, Burruss, Sher, & Johnson, 1997; S. A. Gallagher, Stepien, Sher, & Workman, 1995). Thus instructional policy must include the selection of a few core teaching models that successfully highlight the intended outcomes of the curriculum. Administrators must ensure that teachers have the opportunity to learn such models deeply and well.

Just as differentiation involves careful selection of core materials and curriculum that underlies them and the deliberate choice of high-powered instructional approaches, it also requires the choice of differentiated assessment protocols that reflect high-level learning. High-stakes assessments such as the

Scholastic Aptitude Test (SAT), AP exams, and even state assessments are the standardized symbols of how well students are doing in comparison with others of their age. School districts, in order to be considered high-quality, must be producing students scoring at the top levels on these nationally normed instruments. Yet deep preparation for success on these tests rests in individual classrooms. Even strong learners like the gifted cannot do as well as they could without adequate preparation in relevant content-based curriculum archetypes. Thus, the use of these assessments as planning tools for direct instruction in each relevant subject area is a key to overall improvement in student performance. Administrators responsible for the review of teacher lesson plans need to know how such assessment models are being converted into work in classrooms. School-based teams and secondary departments should spend planning time on strategies for incorporating such elements. Since such assessments are a reality viewed by our society as crucial indicators of student progress in school, we need to make them work for us rather than against us in the public arena.

In addition to standardized measures to assess student learning, it is crucial that performance-based tools be employed to assess individual growth and development (Wiggins, 1996). In tandem with more standardized measures, these provide a more complete picture of individual progress toward specific education goals. For gifted learners, in particular, the quality of performance on such measures may be a better indicator of skills and concepts deeply mastered than are traditional paper-and-pencil measures. In truth, gifted education has long favored such approaches since they match well with the goal structure of many gifted programs. For example, to use a rubric to assess a research project holistically has long been a standard practice in strong gifted programs. The important issues to consider for gifted learners in the use of such assessments, however, are concern about real growth over time, revealed through careful pre- and post-assessment procedures, and the use of pre-assessment results in instructional planning for individuals and small groups. Too frequently, students are assessed on what they already know or are not held accountable for reaching new thresholds of learning.

A final consideration in the use of alternative assessment approaches with gifted learners involves attention to teaching students the rubrics for assessment at the time the assignment is given so that students can understand expectation levels required for any given assignment at conception rather than at the end. This approach also ensures that criteria for judgment are both well defined by the teacher and well understood by the student.

Policy on Articulation

A third policy initiative necessary to create program coherence is one dealing with curriculum articulation and alignment. Gifted learners need to be assured early on in their school careers that their advancement at earlier stages can continue and be supplemented by even more challenging offerings across years in school (VanTassel-Baska, 1992). Consequently, careful attention to scope and sequence of curriculum offerings coupled with alignment with existing curriculum structures is a crucial part of curriculum policy development and implementation. Too frequently, lack of attention to these aspects of curriculum development results in fragmentation of program experiences and lack of consistent curriculum offerings.

Prototypes of K–12 options must be developed for each subject area so that decisions can be made about the overall approach to be employed in curriculum-making in discrete areas. For example, if the major approach to differentiating mathematics curriculum is content acceleration, the overall schema for this approach should be laid out so that appropriate options might be included at the senior high school level to ensure that students don't "run out of" mathematics. If a combined approach is to be employed, delineating the connections between the components is essential. For secondary schools, developing grade 6–12 prototypes may also be an important function if no models exist for the elementary program. Obviously middle-school models must align well with high school options; scope and sequence prototypes force the discussion around how to make that happen and can provide a way to communicate to parents and other educators the salient aspects of a curriculum for gifted learners.

While differentiated prototypes of subject area offerings can serve a helpful function in curriculum policy, equally important is curriculum alignment with state standards of learning. This process answers the question of the relationship between gifted-learner curriculum and the curriculum for everyone at given levels of development and in given subject areas. To what extent do gifted students' expectations exceed state standards and extend into areas beyond them? This core issue is central to communication about curriculum for a school's best learners to various internal and external publics. Strong gifted curriculum should be designed to ensure passages through state standards, not around them. Articulation documents provide a mechanism to accomplish this task. Consequently, educators and the lay public begin to understand how gifted-learner curriculum is the same as, as well as different from, the norm for all students.

A frequent criticism is that state standards may hold gifted students back and severely retard their learning (Reis, 1999). However, after close analysis of a dozen or more state standards documents, it is difficult to understand this concern. The new standards were developed based on the latest research on effective learning within each subject area and call for extensive use of higher-level skills by students. Strands such as research, historical analysis, literary interpretation, and experimental design all feature these skills at all stages of development across subject areas. While gifted learners may master them sooner, such skills constitute important learning that requires practice over time for gifted as well as more typical learners. Thus, the crux of the concern rests not with the standards themselves but with how they may be translated by individual teachers. The key to effective implementation of these standards rests with the inferences made by teachers about each student's level of functioning within each strand of a given subject. If no attention is given to diagnostic assessment or careful clustering of standards, gifted students may in fact be penalized.

A final consideration for alignment rests with how the curriculum for gifted learners aligns vertically with Advanced Placement and International Baccalaureate programs. This is also essential to sound policy development. Teachers at all levels need to understand the highest-level skills that students attain in subject matter areas before they leave a school district so that the core skills can be introduced and addressed early rather than late in their school experience when it may be more difficult to bring many students up to the rigorous levels required by the standardized exams in these programs. Thus, an effective design-down process must be developed to ensure continuity and reasonable levels of rigor at all stages of schooling.

Policy on Grouping

Given the current research on the positive use of ability grouping with the gifted (Kulik & Kulik, 1992; Rogers, 1998), it is critical that school district policy attend to this facet of a support structure in evolving programs. Important components for such a policy would include attention to within-class flexible grouping and differentiated assignments as well as opportunities for special-class and independent-grouping options such as mentorships and internships.

The use of within-class grouping is critical at all levels of schooling. At the elementary level, many classrooms now are heterogeneous and inclusive. Such settings typically provide little differentiation or challenge for the gifted learner and may not be as beneficial for any group as are within-class grouping approaches that allow for a cluster group of similar-ability students within a mixed class (Lou, Abrami, Spence, Poulson, Chambers, & D'Apollonia, 1996). At the secondary level, the norm for honors and even Advanced Placement grouping is across high-ability and gifted ranges. Consequently, the pace of the class and the opportunity for in-depth work may be lost to gifted students as the teacher struggles to cover all of the material with everyone. In-class grouping according to student capacity provides teachers alternative ways to handle certain aspects of learning. For example, differentiating paper assignments by group allows advanced students both more latitude and depth potential for their work. Differentiating readings by group may have the same effect. More in-class writing practice may be given to groups already skilled at peer critique. All of these approaches to vary "within-group" work will help the teacher ensure that each student receives appropriate levels of instruction.

Special class grouping of gifted learners by subject area has historically been the most frequently utilized approach at the secondary level, while pull-out by program focus has predominated at the elementary level (VanTassel-Baska, 1998a). Because it is so widely practiced, special class grouping is an important area to consider for establishing district policy and is one of the primary ways to deliver differentiated curriculum, which is difficult without such grouping arrangements. Research has shown that 84% of the time in heterogeneous classroom settings is spent on whole-class activities, with no attention to differentiating for the gifted (Archambault et al., 1993). More-over, special classes are where good acceleration practices for individual students can be applied as the level of the class by necessity is more advanced in content.

Many schools have provided special grouping for mathematics and language arts, but not for science and social studies. Again, it is critical that a grouping policy apply to all relevant academic subjects, where size of school can allow for such clusters to be formed. Students advanced in all areas need the opportunity to interact with others at their ability levels and to advance academically at a rate and pace consonant with their abilities. Such a situation can typically occur only in a specialized group setting.

Grouping for more independent types of work is also a critical part of a grouping policy at all levels. Students may select among options geared at providing them more personalized opportunities for intellectual growth, whether through a well-designed independent project or through work in a professional setting or through an "optimal match" with an adult in an area of expertise in which the student is interested. Each of these arrangements calls for schools to adopt a policy that allows for one-on-one interactions with members of the community as well as more individualized use of school time.

Policy on Teacher Development

The last support structure necessary for inclusion in a policy statement on curriculum should focus on a mechanism for ensuring teacher development that supports the components of policy already delineated in this chapter. The careful nurturing and socializing of teachers to the demands of working effectively with gifted learners is a long-term process. Yet it must be accomplished within the framework of areas of content expertise so that the incentive to grow in one's work with a particular group of learners is carefully embedded within the overall expectations of the job. Rarely does a teacher work only with high-ability and gifted learners. Thus, the emphasis has to be on modifying curriculum and instruction in an efficient and effective manner, given limited time to do so. Such issues impact greatly on components of and approaches to staff development.

One important component of basic staff development is understanding the characteristics and educational needs of the gifted learner. This is essential for effectively manipulating a curriculum plan. It is also an essential backdrop for any teacher being assigned gifted students. All teachers must take a course in understanding disabilities before they leave college, yet no analogue currently exists for understanding gifted learners. State certification standards may be one viable way to ensure that even regular classroom teachers have such education if gifted learners are to be assigned to them.

A second component of staff development structural support is to address relevant content and its supportive pedagogy. Teachers who work effectively with gifted learners need to be very knowledgeable about their content and how best to convey it to learners. Such expertise is essential for helping students learn (Shulman, 1987). Workshops available nationally through the College Board provide this mix of content and pedagogy in an effective manner, as do several sessions at national content conferences such as that of the National Council of Teachers of Mathematics. Purchasing journal subscriptions for teachers to publications like *Mathematics Teaching* and *Science Scope* is another way to ensure ongoing engagement with relevant content. As a field, gifted education has not actively promoted a teacher training model that merges content and pedagogical skill development, although it is clearly needed.

A third component of staff development policy must attend to teacher understanding of other aspects of curriculum for the gifted related to acceleration and articulation. Familiarity with the school district and state curriculum at all levels of schooling is an essential part of that education. Knowing relevant standards and assessments to be employed provides teachers with broader knowledge of their own curriculum area, even if they do not have direct responsibility for teaching it. Secondary teachers must also have a working knowledge of both Advanced Placement and International Baccalaureate exams in their subject area, as these are considered the most rigorous secondary options through which gifted students may pass on their path to college. The level of task demand on these exams provides a good model for teachers who work with younger students to emulate, particularly in writing assignments for English and social studies and problem sets assigned in science and mathematics. Thus, the staff development approach must socialize teachers to exit expectations for high-ability learners at secondary levels.

Finally, there must be a core arsenal of strategies teachers feel comfortable using with high-ability and gifted learners in the classroom. Because the goals of gifted programs so frequently stress research, higher-level thinking, and problem solving, teachers need to be able to employ at least one teaching model that addresses each of these goals. Using a consistent model to teach research, employing a deliberate thinking model such as Richard Paul's, and using problem-based learning or creative problem solving as a heuristic to teach problem solving are critical components of staff development. Helping teachers link these models to relevant content is also essential to their being used effectively in the classroom.

CONCLUSION

The need for coherent gifted programs calls for the development of curriculum policy that accounts for flexibility, differentiation, and articulation issues in planning and implementation. Support structures such as grouping and teacher education also must be considered. As the use of state standards and assessments intensifies, it is crucial that gifted programs at all levels of learning use these approaches as the base for building a rich and complex set of options for gifted learners.

CHAPTER 12

Reconsidering Regular Curriculum for High-Achicving Students, Gifted Underachievers, and the Relationship Between Gifted and Regular Education

Sally M. Reis

Almost 24 years ago I returned home to my former school district to teach English in the junior high school I had attended. I began teaching, a veteran of 2 years of experience in another city, filled with excitement and a mission to improve my school, and worked with colleagues who had been my own teachers. After completing graduate courses in gifted and talented education, I faced the challenge of developing a comprehensive gifted program in my hometown. Almost 12 years later that program was in place, and comprehensive services were available to academically and artistically talented students at the elementary, middle, and high school level. Nine full-time faculty, numerous grants, and staff development resulted in a gifted program that provided a wide range of services in a resource setting and in classrooms, some self-contained and some with cluster groups of advanced learners. A theoretical model based on Renzulli's (1978) definition of giftedness and the Enrichment Triad programming model (Renzulli, 1977) was the basis for our efforts. Within 5 years, an effective and popular program was implemented and it continued for many more years. Parent and teacher support was demonstrated in annual evaluation reports, and achievement tests, college placements, and student productivity indicated that opportunities that had not previously existed were now available for students.

Given the same amount of time, effort, and love that created this program, I wonder if a similar program could be created in this district today.

My friends who still teach there paint a changed portrait of my largely blue-collar hometown, one of remediation and lowered expectations from both parents and teachers. A close friend who teaches kindergarten recently told me that the majority of students starting the year in her class had never held a crayon. Most of her students had seldom, if ever, had the opportunity to listen to a much-loved children's book being read by a parent or grandparent. How does a program for gifted students fit into a community committed to remedial instruction and improving scores on the state mastery tests?

My reasons for becoming involved with the education of gifted students are tied to this city. As an advanced learner, I suffered from boredom for years. Never learning how to work, I coasted through high school as a National Honor Society member who did the absolute minimum necessary to achieve high, but not the highest, grades. Few teachers noticed, and the few who tried to get me to work were disappointed, for I had learned the system and was rewarded with good grades, college scholarships, and time to play. In college and graduate school, I encountered opportunities to learn the value of work and the rewards of doing one's best not experienced in elementary and secondary school. I believe that the current climate in America does not always encourage educators to create gifted programs. If we are to be successful at encouraging and providing appropriately high levels of instruction and curriculum for our most talented students, we must reconsider the ways general education has evolved in the last decade, and the relationship between gifted and general education.

In this chapter, I discuss the ramifications of dumbing down curriculum and textbooks, repetition of content, and the ease with which gifted and talented students learn to go to school. The reasons that so many students underachieve are also discussed, as is underachievement in diverse groups. I also discuss the dumbing down of some gifted programs and the need for new directions in our field. These directions include a commitment to address issues such as underachievement, a commitment to investing in the identification and programming for culturally diverse gifted students, and a reconsideration of identification procedures for all gifted students. The crucial partnership between gifted program opportunities and classroom teachers' responsibilities in areas involving the regular curriculum are also highlighted.

DUMBING DOWN AND REPETITION
OF REGULAR CURRICULUM CONTENT

The policy statements of almost every school district in the nation reflect a commitment to meeting students' individual needs, yet many districts lack the capacity to put these policies into practice. What has happened to general education in America to cause us to need gifted education? An almost unlimited amount of remedial curricular material has helped teachers make necessary adjustments for lower-achieving students; however, most schools do not have either a method or a commitment to make comparable adjustments for students who are already achieving at well-above-average levels. It is clear that a major problem facing our schools is the lack of curricular differentiation and academic challenge for many of the most able students. Research supports this claim. In a recent study dealing with average and above-average readers, Taylor and Frye (1988) found that 78% to 88% of fifth- and sixth-grade average readers could pass pretests on basal comprehension skills before they were covered in the basal reader. The average readers were performing at approximately 92% accuracy while the better readers were performing at 93% accuracy on the comprehension skill pretests.

One reason that so many average and above-average students demonstrate mastery of the curriculum is because contemporary textbooks have been "dumbed down," a phrase used in 1984 by Terrel Bell, former secretary of education. Chall and Conard (1991) concur with Bell's assessment, documenting a trend of decreasing difficulty in the most widely used textbooks over a 30-year period (from 1945–1975): "On the whole, the later the copyright dates of the textbooks for the same grade, the easier they were, as measured by indices of readability level, maturity level, difficulty of questions and extent of illustration" (p. 2). Kirst (1982) also believed that textbooks have dropped by two grade levels in difficulty over the previous 10 to 15 years. Most recently, Philip G. Altbach (Altbach, Kelly, Petrie, & Weis, 1991), noted scholar and author on textbooks in America, suggests that textbooks, as evaluated across a spectrum of assessment measures, have declined in rigor.

> Textbooks are a central part of any educational system. . . . American textbooks, according to the critics, are boring and designed for the lowest common denominator. They have been "dumbed down" so that content is diluted and "readability" is stressed. Textbooks have evolved over the past several decades into "products" often assembled by committees in response to external pressures rather than a coherent approach to education. Most important to many of the critics, textbooks do not provide the knowledge base for American schools in a period of reform, renewal and improvement. (p. 2)

Researchers have discussed the particular problems encountered by high-ability students when textbooks are dumbed down because of readability formulas or the politics of textbook adoption. Bernstein (1985) summarized the particular problem with current textbooks used for high-achieving students:

> Even if there were good rules of thumb about the touchy subject of textbook adoption, the issue becomes moot when a school district buys only one textbook,

usually at "grade level," for all students in a subject or grade. Such a purchasing policy pressures adoption committees to buy books that the least-able students can read. As a result, the needs of more advanced students are sacrificed. (p. 465)

Chall and Conard (1991) also cite particular difficulties for the above-average student with less difficult textbooks. "Another group not adequately served was those who read about two grades or more above the norm. Their reading textbooks, especially, provided little or no challenge, since they were matched to students' grade placement, not their reading levels" (p. 111). Further, Chall and Conard stress the importance of the match between a learner's abilities and the difficulty of the instructional task, stating that the optimal match should be slightly above the learner's current level of functioning. When the match is optimal, learning is enhanced. However, "if the match is not optimal [i.e., below or above the child's level of understanding], learning is less efficient and development may be halted" (p. 19). It is clear that the trend of selecting textbooks that the majority of students can read creates a problem for high-ability students.

Findings by Usiskin (1987) and Flanders (1987) indicate that not only have textbooks decreased in difficulty; they also incorporate a lot of repetition to facilitate learning. Usiskin argues that even average eighth-grade students should study algebra since only 25% of the pages in typical mathematics texts in this grade contain new content. Flanders corroborated this finding, investigating the mathematics textbooks of three popular publishers. Students in grades 2–5 who used these textbooks encountered approximately 40 to 65% new content over the course of the school year, which equates to new material 2 to 3 days a week. By eighth grade, the amount of new content had dropped to 30%, which translates to encountering new material once every 1.5 days a week. Flanders (1987) suggests that these estimates are conservative because days for review and testing were not included in his analysis, and concludes, "There should be little wonder why good students get bored: they do the same thing year after year" (p. 22).

In light of the findings by recent researchers, a mismatch seems to exist between the difficulty of textbooks, the repetition of curricular material in these texts, and the needs of our high-ability learners. These students spend much of their time in school practicing skills and "learning" content they already know. All of these factors may cause our most capable children to learn less and may slow their development, thereby creating, or at a minimum encouraging, their underachievement. Many of these bright students learn at an early age that if they do their best in school, they will be rewarded with endless more pages of the same kind of practice materials.

In many schools, the "underachieving" curriculum causes classrooms to be places where students learn to expend minimum effort, creating a perpetual cycle of underachievement. Students identified as gifted learn less, and gifted programs are directly affected as many talented students have not learned to do challenging work. Many lack content that would have been considered core knowledge at an earlier time. In a study of high-ability students in an urban high school, many students were leaving high school without having been exposed to challenging literature, major historical trends or themes, and opportunities for advanced discussions in an academically challenging environment (Reis, Hebert, Diaz, Rattley, & Maxfield, 1995).

My experiences as a gifted program coordinator convinced me that some gifted programs actually serve a remedial purpose, focusing on such basic skills as finding information, taking notes, and understanding the difference between primary and secondary sources so students can complete rudimentary research projects, leaving less time for advanced content or research in gifted programs. This might be referred to as the "Dumbing Down of Gifted Programs"; teachers of talented students spend hours teaching content and skills that would have been considered common knowledge 20 years ago. Coupled with poor work habits and a lack of self-regulation skills, this leads to lower acquisition of skills and less advanced content than what may have been possible 20 years ago. McCall, Evahn, and Kratzer (1992) explain:

> The very fact that underachievers do not learn as much in school as would be expected will mean that their mental ability may decline to match their grades, at which point they will no longer be underachieving. Prolonged underachievement, then, may be unusual, not because of lack of stability in the psychological characteristics of such students, but because their mental ability has not been nurtured by effort in school. (p. 18)

It is interesting to note that the issue of dumbing down may be fairly easy to address given the current explosion of technology and the use of technology in instruction and curriculum. A variety of books, lessons, and interactive web sites currently offer a wide variety of options beyond those available only a few years ago to enable classroom teachers to address the learning needs of advanced students.

UNDERACHIEVEMENT OF HIGH-POTENTIAL STUDENTS

Student performance that falls noticeably short of potential, especially for young people with high ability, is bewildering and perhaps the most frustrating of all challenges facing teachers. The literature describing the problem of academic underachievement among high- ability students dates back to Conklin (1940), who conducted research about students with high IQ scores who were failing. In spite of over five decades of research, underachievement among high-ability students is still considered a major problem. As early as 1955, Gowan described the gifted underachiever as "one of the greatest social wastes of our culture" (p. 247). According to a 1990 national needs assessment survey conducted by the National Research Center on the Gifted and Talented, the problem of underachievement was identified as the number-one concern among educators of high-ability students (Renzulli, Reid, & Gubbins, 1990).

The conceptual and operational definitions of underachievement are problematic. Most people agree on a generic definition of underachievement as it applies to education such as the following: "The underachiever is a young person who performs more poorly in school than one would expect on the basis of his mental abilities" (McCall et al., 1992, p. 2). This conceptual definition represents a discrepancy between actual and expected performance, but categorizing different types of underachievers continues to be problematic.

Since the Soviet launching of Sputnik in 1957, and the resulting concern over our country's technological ability, critics of education alleged that we were not doing enough educationally for our most capable students, many of whom were performing at mediocre levels in school. Social, political, and educational attention began to be focused on the gifted underachiever. Shaw and McCuen (1960) provided educators with an early definition, stating that "the underachiever with superior ability is one whose performance as judged either by grades or achievement test scores, is significantly below his high measured or demonstrated aptitudes or potential for academic achievement" (p. 15).

The label "gifted underachiever" implies that it is important to recognize a learner's level of potential. A belief in this need provides a rationale for considering that appropriate academic performance constitutes fulfillment of potential. Even more difficult than assessing a learner's potential is the task of evaluating at what level of academic performance students should be identified as underachieving. Simply performing below average for the current grade level appears to be the most commonly applied standard (Fitzpatrick, 1978; Morrow & Wilson, 1961; Perkins, 1976). Rather than targeting a particular school year, some researchers regard gifted underachievers as students who evidence a long-standing, and therefore *chronic*, pattern of academic underachievement (Lukasic, Gorski, Lea, & Culross, 1992).

It is commonly reported that underachievement begins during the late elementary grades, certainly by middle or high school, and that it begins earlier for males than for females (McCall et al., 1992; Shaw & McCuen, 1960). The problem of underachievement may not really begin in adolescence; rather, it may simply become more visible in middle or secondary school. For example, homework increases during these years, and students who refuse to complete homework or do so with little care or effort are easily identified.

Some gifted students may achieve easily and without effort through the early years in school but falter when they meet the challenge of strenuous effort, real production, or increased homework, and are then labeled underachievers. The identification of smart students who underachieve raises an important question regarding the stability of underachievement and the resulting problem in defining it.

Causes and Contributors to Underachievement

What can cause a capable learner to mask his or her ability? No definitive answers to this perplexing question exist, but theories discuss a variety of possible causes: biology, environment, self-pressure, school pressure, peer pressure, parental pressure, boredom with school, and inappropriate teaching methods (Lukasic et al., 1992). Many researchers believe that school environments may cause bright students to lose their interest and drive. Some teachers may be too easily satisfied with good work, and their low expectations and an unchallenging curriculum may have a negative impact on the academic achievement of bright youngsters (Pirozzo, 1982). In educational settings in which conformity is valued, classroom teachers may reward rote learning rather than critical or creative thinking and problem solving.

Inappropriate curriculum clearly contributed to underachievement in culturally diverse high-ability urban high school students in a recent study (Reis, Gentry, & Park, 1995). Our research indicated that these young people perceived that they never learned to work primarily because their elementary and middle-school experiences had been too easy, which had a direct impact on their high school experiences. They recalled "breezing through" elementary school, indicating that schoolwork required no major effort. These students did not have appropriate opportunities to develop important academic skills or sophisticated study skills. Students' school work habits and their self-discipline, in their classrooms and at home, were improperly developed, according to data gathered in this study. Students did not have early access to appropriate levels of challenge or educational services either within the regular classroom or in gifted programs. By the time the limited gifted program available in their urban district was offered in fifth grade, many of these students would not have been identified to participate, despite high scores on a number of aptitude and achievement tests.

During upper-elementary, middle, and high school, the students encountered new situations requiring different amounts of effort and more efficient study skills. Consequently, opportunities to acquire new study skills and to improve students' work habits were necessary, but few students received assistance in developing or improving their work habits. Few developed self-discipline as a result of their school experiences, and their underachievement intensified. Many of the participants in this study believed that if they had been identified as having a potential talent in the earlier grades and had been challenged through appropriate programming options, their subsequent underachievement could have been avoided.

EXPERIENCES OF HIGH-ABILITY STUDENTS IN REGULAR CLASSROOMS

Recently, three studies conducted by the University of Connecticut site of the National Research Center on the Gifted and Talented analyzed what occurs in American classrooms for high-ability students. The results portray a disturbing pattern. The Classroom Practices Survey (Archambault et al., 1993) examined the extent to which these students receive differentiated education in regular classrooms. Approximately 7,300 third- and fourth-grade teachers in public and private schools were randomly selected to participate in this research, and over 51% of this national sample responded to the survey. Sixty-one percent of public school teachers and 54% of private school teachers reported that they had no training in teaching gifted students. The major finding of this study is that classroom teachers made only *minor* modifications in the curriculum to meet the needs of gifted students. This result was consistent for all types of schools sampled and for classrooms in various parts of the country and for all types of communities.

The Classroom Practices Observational Study (Westberg, Archambault, Dobyns, & Salvin, 1993) examined the instructional and curricular practices used with gifted and talented students in regular elementary classrooms throughout the United States. Systematic observations were conducted in 46 third- or fourth-grade classrooms identified by school superintendents and principals. The observations were designed to determine if and how classroom teachers meet the needs of gifted students in the regular classroom. Two students, one high-ability student and one average-ability student, were selected as target students for each observation day, and the types and frequencies of instruction that both students received through modifications in curricular activities, materials, and teacher-student verbal interactions were documented by trained observers. The results indicated little differentiation in the instructional and curricular practices, including grouping arrangements and verbal interactions, for gifted students in the regular classroom. In all content areas on 92 observation days, gifted students rarely received instruction in homogeneous groups (only 21% of the time), and more alarmingly, the target gifted students experienced no instructional or curricular differentiation in 84% of the instructional activities in which they participated.

The daily summaries of these observations completed by the trained observers were also examined. The dominant finding was the use of identical practices for all targeted students. Phrases such as "no purposeful differentiation" appeared on 51 of the 92 summaries. Anecdotal summaries such as the following provided poignant glimpses into the daily experiences of high-ability students: "It should be noted that the targeted gifted student was inattentive during all of her classes. She appeared to be sleepy, never volunteered, and was visibly unenthusiastic about all activities. No attempt was made to direct higher order thinking skills questions to her or to engage her in more challenging work. She never acted out in any way."

A third study, the Curriculum Compacting Study (Reis et al., 1993), examined the effects of using curriculum compacting to modify the curriculum and eliminate previously mastered work for high-ability students. Over 400 teachers participated in this study, identifying 783 students as gifted and in need of curriculum differentiation. Students took the next chronological grade level Iowa Test of Basic Skills in both October and May. When classroom teachers in the group eliminated between 40 and 50% of the previously mastered regular curriculum for high-ability students, no differences were found between students whose work was compacted and students who did *all* the work in reading, math computation, social studies, and spelling. In science and math concepts, students whose curriculum was compacted scored significantly higher than their counterparts in the control group. Accordingly teachers could eliminate as much as 40–50% of material without detrimental effects to achievement scores. And in some content areas, scores were actually higher when this elimination of previously mastered content took place. Teachers also identified additional students who had not been identified as gifted in their classrooms who could benefit from curriculum compacting.

EXTENDING GIFTED EDUCATION PEDAGOGY

The application of gifted program know-how to general education is supported by a variety of research on human abilities (Bloom, 1985; H. Gardner, 1983; Renzulli, 1986b; Sternberg, 1984). This research provides a clear justification for much broader conceptions of talent development, and argues against the restrictive student-selection practices that guided identification procedures in the past. Tomlinson and Callahan (1992) cited several contributions of gifted education to general education, including expanded views of intelligence (H. Gardner, 1983; Reis & Renzulli, 1982; Renzulli, 1978; Sternberg, 1985a, 1991); attention to underserved populations (Baldwin, 1985; Frasier, 1989; Whitmore, 1980); instructional techniques (Brandwein, 1981; Maker, 1982; Passow, 1982; Renzulli, 1977; Renzulli & Reis, 1985, 1997; VanTassel-Baska, 1988a; V. S.

Ward, 1961/1980); differentiation of content, process, and product as well as theme-based learning (Kaplan, 1986), self-directed learning (Treffinger, 1986), and student productivity (Renzulli, 1977); individualization (Renzulli & Smith, 1979); teaching models (Feldhusen & Kolloff, 1986; Kaplan, 1986; Renzulli, 1977; Renzulli & Reis, 1997).

Some of the pedagogy used in gifted education programs can be extended to students who are not usually included in special programs for talented students. In a recent study, enrichment clusters (Renzulli, 1994; Renzulli & Reis, 1997) were implemented in two culturally diverse urban school districts during specially designated times each week (Reis et al., 1995). During these cluster programs, everything in the school changed. Students left their classrooms and, in a minute or two, sped joyfully down the hallways to another room and another adult to a cluster they had selected because of the topic being covered and the adult facilitating the cluster. Clusters are open-ended opportunities for students to work with an adult facilitator to learn new material and produce a service or product. Enrichment clusters in this study were offered in areas such as creative writing, inventions, historical studies, scientific studies, drama, and the arts. The implementation of enrichment clusters affected teachers' use of differentiation, enrichment strategies, and advanced content. The use of advanced content in their enrichment clusters was a by-product of the nature of clusters, the opportunity to delve into advanced issuers and content based on the mutual interests of children and adults.

The study investigated the use of advanced content and the application of advanced opportunities in the cluster facilitator's regular classroom in two urban schools. The introduction of new concepts and advanced content by 95% of the cluster facilitators was both gratifying and somewhat expected, given the design of the clusters, but the addition of a number of other strategies for providing advanced opportunities was higher than we had expected or even hoped for. These included (in decreasing frequency of use) the development of a product or service by the facilitators; the teaching of specific, authentic methodologies; the use of advanced vocabulary; the use of authentic "tools" related to the topic; the use of advanced resources and reference materials; the use of advanced thinking and problem-solving strategies; the integration of creative thinking and historical perspectives; and the development of presentations or performances.

The frequency with which these advanced strategies were used within the clusters indicated that some transfer would occur from cluster to classroom. Many teachers reported that they began using the strategies employed in their cluster in their classrooms. It appears that classroom teachers who receive appropriate professional development can implement differentiation strategies suggested in gifted education. The more time that teachers had to work on their clusters and to experiment with this more inductive way to teach, the more advanced the content and the more diverse the products and services became.

Based on previous findings of classroom practices studies by Archambault et al. (1993) and Westberg et al. (1993), it would appear that the opportunity to teach in an enrichment cluster may result in much higher levels of use of differentiation strategies by classroom teachers in their own classroom teaching situations. The implementation of enrichment clusters may then provide the opportunity: high-end learning (Renzulli, 1994), more advanced opportunities for all children, and professional development for teachers in differentiation strategies.

REEXAMINING GIFTED EDUCATION PRACTICES RELATED TO IDENTIFICATION, CURRICULUM ISSUES, AND THE UNDERACHIEVEMENT OF STUDENTS WITH HIGH POTENTIAL

Reconsidering basic premises within our field results in a series of beliefs emerging from my more than two decades of work in gifted education. The following propositions come from my thoughts regarding these issues.

Proposition One: We must systematically overhaul the ways we define and identify high-potential students, and question whether formal identification is warranted if current systems continue to fail to identify many students.

In the past, the general approach to the study of giftedness has led some to believe that giftedness is an absolute condition magically bestowed in much the same way that nature endows us with blue eyes or a dark complexion (Renzulli, 1980). This is simply not supported by current research. Multiple lists of traits exist, some for girls and some for boys; some for students from the majority culture, others for students from diverse cultural and economically disadvantaged backgrounds (Borland & Wright, 1994). For too many years we have pretended that we can identify *the* traits of gifted children in an unequivocal fashion. Too many lists provide these traits and the "Termanology" by which we define "truly" gifted students.

Many people have been led to believe that certain individuals have been endowed with a golden chromosome (Renzulli, 1980) that makes them "gifted persons." This belief has further led to the mistaken idea that all we need to do is find the right combination of traits that prove the existence of this "gift." The further use of such terms as *the truly gifted, the highly gifted, the moderately gifted, the profoundly gifted,* and *the borderline gifted* serves only to confound the issue. The misuse of the concept of giftedness has given rise to both criticism and confusion about identification and programming. The result of this criticism has been mixed messages sent to educators and the public at large, resulting in a justifiable skepticism about the credibility of gifted education and the inability of some educators of gifted students to offer services that are qualitatively different from those offered in general education.

Most of the confusion and controversy surrounding characteristics of giftedness can be placed in perspective if we examine a few key questions. Do we use specific characteristics of one group of people to identify another group? Are the characteristics of giftedness reflected in high-ability Puerto Rican students in Willimantic, Connecticut, the same as those demonstrated by above-average Mexican students in Texas? Do common characteristics exist within each group? If so, how are they exhibited? What happens to a child who consistently manifests these characteristics in the primary grades but who learns to underachieve in school because of an unchallenging curriculum? What curriculum adjustments can be made for an intelligent child with a learning disability whose disability masks the talents? Are characteristics of giftedness static (i.e., you have or you don't have them) or are they dynamic (i.e., they vary within persons and among learning and performance situations) (Renzulli & Reis, 1985, 1997)?

A fundamental change is needed in the ways the characteristics and traits of giftedness are viewed in the future. The characteristics of any group of advanced learners must be identified within the specific population group. That is, we should attempt to identify the characteristics of talented students both in the educational context and within the population group, and use this information to help us differentiate between all students and those who need different levels of service in school to realize their potential. These different levels of services may result in a wider range of students being served by a continuum of services that is broader and much more inclusive. This has implications for considerations of characteristics of giftedness and the ways in which we should structure our programming endeavors. This change may also provide the flexibility in both identification and programming endeavors that will encourage the inclusion of diverse students in our programs, thereby addressing the critical issue of widespread underachievement of high-potential economically disadvantaged and culturally and linguistically diverse populations.

Proposition Two: The lines between gifted programs and regular education must become less sharply defined, and gifted education specialists should serve a dual role, providing direct service to students and professional development and consultation services to classroom teachers. In this way, we can apply some of what has been the pedagogy of "gifted" education to the development of talents in all students.

The issues relating to dumbing down and a lower degree of challenge both in gifted programs and in regular education programs provide a superb rationale for why some gifted education practices and principles should be infused into regular education to upgrade the challenge level for all students. To some extent, this has already begun.

Renzulli (1994) believes there are two reasons why practices that have been a mainstay of gifted programs are being absorbed into general education. The first reason concerns the limited success of remedial-oriented compensatory education programs and practices, and the second reason is the success of practices developed in gifted programs and the need for these practices to be included in the regular curriculum. All students should have the opportunities to develop higher-order thinking skills, to pursue more creative work, to select some of what they do in school, and to develop self-directed work habits. Not all students can, of course, participate in all advanced opportunities, but many can work far beyond what they are currently asked to do. It is clear that our most advanced students need different types of educational experiences than they are currently receiving and that without these services, talents may not be nurtured in many American students, especially those who attend schools in which survival is a major daily goal. What is seldom discussed is whether and how these different types of educational experiences can help improve education for all students.

Efforts to change and improve education have been around for decades, but many of them ignore talent development in our schools. Time must be provided in school to enable students who want to work to be able to learn at an appropriate and challenging pace. Unless proactively addressed, the result of the dumbing down of the curriculum and the proliferation of basic-skills practice material may result in the creation of the largest percentage of high-ability underachievers in the history of public schools in America.

Our field's pedagogy and innovative programs admittedly will not provide quick-fix solutions to issues such as these, but they can offer numerous creative alternatives for instruction and curriculum. In our relatively short history we have achieved a rather impressive array of exciting curricular adaptations, thinking-skills applications, methods for teaching independent study, and numerous other innovations. Specialists in the education of the gifted have concentrated on identifying student interests and learning styles and providing relevant and challenging curricular experiences to individual students instead of identical experiences to 30 students in a classroom without consideration of their previous knowledge or background.

Specialists in gifted education also have expertise in adjusting the regular curriculum to meet the needs of advanced students in a variety of ways including accelerating content, incorporating a thematic approach, and substituting more challenging textbooks or assignments. The range of instructional techniques used in most classrooms observed by Goodlad (1984) and his colleagues is vastly different from what is currently recommended in gifted programs. It seems clear that gifted education can help to bring creativity and innovation to regular education by challenging conventional practices and offering stimulating alternatives. Flexible grouping encouraged in many gifted programs might also be helpful in other types of educational settings. For example, interest groups, achievement groups, and grouping based on preferred styles of learning are often used in gifted education programs and could be used in regular education.

We can, therefore, make every attempt to share with other educators what we have learned about teaching process and thinking skills, modifying and differentiating the regular curriculum, and helping students learn advanced reference skills and how to do independent, self-directed work. We can extend enrichment activities and provide staff development in the many principles that guide our programming models. Yet, without the changes at the local, state, and national policymaking levels that will alter the current emphasis on raising test scores and the purchase of unchallenging, flat, and downright sterile textbooks, our efforts may appear insignificant.

Proposition Three: We must maintain our identity as a field while continuing to ask difficult questions and reexamining and reconsidering basic tenets in gifted education.

Fiscal constraints in many geographical areas are causing the elimination of gifted programs (Purcell, 1993), and many above-average students remain unchallenged by the regular curriculum. While sharing our knowledge is, indeed, one of our goals, we must continue to create and maintain exemplary programs and practices that serve as models of what can be accomplished for high-ability students. We must continue to advocate for the needs of high-ability students. We must argue logically and forcefully to maintain the programs, grouping practices, and differentiated learning experiences that the students we represent need. To allow these youngsters to be placed in classrooms in which no provisions are made for their needs would be an enormous step backward. To lose our quest for excellence in the current move to guarantee equity would undoubtedly result in a disappointing education for our most potentially able children.

Although the use of gifted program pedagogy has been suggested as a way to improve the challenge level for all children, little research exists on whether this can be implemented. Which strategies used in gifted programs can be extended to benefit more students? Can students who are not traditionally identified as gifted benefit from some of the innovative curriculum being developed for gifted students in Javits projects such as those developed by Baum, Owen, and Oreck (1996); VanTassel-Baska (1998d); Borland and Wright (1994); and Kaplan (1986)? Can we make adaptations to gifted program strategies or instructional materials to make them more meaningful and appropriate for all children? How much advanced content can be introduced when opportunities to participate in these classes are made available to all interested students? Does the use of gifted education teaching strategies have an impact on all children's love of learning and interest in school? Can parental attitudes about school be changed by implementing strategies advocated by gifted education specialists, such as differentiation of content and instruction? Most important, can we develop a plan for implementing these strategies that can be used with ethnically diverse populations and economically disadvantaged students? If so, then the potential significance of further research in this area may be far-reaching. As the federal report *National Excellence: A Case for Developing America's Talent* (U.S. Department of Education, 1993) stated: "Over the past 20 years, while the regular school program focused on basic skills and minimum standards, programs for gifted and talented students served as laboratories for innovative and experimental approaches to teaching and learning" (p. 23).

Longitudinal studies of participants in these programs may also provide information for future program innovations (Subotnik & Arnold, 1994). We seldom ask how gifted program participants benefit from their experiences, and we rarely ask what else we should have been doing for gifted students who had some program involvement. It is clear that a continuum of services should be made available representing a variety of different approaches, including acceleration, counseling, regular curriculum modification and differentiation, separate classes, and a pull-out or resource room component. Longitudinal studies should also investigate the acquisition of self-regulated, self-directed learning, given the current explosion of knowledge available on the web. We must start to investigate how gifted students can gain access to this information while also learning the skills of synthesis, analysis, and evaluation necessary to understand how to interpret the large body of information they encounter.

The new millennium is causing us to ask questions about every area of our personal and professional lives. The knowledge explosion has yet to be completely explored in education. If we could imagine a perfect learning situation for every advanced learner, it might include some of the following: opportunities for advancement through the regular curriculum at an appropriately challenging rate and pace; depth and advanced content; independent, self-directed learning challenges; independent study; and varied learning opportunities based on interest, learning styles, product preferences, and modality preferences. We must also ask what learning situation we would want for other students. Is what we might want for them so different?

CHAPTER 13

Issues in the Assessment of Talent Development

Susan K. Johnsen

For nearly a century, professionals have been developing instruments for assessing individual differences. In 1905 Binet and Simon designed the Metrical Scale of Intelligence to identify children who might profit from an education in the French schools. By 1916 Edward Thorndike and his graduate students at Columbia University had created scales of achievement that established norms for comparing student performance in academic areas. The new century has begun with a continuing focus on the assessment of individual differences. School districts use assessment to determine who needs educational programming for gifted students. State and national agencies use assessment to compare student achievement between schools, across school districts within states, across states, and among different countries. Have we progressed? Do professionals use assessment primarily for categorizing and rating or for instructional planning? What influences tend to sustain or to change the uses of assessment? In gifted education, is the movement toward talent development a significant influence? This chapter will address these important questions by examining issues related to the development of talents and assessment reform.

OVERVIEW OF ASSESSMENT

Assessment is a broad term. Linn and Gronlund (1995) describe assessment as simply the procedures used to gather information about student performance. The information may be both quantitative (measurement) and qualitative (non-measurement). Different types of assessment may be used for identification and accountability, as mentioned previously, or for diagnosis, instructional planning, program implementation, evaluation, and even policy analysis. The results are always interpreted according to the overall purpose.

Alternative Assessments

While the above-mentioned uses of assessment may not have changed over the past century, new forms have emerged with such titles as "performance," "authentic," "reflective," "dynamic," and "portfolio." These alternative assessments provide evidence of student achievement and talents that do not use the traditional fixed-response closed formats. Some of these *performance-based* alternatives are "testing that calls for demonstration of understanding and skill in applied, procedural, or open-ended settings" (Baker, O'Neil, & Linn, 1994, p. 322). These tasks may be presented in concrete formats such as blocks and puzzles, or embedded in more realistic contexts, such as auditions and apprenticeships. The latter types are frequently called *authentic* because they are used to denote assessment tasks that contain genuine, true-to-life problems within naturally occurring situations (Baker et al., 1994; Maker, 1994). In some cases, the tasks attempt to replicate the actual working conditions that may face an individual in a specific profession or involve *self-reflections* that are discussed or written in learning logs, journals, or checklists (Maker, 1994). They may also involve ratings on *rubrics* that are based on a set of standards or *anchor* products. These criteria are used for scoring students' performances and developing *benchmarks* for comparisons (Freedman, 1994). Authentic assessments may also be ongoing and interwoven with teaching and learning (Hancock, Turbill, & Cambourne, 1994). If instruction is used diagnostically, then the assessment may be called *dynamic* and used to discover the student's ability to learn from experience within the context (Borland & Wright, 1994; Kirschenbaum, 1998). In this case, the teacher may administer a pretest to establish a level of proficiency, instruct the student at slightly beyond level, observe the performance, and then assess again in one setting. Vygotsky (1978) described the distance between this independent or proficient level and the new level that requires assistance as the "zone of proximal development" (p. 93). All of this assessment information may be kept in a *portfolio* of work that evidences the students' accomplishments and progress over time. These portfolios may contain, for example, selected pieces of writing that document a students' learning and provide opportunities for the students to engage in self-reflection, examining their strengths and weaknesses as writers.

ASSESSMENT IN GIFTED EDUCATION

Alternative assessments have become increasingly popular among professionals who view the goal of gifted education as talent development. Proponents of this view believe that "giftedness" is socially constructed (Borland, 1997b), multidimensional (H. Gardner, 1983; Sternberg, 1986), qualitatively different (Neisser et al., 1996), and not stable, but related to influences within the environment (Renzulli, 1986b; Tannenbaum, 1983). For example, gifted individuals not only possess a greater knowledge base, but they use it in qualitatively different ways such as identifying and discarding irrelevant information; understanding, retrieving, and responding to tasks more quickly and efficiently; organizing knowledge in generalizable categories; and selecting problem-solving strategies (Neisser et al., 1996).

For abilities to emerge, the right combination of factors must be present. Renzulli (1986b) represents this view by suggesting that "gifted behaviors take place in certain people (not all people), at certain times (not all the time), and under certain circumstances (not all circumstances)" (p. 76). To describe the multifaceted nature of talent and needed strategies for its development, Talent Profiles (Feldhusen, 1992b; Isaksen, Puccio, & Treffinger, 1993) and Total Talent Portfolios (Renzulli & Reis, 1991) summarize ongoing assessments and may include teacher classroom observations and checklists, student reflections about their work, interviews, videos of performances, and activities completed at home and school to document children's interests and abilities.

The focus on assessing "giftedness" and/or "talents" by describing qualitative differences among students' responses to a variety of tasks in many subject areas and within varied environments is a departure from the traditional model, in which the focus is on quantitative differences that are viewed as more inherent and stable. Students are described as "being gifted" or "not being gifted" based on their performance on norm-referenced standardized tests. Higher scores indicate that the students have more of the traits that are associated with giftedness. As opposed to the development of talents within a particular academic subject area or field of interest, the goal of gifted education in the traditional model is to enhance students' traits such as critical and creative thinking so that they can realize their potential.

While many school districts still use this more traditional, static model in identifying students, some writers in gifted education have encouraged their colleagues to focus on the developmental nature of gifts and talents and the use of alternative assessments (Gardner, 1997; Maker, 1994; Wiggins, 1996). Treffinger (1995) asserts, "We need to continue and expand our efforts to apply profiling, performance assessment, and portfolio approaches for documenting students' progress, growth, and success, and not be limited to a view in which local, state, national or international comparisons of test scores become our only defining criteria of excellence" (p. 94). However, these alternatives are not widely used by state and national agencies that are engaged in accountability issues and high-stakes testing. Why not? The next section will explore the reasons in some detail.

OBSTACLES TO THE ASSESSMENT OF TALENTS

Reforming educational assessment requires attention to how the elements of a system function together, how they influence one another in a period of change, and which elements might be the most susceptible to modification. If susceptible elements are modified, then the likelihood of reform is greater. Assessment reform, particularly the assessment of talent development, has not occurred on a larger scale because of obstacles that have supported more traditional types of testing: contextual beliefs and values, technical qualities of alternative assessments, and diversity within the area of talent development.

Contextual Beliefs

In our society, everybody believes that he or she know something about schools and testing because everybody was once a student and took tests. Tests, for the most part, have always had a certain aura of respectability among consumers because they produce scores (Paris, Lawton, Turner, & Roth, 1991). Quantifiable scores are viewed as much more "scientific" than subjective teacher judgments. Parents believe that tests show what their children know in basic skill areas, how well they are doing in relationship to other students, and to some degree their ability levels. For example, school districts that attempt to use nontraditional means of identifying gifted and talented students such as products or portfolios quickly retreat to percentile ranks and standard scores when parents challenge a placement. Given the threat of hearings and due-process procedures, innovative school districts may incorporate one or two nontraditional assessments but still rely on the quantitative measures. This belief in the sanctity of numbers tends to perpetuate the traditional view that giftedness is a binary construct, that is, a student is or is not gifted. In fact, if students produce products of high quality but have average scores on an intelligence test, they might be labeled "overachievers" or "talented," but certainly not "gifted." For these reasons, the trend toward nontraditional assessments and talent-development programs is viewed by some professionals in the field of gifted and talented education as the beginning of the elimination of specialized programs for gifted students (because all children are gifted and talented) (Delisle, 1998).

Another contextual belief that works against the use of nontraditional assessments is the assumption that improved performance on tests means improved student learning. To ensure maximum comparability, standardized tests are now aligned with state and national curriculum standards that are used to judge the overall quality of schools and programs. These tests are used in high-stakes situations. In 1998, 50 states had tests that measured student achievement, 36 used these data to compare performance across schools, 19 rated each school's performance, 14 provided monetary rewards for teachers and/or schools, and 16 allowed the state to close down or take over failing schools. School content has increasingly become more focused on the test and thus more narrowly defined. Professionals have expressed fears that more performance-based and nontraditional talent areas such as the arts and leadership will be eliminated from the school curriculum because teachers won't teach what is not on the test (Resnick & Resnick, 1992). The multifaceted nature of talents and their development is therefore being lost with the narrowing of the curriculum to minimum standards and the "basics."

Technical Qualities of Alternative Assessments

Another argument against the use of alternative assessments to assess talent development has to do with technical qualities, that is, reliability and validity. The empirical literature on performance-based assessment is limited primarily to reliability of scoring procedures, models for rater training, maintenance of scale reliability, and the verification of raters' use of predefined scoring rubrics (Baker et al., 1994). Limited validity evidence is available. Linn, Baker and Dunbar (1991) argue that "simply because the measures are derived from actual performance or relatively high-fidelity simulations of performance, it is too often assumed that they are more valid than multiple-choice tests" (p. 16). Since many alternative assessments are simulations, examinees may just not behave in the same way that they would in real life (Swanson, Norman, & Linn, 1995). Consequently, generalization between raters may be better than generalization across contexts. This lack of generalization is also true for traditional assessments. For example, experts who perform at a high level when engaged in ordinary tasks or in more authentic situations frequently perform poorly on formal measures of problem solving (Kay, 1991; Rogoff, 1982; Scribner, 1986). To remedy this problem of generalization, Messick (1994) argues for a construct-driven approach in which both complex and component skills are tested across situations, rather than a task-driven approach to performance assessment. This would require that talents be clearly defined and assessed across settings in which they would most likely appear.

In summary, the use of alternative assessments that are necessary in determining the development of talents raises many validity and reliability questions. How do traditional methods for item discrimination indices relate to variations in products within and across groups such as those collected for a portfolio? Is the sample of portfolio items systematically collected and representative of an individual student's work (i.e., internal validity)? Do holistic scores on various alternative assessments relate to outstanding performance outside the setting (i.e., external validity)? Given the substantial time requirement needed to assess performance across tasks and talent areas, proponents of alternative assessments must find ways to demonstrate alternative assessments' efficiency, reliability, and validity for accountability.

Diversity within the Area of Talent Development

Moving away from a conception of intelligence as a unitary trait, researchers have reviewed the nature of giftedness from a talent-development viewpoint (Gagné, 1985; Treffinger & Feldhusen, 1996). Their approach has a more developmental orientation to human abilities and represents a broad range of talents among students with many levels of abilities—in the artistic, vocational, athletic or psychomotor, cognitive or intellectual, and social-interpersonal areas (Bloom, 1985; Treffinger & Feldhusen, 1996). In his model, Gagné (1985) discriminated between giftedness and talent by saying that giftedness is associated with *g*, and talent denotes more specific skills or aptitudes. Talents emerge from the "progressive transformation of these aptitudes into the systematically developed skills characteristic of a particular occupational field" (Gagné, 1995, p. 353). These talents are mediated by family, school, personality, interests, attitudes, and identification experiences. While Gagné (1995b) believes that most children and adults can become competent in many activities, he does not believe that all will become exemplary. He does recommend early screening of specific aptitudes and emerging talents outside the school curriculum and more frequent measurement of specific aptitudes.

Using Nobel laureates as a sample, Stewart (1994) described a *Laureate Learning Cycle* that includes five stages of talent development. The cycle begins with the *Romance Stage* or "falling in love" with an idea. During the next stage, *Inquiry*, resources are provided that support questions leading to the next stage of involvement in which the individual is immersed in the talent area. Finally, the individual moves to *Expansion*, creating fresh or original thinking, and finally into the *Insight Phase* of finding new meaning, which leads back to the *Romance Stage*.

Including more cognitive characteristics, Sternberg (1998) created a "developing-expertise" model that includes five key interacting elements: metacognitive skills, learning skills, thinking skills, declarative and procedural knowledge, and motivation. While contextual factors and deliberate practice are important, these student characteristics must be present for a novice to develop expertise and become a reflective practitioner. Sternberg believes that all types of assessments provide information about developing expertise and that "there is no one right kind of assessment" (p. 18).

Researchers debate the age at which talents emerge and might be assessed. While Sloboda (1996) and Winner (1996) report that early talent indicators are difficult to identify, other researchers disagree. For example, Roe (1953) found that her subjects discovered their passion for science around the age of seven. With the help of mentors, specialized teachers, and programs, gifted young people do become increasingly engaged in a talent area (Bloom, 1985; Csikszentmihalyi et al., 1993). Feldman (1986) even identified a critical period—between the ages of 10 and 13—for prodigies to formally begin the development of their talent with mentors, models, contests, and apprenticeships.

In summary, the majority of researchers believe that a base of innate ability contributes to exceptionally high performance and accelerated acquisition in a specific field (Gagné, 1985, 1995b; Simonton, 1999b; Sternberg, 1998). The talent or area of expertise is progressive—whether in a cyclical, linear, additive, and/or multiplicative combination—and needs systematic development (Gagné, 1995b; Renzulli & Reis, 1991; Simonton, 1999b; Stewart, 1994). While the talent is related to one field, the field itself is quite complex and has separate components. Simonton (1999b) states that a child "might exhibit accelerated development on one component while displaying retarded or arrested development on another. Talent development can thus entail a highly idiosyncratic process" (p. 442). Adding to this complexity of factors, talent is developed through a dynamic interaction among a variety of personal and environmental variables—interests, energy, perseverance, motivation to excel, personality traits, openness to experience, independence, values, mentors, and role models (Amabile & Tighe, 1993; Bloom, 1985; Csikszentmihalyi et al., 1993; Gagné, 1985; Renzulli & Reis, 1991; Simonton, 1999c; Treffinger & Feldhusen, 1996). H. Gardner (1993), who believes that creative productivity emerges after 10 years of work in a field of study, also stresses cultural factors such as the period of time in which the individual lives and the maturity of the field itself.

The diversity of the field of talent development raises many assessment questions. How does an examiner create a sample of a developing talent that is dynamic and idiosyncratic? What components should be assessed that will represent and contribute significantly to the growth of talents? How are these components similar within or across talent areas and contexts? What personal and environmental variables should be assessed simultaneously? How might one assess performance in a field not yet fully created or manifested in a short period of time? If talent development is to assume a position within this current age of accountability, then talent fields and their development must be clearly defined and linked to improved student performance, and must have practical significance for teachers and other professionals in the field of gifted education.

Reciprocal Effects of Obstacles

These three obstacles have reciprocal effects on one another and on assessment reform. Since the diverse field of talent development is ill defined, it is difficult to design alternative assessments that would be construct-driven, dynamic, and generalizable. This lack of clarity, in turn, presents particular problems for educators who want to use alternative assessments for accountability and identification but find that these methods do not have adequate studies demonstrating their reliability and validity. Without technically adequate alternative assessments, contextual beliefs about the sanctity of numbers that provide important comparison information about schools and learning tend to sustain traditional types of assessment and binary views of giftedness. All of these interactive effects influence the school programs and instructional tasks that are offered to students, particularly those who are gifted and talented.

The best opportunity for institutionalizing the assessment of talent development may lie in addressing each of these obstacles, which will eventually alter educational programming for gifted and talented students. The changes in programming that focus more on talent development will, in turn, sustain and even require the use of more dynamic alternative assessments. This approach of simultaneously addressing influences to effect system reform requires the development of procedures that are valid for identifying and developing talents, which will be described in the next section.

THE ASSESSMENT OF TALENT DEVELOPMENT

While some have questioned whether traditional psychometric standards should be applied to alternative assessments (Baker et al., 1994; Wiggins, 1993), other professionals believe that they must meet the same standards as more traditional forms since they have meaning and influence on teachers and other decision makers (Messick, 1994; Worthen, 1993). These standards primarily relate to reliability and validity.

Reliability Standards

Two criteria are crucial in developing reliable tasks that assess talent development: Can professionals rate student products and performances effectively? Is there enough evidence of students' abilities to translate knowledge meaningfully across time and situations? Researchers have found that raters can be trained to score complex performance reliably across a variety of subject areas—problem solutions and essays in math (77.6%–98.5%)(Niemi, 1996), hands-on tasks in science (above .80)(Shavelson & Baxter, 1992), activities in language arts (.88) (Hatch & Gardner, 1997), and performances in drama (.65–.82) (Baum, Owen, & Oreck, 1996). This consistency, however, is not present in performance across time and situations. Different explanations have been offered for this variation in performance across tasks—including different instructional demands (Baum et al., 1996) and a limited sample (Shavelson & Baxter, 1992). Shavelson and Baxter suggested that 10 to 20 investigations are needed to get an accurate assessment of an individual student's science achievement. Messick (1994) and Baker et al. (1994) would explain this lack of generalization by describing the task-driven nature of performance assessment. They argue that reliability will not improve until complex and component skills are identified and sampled across situations, which is a validity issue.

Validity Standards

It is also not easy to establish *content validity* in the area of talent development. First, expertise is subject-specific (Chi, Glaser, & Farr, 1988; Gelman, 1978). Second, talents are quite diverse and cover many fields of study. Third, these fields also include both declarative (i.e., knowledge about facts, concepts, and principles), and procedural knowledge (i.e., knowing how to do something), which may vary during different phases of talent development. Simonton (1999a) reports that some components may function primarily in the acquisition phase whereas other components may have the most impact in the performance phase. Fourth, the sample of items or tasks must be in an order that represents the development of expertise in the talent area. These characteristics may progress in a cyclical, linear, additive, and/or multiplicative fashion. Some researchers are concerned that expert performance, frequently automatized after years of experience, may not be a developmentally appropriate standard for younger children. They suggest that high-performing students or beginning experts might be used to set benchmarks (Baker & Schacter, 1996). Fifth, the tasks must not only resemble the content knowledge of the field but must elicit the complex processes that are used within the talent area. Test situations can become oversimplified and not assess the complexity of natural settings (Linn, Baker, & Dunbar, 1991; Messick, 1994). Sixth, many tasks are needed to measure both declarative and procedural knowledge across a variety of situations (Shavelson, Baxter, & Pine, 1992). Few researchers have examined the developmental nature of talents. Davidson and Scripp (1994) did describe the evolution of musical reasoning, the nature and timing of interventions, and differences between gifted students and their peers. While the vast majority of researchers have tended to develop performance tasks or observational checklists that *resemble* a specific talent area (i.e., face validity), Baum et al. (1996) attempted to identify characteristics systematically for the areas of dance and music. Using a panel of arts educators and professional artists, they identified behavior-based criteria that could be observed by both novices and experts (p. 95). Baum and her colleagues addressed many of the suggestions for ensuring content validity—identifying characteristics specific to the talent area, including knowledge and procedural skills; using experts in describing behaviors; and varying and increasing the difficulty of tasks over time. While this study is promising, much work remains to be done in designing alternative assessments whose tasks elicit desired processes, in a developmental framework aligned with benchmark performances within a specific talent area.

The majority of the studies examined the relationship between the alternative assessment and other standardized instruments in establishing *criterion-related validity*. For instance, Niemi (1996) found a relationship between high scores on a norm-referenced achievement test and on mathematical problem solving tasks; Shavelson and Baxter (1992) similarly reported a relationship between science tasks and traditional achievement tests (r = .45). On the other hand, Baum et al. (1996) found a relationship between artistic talent and teacher ratings (r = .40 to .49), but they did not find a relationship between artistic talent and academic achievement (r = .08 to .25), supporting their theoretical understanding of the nature of the construct. Predictive-validity studies have tended to examine short-term results. For example, using different professional artists, Baum et al. (1996) reported that students who were selected during initial auditions received higher ratings than students who were not selected from previous auditions. Johnsen and Ryser (1997) discovered that portfolios used in identifying young gifted kindergarten students predicted their achievement in the fourth grade. Unfortunately, few studies report how alternative assessments predict an individual's long-term success in a chosen field. Getzels and Csikszentmihalyi's (1976) classic study found that an alternative assessment, in which students created a problem from a given set of objects, was a key predictor of successful artists 7 years after they graduated from the Art Institute in Chicago. Milgram and Hong (1994) found that teenage leisure-time activities in science and the performing arts are better predictors of adult career fields than are standardized tests. Longitudinal studies in talent development present many problems for researchers: subject attrition, adequate control groups, operationalizing criteria that measure talent development over time and successful performance, and finding teachers and experts at each level of mastery (Arnold & Subotnik, 1994). Albert (1994) suggests that researchers may have problems predicting future success because highly talented students demonstrate less stability in their expressed interests than do average students (i.e., one-third change interests from high school to college). Again, much work remains before professionals understand the complex interactions within a talent area, other variables, and future success.

Models that have been proposed in talent development raise interesting questions for the *construct validity* of alternative assessments. If a base of aptitude or achievement exists before talents emerge (Gagné, 1985; H. Gardner, 1983), what level is required for success on components within the area? If expertise or talent in an area is developmental (Bloom, 1985; Csikszentmihalyi et al., 1993; Gagné, 1985; Stewart, 1994), how might progressive increases in performance be demonstrated? If talent development is cyclical (Stewart, 1994), how might critical points of intervention be identified? If talent is developed through systematic training (Bloom, 1985; Gagné, 1985; Stewart, 1994), what types of interventions influence performance (and how)? If the talent area is complex (Simonton, 1999a), how do different components relate to different aspects of the criterion performance? If metacognitive skills must be present (Ericsson, 1987; Sternberg, 1998), how does one's approach to problem finding or solving compare with experts' approaches? If talent is developed through an interaction with a number of variables (Bloom, 1985; Gagné, 1985), what types of and at what times do variables exert the most influence on the individual's development of talent? Some researchers have used factor analysis to examine the nature of the field being measured by alternative assessments. Results have often indicated fewer factors than hypothesized. For example, Plucker, Callahan, and Tomchin (1996) confirmed the presence of only two subscales—linguistic and logical-mathematical—in a battery of 13 activities that were supposed to be assessing four intelligences. They also discovered that the Iowa Test of Basic Skills language subtest correlated more highly with the math teacher checklist than with the linguistic teacher checklist, raising questions as to the construct validity of the tasks.

Some researchers have observed and analyzed how students demonstrate knowledge and use general strategies within and across authentic contexts. In identifying general strategies within mathematics, Niemi (1996) identified key elements of a strategy for assessing conceptual understanding across elementary math curriculum tasks using student explanations. Similarly, Maker (1994) used real and simulated problem-solving situations, both in and out of the classroom setting, to observe students' problem-solving abilities. These methods have a greater likelihood than traditional instruments of addressing the above questions about the complex nature of talent development. In observing the dynamic interaction between the learner and tasks across diverse settings, one will be able to discover general construct-driven strategies, approaches to solving problems, knowledge and strategies that lead to increases in performance, and intervention points for successful talent development.

Tasks for dynamic assessment should be carefully selected and used within the most authentic contexts. Not only must they resemble declarative and procedural knowledge within the talent area, but they also must provide opportunities for students to use complex thinking (Baker et al., 1994). Once the tasks are designed and the contexts selected, one will be able to identify potential in a particular talent area by using a three-phase process: identifying baseline abilities, teaching, and reassessing. The observer must be familiar with the area of talent development for the assessment to be valid. For example, Terry and Pantle (1994) describe how teachers knew what to observe and methods for describing the writing process—what the student did over time in particular areas such as prewriting, drafting, and revising in both persuasive and narrative formats across settings. As instruction occurs, the trained observer can watch the critical strategies emerge and assess talent "potential," the distance between the initial baseline level and the new instructed level. The greater the distance that is achieved by the learner, the greater may be the potential in the talent domain (Vygotsky, 1978). This approach to examining the theoretical construct within specific talent areas may help in specifying the knowledge and procedural skills necessary for successful performance across tasks and in future settings.

ISSUES

This chapter has examined a number of issues that relate to systemic assessment reform, particularly the assessment of talent development. Three primary obstacles tend to sustain traditional forms of assessment—contextual beliefs, technical qualities of alternative assessments, and the diversity of the domain of talent development. Since declarative and procedural knowledge within talent areas has not been well defined and technical qualities of alternative assessments have been questioned, traditional achievement tests will continue to be used as the primary means of determining accountability. Because these tests have a strong influence on the classroom, the majority of teachers most likely will not incorporate talent development activities into their daily instructional practices. Indeed, the field of gifted education is struggling with the amorphous concept of talent development and the design of technically sound alternative procedures. Significant issues must be addressed before the promise of developing talents is realized.

1. *What is the important declarative and procedural knowledge within each talent area?* Alternative assessments must be based on a clear conceptual understanding of the construct of talent development (i.e., declarative knowledge). While many characteristics checklists are available, studies in the development of expertise or procedural knowledge in different fields are quite limited. Without this understanding, assessment tasks cannot be designed to examine the growth of complex thinking processes within and outside the classroom setting.

2. *What is the criterion for successful talent development?* Will the teacher, the school, the field, and/or the individual define this success? For

example, the teacher might define success as student growth in product improvement or receipt of awards in competitions. The school, on the other hand, might define success as the number of students who are involved in AP programs or who attend prestigious universities or who attain high scores on SAT tests. Experts in a talent field may define success as being prolific and attaining special recognition, or even eminence. Individuals may define success in similar ways or idiosyncratically based on opportunities, personal interests, and motivations. For example, a talented middle-school student who makes acceptable grades in school may link his success more to inventions that he is creating at home (e.g., Will the roller coaster in the back yard run?).

If accountability is going to include talent development, then the criterion for success must be identified and must also relate to other high-stakes measures. If it doesn't relate to any of the measures that are viewed as important by decision makers, then the likelihood of its becoming a part of the mainstream of education is limited.

3. *How might the technical qualities of alternative assessments be improved?* If alternative assessments are going to be taken seriously by the larger professional community, they must be improved technically. First, they must *reliably* sample a variety of tasks within the talent domain so that generalization to other settings across time can be ensured. For example, in building a portfolio, does the teacher collect samples that represent the student's work as a whole? Were they collected across situations? Does the student have the opportunity to exhibit the talent in the school? Do evaluators or experts in the talent field interpret the samples in a similar fashion? Second, they must relate to criteria for successful performance in a field and must be driven by the constructs that underlie the specific talent area. For example, to ensure the internal *validity* of portfolio assessment, is the teacher collecting samples that assess the area of talent development? Are these work samples worthy of being collected? Does the sample represent what the student is intending or attempting to do? While alternatives are increasingly being used as one part of high-stakes assessment, they may not survive without a strong empirical research base.

4. *Should talent development be a part of high-stakes accountability testing?* Alternative assessments are time-consuming. They require intensive teacher training in observational and scoring procedures, a variety of tasks that are sequenced and embedded within authentic settings and collected over a period of time, and a considerable knowledge base of techniques and strategies within the talent domain. They may simply be too expensive and cumbersome to use within a broader accountability system. In fact, professionals may lose the dynamic, individualistic nature of talent-development assessments if

they attempt to align with state or national standards. With teachers teaching to the test, this alignment may actually work against the design of tasks that demand novel and more complex student responses.

So have we progressed? Will talent development be a significant influence on assessment reform? With such a limited research base and with such strong external influences, alternative assessments in talent development may never assume a prominent role in high-stakes situations. But is that really the goal? The goal is actually to encourage teachers to use dynamic forms of assessment in gathering diagnostic information so that special talents are identified, individual plans are developed, interventions are implemented, and appropriate placements are made. If researchers address the issues—define the talent areas, identify criteria for success, develop quality assessment tasks—then talent development may assume a more important role in the classroom and in the lives of gifted children.

CHAPTER 14

Why Not Be Creative When We Enhance Creativity?

Jonathan A. Plucker and Ronald A. Beghetto

In 1958, during an era marked by considerable research and education on creativity, Harold Anderson noted that a great unanswered question in psychology was why adults possess so little of the creativity and curiosity that children universally possess. During the current explosion in creativity research and education, one would expect Anderson's question to have been answered, and to a point it has been. Yet our creativity-enhancement efforts look surprisingly like those used 20, 30, or even 50 years ago. What are we doing wrong?

THE NECESSITY AND POPULARITY OF CREATIVITY

According to Sternberg and Lubart (1996), the ability to think creatively is important to both individual problem solving and societal advancement. Smith (1993) echoes this sentiment in stating that innovative thinking and creative problem solving are skills that allow for the redefinition of boundaries, continual advancement, increased productivity, and possibly revolutionary change. Nadler, Habino, and Farrell (1995) take this notion a bit further by asserting that innovation is critical to our continued survival. These authors argue that the times in which we live demand that people make fundamental changes in their personal lives, their societies, and their work-related organizations. As Albert Einstein reportedly said, "We shall require an entirely new way of thinking if we are to survive" (quoted in Nadler et al., p. 2). The sentiments attributed to the value of creative/innovative thinking are not hyperbole and have resulted in countless individuals and organizations investing in and at-

tending to a vast continuum of programs that claim to enhance creative thinking—some worthwhile, some ridiculous.

For these reasons, among others, creativity has become highly valued
over the past 50 years. It has always been a topic in artistic and, more recently,
educational circles, and as we enter the 21st century the corporate sector is
becoming increasingly interested in the study and enhancement of innovation.
Indeed, it is nearly impossible to pick up a business magazine and not find an
article or advertisement about creativity. Research and theory involving creativity are also flourishing, especially among social scientists. Learning theory,
which rejected the role of creativity when behaviorists held sway, has gradually
turned toward constructivism, which is based on the idea that humans create
knowledge, either individually or in social units.

Given all of this emphasis, one could reasonably conclude that creativity
education (i.e., efforts to enhance creativity) is enjoying a similar renaissance.
One would be wrong. Stereotypes about creativity abound, and methods for
teaching creativity look frighteningly similar to techniques used decades ago.
Stereotypes about creativity abound, and methods for teaching creativity look
frighteningly similar to techniques used decades ago (e.g., Guilford, 1950;
Osborn, 1963; Torrance, 1972, 1987; Renzulli & Reis, 1985). Why haven't we
had a greater impact? We believe that the answer to this question has, at its
foundation, two parts: unacceptably broad definitions and lack of innovation
in enhancement methods. We focus on the second of these in this chapter and deal with the definition issue in a separate manuscript (Plucker,
Beghetto, & Dow, in preparation).

The purpose of this chapter is to explore the lack of creativity in creativity
education. We begin with the question of whether creativity can be enhanced,
provide a brief overview of traditional enhancement strategies, explore reasons
for the apparent lack of change in creativity education over the past several
decades, and suggest alternative directions in creativity education that may
one day bear fruit.

CAN CREATIVITY BE ENHANCED THROUGH TRAINING?

Leaders in the study of creativity have long held that it can be enhanced.
Osborn (1963) argued that creative-thinking skills are available to all people
and that these skills can be nurtured through training. E. P. Torrance (1972,
1987; E. P. Torrance & J. P. Torrance, 1973) has spent much of his prodigious
career documenting the success of creativity training programs. Several studies and reviews of the literature provide empirical support for the idea that
creativity can be enhanced through training (e.g., Fontenot, 1993; Grossman & Wiseman, 1993; Higgins, 1994; Nadler et al., 1995; Pyryt, 1999; Stern-

berg & Lubart, 1996; Treffinger, Isaksen, & Dorval, 1996). Important work in social psychology provides evidence that environmental constraints and motivation can also have an effect on creativity (e.g., Amabile, 1979, 1996; Hennessey & Amabile, 1988; Sternberg & Lubart, 1992), reinforcing similar, earlier work of E. P. Torrance (1965, 1977) among others. Considerable pragmatic evidence exists in the growth of corporate training programs in creativity, with "more than half of the nation's 500 largest corporations hav[ing] adopted some type of training in creative thinking or innovative problem solving" (Ford & Harris, 1992, p. 188), a number that has surely grown in the past decade. However, in the face of all of this evidence, a widespread belief still exists that creativity is something people either have or do not have (Treffinger et al., 1996).

In response to this belief, Osborn (1963) argued that everyone has the potential for creatively productive and meaningful contributions. More recently, Halpern (1996) reported that there is little evidence to support the notion that only a select group of people has what it takes to be highly creative. According to Halpern, most people have the potential to produce novel and valuable ideas, "all we need to do is learn how" (p. 368). Higgins (1994), among many others, has also strongly asserted that there is nothing exclusive about the skills necessary for innovative thinking, thus anyone can learn and effectively utilize creative-thinking techniques.

Given this evidence, we believe that Plucker and Runco's (1999) recent comments are a reasonable conclusion about the possibility of fostering creativity: "In response to the question 'Can creativity be enhanced?' the best answer is yes, because creative potentials can be fulfilled. Efforts to enhance creativity will not expand one's in-born potentials but can insure that potentials are maximized" (p. 670).

ENHANCEMENT OF CREATIVITY

In 1972, E. P. Torrance classified 142 enhancement studies into nine "categories of ways of teaching children to think creatively." In approximate order of effectiveness, they included Creative Problem Solving (CPS) programs based on the Osborn-Parnes model; other "disciplined approaches," such as training in semantics and conducting research; creative arts programs; media and reading programs; packaged programs for creative thinking; modification of testing conditions; use of motivation, reward, and competition; teacher-classroom variables, including level of control and classroom climate; and curricular and administrative arrangements to facilitate creativity-fostering conditions. Torrance found the most research on the CPS and packaged programs, with the least on curricular and administrative arrangements and other disciplined approaches. Of special interest to this chapter is the fact that over 80% of these evaluation studies used divergent thinking as an outcome variable. Torrance's follow-up in 1987 found similar results, with a moderation in emphasis on divergent thinking. However, divergent thinking was still the foundation of most program evaluations at the K–12 levels.

The reliance on divergent thinking as an outcome of enhancement programs is not surprising. Many of these programs were inspired by Guilford's (1967) research in this area with its emphasis on divergent thinking. Other programs were based on the work of Wallach or E. P. Torrance and their colleagues (e.g., Torrance, 1962, 1965, 1971; Wallach & Kogan, 1965; Wallach & Wing, 1969), both of whom were inspired to a point by Guilford's work. Torrance (1987) found that even CPS programs, with explicit components on both divergent *and* convergent thinking, often focused on divergent-thinking outcomes.

Much has changed in theory and research since E. P. Torrance's seminal analyses (1987), but the same has not occurred in the development of new and innovative programs for enhancing creativity (cf. Meador, Fishkin, & Hoover, 1999; Nickerson, 1999). For example, perhaps the most important theoretical advance is the creation of complex systems theories to explain creative development and production. These theories (e.g., Csikszentmihalyi, 1988; Rubenson & Runco, 1992; Sternberg & Lubart, 1992; Walberg, 1988) promote a much broader conceptualization of creativity by including affective, social, political, and economic considerations in addition to cognitive ones. Yet education programs generally focus only on cognitive aspects of creativity; even then, they usually are based largely on divergent-thinking exercises.

Problems

Although traditional approaches to creativity training have enjoyed wide acceptance and often have a positive effect, the efficacy data on such programs are inconsistent, rely largely on anecdotal support, are dated, and typically are restricted to business settings. Furthermore, programs developed recently have a restricted audience (i.e., gifted students), are not widely used in American schools and workplaces, or—in the face of broader, more inclusive systems theories—are still narrowly focused (usually on divergent thinking as a program outcome). Current approaches to teaching creativity sprang from once-fresh ideas and models for enhancing creative thinking (Osborn/Parnes 1950s, Torrance 1960s, Renzulli, 1970s) but have largely become stagnant. It is our contention that the enhancement of creativity has generally benefited from early pioneering efforts, but that stereotypes and problems surrounding the effort abound. Currently, and most specifically in educational settings, there is need for alternative, innovative approaches to the enhancement of education.

POSSIBLE EXPLANATIONS FOR THE LACK OF CREATIVITY WITHIN CREATIVITY EDUCATION

We explore three possible causes for the lack of originality in creativity enhancement over the past few decades: the overemphasis and misunderstanding of "Big C" creativity, which leads to the creation of damaging stereotypes and myths about creativity; an overemphasis on psychometric approaches to the study of creativity as manifest in the obsession with divergent thinking; and insularity of research efforts in the areas of creativity and innovation.

Big C Versus Little C Creativity: The Origins of Damaging Stereotypes

The issue of what *degree* of creativity to study and enhance has clouded issues related to enhancement for decades. "Big C" creativity is often used to refer to genius-level, relatively clear cut examples of creativity (e.g., the work of Einstein, Mozart, Gandhi, Graham), whereas "little c" creativity refers to common, everyday creativity of an unremarkable, more ambiguous sort (e.g., a new way to bake a cake, a unique solution to a math homework problem). Csikszentmihalyi (1996) has described Big C creativity as the kind that results in changes in some aspect of the culture, with little c creativity leading to original changes that are not on the level of Big C change. Sternberg and Lubart (1996) have reported that many scholars of creativity recognize only the type of creativity that falls in the Big C or genius-level creativity, with considerable debate about whether little c creativity is significant enough even to warrant being labeled creativity. Focusing on Big C creativity is also a solution to the criterion problem in creativity research, since only unambiguously creative achievements are studied.

But is the evidence in favor of Big C Creativity really that compelling? The creativity literature offers little support that Big C Creativity exists, let alone that it can be taught. Weisberg (1986) has offered a potential reason for this in stating that "genius is a characteristic that society bestows upon an individual in response to his or her work. Since the sensibilities of society change, so do its judgments of genius" (p. 88). Being that Big C creativity is tied to the judgment of society, any effort to teach or even identify specific characteristics of this kind of creativity seems virtually impossible.

In addition to criticisms of the Big C approach, several authors have made strong cases for the usefulness of little c creativity, asserting that it can be enhanced through training and often produces meaningful and useful results (DeBono, 1992; Fontenot, 1993; Grossman & Wiseman, 1993; Noone, 1993; Osborn, 1963; Treffinger et al., 1996; Wise, 1991). For example, Halpern (1996) asserts that creativity exists in degrees and thereby does not only exist in eminent, revolutionary breakthroughs. Sternberg and Lubart (1996) note that recent studies in cognitive psychology propose that creativity involves essentially ordinary cognitive processes. These authors have reported that numerous research investigations suggest that creativity requires interrelated resources that all people have the potential to possess. These resources are tied to the freedom and willingness to generate unique ideas, select the most favorable ideas, and effectively implement those ideas.

H. Gardner (1993), in his well-regarded study of eminent creators, actually provides additional evidence against the "genius" view of creativity. His subjects, who included Freud, Einstein, Picasso, Stravinsky, Eliot, Graham, and Gandhi, nearly all exhibited talents in the area of selling or marketing their creativity. Quick perusals of biographies of Michelangelo, Frank Lloyd Wright, and countless others also reveal a skill in promoting their creativity. In other words, one reason we perceive them to be Big C creators is because they deliberately set out to convince us that they were!

Further, even though the enhancement of little c creativity may be the focus of creativity training, there is no reason to exclude the possibility of achieving Big C creativity through such training. As O'Neill and Shallcross (1994) have suggested, all people have the ability to be sensational thinkers; getting them to actualize their potential may simply rely on helping them discover and articulate their abilities. Further, Big C creativity may in fact arise not from being a true visionary, but rather from being a highly productive individual. Simonton (1994) presents a compelling argument in stating that "quality is a function of quantity" (p. 184) because of the equal odds rule. In other words, the more products produced in a given time period, the greater the chance of producing a truly eminent or Big C product. This finding has been uncovered repeatedly in the study of "greatness" and other forms of eminence (see Simonton, 1994, 1999a). Simonton concedes that there are exceptions to this rule (i.e., some mass producers produce masses of mediocrity as well as quality), but on average the more produced the greater the chance that Big C creativity will be achieved. These observations, taken in concert with many recent systems theories (here we are thinking specifically of Csikszentmihalyi's 1988 model), lead us to the conclusion that the key to achieving Big C status for one's work is to produce a large body of high-quality work and market it effectively.

In summary, Big C creativity has received a great deal of attention in the creativity literature, yet evidence supporting the importance of and ability to teach Big C creativity is scarce. Our position is that Big C creativity research has made and is making major contributions to the field, but that its traditional emphasis in creativity theory and research has had unintended and negative consequences for enhancements efforts. These efforts should focus on the more common, everyday types of creativity, often referred to as little c creativity. Little c creativity does exist, can be enhanced, and does warrant serious study and enhancement efforts regardless of whether those efforts will eventually lead to designation of Big C status.

Myths and Stereotypes About Creativity. We are aware that a possible reaction to the previous section could be, "Is Big C creativity really that bad? I don't see how it hurts enhancement efforts." We have three responses: One, it detracts attention from little c creativity. Two, it hurts enhancement efforts by putting the focus strongly on personality characteristics related to creativity and not on the creative process or environment. In other words, rather than focus on making every thought and effort truly eminent and innovative, it is often more fruitful to get to the hard, ubiquitous work of producing whatever it is that you produce. Third, because Big C creativity is so elusive and foreign to the vast majority of people, the idea of enhancing "creativity" conjures up images of people running around barefoot rubbing crystals on their foreheads, an idealized version of a 1960s commune more than the nature of creativity. As a result of focusing on Big C creativity, these stereotypical images have fallen under the care of pop psychology. This is unfortunate. As more pop psychology books are sold, serious scholars dissociate themselves from the study of creativity, and the empirically supported knowledge base continues to shrink relative to that of other psychological constructs.

Like many creativity scholars (DeBono, 1992; Halpern, 1996; Treffinger et al., 1996; Weisberg, 1986), we have observed—both in our classrooms and at professional conferences—that creativity is plagued by grave misconceptions and mystical overtones and we think that efforts should be taken to dispel these misconceptions that distort the understanding and study of creativity. This will undoubtedly take time; Treffinger et al. (1996) note that even though many myths and misconceptions continue to be refuted, many are still widely held. It is, therefore, important to understand the historical and conceptual roots of these myths if we are to dispel them effectively. According to Treffinger et al., over the course of history, those who are called creative have been regarded as divinely inspired, or in secret communion with the Muses (Sternberg & Lubart, 1996; Treffinger et al., 1996; Weisberg, 1986). Indeed, inspiration is derived from the Latin for "breathe in," so those that are inspired have been said to be breathing in divinity.

The mystical view of creativity presents several difficulties to creativity educators. The myths create perceptions that creativity is a process that is out of the control of the individual, that enhancement is impossible, and that creative people are eccentric and engage in deviant behaviors. In addition, Sternberg and Lubart (1996) suggest that mystical views of creativity do not lend themselves well to study because it may be felt that scholars are treading in the spiritual realm—forbidden ground for most academics. Our goal is not to get into a metaphysical debate regarding creativity but rather to embrace the notion that people can deliberately and effectively enhance their use of creative thinking. This notion moves away from a passive reliance on mystical inspiration, away from the grandiose focus on Big C creativity, to a realistic, active approach to creative thinking and creative action.

Divergent Thinking: When Is Too Much Enough?

The third issue involves a lopsided focus on divergent-thinking skills. Theory and research have begun to stress the influence of noncognitive factors on creativity (Plucker & Runco, 1999), and our understanding of the role of cognitive factors has broadened substantially (see T. B. Ward, Smith, & Vaid, 1997). Yet, as noted earlier, many current creativity programs primarily stress the importance of divergent-thinking skills, possibly due to a belief that enhancing divergent-thinking skills leads to enhanced creative ability (Fontenot, 1993)—a belief that has some empirical support. Yet the creativity literature is marked by criticisms of the overemphasis on the role of divergent thinking in the training of creativity and problem solving (Clapham, 1997; Treffinger et al., 1996; Wallach, 1976).

Clapham (1997) reports that training programs with the highest success rate contained procedures that involve divergent and convergent-thinking. Unfortunately, many programs fail to teach convergent-thinking skills and even fewer address the final step, implementation of ideas. As a result, creativity enhancement programs that are enjoyable and effective in producing multiple ideas proliferate. When the positive affect dissipates, the participants are left with a mountain of ideas with little understanding of how to identify the most promising ideas and virtually no guidance in regard to how to put the good ideas to use (see research on this issue by Cramond, Martin, & Shaw, 1990; Eriksson, 1990). The overemphasis on divergent-thinking techniques has helped fuel the fire from critics regarding the teaching of creative thinking—a criticism that started in the 1960s and continues today (Halpern, 1996; Treffinger et al., 1996).

As Treffinger et al. (1996) suggest, overemphasizing divergent thinking leads to frivolous and undisciplined rambling and may result in "nothing more than cerebral popcorn popping" (p. 225). This not only produces weak results, but as Sternberg and Lubart (1996) claim, a focus on technique (such as divergent-thinking activities) while neglecting theory suggests a commercialized phenomenon rather than "a serious endeavor for psychological study" (p. 680).

The trend of commercialization is evident in the late 1980s enhancement of creative thinking being driven by a focus on real-world performance. In other words, there is a trend to try something—anything—that might increase creative thinking without first considering the objectives, goals, and potential outcomes. This continued through the 1990s as more companies turned to creativity training to increase innovation and productivity at nearly any cost, even though the demand for this training outpaced resources to provide it (Clapham, 1997; Higgins, 1994; Wise, 1991). Casual observation of corporate training programs usually reveals high-priced consultants quoting "research" about their techniques, most of which are repackaged divergent-thinking activities that are decades old.

Insularity of Theory and Research

Why not share with other fields addressing similar issues? Several fields explicitly study creativity, such as diffusion of innovation, entrepreneurship, and product development, yet their contributions are infrequently cited in the creativity and gifted education journals. Other fields, such as counseling, business management, marketing, complexity, learning theory, and language education, grapple with similar issues, yet potential linkages to creativity theory and research are rarely explored, and applications to creativity training are negligible. For example, the role of group versus individual creativity is a hot topic, yet few educators look to the business management literature to see if the many studies on this topic would inform enhancement with younger people. This insularity goes both ways—since constructivist learning theories involve the creation of knowledge, information may be gained (and considerable time saved) by investigating the creativity literature. Creativity educators often preach about the dangers of functional fixedness and groupthink, yet they only sporadically look beyond their academic boundaries for new information and inspiration. A few gatekeepers to the field, such as Mark Runco, the editor of the *Creativity Research Journal*, have made headway in encouraging authors to investigate relevant material from other fields, but significant room for improvement remains in this area.

Summary

The combination of these causes—the emphasis on Big C creativity, resultant myths and stereotypes, the focus on divergent thinking, and insularity of theory and research—has narrowed educators' perspectives on creativity. Theory and research can improve greatly, but if the underlying problems are not aggressively addressed, creativity education will remain grounded.

AN EXAMPLE OF A PROMISING ALTERNATIVE APPROACH
TO CREATIVITY EDUCATION

Rather than provide a list of promising approaches, we will highlight one such approach: the use of problem-based learning (PBL) to enhance creativity. PBL is based on theories of situated cognition in learning, which posit that transfer from traditional classroom learning to real-life application occurs infrequently, and that learning requires situation-specific competence (Brown, Collins, & Duguid, 1989). Problem-based learning initiates learning by exposing students to an ill-structured, real-world problem. The problem is often interdisciplinary, since solving real problems often requires the crossing of traditional disciplinary boundaries. Important components of PBL include an instructional unit that is anchored to an authentic ill-structured problem (i.e., information readily available to the students is not sufficient to solve the problem; a single, correct process for solving the problem is not readily apparent or does not exist; the problem may change as the students attempt to solve it); the teacher serves as a facilitator; student choice promotes ownership of learning; thinking and procedural skills training and content mini-lectures are available as needed; and social interaction and collaboration are required to solve the problem.

Variations on problem-based learning, under different labels, have been used in gifted education for many years. One of the most popular models for educating gifted students, the Schoolwide Enrichment Model (Renzulli & Reis, 1985, 1986), stresses the need for experiences through which students solve real-world problems. The research literature strongly suggests that problem-based learning is an effective curricular approach to developing student talent and creativity (e.g., Barron et al., 1998; Gallagher & Stepien, 1996; Krajcik et al., 1998; Reis & Renzulli, 1999; Renzulli & Reis, 1994), although creativity is rarely considered to be an outcome of PBL activities. In our experience, students engaged in PBL activities generally gain a greater grasp of the content, develop and refine specific technological and creative skills, and report greater understanding of the creative process (Gorman, Plucker, & Callahan, 1998; Plucker & Gorman, 1995, 1999; Plucker & Nowak, 2000).

Problem-based programs are not without their own concerns (e.g., see Coleman, 1999, for commentary on the Renzulli approach). PBL is resource-intensive in terms of preparation and instructional time and physical resources (Plucker & Nowak, 2000). The debate about transfer applies to directly to PBL and situated learning (Anderson, Reder, & Simon, 1996; Plucker, 1998). From the teacher's perspective, one of the most important concerns is that time spent on PBL detracts from teaching required content, although this does not appear to be supported by the research literature (e.g., Gallagher & Stepien, 1996).

Application to Creativity Education

PBL has several advantages for creativity education. First, the broader, real-world approach models systems theories of creativity to a greater extent than do traditional approaches to creativity education. In the same vein, the need to disseminate and argue in favor of one's solution develops valuable skills regarding marketing one's creative ideas. Second, the approach is decidedly little c creativity in nature, combating the stereotypes of creative individuals that many young people have already developed. Third, setting the cultural and political context of the problem and encouraging students to reach out to other information sources creates an interdisciplinary context for the activities. Finally, the problem-based approach is flexible: It can focus explicitly on creativity enhancement, emphasize content to a greater agree, or emphasize process and content (as the example provided above demonstrates).

HOW CAN WE MAKE AND KEEP CREATIVITY EDUCATION CREATIVE?

The following list of suggestions is by no means comprehensive, yet the suggestions may serve as starting points in the effort to improve the effectiveness of creativity education. Readers should compare the suggestions with those of Sternberg and Williams (1996), Hennessey and Amabile (1987), Nickerson (1999), and others, although the purpose of those recommendations is to enhance creativity, while the following suggestions are aimed at improving the effectiveness of enhancement efforts.

- Distinguish between the kind of creativity that is being emphasized (i.e., Big C versus little c) and be certain not to overemphasis Big C conceptions in the training. As DeBono (1992) observed, "It may not be possible to train genius—but there is an awful lot of useful creativity that takes place without genius" (p. 31).
- Dispel the numerous myths, misconceptions, and stereotypes about creativity and creative individuals and organizations. The first step is to understand the origins of these stereotypes.
- Scrutinize the claims and theoretical and empirical support of the growing number of "popular" creativity training programs.
- Do not neglect the importance of divergent thinking in training but rather balance the training of divergent thinking with the training of convergent thinking and other noncognitive aspects of creativity.
- Consider the use of problem-based learning and other approaches that

are based on systems theories of creativity. Similarly, conceptualize programs such as the Schoolwide Enrichment Model as creativity-development programs and learn from the extensive research base attached to these programs.

- Search for and apply innovative approaches from various fields to help guide students' creative endeavors. For example, Sternberg's (1999) typology of creative contributions is an excellent framework for understanding the qualitatively different types of creativity, which should benefit people who are trying to achieve creatively. Chaos and complexity theory, which receive a great deal of attention in the physical, life, and social sciences, should also be explored for possible applications to the enhancement of creativity (e.g., Arthur, 1989, 1990; Kauffman, 1991, 1993; Nicolis & Prigogine, 1989; Schuldberg, 1999).

CHAPTER 15

Beyond Bloom: Revisiting Environmental Factors That Enhance or Impede Talent Development

Rena F. Subotnik, Paula Olszewski-Kubilius, and Karen D. Arnold

Classic studies of talent development involve reflections by accomplished or even eminent individuals on the parenting, education, and training they received in preparation for their careers. Roe (1953) discovered that her subjects, eminent scientists, typically began their passionate pursuit of collection, experimentation, or theorizing around the age of seven. Zuckerman (1977), surveying American Nobel laureates, reported that a large majority were themselves students of previous laureates. The laureate mentor auditioned various brilliant students in order to select those most likely to carry on his laboratory's line of work while the student sought guidance and association with recognized greatness. The chief benefit for the protégé was the communication of tacit knowledge (Wagner & Sternberg, 1986) on how to identify scientific problems with great potential for discovery and impact.

Bloom (1985), in collaboration with several students and colleagues, studied musicians, athletes, and scholars who had achieved high-level public recognition, focusing on the development of talent as expressed through the efforts of families and teachers. Roe's (1953) research addresses the first stage, "falling in love" with science. Zuckerman's (1977) study dwells mostly on the "mastery" stage, where unique aspects of performance are refined and professional reputation is enhanced. The middle period of disciplined practice of technique has, until recently, been largely ignored by our field (Ericsson, 1996). Educational institutions, peers, and families play a key role in assisting young people through this challenging yet essential developmental period.

SOME QUESTIONS THAT EMERGE FROM BLOOM'S STUDY

Developing Talent in Young People (Bloom, 1985) addresses the issue of whether the design and purpose of schools conflict with talent development. Bloom's work also raises a set of questions about the role of parents, teachers, and mentors:

- For which talent domains should schools be responsible? Should the culture of families in a particular school community influence this decision?
- Most talent domains include a "high" form and a "low" form. For example, dancers may perform in classical ballet or in musical theater. Should parents and teachers be equally supportive of students missing school to rehearse or perform in both cases?
- How much talent must be demonstrated in order to convince families and teachers that a child should be tracked into a serious talent-development program? Should sheer motivation and interest count as much as demonstrated talent?
- At what age should talent development begin? What criteria should be used to decide about moving a child into more narrowly focused training?
- Since lack of early opportunity precludes assessing talent on a level playing field, how should the needs of children outside the mainstream be addressed?

ENVIRONMENTAL FACTORS THAT AFFECT
THE DEVELOPMENT OF TALENT

Families clearly play a very important role in the realization of promise and potential (Bloom, 1985). At the most fundamental level, parents provide two critical resources: money and time. Parental financial support for lessons, instruments, equipment, and outside-of-school educational opportunities is as essential as their role in arranging lessons, searching out programs, driving to and monitoring practices.

Parents, overtly or covertly, espouse values conducive to talent development (Olszewski, Kulieke, & Buescher, 1987). These may include the importance of finding and developing one's abilities; aspiring to achievement at the highest levels possible; independence of thought and expression; and favoring active-recreational, cultural, and intellectual pursuits (Olszewski et al., 1987). Csikszentmihalyi and Beattie (1979) assert that families have systems of cognitive coding as well as patterns of explanations for events or circumstances that determine values and attitudes. Parents can model a love of work and learning, including learning outside of structured or traditional activities and settings. Parents also model personality dispositions that are essential to talent development, such as risk taking and coping with setbacks and failures. They demonstrate that success requires a great deal of hard work and sustained effort over long periods of time (Olszewski et al., 1987).

Another very important role for parents is helping their talented child build supportive social networks (Subotnik & Olszewski-Kubilius, 1997). Although the social world of the child begins with the family, over time, as higher levels of performance are achieved, that world expands to include teachers, coaches, mentors, and talented peers. Social networks evolve naturally, but parents can help children build connections that support not only general social and emotional development, but talent development as well. Participation in special activities, such as competitions or after-school or summer programs, can augment social networks with peers that provide specific emotional support for achievement—friends and companions who are also involved in the talent field can be essential to sustaining commitment during times of flagging interest or disappointing performance. Parents can take an active and deliberate role in constructing these social-support networks for their children by providing a rich array of opportunities to connect with other talented children. Parents also assist by managing social relations (e.g., dates to play with other children) until the child is able to do so him or herself.

Although research generally supports the positive role that families can play in developing talent, the literature also suggests that different kinds of family interactions yield different outcomes for children. Specifically, family dynamics, attitudes, and behaviors and parenting styles greatly influence children's motivations to achieve or produce. Creatively gifted children tend to come from families that stress independence rather than interdependence between family members, are less child-oriented, have tense or imbalanced family relationships, and express negative affect and competition between family members, resulting in motivation toward power and dominance. High scholastic achievers come from families that are cohesive and child-centered, and where parent-child identification is strong, resulting in high levels of achievement motivation (Albert, 1978, 1983; Arnold, 1995).

Research studies of eminent adults yield retrospective accounts of family environments characterized by stress, trauma, conflict, and dysfunction (Ochse, 1993). Research on high-IQ individuals, most of whom do not end up being eminent, describes families that are intact and happy with normal and moderate levels of stress (Olszewski-Kubilius, 2000). What can we glean from these profiles of families of gifted individuals? Different mixtures of family variables may, in fact, yield different outcomes that are more or less supportive of creativity, scholastic achievement, talent development, and general mental health.

Question: Should we actively seek to help parents and educators promote one of these outcomes over others? Studies suggest that an important factor in the lives of eminent individuals is the degree to which children freely develop a unique identity and express their own thoughts. Individuals who do so are more likely to produce ground-breaking work in their talent domain as opposed to high levels of achievement. The circumstances within homes and families that create environments conducive to the development of independent identities and thought are many and varied. They include a reduction in parent-child identification, an emotional distance between parent and child, lower levels of parental monitoring of children, and less conventional socialization of children by parents (Ochse, 1993; Olszewski-Kubilius, 2000). The literature cites negative circumstances that create this "distance," such as imbalanced or difficult family relationships, parental alcoholism or mental illness, death of a parent or sibling, or more benign circumstances such as parents who are less involved with children because they are involved with their own interests or careers (Ochse, 1993; Olszewski-Kubilius, 2000). These conditions are thought to result in children's being more independent and autonomous, and less sex-stereotyped. They also cause children to retreat or shy away from interpersonal interactions at home and spend more time alone, which can facilitate practice and skill acquisition in the talent area and promote an inward focus (Ochse, 1993; Simonton, 1992).

A second family variable that appears to play an important role in achievement motivation is stress. Stress is a broad concept and difficult to define. What is very stressful for one person may be only moderately stressful for another. As mentioned above, many eminent individuals report difficult childhood circumstances, including parental loss, parental dysfunction, neglect, harsh parenting, lack of family stability, rejection due to physical handicaps, and poverty. Researchers speculate on the role of stress in engendering powerful motivations to succeed. Specifically, individuals may strive to acquire admiration and affection from others and compensate for that which was not obtained from family, to ameliorate rejection, or to prove that they are worthwhile (Ochse, 1993; Rhodes, 1997). Stressful family circumstances may propel a child to seek refuge in safe, controllable intellectual activities or to use creative activity as an outlet for emotions (Ochse, 1993, Piirto, 1992), or it may force an early psychological maturity for the child (Albert, 1978, 1980). Further, stressful childhoods may prepare individuals to cope with the intellectual tensions and marginal existence characteristic of many highly creative people (Feldman, 1994b; H. Gardner, 1994).

Traumatic childhood events galvanize some individuals to devote their life's work to righting a perceived wrong. Csikszentmihalyi (1990) refers to the process by which some individuals take stressful circumstances and turn them into positive ones as "transformational coping," whereby an individual redefines the situation into a broader existential problem and seeks a creative solution (i.e., creative work), thereby reducing or assuaging the emotions associated with the initial event or situation (Ochse, 1993)

Although research on eminent individuals seems to suggest that family stress and unhappy childhoods are associated with producing a creative individual, are they necessary ingredients? Not according to Csikszentmihalyi et al. (1993). They talk about a balance of support and tension within the family as conducive to high levels of talent development. These families provide contexts for children that are both integrated (family members are connected and supportive of one another) and differentiated (there are high expectations from parents that individual children will develop their talents to the highest degree possible through individual thought and expression). Such families produce autotelic personalities, or individuals who are self-motivated and self-directed. According to Csikszentmihalyi et al., an overemphasis on integration or differentiation can result in individuals who are eminent but not well adjusted (primacy of differentiation) or very well adjusted but not talented or creative (primacy of integration). They suggest that the development of high levels of talent requires the motivation and characteristics born of childhood trauma—other levels of talent result from a more balanced blend of tension and support.

Similarly, Therival (1999a, 1999b) asserts that stress and tragedy are not essential to creative productivity. He offers a model of creativity that includes the following components: genetic endowment (G), parental or other "confidence building" assistances (A), and misfortunes (M). According to Therival, creativity can develop in individuals who experience great misfortune as long as there is also assistance present. He distinguishes between creators who are dedicated (have high levels of G, many A's in youth, and no major M's) and creators who are "challenged" (high G, some A's, and some M's). Both produce creative work, but the challenged personalities are more overtly driven to prove themselves and to receive recognition (Therival, 1999b). Parenting styles that help a child to find his or her own identity, allow for open expression of ideas and independent thought, reduce parent-child identification but not necessarily affiliation or affection, and provide support in the presence of trauma or tragedy will be supportive of talent development, creativity, and good mental health.

Parents also help children succeed by not shielding or protecting them from risks or hard work and allowing them to experience the tensions that arise from high expectations. They can also support a rich internal fantasy life, use of time alone to decompress and rejuvenate, expression of emotions via creative work, active use of leisure time, and other ways for children to gain control over their life circumstances.

A THEORETICAL FRAMEWORK FOR ENVISIONING ENVIRONMENTS FOR TALENT DEVELOPMENT

Thus far, the discussion has centered on a psychological view of individuals in family settings. Cultural psychologists, anthropologists, and sociologists define environment in different ways that can illuminate early pathways to eminence and creative productivity. Bronfenbrenner's (1977, 1979, 1993) theory of eco-logical development places individual development within nested contexts ranging from those in which an individual actively participates (*microsystems* of family, classroom, and peer group) to those framing society at the broadest level (*macrosystems* of opportunity structures and ideologies). Both immediate environments and systems in which an individual does not directly participate strongly influence the probability of fulfilling one's potential. In Bronfenbren-ner's terms, the macrosystem "of overarching institutional patterns of the cul-ture or subculture, such as the economic, social, educational, legal, and politi-cal systems" (1977, p. 515) manifests itself through interactions of individuals with their environments. Analysis of these interactions provides a deep and complex picture of the relationship between family, education, society, and the production of eminence. Bronfenbrenner's model also enables investiga-tion of historical time as it affects reciprocal interactions between individuals and social systems, such as education.

Bronfenbrenner's (1977) framework presents levels of the environment that interact and ultimately affect the family system of the developing child. At the center are the individual and his or her personality, genetic endow-ment, and other personal variables. Individual attributes are developmentally characteristic ways of interacting with one's immediate environment. A predis-position to seek challenge and eliciting the attention of mentors, for instance, are instigative traits common to talented individuals. The lowest level of envi-ronment, the microsystem, encompasses the individual's direct interactions with his or her interpersonal and physical surroundings. A child's immediate environment is a dynamic system in which parents both influence and are influenced by their talented son or daughter (Lerner, 1996). To take a dra-matic case, the young violin prodigy is influenced by family values and re-sources to begin the instrument at a young age and to work diligently to master it. At the same time, evidence of exceptional talent leads the family to attend to the young violinist in particular ways, to treat him or her differently from siblings, even to change the family life-style to afford expensive training, relocate for a specific teacher, or undertake extensive travel to competitions and concerts. The reciprocal effects of child and family lead to a dynamic environment that may be underestimated, for example, in retrospective studies investigating the relationship of early stress and subsequent eminence. It could be the child's own reactions to family conditions and resulting modifications of the family system that lead to different outcomes in terms of talent development.

Ecological frameworks of development go beyond the immediate family and peer system to consider three additional hierarchical levels of environment. The *mesosytem* encompasses relationships between a child's immediate surroundings, or microsystems. Peer group and family, or school and science club, are examples of interacting environments. For a gifted child, contradictory family messages and peer-group influence may serve to inhibit dedicated work in a talent domain. Conversely, when mentors and teachers in a talent domain align with supportive peers, parents, and school environments, the conditions for talent development should be maximized (Olszewski-Kubilius, Grant, & Seibert, 1993). One microsystem can influence another, as when parents step in to influence peer contacts or to establish a specialized network in the child's talent area. Consideration of the multiple and interacting environments in which a child participates is a necessary practical and research strategy for understanding the role of family more broadly and thoroughly in talent development. The family can alternatively buffer or intensify the effects of environmental factors and always acts as a filter of events and circumstances (Olszewski-Kubilius, 2000).

The *exosystem*, the next nested level of environment, refers to environments that affect a child, but in which the child does not directly participate. The work lives of parents, for instance, affect household resources and parental stress, which in turn act on family dynamics and the life of the child. The bureaucracies of school districts and state legislatures offer another example of exosystem environments that affect the lives of talented children through decisions about gifted programs, school orchestras, science facilities, and advanced academic options.

The broadest level of environment is the macrosystem, defined as "the overarching pattern of *micro, meso,* and *exosystems* characterizing a given culture, subculture or other broader social context, with particular reference to the developmentally instigated belief systems, resources, hazards, lifestyles, opportunity structures, life course options and patterns of social interchange that are embedded in each of these systems" (Bronfenbrenner, 1979, p. 228). It is within the macrosystem that cultural views of child rearing, giftedness and talent, and achievement pathways emerge to affect the beliefs and behaviors of parents and teachers. Widespread beliefs about the importance of being well-rounded, for instance, characterize much of contemporary American society and work against intensive early training in many talent areas. Similarly, intensifying social ideologies of equality have led to an anti-elitist bias and the dismantling of ability tracking in schools. The ideal of meritocracy continues as a strong component of the contemporary macrosystem, despite compelling evidence of limited social mobility in the general population (Lemann, 1999). Which talent areas are valued, which kinds of people advance, and what kinds of achievement pathways are available are all functions of the broad macrosystem of a society. An individual's cultural attributes and orientation, socialized primarily through the family but also in education, determine his or her success and social standing (Bourdieu, 1977; Meyer, 1994). Just as important, the cultural attributes that are valued and rewarded in education and the professions are those a society deems valuable (Feldman et al., 1994). The composition of elites interacts with the larger cultural context; eminent individuals and creative producers are both shapers and products of society.

Studying talent development requires understanding individual pathways within cultural and historical contexts. Cultural capital theory (Bourdieu, 1977) provides a useful framework as it moves beyond family environment to consider the content of the values, tastes, and personal presentation style that affect an individual's acceptance into professional and social elites. In the study of social stratification, Bourdieu's work has inspired a body of empirical research on the origins and effects of "cultural capital," usually operationalized as an individual's knowledge of or access to cultural resources (e.g., DiMaggio, 1982). Bourdieu asserts that schools offer the primary institutional setting for production, transmission, and accumulation of the various forms of cultural capital. He treats cultural capital as cumulative, arguing that the greater the early endowment, the easier the further attainments. Family preference for high culture, verbal fluency, and upper-class personal tastes and presentation ("habitus"), according to this theory, provide gifted children with cultural resources that are rewarded in school and among mentors and gatekeepers in talent domains. Merton (1988) refers to this as the "Matthew Effect" or accumulation of advantage. Child-rearing patterns stressing independence, critical thinking, and creativity are associated with high levels of cultural capital (Wachs, 1992). Along with cultural capital, a family's social capital of contacts and networks permeates the environments of gifted children and affects their talent development. Sociologists have investigated how differences in cultural capital reinforce inequality regardless of specific and current family circumstances such as stress or family dysfunction (DiMaggio, 1982; Swartz, 1997).

Time is the final element of environment that surrounds a gifted child and family. Both the historical era and a person's age affect how an individual experiences life events and family systems. Combining psychological and sociological approaches, life-course analysis focuses on the dynamic interaction of individual agency, age cohort, historical conditions, and social ties linked through chronologically ordered life events (Clausen, 1993; Elder, 1974; Giele, 1993; Giele & Elder, 1998). Successive cohorts of individuals are framed and influenced by their formal educational experiences, peer-group socialization, and experience in unique historical and cultural events (Ryder, 1965). The variation that arises from each cohort's unique location in the stream of history "provides an opportunity for analyzing social transformation" (Ryder, 1965, p. 843). Personal characteristics and the timing of life events also interact with individuals' cultural and historical location and their connections to institutions and groups (Arnold, Youn, & Salkever, 1999) to influence development.

The seemingly contradictory findings about the role of adverse circumstances in the childhoods of eminent individuals could be examined through the lens of a life-course approach. As with Elder's (1974) findings about children of the Great Depression, the age at which children experience hardship may play a role in their eventual adaptations. The ideology of the era (its macrosystem) also makes a difference, as, for example, the Depression era valued stoicism and the 1960s expressiveness. Clearly, the relationship between early family factors such as adversity and later eminence is very complex, and the influence of multiple and interacting contexts and historical events must be taken into consideration (Feldman, with Goldsmith, 1991; Jacobi, 1991; Subotnik, 1995; Subotnik & Arnold, 1995; Subotnik & Steiner, 1993; Tannenbaum, 1983).

CASE STUDIES

Over the years, we have been working closely with gifted adolescents and adults, focusing on the variables that either enhance or impede the development of talent over time. Below are some case studies from our work: two in academics, one in instrumental music, and one in dance. These case studies illustrate the broader environmental and cultural issues involved in the talent-development process that were described in previous sections. They also provide real-life examples of the issues posed in the questions at the beginning of this chapter.

> At age 10, Lyle has mastered the secondary school mathematics curriculum. Throughout his elementary years, his teachers have tried to accommodate him with tutoring sessions and visits to high school classes. Lyle has always wanted more from his mathematics classes: more theory, more history, more "What if's." At home, Lyle creates poems with cadences based on mathematical patterns and writes stories about geometric figures. He attends graduate-level mathematics classes at a local university one afternoon a week after school.

Question: How will ecosystem factors that place emphasis on being well-rounded and socially adept affect Lyle's talent development?

Alex is a fifth grader enrolled in eighth-grade mathematics at a highly selective school for academically gifted students. If it were up to him, he would take math all day long at school. He loves to show the teacher and his older classmates that he has mastered the homework or lesson at hand. Alex turned down an opportunity to participate in an after-school mentorship program with a mathematics professor, preferring instead to play Nintendo and participate in sports. It would not occur to him to pose math problems for himself or to create mathematics-related projects on his own.

Question: Should effort be invested in developing Alex's mathematical creativity and, if so, what form should this effort take? What factors contribute to Alex's low levels of extracurricular motivation related to mathematics?

Michael Y. is 4 years old and is the youngest child in a musical family. His mother has nurtured the talents of internationally renowned violinists and has great hopes for Michael. He began practicing at the age of 2-1/2 and now practices up to 2 hours a day. Mrs. Y. provides him with daily lessons. Sometimes he cries during his practice sessions, but when he does, his parents pick up their violins and practice along with him. They believe that if Michael proves to be extraordinarily talented, he will be poised to make his debut as a teenager. Based on her experience, Mrs. Y. feels strongly that although it is hard to tell at this stage whether Michael is indeed truly talented, without this intensive investment in Michael's early potential there will be little chance for him to perform as a violin soloist in the world's finest concert halls.

Question: How much time and effort should be invested in potential talent before adolescence? What are the effects of these efforts on general development?

Maggie and her mother just moved from New York City to a lovely semi-rural community to start a new life after a nasty divorce. Ten-year-old Maggie requested ballet lessons, so she was enrolled in a local ballet school. The teacher noted after just a few sessions that Maggie was far too talented to be served well by the limited offerings of her school and suggested she attend the regional ballet preparatory program. Maggie's mother drove her 90 miles each way several times a week to the regional center. One year later, the center director suggested that Maggie had sufficient talent to audition for the nation's premier ballet company in New York City.

Question: How much should parents sacrifice for their children's talent development? What are the costs of great parental investment to the family system and to other family members?

About the Cases

Each case study raises questions about the desirability of intensive early talent development. Both the child's personality and the family environment play central roles in how (or whether) early talent unfolds. The parents of Lyle and Michael hold the values and the cultural capital to commit unambiguously to all-out efforts to develop their children's gifts. From the brief case study, it seems that Lyle's personal drive and love of mathematics have been supported by his parents' willingness to supply him with time, resources, and transportation. Lyle's parents' values for independence and unconventionality fit the findings from family-environment studies of eminent individuals. Lyle also receives substantial reinforcement from educational settings and mentors, including those to which his parents have connected him (mesosystems). In Michael's case, his family made the decision to invest in musical education before any particular evidence of desire or talent appeared. Each boy's immediate environment (microsystem) reflects his parents' backgrounds, values, and expertise (exosystems). Both families clearly believe that concentrated talent development and being different from peers are perfectly consonant with a happy life.

The cases of Alex and Maggie illustrate microsystems that are less supportive of maximal talent development. The values of Alex's parents and the resources of Maggie's mother do not necessarily favor sacrificing well-roundedness or family life-style for the chance of future eminence. The exosystem of American education does not provide students like Alex and Maggie with automatic, affordable mathematics or dance training at the highest levels. Left for the family to support, such intensive talent development also contradicts macrosystem American ideologies about child rearing and the nature of happiness. Being well-rounded, "normal," socially integrated, and family-oriented takes precedence over sacrifice, solitary endeavor, individualized education, and emphasis on a particular family member.

These four individuals illustrate how interacting environments serve to determine whether childhood gifts progress to adult eminence. Direct interactions of personality, family, school, and peers determine whether a talented child delves into his or her domain. Individual decisions about such talent development, however, are nested in broader environments that ultimately affect the opportunities and values surrounding the school and family.

CHALLENGE FOR OUR FIELD

Given the ambivalence of our culture and schools about the desirability of intensive talent development, how can educators support gifted children and their families? Let us end with a challenge to researchers in our field:

Question: Is a chance at greatness worth the price of failure?

We believe that intensive talent development is extraordinarily worthwhile for both the individual and society. Research on talent and eminence consistently shows that the pleasures of engaging in high-level talent expression (Csikszentimihalyi et al., 1993) along with public recognition and identity as a high achiever (Bloom, 1985; Subotnik & Arnold, 1995) offer ample compensation for the rigors of talent development. Competition and critical analysis of creative work do not elicit a turning away from the pursuit of talent development. In fact, feedback and comparisons with others are essential to outstanding performance and creative productivity. Serious devotees of a talent domain learn to endure occasional failure and to distinguish derogatory comments about one's work from personal attacks.

We strongly support intensive engagement in a talent domain and look to environmental theory as a guiding force for intervention. Returning to the discussion on family that appears earlier in this chapter, we can draw some parallels with how educators might bolster children's psychological strength when it comes to competition or bucking the tide of conventionality. Educators can work with families to examine negative assumptions about talent engagement, provide cultural capital resources in the form of tacit knowledge and connections, and reduce financial and other barriers to top-level training. At the macrosystem level, we need to continue working for equal opportunity for talented people from underrepresented groups.

Playing it safe with a career or interest should be encouraged if it protects a young person in physical danger or if it leaves open other future paths of creative or intellectual development. Otherwise, there is much to be learned in the deep and persistent pursuit of a goal. In earlier times, women and people of color could not pursue their ambitions. Being condemned to speculate whether one could have been "a contender" is a sad way to live, whether imposed by racism, sexism, or well-meaning protectiveness.

We must redefine the meaning of happiness for individuals with great talent. Too often we operate under the impression that conventional conceptions of happiness are universal in their appeal. Imposing this value on individuals with a drive to excel or create makes their lives more difficult. Understanding and supporting that drive, especially when it is constructive in result and does not impede mental and physical health, can go a long way toward supporting our most talented youth.

References

Achter, J., Lubinski, D., & Benbow, C. (1996). Multipotentiality among the gifted: "It was never there in the first place and already it's vanishing." *Journal of Counseling Psychology, 43*(1), 65–76.

ACORN. (1996). *Secret apartheid.* Available on the World Wide Web, http://www.acorn.org/ACORNarchives/studies/secretapartheid/index.html.

Albert, R. S. (1978). Observation and suggestions regarding giftedness, familial influence and the achievement of eminence. *Gifted Child Quarterly, 28*(2), 201–211.

Albert, R. S. (1980). Family positions and the attainment of eminence: A study of special family positions and special family experiences. *Gifted Child Quarterly, 24*(2), 87–95.

Albert, R. S. (Ed). (1983). *Genius and eminence: The social psychology of creativity and exceptional achievement.* New York: Pergamon Press.

Albert R. S. (1994). The achievement of eminence: A longitudinal study of exceptionally gifted boys and their families. In R. F. Subotnik & K. D. Arnold (Eds.), *Beyond Terman: Contemporary longitudinal studies of giftedness and talent* (pp. 282–315). Norwood, NJ: Ablex.

Altbach, P. G., Kelly, G. P., Petrie, H. G., & Weis, L. (1991). *Textbooks in American society.* Albany: State University of New York Press.

Altizer, T. J. J. (1967). *Toward a new Christianity: Readings in the death of God theology.* New York: Harcourt, Brace & World.

Amabile, T. M. (1979). Effects of external evaluation on artistic creativity. *Journal of Personality and Social Psychology, 37,* 221–233.

Amabile, T. M. (1996). *Creativity in context: Update to the social psychology of creativity.* Boulder, CO: Westview.

Amabile, T. M., & Tighe, E. (1993). Questions of creativity. In J. Brockman (Ed.), *Creativity* (pp. 7–27). New York: Simon & Schuster.

Ambrose, D. (1998). A model for clarification and expansion of conceptual foundations. *Gifted Child Quarterly, 42*(2), 77–86.

Ambrose, D. (2000). World view entrapment: Moral-ethical implications for gifted education. *Journal for the Education of the Gifted, 23*(2), 159–186.

Ambrose, D., Cohen, L. & Coleman, L. (Eds.). (1999). [Special issue]. *Journal for the Education of the Gifted, 22*(4), 321–419.

American Psychological Association. (1997, November). *Learner-centered psychological principles: A framework for school reform and redesign.* Prepared by the Learner-Centered Principles Work Group of the American Psychological Association's Board of Educational Affairs, Retrieved January 30, 2002. Available on the World Wide Web, http://www.apa.org/ed/lcp2/homepage.html.

Anderson, H. H. (1958). Preface. In H. H. Anderson (Ed.), *Creativity and its cultivation* (pp. ix xiii). New York· Harper & Row.

Anderson, J. R., Reder, L. M., & Simon, H. A. (1996). Situated learning and education. *Educational Researcher, 25*, 5–11.

Archambault, F. X., Westberg, K. L., Brown, S. W., Hallmark, B. W., Zhang, W., & Emmons, C. (1993). Classroom practices used with gifted third and fourth grade students. *Journal for the Education of the Gifted, 16*, 103–119.

Arellano, A. R., & Padilla, A. M. (1996). Academic invulnerability among a select group of Latino university students. *Hispanic Journal of Behavioral Sciences, 18*(4), 485–507.

Armenta, C. (1999). A shift to identity: A journey to integrity in gifted education. *Journal for the Education of the Gifted, 22*(4), 384–401.

Arnold, K. D. (1995). *Lives of promise: What becomes of high school valedictorians.* San Francisco: Jossey-Bass.

Arnold, K. D., Noble, K. D., & Subotnik, R. F. (1996). *Remarkable women: Perspectives on female talent development.* Cresskill, NJ: Hampton Press.

Arnold, K. D., & Subotnik, R. F. (1994). Lessons from contemporary longitudinal studies. In R. F. Subotnik & K. D. Arnold (Eds.), *Beyond Terman: Contemporary longitudinal studies of giftedness and talent* (pp. 2–51). Norwood, NJ: Ablex.

Arnold, K. D., Youn, T. I. K., & Salkever, K. (1999). *Comparing lives of leaders: Effects of baccalaureate experience on inequalities of privilege and power.* Paper presented at the annual meeting of the Association for the Study of Higher Education, San Antonio, TX.

Arthur, W. B. (1989, November). Competing technologies, increasing returns, and lock-in by historical events. *The Economic Journal, 99*, 116–131.

Arthur, W. B. (1990). Positive feedbacks in the economy. *Scientific American*, 92–99.

Ausubel, D., & Robinson, F. (1969). *School learning.* New York: Holt, Rinehart & Winston.

Ayers, W. & Ford, P. (Eds.). (1996). *City kids, city teachers: Reports from the Front Row.* New York: The New Press.

Baker, E. L., O'Neil, Jr., H. F., & Linn, R. L. (1994). Policy and validity prospects for performance-based assessment. *Journal for the Education of the Gifted, 17*(4), 332–353.

Baker, E. L., & Schacter, J. (1996). Expert benchmarks for student academic performance: The case for gifted children. *Gifted Child Quarterly, 40*(2), 61–65.

Baldwin, A. (1985). Programs for the gifted and talented: Issues concerning minority populations. In F. Horowitz & M. O'Brien (Eds.), *The gifted and talented: Developmental perspectives* (pp. 223–250). Washington, DC: American Psychological Association.

Bamberger, J. (1991). *The mind behind the musical ear.* Cambridge: Harvard University Press.

Banks, J. A. (1992). African American scholarship and the evolution of multicultural education. *Journal of Negro Education, 61*(3), 273–286.

Banks, J. A. (1995a). Multicultural education and the modification of students' racial attitudes. In W. D. Hawley & A. W. Jackson (Eds.), *Toward a common destiny: Improving race and ethnic relations in America* (pp. 315–339). San Francisco: Jossey-Bass.

Banks, J. A. (1995b). Multicultural education: Historical development, dimensions, and practice. In J. A. Banks & C. A. M. Banks (Eds.), *Handbook of research on multicultural education* (pp. 3–24). New York: Macmillan.

Banks, J. A., & Banks, C. A. M. (Eds.). (1995). *Handbook of research on multicultural education*. New York: Macmillan.

Baptiste, Jr., H. P. (1995). *Definition of multicultural education*. Proposed comprehensive remedial plan and order for Rockford School District, Rockford, IL.

Barber, C., Bledsoe, T., Pequin, L., & Montgomery, D. (1999, March). *Increasing Native American involvement in gifted programs through authentic discovery and rural linkages*. Paper presented at the annual meeting of the American Council on Rural Special Education, Albuquerque, NM. (ERIC Document Reproduction Service No. ED 429 749)

Barron, B. J. S., Schwartz, D. L., Vye, N. J., Moore, A., Petrosino, A., Zech, L., Bransford, J. D., & The Cognition and Technology Group at Vanderbilt. (1998). Doing with understanding: Lessons from research on problem- and project-based learning. *The Journal of the Learning Sciences, 7*, 271–312.

Baum, S. M., Owen, S. V., & Oreck, B. A. (1996). Talent beyond words: Identification of potential talent in dance and music in elementary students. *Gifted Child Quarterly 40*(2), 93–101.

Bellah, R. N., Madsen, R., Sullivan, W. M., & Tipton, S. M. (1985). *Habits of the heart: Individualism and commitment in American life*. Berkeley: University of California Press.

Benard, B. (1994). Fostering resiliency in kids. *Educational Leadership, 51*(3), 44–48.

Benbow, C. P. (1986). SMPY's model for teaching mathematically precocious students. In J. S. Renzulli (Ed.), *Systems and models for developing programs for the gifted and talented* (pp. 1–26). Mansfield Center, CT: Creative Learning Press.

Benbow, C. P. (1997). Intellectually talented children: How can we best meet their needs? In N. Colangelo & G. Davis (Eds.), *Handbook of gifted education* (2nd ed.). (pp. 155–169). Boston: Allyn & Bacon.

Benbow, C. P. (1998). Acceleration as a method for meeting the academic needs of intellectually talented children. In J. VanTassel-Baska (Ed.), *Excellence in educating the gifted* (3rd ed.) (pp. 279–294). Denver, CO: Love.

Bentham, J. (1843). *Collected works* (J. Bowring, Ed.). London: University of London.

Bereiter, C., & Scardamalia, M. (1993). *Surpassing ourselves, An inquiry into the nature and implications of expertise*. Chicago: Open Court.

Berlin, I. (1990). *The crooked timber of humanity Chapters in the history of ideas* (H. Hardy, Ed.). Princeton, NJ: Princeton University Press.

Bernstein, H. T. (1985). The new politics of textbook adoption. *Phi Delta Kappan, 66*, 463–466.

Berry, J. W. (1969). On cross-cultural comparability. *International Journal of Psychology, 4*, 119–128.

Berry, W. (1990a). *Unsettling America* (3rd ed.). San Francisco: Sierra Club Books. (Original work published 1978)

Berry, W. (1990b). *What are people for?* San Francisco: North Point Press.

Binet, A., & Simon, T. (1905). The development of intelligence in children. *L'Annee Psychologique, 11,* 191–244. (Published in book form, E. S. Kit, Trans., Baltimore, MD: Williams & Wilkins, 1916.)

Bland, L. C., Sowa, C. J., & Callahan, C. M. (1994). An overview of resilience in gifted children. *Roeper Review, 17*(2), 77–80,

Bloom, B. S. (Ed.). (1985). *Developing talent in young people.* New York: Ballantine Books.

Borko, H., Mayfield, V., Marion, S., Flexer, R., & Cumbo, K. (1997). Teachers? developing ideas and practices about mathematics performance assessment: Successes, stumbling blocks, and implications for professional development. *Teaching and Teacher Education, 13,* 259–278.

Borland, J. H. (1986). IQ tests: Throwing out the bathwater, saving the baby. *Roeper Review, 8*(3), 163–167.

Borland, J. H. (1989). *Planning and implementing programs for the gifted.* New York: Teachers College Press.

Borland, J. H. (1996a). Gifted education and the threat of irrelevance. *Journal for the Education of the Gifted, 19,* 129–147.

Borland, J. H. (1996b). [Review of *Playing Favorites* by Mara Sapon-Shevin]. *Roeper Review, 18,* 309–311.

Borland, J. H. (1997a). Evaluating gifted programs. In N. Colangelo & G. Davis (Eds.), *Handbook of gifted education* (2nd ed.) (pp. 253–266). Boston: Allyn & Bacon.

Borland, J. H. (1997b). The construct of giftedness. *Peabody Journal of Education, 7,* 6–20.

Borland, J. H. (1999). The limits of consilience: A reaction to Françoys Gagné's "My convictions about the nature of abilities, gifted, and talents." *Journal for the Education of the Gifted, 22,* 137–147.

Borland, J. H., & Wright, L. (1994). Identifying young, potentially gifted, economically disadvantaged students. *Gifted Child Quarterly, 38,* 164–171.

Borland, J. H., & Wright, L. (2001). Identifying and educating poor and under-represented gifted students. In K. A. Heller, F. J. Mönks, R. J. Sternberg, & R. F. Subotnik (Eds.), *International handbook of research and development of giftedness and talent* (pp. 587–594). Oxford, UK: Pergamon Press.

Bourdieu, P. (1977). Cultural reproduction and social reproduction. In J. Karabel & A. H. Halsey (Eds.), *Power and ideology in education* (pp. 487–511). New York: Oxford University Press.

Boyce, L. N., VanTassel-Baska, J., Burruss, J. D., Sher, B. T., & Johnson, D. T. (1997). A problem-based curriculum: Parallel learning opportunities for students and teachers. *Journal for the Education of the Gifted, 20,* 363–379.

Boyer, J. B., & Baptiste, Jr., H. P. (1996). *Transforming the curriculum for multicultural understandings: A practitioner's handbook.* San Francisco: Caddo Gap Press.

Brandwein, P. F. (1981). *Memorandum: On reviewing schooling and education.* New York: Harcourt, Brace and Jovanovich.

Bringuier, J. C. (1980). *Conversations with Jean Piaget*. Chicago: University of Chicago Press.

Bronfenbrenner, U. (1977). Toward an experimental ecology of human development. *American Psychologist, 32*, 515–531.

Bronfenbrenner, U. (1979). *The ecology of human development*. Cambridge: Harvard University Press.

Bronfenbrenner, U. (1993). The ecology of cognitive development: Research models and fugitive findings. In R. H. Wozniak & K. Fischer (Eds.), *Scientific environments* (pp. 3–44). Hillsdale, NJ: Erlbaum.

Brown, J. S., Collins, A., & Duguid, P. (1989). Situated cognition and the culture of learning. *Educational Researcher, 18*(1), 32–42.

Brown v. Board of Education of Topeka, Kansas. (1954). 347 U.S. 483.

Bruner, J. (1972). The nature and uses of immaturity. *American Psychologist, 27*, 1–22.

Bugental, J. F. T. (1989). Foreword. In R. S. Valle & S. Halling, *Existential-phenomenological perspectives in psychology: Exploring the breadth of human experience* (pp. ix–xi). New York: Plenum Press.

Burnette, E. (1997, June). Talking openly about race thwarts racism in children. *APA Monitor*, p. 33.

Butts, R. F., & Cremin, L. A. (1953). *A history of education in American culture*. New York: Holt.

Cain, K. M., & Dweck, C. S. (1989). The development of children's conceptions of intelligence: A theoretical framework. In R. J. Sternberg (Ed.), *Advances in the psychology of human development* (Vol. 5, pp. 47–82). Hillsdale, NJ: Lawrence Erlbaum Associates.

Cairns, R. B., Elder, G. H., & Costello, E. J. (Eds.). (1996). *Developmental science*. New York: Cambridge University Press.

Callahan, C. M. (1996). A critical self-study of gifted education: Healthy practice, necessary evil or sedition? *Journal for the Education of the Gifted. 19*(2), 148–163.

Campbell, D. T., & Stanley, J. C. (1963). *Experimental and quasi-experimental designs for research*. Chicago: Rand McNally.

Carroll, J. B. (1993). *Human cognitive abilities: A survey of factor-analytic studies*. New York: Cambridge University Press.

Case, R. (1991). *The mind's staircase*. Hillsdale, NJ: Lawrence Erlbaum Associates.

Cattell, R. B. (1963). Theory of fluid and crystallized intelligence: A critical experiment. *Journal of Educational Psychology, 54*, 1–22.

Chall, J. S., & Conard, S. S. (1991). *Should textbooks challenge students?: The case for easier or harder textbooks*. New York: Teachers College Press.

Chandler, D. (2001). *Semiotics for beginners*. Available on the World Wide Web, http://www.aber.ac.uk/media/ Documents/S4B/sem02a.html.

Chang, D., and Sugarman, R. (1997, March 23). Test scores split up twins. *New York Daily News*, p. 6.

Charlton, J. C., Marolf, D., & Stanley, J. C. (1994). Follow-up insights on rapid educational acceleration. *Roeper Review, 17*, 123–130.

Chevalier, M. (1995). Maintaining an ethnic identity in school: A folkloric perspective. *Equity & Excellence in Education, 28*(2), 26–35.

Chi, M. T. H., Glaser, R., & Farr, M. (Eds.). (1988). *The nature of expertise*. Hillsdale, NJ: Erlbaum.

Christian, D., & Wolfram, W. (1979). *Exploring dialects*. Arlington, VA: Center for Applied Linguistics

Christopherson, S. L. (1981). Developmental placement in the regular school program. *G/C/T, 19*, 40–41.

Clapham, M. (1997). Ideational skills training: A key element in creative training programs. *Creativity Research Journal, 10*, 33–44.

Clark, G., & Zimmerman, E. (1992). *Issues and practices related to identification of gifted and talented students in the visual arts*. Storrs, CT: The National Research Center on the Gifted and Talented.

Clark, G., & Zimmerman, E. (1994). *Programming opportunities for talented in the visual arts students*. Storrs, CT: The National Research Center on the Gifted and Talented.

Clark, G., & Zimmerman. E. (1995). You can't just scribble: Art talent development. *The Educational Forum, 59*(4), 400–408.

Clark, G., & Zimmerman, E. (1998). Nurturing the arts in programs for the gifted and talented. *Phi Delta Kappan. 79*(10), 747–751.

Clausen, J. A. (1993). *American lives: Looking back at the children of the Great Depression*. New York: Free Press.

Cleary, T. A., Humphreys, L. G., Kendrick, S. A., & Wesman, A. (1975). Educational uses of tests with disadvantaged students. *American Psychologist, 3*, 15–41.

Clune, W. H. (1993). Systemic educational policy: A conceptual framework. In S. H. Fuhrman (Ed.), *Designing coherent education policy: Improving the system* (pp. 125–140). San Francisco: Jossey-Bass.

Cohen, D., & Hill, H. (1998). *Instructional policy and classroom performance: The mathematics reform in California* (Research Report No. RR-39). Philadelphia: University of Pennsylvania, Consortium for Policy Research in Education.

Cohen, L. (1988). To get ahead, get a theory. *Roeper Review, 11*, 95–99.

Colangelo, N., & Brower, P. (1987a). Gifted youngsters and their siblings: Long term impacts of labeling on their academic and personal self concepts. *Roeper Review, 10*(2), 101–103.

Colangelo, N., & Brower, P. (1987b). Labeling gifted youngsters: Long term impact on families. *Gifted Child Quarterly, 31*(2), 75–78.

Cole, M., & Bruner, J. S. (1971). Cultural differences and inferences about psychological processes. *American Psychologist, 26*(10), 867–876.

Coleman, E. B., & Shore, B. (1991). Problem-solving processes of high and average performers in physics. *Journal for the Education of the Gifted, 14*(4), 366–379.

Coleman, L. J. (1997). Studying ordinary events in a field devoted to the extraordinary. *Peabody Journal of Education, 72*(3 & 4), 117–132.

Coleman, L. J. (Ed.). (1999). [Special issue]. *Journal for the Education of the Gifted, 23*(1).

Coleman, L. J. (2001). "A Rag Quilt": Social relationship among students in a special high school. *Gifted Child Quaterly, 45*, 164–173.

Coleman, L. J., & Cross, T. L. (1988). Is being gifted a social handicap? *Journal for the Education of the Gifted, 11*, 41–56.

Coleman, L. J., & Cross, T. L. (2001). *Being gifted in school: An introduction to development, guidance, and teaching*. Waco, TX: Prufrock Press.

Coleman, L. J., Sanders, M. D., & Cross, T. C. (1997). Perennial debates and tacit assumption in the education of gifted children. *Gifted Child Quarterly, 41*(3), 44–50.

Conklin, A. M. (1940). *Failure of highly intelligent pupils: A study of their behavior*. New York: Teachers College Press.

Cooper, C. R. (1998). For the good of humankind: Matching the budding talent with a curriculum of conscience. *Gifted Child Quarterly, 42*, 238–244.

Cornell, D. G., Delcourt, M. A. B., Goldberg, M. D., & Bland, L. C. (1995). Achievement and self-concept of minority students in elementary school gifted programs. *Journal for the Education of the Gifted, 18*(2), 189–209.

Cox, J., Daniel, N., and Boston, B. (1985). *Educating able learners: Programs and promising practices*. Austin: University of Texas Press.

Cowen, E. L., Wyman, P. A., Work, W. C., & Iker, M. R. (1995). A preventive intervention for enhancing resilience among highly stressed urban children. *The Journal of Primary Prevention, 15*(3), 247–260.

CQ Researcher. (1997). Educating Gifted Students. 7(12).

Cramond, B., Martin, C. E., & Shaw, E. L. (1990). Generalizability of creative problem solving procedures to real-life problems. *Journal for the Education of the Gifted, 13*, 141–155.

Critical Appraisals of Gifted Education. (1996). [Special issue]. *Journal for the Education of the Gifted, 19*(2).

Cross, T. L. (1990). Making research in education meaningful: Existential phenomenology and a critique of the politics of methodology. *Journal of Humanistic Education, 14*(1), 98–101.

Cross, T. L. (1994). Alternative inquiry and its contributions to gifted education: A commentary. *Roeper Review, 16*(4), 284–285.

Csikszentmihalyi, M. (1988). Society, culture, and person: A systems view of creativity. In R. Sternberg (Ed.), *The nature of creativity* (pp. 325–339). New York: Cambridge University Press.

Csikszentmihalyi, M. (1990). *Flow: The psychology of optimal experience*. New York: HarperCollins.

Csikszentmihalyi, M. (1993). *The evolving self*. New York: HarperCollins.

Csikszentmihalyi, M. (1996). *Creativity: Flow and the psychology of discovery and invention*. New York: Harperperennial.

Csikszentmihalyi, M. (1997). *Creativity*. New York: HarperCollins.

Csikszentmihalyi, M., & Beattie, O. (1979). Life themes: A theoretical and empirical exploration of their origins and effects. *Journal of Humanistic Psychology, 19*, (1), 45–63.

Csikszentmihalyi, M., & Rathunde, K. (1997). The psychology of wisdom: An evolutionary interpretation. In R. J. Sternberg (Ed.), *Wisdom: Its nature, origins, and development* (pp. 25–51). Cambridge, UK: Cambridge University Press.

Csikszentmihalyi, M., Rathunde, K., & Whalen, S. (1993). *Talented teenagers*. New York: Cambridge University Press.

Dacquel, L., & Dahmann, D. (1993). *Residents of farms and rural areas: 1991* (Current Population Reports, pp. 20–472). Washington, DC: Bureau of the Census.

Darling-Hammond, L. (1997). *The right to learn: A blueprint for creating schools that work.* San Francisco: Jossey-Bass.

Davidson, L., & Scripp, L. (1994). Conditions of giftedness: Musical development in the preschool and early elementary years. In R. F. Subotnik & K. D. Arnold (Eds.), *Beyond Terman: Contemporary longitudinal studies of giftedness and talent* (pp. 155–185). Norwood, NJ: Ablex.

DeBono, E. (1992). *Serious creativity: Using the power of lateral thinking to create new ideas.* New York: HarperBusiness.

DeHaan, R. F., & Kough, J. (1956). *Identifying students with special needs.* Chicago: Science Research Associates.

Delcourt, M. A. B., Loyd, B. H., Cornell, D. G., & Goldberg, M. D. (1994). Evaluation of the effects of programming arrangements on student learning outcomes. Charlottesville, VA: The National Research Center on the Gifted and Talented.

Delisle, J. (1998). Zen and the art of gifted child education. *Gifted Child Today, 21*(3), 38–39.

Delpit, L. D. (1988). The silenced dialogue: Power and pedagogy in educating other people's children. *Harvard Educational Review, 58*(3), 280–298.

Derber, C. (1995). The politics of triage: The contract with America's surplus populations. *Tikkun, 10*(3), 37–43, 86–88.

DeYoung, A., & Lawrence, B. K. (1995). On Hoosiers, Yankees, and mountaineers. *Phi Delta Kappan, 77*(2), 104–112.

DeYoung, A., & Theobald, P. (1991). Community schools in the national context: The social and cultural impact of educational reform movements on American rural schools. *Journal of Research in Rural Education, 7*(3), 3–14.

DiMaggio, P. (1982). Cultural capital and school success: The impact of status culture participation on the grades of U.S. high school students. *American Sociological Review, 47*, 189–201.

Duncan, C. (1999). *Worlds apart: Why poverty persists in rural America.* New Haven, CT: Yale University Press.

Elder, G. H. (1974). *Children of the Great Depression: Social change in life experience.* Chicago: University of Chicago Press.

Ericsson, K. A. (1987). Theoretical implications from protocol analysis on testing and measurement. In R. R. Ronning, J. A. Glover, J. C. Conoley, & J. C. Witt (Eds.), *The influence of cognitive psychology on testing* (pp. 191–226). Hillsdale, NJ: Erlbaum.

Ericsson, K. A. (1996). The acquisition of expert performance: An introduction to some of the issues. In K.A. Ericsson (Ed.), *The road to excellence: The acquisition of expert performance in the arts, sciences, sports, and games* (pp. 1–52). Mahwah, NJ: Erlbaum.

Eriksson, G. I. (1990). Choice and perception of control: The effect of a thinking skills program on the locus of control, self-concept and creativity of gifted students. *Gifted Education International, 6*, 135–142.

Europa World Year Book: Vol. 2 (40th ed.). (1999). London: Europa.

Fasold, R. (1990). *The sociolinguistics of language*. Cambridge: Blackwell.

Feagin, J. R., & Sikes, M. P. (1994). *Living with racism: The Black middle-class experience*. Boston: Beacon.

Feldhusen, J. F. (1992a). From the editor: Talent identification and development in education. *Gifted Child Quarterly, 36*, 123.

Feldhusen, J. F. (1992b). *Talent identification and development in education (TIDE)*. Sarasota, FL: Center for Creative Learning.

Feldhusen, J. F. (1995). *Talent identification and development in education (TIDE)* (2nd ed.) Sarasota, FL: Center for Creative Learning.

Feldhusen, J. F. (1997). Secondary services, opportunities, and activities for talented youth. In N. Colangelo & G. A. Davis (Eds.), *Handbook of gifted education* (pp. 547–552). Boston: Allyn & Bacon.

Feldhusen, J. F. (1998). Strategies and methods for teaching the talented. In J. Van-Tassel-Baska, *Excellence in educating gifted and talented learners* (3rd ed.) (pp. 363–379). Denver: Love Publishing Co.

Feldhusen, J. F., Hoover, S. M., & Sayler, M. F. (1990). *Tide: Identification and education of the gifted and talented at the secondary level*. New York: Trillium Press.

Feldhusen, J. F., Jarwan, F, & Holt, D. (1993). Assessment tools for counselors. In L. K. Silverman (Ed.), *Counseling the gifted and talented* (pp. 239–259). Denver: Love Publishing Co.

Feldhusen, J. F., & Kolloff, P. B. (1986). The Purdue three-stage enrichment model for gifted education at the elementary level. In J. S. Renzulli (Ed.), *Systems and models for developing programs for the gifted and talented* (pp. 126–152). Mansfield Center, CT: Creative Learning Press.

Feldhusen, J. F., & Wood, B. K. (1997). Developing growth plans for gifted students. *Gifted Child Today, 20*(6), 24–26, & 48–49.

Feldhusen, J. F., Wood, B. K., & Dai, D. Y. (1997). Gifted students perceptions of their talents. *Gifted and Talented International, 12*(1), 42–45.

Feldman, D. H. (1974). Universal to unique: a developmental view of creativity and education. In S. Rosner & L. Abt (Eds.), *Essays in creativity* (pp. 45–85). Croton-on-Hudson, NY: North River Press.

Feldman, D. H. (1976). The child as craftsman. *Phi Delta Kappan, 56*, 143–149.

Feldman, D. H. (1986). How development works. In I. Levin (Ed.), *Stage and structure: Reopening the debate* (pp. 284–306). Norwood, NJ: Ablex.

Feldman, D. H. (with Goldsmith, L. T.). (1991). *Nature's gambit: Child prodigies and the development of human potential*. New York: Teachers College Press (Original work published 1986)

Feldman, D. H. (1992). Has there been a paradigm shift in gifted education? In N. Colangelo, S. Assouline, & D. Ambroson (Eds.), *Talent development: proceedings from the 1991 Henry B. and Jocelyn Wallace National Research Symposium on Talent Development* (pp. 89–94). Unionville, NY: Trillium Press.

Feldman, D. H. (1993a). Child prodigies: A distinctive form of giftedness. *Gifted Child Quarterly, 37*, 188–193.

Feldman, D. H. (1993b). Cultural organisms in the development of great potential: Referees, termites, and the Aspen Music Festival. In R. Wozniak & K. W.

Fischer (Eds.), *Development in context: Acting and thinking in specific environments* (pp. 225–251). Hillsdale, NJ: Erlbaum.

Feldman, D. H. (1994a). *Beyond universals in cognitive development.* (2nd ed.). Norwood, NJ: Ablex.

Feldman, D. H. (1994b). Creativity: Dreams, insights, and transformations. In D. H. Feldman, M. Csikszentmihalyi, & H. Gardner (Eds.), *Changing the world: A framework for the study of creativity* (pp. 85–102). Westport, CT: Praeger.

Feldman, D. H. (1994c). Mozart and the transformational imperative. In J. Morris (Ed.), *On Mozart* (pp. 52–71). New York: Cambridge University Press.

Feldman, D. H. (1995). Learning and development in nonuniversal theory. *Human Development, 38,* 315–321.

Feldman, D. H. (1999). A developmental, evolutionary perspective on gifts and talents. *Journal for the Education of the Gifted, 22,* 159–167.

Feldman, D. H. (2000). Developmental theory and the expression of gifts and talents. In C. Van Lieshout &.P. Heymans (Eds.), *Talent, resilience, and wisdom across the life span: A festschrift for Franz Monks.* East Sussex, UK: Psychology Press.

Feldman, D. H. (In press). Piaget's stages revisited and (somewhat) revised. *New Ideas in Psychology.*

Feldman, D. H., & Fowler, R. C. (1998). The nature(s) of developmental change: Piaget, Vygotsky, and the transition process. *New Ideas in Psychology, 15,* 195–210.

Feldman, D. H., Csikszentmihalyi, M., & Gardner, H. (1994). *Changing the world: A framework for the study of creativity.* Westport, CT: Greenwood/Praeger.

Fiene, J. I. (1993). *The social reality of a group of rural, low-status, Appalachian women: A grounded theory study.* New York: Garland.

Fitzpatrick, J. L. (1978). Academic underachievement, other-direction, and attitude toward women's roles in bright adolescent females. *Journal of Educational Psychology, 70,* 645–650.

Flanders, J. R. (1987). How much of the content in mathematics textbooks is new? *Arithmetic Teacher, 35,* 18–23.

Fontenot, N. A. (1993). Effects of training in creativity and creative problem finding upon business people. *The Journal of Social Psychology, 133,* 11–22.

Ford, D. Y. (1994). Nurturing resilience in gifted Black youth. *Roeper Review, 17*(2), 80–85.

Ford, D. Y. (1994/1995). Underachievement among gifted and non-gifted Black females. *Journal of Secondary Gifted Education, 6,* 165–175.

Ford, D. Y. (1996). *Reversing underachievement among gifted Black students.* New York: Teachers College Press.

Ford, D. Y. (1998). *A study of factors affecting the recruitment and retention of minority teachers in gifted education.* Storrs, CT: National Research Center on the Gifted and Talented.

Ford, D. Y., Grantham, T. C., & Harris III, J. J. (1997). The recruitment and retention of minority teachers in gifted education. *Roeper Review, 19*(4), 213–220.

Ford, D. Y., & Harris, J. J. (1992). The elusive definition of creativity. *Journal of Creative Behavior, 26,* 186–198.

Ford, D. Y., & Harris III, J. J. (1999). *Multicultural gifted education*. New York: Teachers College Press.

Ford, D. Y. & Harris III, J. J. (2000). A framework for infusing multicultural curriculum into gifted education. *Roeper Review, 23*(1), 4–9.

Ford, D. Y., Howard, T. C., & Harris III, J. J. (1999, July/August). Using multicultural literature in gifted education classrooms. *Gifted Child Today*, pp. 14–21.

Foucault, M. (1984). The means of correct training. In P. Rabinow (Ed.), *The Foucault reader* (pp. 188–205). New York: Random House.

Foucault, M. (1995). *Discipline and punish: The birth of the prison* (A. Sheridan, Trans.). New York: Vintage. (Original work published 1975)

Fowler, W. (1992, March). *The influence of early language stimulation on the short and long term development of abilities*. Paper presented at the Esther Katz Rosen Symposium, Lawrence, Kansas.

Fradd, S. H., & Lee, O. (1999). Teachers' roles in promoting science inquiry with students from diverse language backgrounds. *Educational Researcher, 28*(6), 14–20.

Frankl, V. E. (1984). *Man's search for meaning*. New York: Washington Square Press.

Franklin, B. M. (1987). The first crusade for learning disabilities: The movement for the education of backward children. In T. Popkewitz (Ed.), *The formation of school subjects: the struggle for creating an American institution* (pp. 190–209). London: Falmer Press.

Frasier, M. (1989). The identification of gifted black students: Developing new perspectives. In J. Maker (Ed.), *Critical issues in gifted education: Defensible programs for cultural and ethnic minorities* (pp. 213–225). Austin, TX: PRO-ED.

Frasier, M. M. (1997). Gifted minority students: Reframing approaches to their identification and education. In N. Colangelo and G. Davis (Eds.), *Handbook on gifted education* (pp. 498–515). Needham Heights, MA: Allyn and Bacon.

Freedman, R. L. H. (1994). *Open-ended questioning: A handbook for educators*. Menlo Park, CA: Addison-Wesley Publishing Co.

Frey, C. (1998). Struggling with identity: Working with seventh- and eight-grade gifted girls to air issues of concern. *Journal for the Education of the Gifted, 21*(4), 437–451.

Friedman, R. C., & Rogers, K. B. (1998). *Talent in context: Historical and social perspectives on giftedness*. Washington, DC: American Psychological Association.

Fullan, M., & Stiegelbauer, S. (1991). *The new meaning of educational change*. New York: Teachers College Press.

Fuller, W. E. (1982). *The old country school: The story of rural education in the Middle West*. Chicago: University of Chicago Press.

Gagné, F. (1985). Giftedness and talent: Reexamining a reexamination of the definition. *Gifted Child Quarterly, 29*(3), 103–112.

Gagné, F. (1993). Constructs and models pertaining to exceptional human abilities. In K. A. Heller, F. J. Mönks, & A. H. Passow (Eds.), *International handbook of research and development of giftedness and talent* (pp. 69–87). New York: Pergamon Press.

Gagné, F. (1995a). From giftedness to talent: A developmental model and its impact on the language of the field. *Roeper Review, 18*(2), 103–111.

Gagné, F. (1995b). Hidden meanings of the "talent development" concept. *The Educational Forum, 59,* 350–362.

Gagné, F. (1998). A proposal for subcategories within the gifted or talented populatiuus. *Gifted Child Quartorly, 42,* 87–95

Gagné, F. (1999). My convictions about the nature of abilities, gifts, and talents. *Journal for the Education of the Gifted, 22,* 109–146.

Gallagher, J. J. (1996). A critique of critiques of gifted education. *Journal for the Education of the Gifted, 19,* 234–249.

Gallagher, J. J. (1997). Should public schools devote more resources to special programs for gifted students? Yes. In K. Jost (Ed.), Educating gifted students. *The CQ Researcher, 7*(12), 281.

Gallagher, S. (1999). An exchange of gazes. In J. L. Kinchloe, S. R. Steinberg, & L. E. Villeverde (Eds.), *Rethinking intelligence* (pp. 69–84). New York: Routledge.

Gallagher, S. A., & Stepien, W. J. (1996). Content acquisition in problem-based learning: Depth versus breadth in American studies. *Journal for the Education of the Gifted, 19,* 257–275.

Gallagher, S. A., Stepien, W. J., Sher, B. T., & Workman, D. (1995). Implementing problem-based learning in science classrooms. *School Science and Mathematics, 95,* 136–146.

García, E. (1999). *Student cultural diversity:Understanding and meeting the challenge* (2nd ed.). Boston: Houghton Mifflin.

Gardner, H. (1983). *Frames of mind* (2nd ed.). New York: Basic Books. (Original work published 1983)

Gardner, H. (1993). *Creating minds.* New York: Basic Books.

Gardner, H. (1994). The fruits of asynchrony: A psychological examination of creativity. In D. H. Feldman, M. Csikszentmihalyi, & H. Gardner (Eds.), *Changing the world: A framework for the study of creativity* (pp. 47–68). Westport, CT: Praeger.

Gardner, H. (1995). *Extraordinary minds.* New York: Basic Books.

Gardner, H. (1997). Assessment in context: the alternative to standardized testing. In B. Roff (Ed.), *Multiple intelligences and assessment* (pp. 153–208). Arlington Heights, IL: Skylight.

Gardner, H. (1999). *The disciplined mind.* New York: Simon & Schuster.

Gardner, H., Kornhaber, M., & Wake, W. (1996). *Intelligence: Multiple perspectives.* Fort Worth: Harcourt Brace.

Gardner, H., Walters, J., & Hatch, T. (1992). If teaching had looked beyond the classroom: The development and education of intelligences. *Innotech Journal, 16*(1), 18–35.

Gardner, J. W. (1984). *Excellence: Can we be equal and excellent too?* New York: W. W. Norton and Company. (originally published in 1961)

Gaventa, J. (1980). *Power and powerlessness: Quiescence and rebellion in an Appalachian valley.* Urbana: University of Illinois Press.

Gelman, R. (1978). Cognitive development. *Annual Review of Psychology, 29,* 297–332.

George, W. C., Cohn, S. J., & Stanley, J. C. (1977). *Educating the Gifted: Acceleration and Enrichment. Proceedings of the Ninth Annual Hyman Blumberg Symposium on Research in Early Childhood Education.* Baltimore: Johns Hopkins University Press.

Gersten, R., Brengelman, S., & Jiménez, R. (1994). Effective instruction for culturally and linguistically diverse students: A reconceptualization. *Focus on Exceptional Children, 27*(1), 1–16.

Getzels, J. W., & Csikszentmilhalyi, M. (1976). *The creative vision: A longitudinal study of problem finding in art.* New York: Wiley.

Giele, J. Z. (1993). Women's role change and adaptation 1920–1990. In K. D. Hulbert & D. T. Schuster (Eds.), *Women's lives through time: Educated American women of the twentieth century.* San Francisco: Jossey-Bass.

Giele, J. Z., & Elder, Jr. G. H., (1998). (Eds.). *Methods of life course research.* Thousand Oaks, CA: Sage.

Gilmore, W. J. (1982). *Elementary literacy on the eve of the industrial revolution: Trends in rural New England.* Worcester, MA: American Antiquarian Society.

Ginsburg, H. P. (1997). *Entering the child's mind: The clinical interview in psychological research and practice.* Cambridge, UK: Cambridge University Press.

Ginzburg, N. (1989). *The little virtues.* New York: Arcade.

Giorgi, A. (1970). Psychology as a human science: A phenomenological approach. New York: Harper and Row.

Glaser, B., & Strauss, A. (1967). *The discovery of grounded theory: Strategies for qualitative research.* New York: Aldine de Gruyter.

Global competitiveness ranking. (2000, September 7). *The Singapore Straits Times,* p. 77.

Goddard, H. H. (1919). *Psychology of the normal and the subnormal.* New York: Dodd, Mead and Company.

Goldsmith, L.T., & Feldman, D. H. (1988). Idiots savants—Thinking about remembering: A response to White. *New Ideas in Psychology, 6,* 15–23.

Goleman, D. (1995). *Emotional intelligence.* New York: Bantam Books.

Gonzalez, R., & Padilla, A. M. (1997). The academic resilience of Mexican American high school students. *Hispanic Journal of Behavioral Sciences, 19*(3), 301–317.

Goodlad, J. (1984). *A place called school.* New York: McGraw Hill.

Gorman, M. E., Plucker, J. A., & Callahan, C. M. (1998). Turning students into inventors: Active learning modules for secondary students. *Phi Delta Kappan, 79*(7), 530–535.

Gould, S. J. (1981). *The mismeasure of man.* New York: Norton.

Gowan, J. C. (1955). The underachieving gifted child: A problem for everyone. *Exceptional Children, 22,* 27–249, 270–271.

Grant, B. (1995). The place of achievement in the life of the spirit and the education of gifted students. *Roeper Review, 18*(2), 132–134.

Gray, J. (1996). *Isaiah Berlin.* Princeton, NJ: Princeton University Press.

Gross, M. (1998). Issues in assessing the highly gifted. *Understanding Our Gifted, 10,* 3–8.

Grossman, S. R., & Wiseman, E. E. (1993). Seven operating principles for enhanced creative problem solving training. *Journal of Creative Behavior, 27,* 1–17.

Guba, E. (Ed.). (1990). The paradigm dialogue. Newbury Park, CA: Sage.

Guilford, J. P. (1950). Creativity. *American Psychologist, 5*, 444–454.

Guilford, J. P. (1967). *The nature of human intelligence.* New York: McGraw Hill.

Gundry, S. N. (n.d.). *Death of God theology.* Retrieved June 2, 2000, from the World Wide Web: http://www.mb-soft.com/believe/txn/deathgod.htm.

Guttmann, A. (1987). *Democratic education.* Princeton, NJ: Princeton University Press.

Habermas, J. (1984). *The theory of communicative action* (Vol. 1; T. McCarthy, Trans.). Boston: Beacon Press.

Habermas, J. (1987). *Lifeworld and system: A critique of functionalist reason, the theory of communicative action* (Volume 2, T. McCarthy, trans.). Boston: Beacon Press.

Hall, S. (Ed.) (1997). *Representation: Cultural representations and signifying practices (Culture, media and identities , Vol. 2).* Thousand Oaks, CA: Sage.

Halpern, D. F. (1996). Creative thinking. *Thought and knowledge: An introduction to critical thinking* (3rd ed.). Mahwah, NJ: Lawrence Erlbaum Associates.

Hancock, J., Turbill, J., & Cambourne, B. (1994). Assessment and evaluation of literacy learning. In S. Valencia, E. Hiebert, & P. Afflerback (Eds.), *Authentic reading assessment: Practices and possibilities* (pp. 46–62). Newark, DE: International Reading Association.

Handy, C. (1994). *The empty raincoat.* London: Arrow Books.

Handy, C. (1995). *Waiting for the mountain to move.* London: Arrow Books.

Handy, C. (1998). *The hungry spirit.* London: Arrow Books.

Hansen, J. B., & Feldhusen, J. F. (1994). A comparison of trained and untrained teachers of gifted students. *Gifted Child Quarterly, 38*(3), 115–123.

Haroutounian, J. (1995). Talent identification and development in the arts: An artistic/educational dialogue. *Roeper Review, 18*(2), 112–117.

Harris, C. R. (1993). *Identifying and serving recent immigrant children who are gifted.* (Report No. ED358676). Reston, VA: Clearinghouse on Disabilities and Gifted Education. (ERIC Document Reproduction Service No. ED 358676)

Harris, C. R. (1995). Wing and flame: Ability grouping and the gifted. In K. Ryan & J. Cooper (Eds.), *Kaleidoscope: Readings in Education* (7th ed.) (pp. 301–307). Boston: Houghton Mifflin Co.

Hartley, E. (1991). Through Navajo eyes: Examining differences in giftedness. *Journal of American Indian Education, 31*(1), 53–64.

Hatch, T., & Gardner, H. (1997). If Binet had looked beyond the classroom: The assessment of multiple intelligences. In B. Roff (Ed.), *Multiple intelligences and assessment* (pp. 5–26). Arlington Heights, IL: Skylight.

Hébert, T. P. (1996). Portraits of resilience: The urban life experience of gifted Latino young men. *Roeper Review, 19*(2), 82–90.

Hébert, T. P. (1998). Gifted black males in an urban high school: Factors that influence achievement and underachievement. *Journal for the Education of the Gifted, 22*(4), 385–414.

Heidegger, M. (1927). *Sein und zeit* (1st ed.). Halle: Niemeyer. English translation by John Macquarrie and Edward Robinson as *Being and time.* Blackwell: Oxford, 1962.

Heilbroner, R. (1993). *Twenty-first century capitalism.* New York: Norton.

Heng, M. A. (1998). *Scrutinizing common sense: The role of practical intelligence in intellectual giftedness.* Unpublished doctoral dissertation, Teachers College, Columbia University, New York.

Heng, M. A. (2000). Scrutinizing common sense: The role of practical intelligence in intellectual giftedness. *Gifted Child Quarterly, 44,* 171–182.

Hennessey, B. A., & Amabile, T. M. (1987). *Creativity and learning: What research says to the teacher.* Washington, DC: National Education Association.

Hennessey, B. A., & Amabile, T. M. (1988). The conditions of creativity. In R. J. Sternberg (Ed.), *The nature of creativity: Contemporary psychological perspectives* (pp. 11–38). New York: Cambridge University Press.

Henry, T. S. (1920). *Classroom problems in the education of gifted children. The nineteenth yearbook of the National Society for the Study of Education (Part II).* Chicago: University of Chicago Press.

Herrnstein, R. J., & Murray, C. (1994). *The bell curve: Intelligence and class structure in American life.* New York: Free Press.

Herzog, M. J., & Pittman, R. B. (1995). Home, family, and community: Ingredients in the rural education equation. *Phi Delta Kappan, 77*(2), 113–118.

Higgins, J. M. (1994, November). Training 101: Creating creativity. *Training and Development,* pp. 11–15.

Hilliard, III., A. G. (1991/1992). Why we must pluralize the curriculum. *Educational Leadership, 49*(4), 12–15.

Hobsbawm, E. (1990). *Nations and nationalism since 1780: Programme, myth, reality.* New York: Cambridge University Press.

Hofstadter, D. (1979). Godel, Escher, Bach: An eternal golden braid. New York: Vintage.

Hollingworth, L. (1942). *Children above 180 IQ.* Yonkers-on-Hudson, NY: World Book Company.

Horowitz, F. D. (Ed.). (1989). Children and their development [Special issue]. *American Psychologist, 44.*

Horowitz, F. D., & O'Brien, M. (Eds.), (1986). *The gifted and talented: Developmental perspectives* (pp. 99–123). Washington, DC: American Psychological Association.

Hostetler, J. A., & Huntington, G. E. (1992). *Amish children: Education in the family, school, and community* (2nd ed.). Fort Worth, TX: Harcourt Brace Jovanovich.

Howley, C. B. (1991). The rural education dilemma as part of the rural dilemma: Rural education and economics. In A. DeYoung (Ed.), *Rural education: Issues and practice* (pp. 73–145). New York: Garland.

Howley, C. B. (1996). Sizing up schooling: A West Virginia analysis and critique. *Dissertation Abstracts International*(A), 57(3), 940. (University Microfilms No. AAT 9622575)

Howley, C. B., & Eckman, J. (Eds.). (1996). *Sustainable small schools: A handbook for communities.* Charleston, WV: ERIC Clearinghouse on Rural Education and Small Schools.

Howley, C. B., Harmon, H., & Leopold, G. (1996). Rural scholars or bright rednecks? Aspirations for a sense of place among rural youth in Appalachia. *Journal of Research in Rural Education, 12*(3), 150–160.

Howley, C. B., Howley, A., & Pendarvis, E. D. (1995). *Out of our minds: Anti-intellectualism and talent development in American schooling.* New York: Teachers College Press.

Hunt, E. B. (1997). Nature vs. nurture: The feeling of vuja de. In R. Sternberg & E. Grigorenko (Eds.), *Intelligence, heredity, and environment* (pp. 531–551). New York: Cambridge University Press.

Hurn, C. J. (1993). *The limits and possibilities of schooling. An introduction to the sociology of education.* Boston: Allyn and Bacon.

Husserl, E. (1962). Cartesian meditations (D. Cairns, Trans.). The Hague: Matius Nijhof.

Hutchins, R. M. (1947). *The education we need.* Chicago: Henry Regnery.

Isaksen, S.G., Dorval, K. B., & Treffinger, D. J. (1991). *Creative approaches to problem solving.* Dubuque, IA: Kendall-Hunt Publishers.

Isaksen, S. G., Puccio, G. J., & Treffinger, D. J. (1993). An ecological approach to creativity research: Profiling for creative problem solving. *Journal of Creative Behavior, 27*(3), 149–170.

Jacobi, M. (1991). Mentoring and undergraduate academic success: A literature review. *Review of Educational Research, 61,* 505–532.

Jatko, B. (1995). Using a whole class tryout procedure for identifying economically disadvantaged students in three socioeconomically diverse schools. *Journal for the Education of the Gifted, 19,* 83–105.

Jeffries, R. B. (1994). The trickster figure in African-American teaching: Pre- and post-desegregation. *Urban Review, 26*(4), 289–304.

Jensen, A. (1997). The puzzle of nongenetic variance. In R. J. Sternberg & E. Grigorenko (Eds.), *Intelligence, heredity, and environment* (pp. 42–48). Cambridge, UK: Cambridge University Press.

Johnsen, S. K., & Ryser, G. (1997). The validity of portfolios in predicting performance in a gifted program. *Journal for the Education of the Gifted, 20*(3), 253–267.

Johnson, D. T., Boyce, L. N., & VanTassel-Baska, J. (1995). Science curriculum review: Evaluating materials for high-ability learners. *Gifted Child Quarterly, 39,* 36–43.

Johnson, D. W. & Johnson, R. T. (1993). Gifted students illustrate what isn't cooperative learning. *Educational Leadership, 50*(6), 60–61.

Johnson, S. (1994). Editor's comments. *Journal of Negro Education, 63*(3), 271–273.

Jones, T., & Young, G. S. A. (1997). Classroom dynamics: Disclosing the hidden curriculum. In A. I. Morey & M. K. Kitano (Eds.), *Multicultural course transformation in higher education: A broader truth* (pp. 89–103). Boston: Allyn and Bacon.

Kaestle, C. F. (1983). *Pillars of the republic: Common schools and American society, 1780–1860.* New York: Hill and Wang.

Kalmar, D. A., & Sternberg, R. J. (1988). Theory knitting: An integrative approach to theory development. *Philosophical Psychology, 1*(2), 153–170.

Kanevsky, L. (1990). Pursuing qualitative differences in the flexible use of problem-solving strategy by young children. *Journal for the Education of the Gifted, 13*(2), 115–140.

Kannapel, P., Aagaard, L., Coe, P., & Reeves, C. (2000). Implementation of the Kentucky nongraded primary program. *Education Policy Analysis Archives, 8*(34). Retrieved October 16, 2002 from: http://epaa.asu.edu/epaa/v8n34.html

Kaplan, S. (1986). The grid: A model to construct differentiated curriculum for the gifted. In J. S. Renzulli (Ed.), *Systems and models for developing programs for the gifted* (pp. 180–193). Mansfield Center, CT: Creative Learning Press.

Karnes, M. B., & Johnson, L. J. (1987). Bringing out Head Start talents: Findings from the field. *Gifted Child Quarterly, 31*, 174–179.

Kaufman, M. (1997, February 2). The best for the brightest. *The Washington Post Magazine*, pp. 18–20, 32–35.

Kauffman, S. A. (1991). Antichaos and adaptation. *Scientific American, 46*, 78–84.

Kauffman, S. A. (1993). *The origins of order: Self-organization and selection in evolution*. New York: Oxford University Press.

Kay, S. I. (1991). The figural problem solving and problem finding of professional and semi-professional artists and nonartists. *Creativity Research Journal, 4*(3), 233–252.

Kay, S. I. (1999). The talent profile as a curricular tool for academics, the arts, and athletics. In S. Kline (Ed.), *Gifted education in the 21st century: Issues and concerns* (pp. 47–59). New York: Winston Press.

Keil, F. (1984). Mechanisms in cognitive development and the structure of knowledge. In R. Sternberg (Ed.), *Mechanisms of cognitive development* (pp. 81–99). San Francisco: Freeman.

Keil, F. (1989). *Concepts, kinds, and cognitive development*. Cambridge: MIT Press.

Kennedy, M. (1999). Form and substance in mathematics and science professional development. *NISE Brief, 3*(2), 1–7.

Keys, W., Harris, S., & Fernandes, C. (1996). *Third international mathematics and science study: First national report* (Part 1). Berkshire, UK: National Foundation for Educational Research.

Khattri, N., Riley, K., & Kane, M. (1997). Students at risk in poor, rural areas: A review of the research. *Journal of Research in Rural Education, 13*(2), 79–100.

King, M. L., Jr. (1963/1997). *I have a dream*. New York: Scholastic Press.

Kingsolver, B. (1992). *Animal dreams*. London: Abacus.

Kirschenbaum, R. J. (1998). Dynamic assessment and its use with underserved gifted and talented populations. *Gifted Child Quarterly, 42*(3), 140–147.

Kirst, M. W. (1982). How to improve schools without spending more money. *Phi Delta Kappan, 64*(1), 6–8.

Kitano, M. K. (1994/1995). Lessons from gifted women of color. *The Journal of Secondary Gifted Education, 6*(2), 176–187.

Kitano, M. K. (1997). Gifted Asian American women. *Journal for the Education of the Gifted, 21*(1), 3–37.

Kitano, M. K. (1998a). Gifted African American women. *Journal for the Education of the Gifted, 21*(3), 254–287.

Kitano, M. K. (1998b). Gifted Latina women. *Journal for the Education of the Gifted, 21*(2), 131–159.

Kitano, M. K. (1998c). *Diverse gifted women: Implications for schooling*. Texas Association for the Gifted and Talented. 21st Annual Professional Development Conference. Dallas, December 11, 1998.

Kitano, M. K., & Pederson, K. S. (2002). Action research and practical inquiry. Multicultural content integration in gifted education: Lessons from the field. *Journal for the Education of the Gifted, 25*(3), 269–289.

Kitano, M. K., & Perkins, C. O. (1996). International gifted women: Developing a critical human resource. *Roeper Review, 19*(1), 34–40.

Kitano, M. K., & Perkins, C. O. (2000). Gifted European American women. *Journal for the Education of the Gifted, 23,* 287–313.

Kitchener, K. S., & Brenner, S. G. (1990). Wisdom and reflective judgment: Knowing in the face of uncertainty. In R. J. Sternberg (Ed.), *Wisdom: Its nature, origins, and development* (pp. 212–229). New York: Cambridge University Press.

Kliebard, H. M. (1995). *The struggle for the American curriculum.* New York: Routledge.

Klineberg, O. (1952). Racial and national differences in mental traits. In W. Monroe (Ed.), *Encyclopedia of educational research* (rev. ed.). New York: Macmillan.

Kohn, A. (1998). Only for my kid: How privileged parents undermine school reform. *Phi Delta Kappan. 79*(8), 568–577.

Kozol, J. (1991). *Savage Inequalities.* New York: Crown.

Kozol, J. (1995). *Amazing grace: The lives of children and the conscience of a nation.* New York: Crown.

Kozol, J. (2000). *Ordinary resurrections.* New York: Crown.

Krajcik, J., Blumenfeld, P. C., Marx, R. W., Bass, K. M., Fredricks, J., & Soloway, E. (1998). Inquiry in project-based science classrooms: Initial attempts by middle school students. *The Journal of the Learning Sciences, 7,* 313–350.

Kuhn, T. S. (1996). *The structure of scientific revolutions.* Chicago: University of Chicago Press. (Original work published 1962)

Kulik, J. A. (1992). Ability grouping and gifted students. In N. Colangelo, S. G. Assouline, & D. L. Ambroson (Eds.), *Talent development* (pp. 261–266). Unionville, NY: Trillium Press.

Kulik, J. A., & Kulik, C. L. (1992). Meta-analytic findings on grouping programs. *Gifted Child Quarterly, 36,* 73–77.

Ladson-Billings, G. (1994). *Dreamkeepers: Successful teachers of African American children.* San Francisco: Jossey-Bass.

Learning about real life drives volunteer. (2000, July 23). *The Singapore Sunday Times,* p. 35.

Lee, K. Y. (2000). *From third world to first.* Singapore: Times Editions & Singapore Press.

Lemann, N. (1999, September 6). Behind the SAT. *Newsweek,* pp. 52–57.

Lerner, R. M. (1996). Relative plasticity, integration, temporality, and diversity in human development: A developmental contextual perspective about theory, process, and method. *Developmental Psychology, 2*(4), 781–786.

Lerner, R. M. (1998). Theories of human development: Contemporary perspectives. In R. M. Lerner (Ed.), *Theoretical models of human development: Volume 1, Handbook of Child Psychology* (5th ed.) (pp. 1–24). New York: Wiley.

Levin, H. M. (1990). The educationally disadvantaged are still among us. In J. G. Bain & J. L. Herman (Eds.), *Making schools work for underachieving minority students* (pp. 3–11). New York: Greenwood.

Levine, D. O. (1986). *The American college and the culture of aspiration, 1915–1940.* Ithaca, NY: Cornell University Press.

Link, W. A. (1986). *A hard country and a lonely place: Schooling, society, and reform in rural Virginia, 1870–1920.* Chapel Hill: University of North Carolina Press.

Linn, R. L., Baker, E. L., & Dunbar, S. B. (1991). Complex, performance-based assessment: Expectations and validation criteria. *Educational Researcher, 20*(8), 15–21.

Linn, R. L., & Gronlund, N. E. (1995). *Measurement and assessment in teaching* (7th ed.). Englewood Cliffs, NJ: Prentice-Hall.

Lloyd, L. (1999). Multi-age classes and high-ability students. *Review of Educational Research, 2*(69), 187–212.

Lou, Y., Abrami, P. C., Spence, J. C., & Poulson, C., Chambers, B., & d'Apollina, S. (1996). Within-class grouping: A meta-analysis. *Review of Educational Research, 66,* 423–458.

Lukasic, M., Gorski, V., Lea, M., & Culross, R. (1992). *Underachievement among gifted/talented students: What we really know.* Houston, TX: University of Houston-Clear Lake.

MacPhee, D., Kreutzer, J. C., & Fritz, J. J. (1994). Infusing a diversity perspective into human development courses. *Child Development, 65,* 699–715.

Madaus, G. F. (1994). A technological and historical consideration of equity issues associated with proposals to change the nation's testing policy. *Harvard Educational Review, 64*(1), 76–95.

Mahbubani, K. (1998). *Can Asians think?* Singapore: Times Editions.

Maker, C. J. (1982). *Curriculum development for the gifted.* Austin, TX: PRO-ED.

Maker, C. J. (1994). Authentic assessment of problem solving and giftedness in secondary school students. *The Journal of Secondary Gifted Education, 6*(l), 19–29.

Maker, C. J. (1996). Identification of gifted minority students: A national problem, needed changes and a promising solution. *Gifted Child Quarterly, 40*(1), 41–50.

Maker, C. J., & Nielson, A. B. (1996). *Curriculum development and teaching strategies for gifted learners* (2nd ed.). Austin, TX: PRO-ED.

Margolin, L. (1994). *Goodness personified: The emergence of gifted children.* New York: Aldine de Gruyter.

Margolin, L. (1996). A pedagogy of privilege. *Journal for the Education of the Gifted, 19,* 164–180.

Marland, S. (1972). *Education of the gifted and talented: Report to Congress of the United States by the U.S. Commissioner of Education.* Washington, DC: U.S. Government Printing Office.

Marx, M. (1963). The general nature of theory construction. In M. Marx (Ed.), *Theory in contemporary psychology* (pp. 4–43). New York: Macmillan.

Maxcy, S. (1981). Progressivism and rural education in the deep south, 1900–1950. In R. K. Goodenow & A. O. White (Eds.), *Education and the rise of the new South* (pp. 43–71). Boston: G. K. Hall.

McCall, R. B., Evahn, C. and Kratzer, L. (1992). *High school underachievers: What do they achieve as adults?* Newbury Park: Sage.

McElroy-Johnson, B. (1993). Giving voice to the voiceless. *Harvard Educational Review, 63*(1), 85–104.

McLeod, J., & Cropley, A. (1989). *Fostering academic excellence.* New York: Pergamon.

Meador, K. S., Fishkin, A. S., & Hoover, M. (1999). Research-based strategies and programs to facilitate creativity. In A. S. Fishkin, B. Cramond, & P. Olszewski-Kubilius (Eds.), *Investigating creativity in youth: Research and methods* (pp. 389–415). Cresskill, NJ: Hampton Press.

Meier, D. (1995). *The power of their ideas*. Boston: Beacon Press.

Merton, R. K. (1988). The Matthew Effect in science: Cumulative advantage and the symbolism of intellectual property. *ISIS, 79*, 606–623.

Messick, S. (1994). The interplay of evidence and consequences in the validation of performance assessment. *Educational Researcher, 23*(2), 13–23.

Meyer, J. W. (1994). The evolution of modern stratification systems. In D. B. Grusky (Ed.), *Social stratification in sociological perspective* (pp. 730–737). Boulder, CO: Westview.

Milgram, R. M., & Hong, E. (1994). Creative thinking and creative performance in adolescents as predictors of creative attainments in adults: A follow-up study after 18 years. In R. F. Subotnik & K. D. Arnold (Eds.), *Beyond Terman: Contemporary longitudinal studies of giftedness and talent* (pp. 212–228). Norwood, NJ: Ablex.

Miller, B., & Hahn, K. (1997). *Finding their own place: Youth in three small rural communities take part in instructive school-to-work experiences*. Charleston, WV: ERIC Clearinghouse on Rural Education and Small Schools. (ERIC Document Reproduction Service No. ED 413 127)

Miller, L. (1989). *Musical savants: Exceptional skill in the mentally retarded*. Hillsdale, NJ: Erlbaum.

Miller, N., & Silverman, L. (1987). Levels of personality development. *Roeper Review, 9*, 221–225.

Mohrman, K. (1994). The public interest in liberal education. *New Directions for Higher Education, 85*, 21–30.

Montgomery, D. (1990, March). *Screening for giftedness among American Indian students*. Paper presented at the annual conference of the American Council for Rural Special Educators, Tucson, AZ. (ERIC Document Reproduction Service No. ED 321 918)

Moon, S. M., Jurich, J. A., & Feldhusen, J. F. (1998). Families of gifted children: Cradles of development. In R. C. Friedman & K. B. Rogers (Eds.), *Talent in context: Historical and social perspectives on giftedness* (pp. 81–99). Washington, DC: American Psychological Association.

Morelock, M. J. (1995). *The profoundly gifted child in family context*. Unpublished doctoral dissertation, Tufts University, Medford, MA.

Morelock, M. J. (1996). On the nature of giftedness and talent: Imposing order on chaos. *Roeper Review, 19*, 4–11.

Morelock, M. J., & Feldman, D. H. (1991). Extreme precocity. In N. Colangelo & G. Davis (Eds.), *Handbook of gifted education* (pp. 354–364). Boston: Allyn & Bacon.

Morelock, M. J., & Feldman, D. H. (1993). Prodigies and savants: What they tell us about giftedness and human cognition. In K. A. Heller, F. J. Monks, & A. H. Passow (Eds.), *International handbook of research and development of giftedness and talent* (pp. 161–181). New York: Pergamon.

Morelock, M. J., & Feldman, D. H. (1997). High IQ children, extreme precocity, and savant syndrome. In N. Colangelo & G. Davis (Eds.), *Handbook of gifted education: Second edition* (pp. 439–459). Boston: Allyn & Bacon.

Morey, A. I., & Kitano, M. K. (1997). *Multicultural course transformation in higher education: A broader truth.* Boston: Allyn and Bacon.

Morris, J. M. (Ed.). (1994). *On Mozart.* Cambridge, UK: Cambridge University Press.

Morrow, W. B., & Wilson, R. C. (1961). Family relations of bright high-achieving and underachieving high school boys. *Child Development, 32,* 501–510.

Myrdal, G. (1962). *An American dilemma: The Negro problem and modern democracy.* New York: Harper & Row.

Nachtigal, P., & Haas, T. (1998). *Place value: An educators' guide to good literature on rural lifeways, environments, and purposes of education.* Charleston, WV: ERIC Clearinghouse on Rural Education and Small Schools. (ERIC Document Reproduction Service No. ED 420 464)

Nadler, G., Habino, S., & Farrell, J. (1995). *Creative solution finding.* Rocklin, CA: Prima Publishing.

National Education Commission on Time and Learning. (1994). *Prisoners of time.* Washington, DC: Author.

Navajo Tribe. (1984). *Navajo Tribal education policies.* Approved November 14, 1984 [by the] Navajo Tribal Council. Window Rock, AZ: Division of Education, Navajo Tribe. (ERIC Document Reproduction Service No. ED 289 638)

Neisser, U., Boodoo, G., Bouchard, T. J., Jr., Boykn, A. W., Brody, N., Ceci, S. J., Halpern, D. F., Lehlin, J. C., Perloff, R., Sternberg, R. J., & Urbina, S. (1996). Intelligence: Known and unknowns. *American Psychologist, 51,* 77–101.

Nickerson, R. S. (1999). Enhancing creativity. In R. J. Sternberg (Ed.), *Handbook of creativity* (pp. 392–430). New York: Cambridge University Press.

Nicolis, G., & Prigogine, I. (1989). *Exploring complexity: An introduction.* New York: W. H. Freeman.

Niemi, D. (1996). A fraction is not a piece of pie: Assessing exceptional performance and deep understanding in elementary school mathematics. *Gifted Child Quarterly, 40*(2), 70–80.

Nietzsche, F. W. (1967). *Thus spake Zarathustra* (T. Common, Trans.). New York: Heritage Press. (Original work published 1891)

Nietzsche, F. W. (1974). *The gay science* (W. A. Kaufman, Trans.). New York: Random House. (Original work published 1887)

Nietzsche, F. W. (1990). Maxims and arrows. In R. J. Hollingdale (Trans.), *Twilight of the idols* (pp. 33–37). London: Penguin Books. (Original work published 1889)

Noone, D. J. (1993). *Creative problem solving.* New York: Barron Publications.

Norman, A. (1971). A southeast Texas dialect study. In J. V. Williamson & V. M. Burke (Eds.), *A various language: Perspective on American dialects* (pp. 309–328). New York: Holt, Rinehart, and Winston.

Nothing like a teacher's eye. (1999, September 5). *The Singapore Sunday Times,* p. 2.

Oakes, J. (1985). *Keeping track: How schools structure inequality.* New Haven, CT: Yale University Press.

Ochse, R. (1993). *Before the gates of excellence: The determinants of creative genius.* Cambridge, UK: Cambridge University Press.

O'Connell-Ross, P. (Ed.) (1993). *National excellence: A case for developing America's talent.* Washington, DC: U.S. Government Printing Office.

Oliner, S. P., & Oliner, P. M. (1988). *The altruistic personality.* New York: The Free Press.

Olszewski, P., Kulieke, M. J., & Buescher, T. (1987). The influence of the family environment on the development of talent: A literature review. *Journal of the Education of the Gifted, 11*(1), 6–28.

Olszewski-Kubilius, P. (1995). A summary of research regarding early entrance to college. *Roeper Review, 18,* 121–125.

Olszewski-Kubilius, P. (2000). The transition from childhood giftedness to adult creative productiveness: Psychological characteristics and social supports. *Roeper Review, 23,* 65–71.

Olszewski-Kubilius, P., Grant, B., & Seibert, C. (1993). Social support systems and the disadvantaged gifted: A framework for developing programs and services. *Roeper Review, 17*(1), 20–25.

O'Neill, S., & Shallcross, D. (1994). Sensational thinking: A teaching/learning model for creativity. *Journal of Creative Behavior, 28,* 75–87.

Orr, D. (1995). Re-ruralizing education. In W. Vitek & W. Jackson (Eds.), *Rooted in the land: Essays on community and place* (pp. 226–234). New Haven, CT: Yale University Press.

Osborn, A. (1963). *Applied imagination: Principles and procedures of creative problem-solving* (3rd ed.). New York: Charles Scribner and Sons.

Paris, S. G., Lawton, T. A., Turner, J. C., & Roth, J. L. (1991). A developmental perspective on standardized achievement testing. *Educational Researcher, 20*(5), 12–20.

Passow, A. H. (1982). The relationship between the regular curriculum and differentiated curricula for the gifted/talented. In *Selected proceedings of the first national conference on curricula for the gifted/talented.* Ventura, CA: Ventura Superintendents of Schools Office.

Passow, A. H. (1989). Needed research and development in educating high ability children. *Roeper Review, 11,* 223–229.

Passow, A. H. (1993). National/state policies regarding education of the gifted. In K. A. Heller, F. J. Monks, & A. H. Passow (Eds.), *International handbook of research and development of giftedness and talent* (pp. 29–46). Oxford, UK: Pergamon.

Patton, J. M., & Baytops, J. L. (1995). Identifying and transforming the potential of young, gifted African Americans: A clarion call for action. In B. A. Ford, F. E. Obiakor, & J. M. Patton (Eds.), *Effective education of African American exceptional learners* (pp. 27–67). Austin, TX: PRO-ED.

Peine, M. (1999). *"I just be wanting to go on": Gifted Students talk about waiting in the regular classroom.* Unpublished doctoral dissertation, University of Tennessee, Knoxville.

Pendarvis, E., & Howley, A. (1996). Playing fair: The possibilities of gifted education. *Journal for the Education of the Gifted, 19,* 215–233.

Perkins, H. R. (1976). Gifted underachievers. *North Carolina Association for the Gifted and Talented Quarterly Journal, 2*(2), 39–44.

Peterson, J. S., & Margolin, L. (1997). Naming gifted children: An example of unintended reproduction. *Journal for the Education of the Gifted, 21*(1), 82–100.

Phillips, D. C. (1987). *Philosophy, science, and social inquiry.* Oxford, UK: Pergamon.

Piechowski, M. (1997). Emotional giftedness: The measure of intrapersonal intelligence. In N. Colangelo & G. Davis (Eds.), *Handbook of gifted education,* (2nd ed.). (pp. 366–381). Boston: Allyn & Bacon.

Piirto, J. (1992). *Understanding those who create.* Dayton: Ohio Psychology Press.

Piirto, J. (1999). *Talented children and adults: Their development and education* (2nd ed.). Upper Saddle River, NJ: Prentice-Hall, Inc.

Pirozzo, R. (1982). Gifted underachievers. *Roeper Review, 4*(4), 18–21.

Plomin, R., & Thompson, L. A. (1993). Genetics and high cognitive ability. In G. R. Bock and K. Ackrill (Eds.), *The origins and development of high ability* (pp. 67–78). London: Ciba Foundation.

Plucker, J., & Nowak, J. (2000). Creativity in science for K–8 practitioners: Problem-based approaches to discover and invention. In M. D. Lynch & C. R. Harris (Eds.), Fostering creativity in children, K–8 (pp. 145–158). Boston: Allyn and Bacon.

Plucker, J. A. (1998). Beware of simple conclusions: The case for content generality of creativity. *Creativity Research Journal, 11,* 179–182.

Plucker, Beghetto, & Dow (in preparation). Why isn't creativity more important to educational psychologists? Potential, pitfalls, and future directions in creativity research.

Plucker, J. A., Callahan, C. M., & Tomchin, E. M. (1996). Wherefore art thou, multiple intelligences? Alternative assessments for identifying talent in ethnically diverse and low income students. *Gifted Child Quarterly, 40,* 81–92.

Plucker, J. A., & Gorman, M. E. (1995). Group interaction during a summer course on invention and design for high ability secondary students. *The Journal of Secondary Gifted Education, 6,* 258–272.

Plucker, J. A., & Gorman, M. E. (1999). Invention is in the mind of the adolescent: Evaluation of a summer course one year later. *Creativity Research Journal, 12,* 141–150.

Plucker, J. A., & Nowak, J. (2000). Creativity in science for K–8 practitioners: Problem-based approaches to discovery and invention. In M. D. Lynch & C. R. Harris (Eds.), *Fostering creativity in children, K–8* (pp. 145–158). Boston: Allyn and Bacon.

Plucker, J. A., & Runco, M. (1999). Enhancement of creativity. In M. A Runco & S. Pritzker (Eds.), *Encyclopedia of creativity* (pp. 669–675). San Diego: Academic Press.

Pollard, D. S. (1989). Against the odds: A profile of academic achievers from the urban underclass. *Journal of Negro Education, 58*(3), 297–308.

Popkewitz, T. (1984). Paradigm and ideology in educational research: The social functions of the intellectual. London: Falmer.

Popper, K. (1968). *Conjectures and refutations.* New York: Harper Torchbooks.

Porath, M. (1997). A developmental model of artistic giftedness in middle childhood. *Journal for the Education of the Gifted, 20*(3), 201–223.

Purcell, J. (1993). The effects of the elimination of gifted and talented programs on participating students and their parents. *Gifted Child Quarterly, 37*(4), 177–187.

Pyryt, M. C. (1999). Effectiveness of training children's divergent thinking: A meta-analytic review. In A. S. Fishkin, B. Cramond, & P. Olszewski-Kubilius (Eds.), *Investigating creativity in youth: Research and methods* (pp. 351–365). Cresskill, NJ: Hampton Press.

Rabinow, P. (Ed.) (1984). *The Foucault reader.* New York: Random House.

Reason, P. (1994). Three approaches to participant inquiry. In N. K. Denzin & Y. S. Lincoln (Eds.), *Handbook of qualitative research* (pp. 324–339. Thousand Oaks, CA: Sage.

Reis, S. M., (1999, Winter). Message from the President. *National Association for the Gifted Communique*, p. 1.

Reis, S. M., Gentry, M., & Park, S. (1995). *Extending the pedagogy of gifted education to all students.* Storrs, CT: The National Research Center on the Gifted and Talented.

Reis, S. M., Hébert, T. P., Díaz, E. I., Maxfield, L. R., & Ratley, M. E. (1995). *Case studies of talented students who achieve and underachieve in an urban high school.* [Research Monograph]. Storrs, CT: The National Research Center on the Gifted and Talented.

Reis, S. M., & Renzulli, J. S. (1982). A case for a broadened conception of giftedness. *Phi Delta Kappan, 63*(4), 619–620.

Reis, S. M., & Renzulli, J. S. (1999). Research relating to the development of creative productivity using the enrichment triad model. In A. S. Fishkin, B. Cramond, & P. Olszewski-Kubilius (Eds.), *Investigating creativity in youth: Research and methods* (pp. 367–387). Cresskill, NJ: Hampton Press.

Reis, S. M., Westberg, K. L., Kulikowich, J., Caillard, F., Hébert, T., Plucker, J., Purcell, J. H., Rogers, J. B., & Smist, J. M. (1993). *Why not let high ability students start school in January?* (Research Monograph No. 93106). Storrs, CT: The National Research Center on the Gifted and Talented.

Renzulli, J. S. (1977). *The enrichment triad model.* Mansfield Center, CT: Creative Learning Press.

Renzulli, J. S. (1978). What makes giftedness? *Phi Delta Kappan, 60*, 180–184, 261.

Renzulli, J. S. (1980). Will the gifted child movement be alive and well in 1990? *Gifted Child Quarterly, 24*(1), 3–9.

Renzulli, J. S. (Ed.). (1986a). *Systems and models for developing programs for the gifted and talented.* Mansfield Center, CT: Creative Learning Press.

Renzulli, J. S. (1986b). The three-ring conception of giftedness: A developmental model for creative productivity. In R. J. Sternberg & J. E. Davidson (Eds.), *Conceptions of giftedness* (pp. 53–92). New York: Cambridge University Press.

Renzulli, J. S. (1992). A general theory for the development of creative productivity in young people. In F. Monks & W. Peters (Eds.), *Talent for the future* (pp. 51–72). Assen/Maastricht, The Netherlands: Van Gorcum.

Renzulli, J. S. (1994). *Schools for talent development: A comprehensive plan for total school improvement.* Mansfield Center, CT: Creative Learning Press.

Renzulli, J. S., Reid, B. D., & Gubbins, E. J. (1990). *Setting an agenda: Research priorities for the gifted and talented through the year 2000.* Storrs, CT: The National Research Center on the Gifted and Talented.

Renzulli, J. S., & Reis, S. (1985). *The schoolwide enrichment model.* Mansfield, CT: Creative Learning Press.

Renzulli, J. S., & Reis, S. M. (1986). The enrichment triad/revolving door model: A schoolwide plan for the development of creative productivity. In J. S. Renzulli (Ed.), *Systems and models for developing programs for the gifted and talented* (pp. 216–266). Mansfield Center, CT: Creative Learning Press.

Renzulli, J. S., & Reis, S. M. (1991). The reform movement and the quiet crisis in gifted education. *Gifted Child Quarterly, 35*(1), 26–35.

Renzulli, J. S., & Reis, S. M. (1994). Research related to the schoolwide enrichment triad model. *Gifted Child Quarterly, 38,* 7–20.

Renzulli, J. S., & Reis, S. M. (1997). *The schoolwide enrichment model* (2nd ed.). Mansfield Center, CT: Creative Learning Press.

Renzulli, J. S., & Smith, L. H. (1979). *A guidebook for developing individualized educational programs for gifted and talented students.* Mansfield Center, CT: Creative Learning Press.

Renzulli, J. S., Smith, L. H., White, A. J., Callahan, C. M., & Hartman, R. K. (1976). *Scales for rating the behavioral characteristics of superior students.* Mansfield Center, CT: Creative Learning Press.

Resnick, L. B., & Resnick, D. P. (1992). Assessing the thinking curriculum: New tools for educational reform. In B. R. Gifford & M. C. O'Connor (Eds.), *Changing assessments: Alternative views of aptitude, achievement and instruction* (pp. 37–75). Boston: Kluwer.

Rethinking Schools (2000, Fall). Multiculturalism: What now? A special Rethinking Schools Report.

Revesz, G. (1925). *The psychology of a musical prodigy.* New York: Harcourt Brace.

Reyes, M. de La Luz. (1992). Challenging venerable assumptions: Literacy instruction for linguistically different students. *Harvard Educational Review, 62*(4), 427–446.

Rhodes, C. (1997). Growth from deficiency creativity to being creativity. In M. A. Runco & R. Richards (Eds.), *Eminent creativity, everyday creativity and health* (pp. 247–263). Greenwich, CT: Ablex.

Richert, E. S. (1991). Rampant problems and promising practices in identification. In N. Colangelo & G. A. Davis (Eds.), *Handbook of gifted education* (pp. 81–96). Boston: Allyn & Bacon.

Richie, B. S., Fassinger, R. E., Linn, S. G., Johnson, J., Prosser, J., & Robinson, S. (1997). Persistence, connection, and passion: A qualitative study of the career development of highly achieving African American-Black and White women. *Journal of Counseling Psychology, 44*(2), 133–148.

Rimm, S. B. (1994). *Keys to parenting the gifted child.* Hauppauge, NY: Barron's.

Rimm, S. B. (1995). Impact of family patterns upon the development of giftedness. In C. L. Hollinger (Ed.), *Serving gifted and talented students* (pp. 243–256). Austin, TX: PROED.

Robinson, A. (1986). The identification and labeling of gifted children: What does research tell us? In K. A. Heller & J. F. Feldhusen (Eds.), *Identifying and nurturing the gifted* (pp. 103–109). Toronto: Hans Huber Publishers.

Robinson, N. M., & Noble, K. D. (1991). Social-emotional development and adjust-
ment of gifted children. In M. C. Wang, M. C. Reynolds, & H. J. Walberg (Eds.),
Handbook of special education: Research and practice (pp. 57–76). New York:
Pergamon Press.

Roe, A. (1953). *The making of a scientist.* New York: Dodd, Mead.

Roeper, A. (1990). *Educating children for life: The modern learning community.* Monroe, NY: Trillium Press.

Roeper, A. (1995). *Annemarie Roeper: Selected writings and speeches.* Minneapolis,
MN: Free Spirit.

Roeper, A. (1996). A personal statement of philosophy of George and Annemarie
Roeper. *Roeper Review, 19*, 18–19.

Roeper, A. (1997). Listen to the gifted child. *Roeper Review, 19*, 166–167.

Rogers, K. B. (1998). Using current research to make ?good? decisions about grouping.
NASSP Bulletin, 82 (595), 38–46.

Rogoff, B. (1982). Integrating content and cognitive development. In M. Lamb &
A. Brown (Eds.), *Advances in developmental psychology* (Vol. 2). Hillsdale, NY:
Erlbaum.

Rogoff, B., & Chavajay, P. (1995). What's become of research on the cultural basis of
cognitive development? *American Psychologist, 50*(10), 859–877.

Rubenson, D. L., & Runco, M. A. (1992). The psychoeconomic approach to creativity.
New Ideas in Psychology, 10, 131–147.

Ryder, N.B. (1965, April). The cohort as a concept in the study of social change.
American Sociological Review, 30, 242–258.

Sampson, E. E. (1993). Identity politics: Challenges to psychology's understanding.
American Psychologist, 48(12), 1219–1230.

Sapon-Shevin, M. (1987). Giftedness as a social construct. *Teachers College Record,*
89(1), 39–53.

Sapon-Shevin, M. (1994). *Playing favorites: Gifted education and the disruption of*
community. Albany: State University of New York Press.

Sapon-Shevin, M. (1996). Beyond gifted education: Building a shared agenda for
school reform. *Journal for the Education of the Gifted, 19*, 194–214.

Sapon-Shevin, M. (1999). *Because we can change the world: A practical guide to build-*
ing cooperative, inclusive classroom communities. Boston: Allyn and Bacon.

Sapon-Shevin, M., and Schniedewind, N. (1993). Why (even) gifted children need
cooperative learning. *Educational Leadership. 50*(6), 62–63.

Saracho, O. N., & Gerstl, C. K. (1992). Learning differences among at-risk minority
students. In H. C. Waxman, J. Walker de Felix, J. E. Anderson, & H. P. Baptiste
(Eds.), *Students at risk in at-risk schools: Improving environments for learning*
(pp. 105–136). Newbury Park, CA: Corwin Press.

Sassen, S. (1996). *Losing control? Sovereignty in an age of globalization.* New York:
Columbia University Press.

Schiever, S. (1985). Creative personality characteristics and dimensions of mental functioning in gifted adolescents. *Roeper Review, 7*(4), 223–226.

Schlichter, C. L. (1986). Talents unlimited: Applying the multiple talent approach in
mainstream and gifted programs. In J. S. Renzulli (Ed.), *Systems and models for*

developing programs for the gifted (pp. 352–390). Mansfield Center, CT: Creative Learning Press.

Schuldberg, D. (1999). Chaos theory and creativity. In M. A. Runco & S. Pritzker (Eds.), *Encyclopedia of creativity* (pp. 259–272). San Diego: Academic Press.

Schroeder-Davis, S. (1994). With malice toward some. [Review of Mara Sapon-Shevin's *Playing favorites: Gifted education and the disruption of community*]. *Gifted Education Press Quarterly, 8*(4), 2–7.

Scribner, S. (1986). Thinking in action: Some characteristics of practical thought. In R. Sternberg & R. K. Wagner (Eds.), *Practical intelligence* (pp. 13–30). New York: Cambridge University Press.

Senge, P. M. (1990). *The fifth discipline: The art and practice of the learning organization.* New York: Doubleday.

Shade, B. J., Kelly, C., & Oberg, M. (1997). *Creating culturally responsive classrooms.* Washington, DC: American Psychological Association.

Shavelson, R. J., & Baxter, G. P. (1992). What we've learned about assessing hands-on science. *Educational Leadership, 49*(8), 20–25.

Shavelson, R. J., Baxter, G. P., & Pine, J. (1992). Performance assessments: Political rhetoric and measurement reality. *Educational Researcher, 21*(4), 22–27.

Shaw, M. C., & McCuen, J. T. (1960). The onset of academic underachievement in bright children. *Journal of Educational Psychology, 51*(3), 103–108.

Shore, B. M., Cornell, D. G., Robinson, A., & Ward, V. S. (1991). *Recommended practices in gifted education: A critical analysis.* New York: Teachers College Press.

Shulman, L. S. (1987). Knowledge and teaching: Foundations of the new reform. *Harvard Educational Review, 19*(2) 4–14.

Siegler, R. S. (1996). *Emerging minds: The process of change in children's thinking.* New York: Oxford University Press.

Silverman, L. K. (1997a). Family counseling with the gifted. In N. Colangelo & G. A. Davis (Eds.), *Handbook of gifted education* (pp. 382–397). Boston: Allyn & Bacon.

Silverman, L. K. (1997b). The construct of asynchronous development. *Peabody Journal of Education, 72,* 36–58.

Simon, J. (1995). *Foucault and the political.* London: Routledge.

Simonton, D. K. (1992). The child parents the adult: On getting genius from giftedness. In N. Colangelo, S. G. Assouline, & D. L. Ambroson (Eds.), *Talent development: Proceedings from the 1991 Henry B. and Jocelyn Wallace National Research Symposium on Talent Development* (pp. 278–297). New York: Trillium.

Simonton, D. (1994). *Greatness: Who makes history and why.* New York: The Guilford Press.

Simonton, D. K. (1999a). Creativity from a historiometric perspective. In R. J. Sternberg (Ed.), *Handbook of creativity* (pp. 116–133). New York: Cambridge University Press.

Simonton, D. K. (1999b). *Origins of genius: Darwinian perspectives on creativity.* Oxford, UK: Oxford University Press.

Simonton, D. K. (1999c). Talent and its development: An emergenic and epigenetic model. *Psychological Review, 106,* 435–457.

Singapore population crosses 4 million mark. (2000, September 1). *The Singapore Business Times*, p. 10.

Slavin, R. E. (1990). Achievement effects of ability grouping in secondary schools: A best-evidence synthesis. *Review of Educational Research, 60*, 471–499.

Sleeter, C. E. (1987). Why is there learning disabilities? A critical analysis of the birth of the field in its social context. In T. Popkewitz (Ed.), *The formation of school subjects: The struggle for creating an American institution* (pp. 210–237). London: Falmer Press.

Sleeter, C. E., & Grant, C. A. (1993). *Making choices for multicultural education: Five approaches to race, class, and gender* (2nd ed.). New York: Merrill.

Slife, B., & Williams, R. (1997). Toward theoretical psychology. *American Psychologist, 52*(2), 117–129.

Sloboda, J. A. (1996). The acquisition of musical performance expertise: Deconstructing the "talent" account of individual differences in musical expressivity. In K. A. Ericsson (Ed.), *The road to expert performance: Empirical evidence from the arts and sciences, sports, and games* (pp. 107–126). Mahwah, NJ: Erlbaum.

Smith, B. L. (1993). Interpersonal behaviors that damage the productivity of creative problem solving groups. *Journal of Creative Behavior, 24*(3), 170–185.

Smutny, J. F. (1998). Parenting the gifted child: Enabling and encouraging parents. In J. F. Smutny (Ed.), *The young gifted child* (pp. 217–219). Cresshill, NJ: Hampton Press.

Snow, R. E. (1973). Theory construction for research on teaching. In R. M. Travers (Ed.), *Second Handbook of Research on Teaching* (pp. 77–112). Chicago: Rand McNally.

Southern, W. T., & Jones, E. D. (Eds.). (1991). *The academic acceleration of gifted children*. New York: Teachers College Press.

Spatig, L. (1999, April 19). [Interview with high school students, Mason County, WV].

Spearman, C. (1927). *The abilities of man*. New York: MacMillan.

Spring, J. (1997). *The American school, 1642–1996* (4th ed.). New York: McGraw-Hill.

Stainback, S., & Stainback, W. (1996). *Inclusion: A guide for educators*. Baltimore: Paul H. Brookes.

Stainback, W., & Stainback, S. (1990). *Support networks for inclusive schooling: Interdependent integrated education*. Baltimore: Paul H. Brookes.

Stephens, E. R., & Perry, W. (1991). A proposed state and federal policy agency for rural education in the decade of the 1990s. In A. J. DeYoung (Ed.), *Rural education: Issues and practice* (pp. 333–394). New York: Garland.

Sternberg, R. J. (Ed.). (1984). *Mechanisms of cognitive development*. San Francisco: Freeman.

Sternberg, R. J. (1985a). *Beyond IQ: A triarchic theory of human intelligence*. Cambridge, UK: Cambridge University Press.

Sternberg, R. J. (1985b). Implicit theories of intelligence, creativity, and wisdom. *Journal of Personality and Social Psychology, 49*, 607–627.

Sternberg. R. J. (1986). *Intelligence applied: Understanding and increasing your intellectual skills*. San Diego: Harcourt Brace Jovanovich.

Sternberg. R. J. (1988). *The triarchic mind: A new theory of human intelligence*. New York: Penguin Books.

Sternberg, R. J. (1991). Giftedness according to the triarchic theory of human intelligence. In N. Colangelo & G. Davis (Eds.), *Handbook of gifted education* (pp. 45–54). Boston: Allyn & Bacon.

Sternberg, R. J. (1998). Abilities are forms of developing expertise. *Educational Researcher, 27*(3), 11–20.

Sternberg, R. J. (1999). A propulsion model of types of creative contributions. *Review of General Psychology, 3,* 83–100.

Sternberg, R. J., Conway, B. E., Ketron, J. L., & Bernstein, M. (1981). People's conceptions of intelligence. *Journal of Personality and Social Psychology, 41,* 37–55.

Sternberg, R. J., & Grigorenko, E. (Eds.). (1997). *Intelligence, heredity, and environment.* New York: Cambridge University Press.

Sternberg, R. J., & Lubart, T. I. (1992). Buy low and sell high: An investment approach to creativity. *Current Directions in Psychological Science, 1,* 1–5.

Sternberg, R. J., & Lubart, T. I. (1996). Investing in creativity. *American Psychologist, 51,* 677–688.

Sternberg, R. J., & Williams, W. M. (1996). *How to develop student creativity.* Alexandria, VA: Association for Supervision and Curriculum Development.

Stevenson, H. W., Lee, S-Y., Chen, C., Lummils, M., Fan, L., & Ge, F. J. (1990). Mathematics achievement of children in china and the United States. *Child Development, 61,* 1053–1057.

Stewart, E. D. (1994). On developing gifts and talents: The laureate learning cycle. *The Journal of Secondary Gifted Education, 6*(l), 7–18.

Struck, J. M. (1999). Project Phoenix: A link to multicultural education. *Systems Newsletter, 8*(1), 6–7.

Subotnik, R. F. (1995). Conversations with masters in the arts and sciences: A formative synthesis. *Journal for the Education of the Gifted, 18,* 440–466.

Subotnik, R. F., & Arnold, K. D. (1994). *Beyond Terman: Contemporary longitudinal studies of giftedness and talent.* Norwood, NJ: Ablex.

Subotnik, R. F., & Arnold, K. D. (1995). Passing through the gates: Career establishment of talented women scientists. *Roeper Review, 18,* 55–61.

Subotnik, R. F., & Olszewski-Kubilius, P. (1997). Restructuring special programs to reflect the distinctions between children's and adults' experiences with giftedness. *Peabody Journal of Education, 73*(3&4), 101–116.

Subotnik, R. F., & Steiner, C. L. (1993). Adult manifestations of adolescent talent in science: A longitudinal study of 1983 Westinghouse Science Talent Search Winners. *Roeper Review, 15,* 164–169.

Superintendent of Public Instruction. (1920). *A study of rural school conditions in Ohio.* Columbus, OH: Author.

Swanson, D. B., Norman, G. R., & Linn, R. L. (1995). Performance-based assessment: Lessons from the health professions. *Educational Researcher, 24*(5), 5–11, 35.

Swartz, D. (1997). *Culture and power.* Chicago: University of Chicago Press.

Swiatek, M. A., & Benbow, C. P. (1991). A 10-year longitudinal follow-up of participants in a fast-paced mathematics course. *Journal for Research in Mathematics Education, 22,* 138–150.

Swisher, K., & Tippeconnic, J. (1999). *Next steps: Research and practice to advance*

Indian education. Charleston, WV: ERIC Clearinghouse on Rural Education and Small Schools. (ERIC Document Reproduction Service No. ED 427 902)

Tannenbaum, A. J. (1983). *Gifted children, psychological and educational perspectives*. New York: Macmillan.

Tarnas, R. (1991). *The passion of the Western mind*. New York: Ballantine.

Taylor, B. M., & Frye, B. J. (1988). Pretesting: Minimize time spent on skill work for intermediate readers. *The Reading Teacher, 42*(2), 100–103.

Taylor, C. W. (1968). The multiple talent approach. *The Instructor, 77,* 27.

Taylor, C. W. (1985). Cultivating multiple creative talents in students. *Journal for the Education of the Gifted, 8*(3), 187–198.

Terman, L. M. (1916). *The measurement of intelligence: An explanation of and a complete guide for the use of the Stanford revision and extension of the Binet-Simon Intelligence Scale*. Boston: Houghton Mifflin.

Terman, L. M. (1925–1959). *Genetic studies of genius*. Stanford, CA: Stanford University Press.

Terry, C. A., & Pantle, T. T. (1994). Authentic assessment. *The Journal of Secondary Gifted Education, 6*(1), 44–51.

Tharp, R. G., & Gallimore, R. (1998). *Rousing minds to life: Teaching, learning, and schooling in social context*. Cambridge, UK: Cambridge University Press.

Theobald, P. (1995). *Call school: Rural education in the Midwest to 1918*. Carbondale: Southern Illinois University Press.

Therival, W. A. (1999a). Why are eccentrics not eminently creative? *Creativity Research Journal, 12*(1), 47–55.

Therival, W. A. (1999b). Why Mozart and not Salieri. *Creativity Research Journal, 12*(1), 67–76.

Thomas, G. (1997). What's the use of theory? *Harvard Educational Review, 67,* 75–104.

Thompson, A. (1998). Not the color purple: Black feminist lessons for educational caring. *Harvard Educational Review, 68*(4), 522–554.

Thurstone, L. L. (1938). Primary mental abilities. *Psychometric Monographs* No. 1.

Toffler, A. (1970). *Future shock*. New York: Random House.

Toffler, A., & Toffler, H. (1995). *Creating a new civilization: The politics of the third wave*. Atlanta, GA: Turner.

Tolan, S. (1994). Discovering the gifted ex-child. *Roeper Review, 17,* 134–138.

Tomlinson, C. A. (1996). Good teaching for one and all: Does gifted education have an instructional identity? *Journal for the Education of the Gifted, 20*(2), 155–174.

Tomlinson, C. A., & Callahan, C. M. (1992). Contributions of gifted education to general education in a time of change. *Gifted Child Quarterly, 36,* 183–189.

Tonemah, S. (1991). Perspectives of gifted and talented American Indian education. *Journal of American Indian Education, 31*(1), 3–9.

Torrance, E. P. (1962). *Guiding creative talent*. Englewood Cliffs, NJ: Prentice-Hall.

Torrance, E. P. (1965). *Rewarding creative behavior*. Englewood Cliffs, NJ: Prentice-Hall.

Torrance, E. P. (1971). Stimulation, enjoyment, and originality in dyadic creativity. *Journal of Educational Psychology, 62,* 45–48.

Torrance, E. P. (1972). Can we teach children to think creatively? *Journal of Creative Behavior, 6*, 114–143.

Torrance, E. P. (1977). *Creativity in the classroom: What research says to the teacher.* Washington, DC: National Education Association.

Torrance, E. P. (1987). Recent trends in teaching children and adults to think creatively. In S. G. Isaksen (Ed.), *Frontiers of creativity research: Beyond the basics* (pp. 204–215). Buffalo, NY: Bearly Limited.

Torrance, E. P., & Torrance, J. P. (1973). *Is creativity teachable? (Phi Delta Kappa Foundation Fastback 20).* Bloomington, IN: Phi Delta Kappan Educational Foundation.

Treffert, D. (1989). *Extraordinary people: Understanding "idiot savants."* New York: Harper & Row.

Treffinger, D. J. (1986). Fostering effective, independent learning through individualized programming. In J. S. Renzulli (Ed.), *Systems and models for developing programs for the gifted and talented* (pp. 126–152). Mansfield Center, CT: Creative Learning Press.

Treffinger. D. J. (1991). Future goals and directions. In N. Colangelo & G. Davis (Eds.), *Handbook of gifted education* (pp. 441–447). Boston: Allyn & Bacon.

Treffinger, D. J. (1995). School improvement, talent development, and creativity. *Roeper Review, 18*(2), 93–97.

Treffinger, D. J. & Feldhusen, J. F. (1996). Talent recognition and development: Successor to gifted education. *Journal for the Education of the Gifted, 16*, 181–193.

Treffinger, D. J., Isaksen, S. G., & Dorval, B. K. (1996). Creative problem solving: An overview. In M. A. Runco (Ed.), *Problem finding, problem solving, and creativity* (pp. 223–235). Norwood, NJ: Ablex.

U.S. Department of Education. (1991). *National educational longitudinal study 88: Final report: Gifted and talented education programs for eighth grade public school students.*Washington, DC: Author.

U.S. Department of Education, Office of Educational Research and Improvement. (1993). *National Excellence: A case for developing America's talent.* Washington, DC: Author.

U.S. education chief praises Singapore way. (2000, April 8). *The Singapore Straits Times*, p. 54.

Usiskin, Z. (1987). Why elementary algebra can, should, and must be an eighth-grade course for average students. *Mathematics Teacher, 80*, pp. 428–438.

Vahanian, G. (1961). *Death of God.* New York: George Braziller.

Valle, R., & King, M. (1978). An introduction to existential-phenomenological thought in psychology. In R. Valle & M. King (Eds.), *Existential-phenomenological alternatives for psychology* (pp. 6–17). New York: Oxford University Press.

VanTassel-Baska, J. (1992). *Planning effective curriculum for gifted learners.* Denver, CO: Love Publishing.

VanTassel-Baska, J. (Ed.). (1988a). *Comprehensive curriculum for gifted learners.* Boston: Allyn & Bacon.

VanTassel-Baska, J. (1998b). The development of academic talent: A mandate for educational best practice. *Phi Delta Kappan, 79*, 760–763.

VanTassel-Baska, J. (Ed.). (1998c). *Excellence in educating gifted and talented learners* (3rd ed.). Denver, CO: Love Publishing.

VanTassel-Baska, J. B. (1998d). A national study of science curriculum with high ability students. *Gifted Child Quarterly (42)*4, 200–211.

VanTassel-Baska, J., Bass, G. M., Reis, R. R., Poland, D. L., & Avery, L. D. (1998). A national pilot study of science curriculum effectiveness for high-ability students. *Gifted Child Quarterly, 42*, 200–211.

VanTassel-Baska, J., Johnson, D. T., Hughes, C. E., & Boyce, L. N. (1996). A study of the language arts curriculum effectiveness with gifted learners. *Journal for the Education of the Gifted, 19*, 461–480.

VanTassel-Baska, J., Patton, J., & Prillaman, D. (1989). Disadvantaged gifted learners: At risk for educational attention. *Focus on Exceptional Children, 22*(3), 1–15.

Vaughn, V. L., Feldhusen, J. F., & Asher, W. J. (1991). Meta-analyses and review of research on pull-out programs in gifted education. *Gifted Child Quarterly, 35*, 92–98.

Villa, R. A., & Thousand, J. S., (Eds.). (2000). *Restructuring for caring and effective education: Piecing the puzzle together*, 2nd ed. Baltimore: Brookes Publishing Co.

Vygotsky, L. (1978). *Mind in society: The development of higher psychological processes* (Trans. M. Cole, V. John- Steiner, S. Scribner, & E. Souberman). Cambridge: Harvard University Press.

Wachs, T. D. (1992). *The nature of nurture* (Individual Differences and Development Series, Vol. 3). Newbury Park, CA: Sage.

Wagner, R., & Sternberg, R. J. (1986). Tacit knowledge and intelligence in the everyday world. In R. Sternberg & R. Wagner (Eds.), *Practical intelligence: Nature and origins of competence in the everyday world* (pp. 51–83). New York: Cambridge University Press.

Wake-up call for Singapore youths (2000, February 24). *The Singapore Straits Times*, p. 1.

Walberg, H. J. (1988). Creativity and talent as learning. In R. J. Sternberg (Ed.), *The nature of creativity: Contemporary psychological perspectives* (pp. 340–361). New York: Cambridge University Press.

Waley, A. (1989). *The analects of Confucius*. New York: Macmillan.

Wallach, M. A. (1976, January-February). Tests tell us little about talent. *American Scientist*, pp. 57–63.

Wallach, M. A., & Kogan, N. (1965). *Modes of thinking in young children: A study of the creativity-intelligence distinction*. New York: Holt, Rinehart and Winston.

Wallach, M. A., & Wing, C. W., Jr. (1969). *The talented student: A validation of the creativity-intelligence distinction*. New York: Holt, Rinehart and Winston.

Walzer, M. (1988). *The company of critics: Social criticism and political commitment in the twentieth century*. New York: Basic Books.

Walzer, M. (1997). *On toleration*. New Haven, CT: Yale University Press.

Wang, M. C., & Gordon, E. W. (Eds). (1994). *Educational resilience in inner-city America: challenges and prospects*. Hillsdale, NJ: Lawrence Erlbaum Associates.

Wang, M. C., Haertel, G. D., & Walberg, H. J. (1998). *Building educational resilience*. Fastback 430. Bloomington, IN: Phi Delta Kappa Educational Foundation.

Ward, T. B., Smith, S. M., & Vaid, J. (Eds.). (1997). *Creative thought: An investigation of conceptual structures and processes*. Washington, DC: American Psychological Association.

Ward, V. S. (1980). *Differential education for the gifted*. Ventura, CA: Ventura County Superintendent of Schools. (Original work published 1961)

Webb, C., Shumway, L., & Shute, R. (1996). *Local schools of thought: A search for purpose in rural education*. Charleston, WV: ERIC Clearinghouse on Rural Education and Small Schools. (ERIC Document Reproduction Service No. ED 391 635)

Weiner, J. (1997). *The beak of the finch: A story of evolution in our time*. New York: Knopf.

Weisberg, R. W. (1986). *Creativity: Genius and other myths*. New York: W. H. Freeman and Company.

Weisman, A. (1998). *Gaviotas: A village to reinvent the world*. White River Junction, VT: Chelsea Green Publishers.

Wells, A. S., & Serna, I. (1996). The politics of culture: Understanding local political resistance to detracking in racially mixed schools. *Harvard Educational Review, 66*(1), 93–118.

Weschler, D. (1991). *Manual for the Weschler Intelligence Scale—Third edition*. San Antonio: Author.

Westberg, K. L., Archambault, F. X., Dobyns, S. M., & Salvin, T. J. (1993). *Technical report: An observational study of instructional and curricular practices used with gifted and talented students in regular classrooms*. Storrs, CT: The National Research Center on the Gifted and Talented.

Whitmore, J. R. (1980). *Giftedness, conflict, and underachievement*. Boston: Allyn & Bacon.

Wiggins, G. (1993). Assessment: authenticity, context, and validity. *Phi Delta Kappan, 75*, 200–214.

Wiggins, G. (1996). Anchoring assessment with exemplars: Why students and teachers need models. *Gifted Child Quarterly, 40*, 66–69.

Will straight As matter in tomorrow's world? (2000, March 1). *The Singapore Straits Times*, p. 54.

Williams, R. (1973). *The country and the city*. New York: Oxford University Press.

Williams, R. (1989). *The politics of modernism*. London: Verso.

Winner, E. (1996). *Gifted children: Myths and realities*. New York: Basic Books.

Wise, R. (1991, June). The boom in creativity training. *Across the Board*, pp. 38–42.

Winzer, M. A., & Mazurek, K. (1998). *Special education in multicultural contexts*. Columbus, OH: Merrill.

Witty, P. (1951). *The gifted child*. Boston: D. C. Heath.

Woodhouse, J. (1999, October). *Coming to a pedagogy of place: An autobiographical journey*. Paper presented at the annual meeting of the American Educational Studies Association, Detroit, MI.

Woodson, C. G. (1933). *The mismeasure of the Negro*. Washington, DC: Associated Publishers.

World Bank. (1999, September 15). *World Bank sees "localization" as major new trend in 21st century* (Press Release). (Available World Wide Web: http://www.worldbank.org/.

Worthen, B. R. (1993). Critical issues that will determine the future of alternative assessment. *Phi Delta Kappan, 74,* 444–454.

Yeats, W. B. (1967). *The collected poems of W. B. Yeats.* New York: Macmillan.

Young, R. (1990). *A critical theory of education: Habermas and our children's future.* New York: Teachers College Press.

Zuckerman, H. (1977). *The scientific elite.* New York: Free Press.

About the Editor and the Contributors

Karen D. Arnold is Associate Professor and Director of the Higher Education program at Boston College. She is also director of the Illinois Valedictorian Project, a longitudinal study of academically talented students and co-principal investigator of Generating Leaders: American Rhodes Scholars. Her books include *Lives of Promise: What Becomes of High School Valedictorians* (1995); *Beyond Terman: Contemporary Longitudinal Studies of Giftedness and Talent* (1994, co-edited with Rena Subotnik and Kathleen Noble); *Remarkable Women: Perspectives on Female Talent Development* (1997, co-edited with Rena Subotnik and Kathleen Noble); and *College Student Development and Academic Life* (1997, with Ilda King). In addition to publishing articles and books on talent development in higher education, she has served as Chair of the Committee on the Role and Status of Women of the American Educational Research Association and as Visiting Scholar of the Murray Research Center for the Study of Lives at Radcliffe College. Dr. Arnold is Associate Editor of the *Review of Higher Education*.

Ronald A. Beghetto is Assistant Professor of education at the University of Oregon. His interests include creativity enhancement, improving instructional effectiveness, and teacher change during school reform. He is a former staff member at the Indiana Center for Evaluation at Indiana University.

James H. Borland is Professor of Education and Chair of the Department of Curriculum and Teaching at Teachers college, Columbia University, where he also directs the graduate programs in the education of gifted students. Dr. Borland is the author of the book *Planning and Implementing Programs for the Gifted* and numerous journal articles and book chapters. He is also editor of the *Education and Psychology of the Gifted* series from Teachers College Press, and a former coeditor of the Section on Teaching, Learning, and Human Development of the *American Educational Research Journal*. Dr. Borland has lectured on the education of gifted students across the United States and abroad, and has consulted with numerous school districts, primarily as an evaluator of programs for gifted students. Dr. Borland was awarded the *Gifted*

Child Quarterly Paper of the Year Award in 1994 (with Lisa Wright) and 2000 (with Rachel Schnur and Lisa Wright), in addition to the Award for Excellence in Research from the Mensa Education and Research Foundation (for 1989–1990 and, with Lisa Wright and Rachel Schnur for 1999–2000).

Laurence J. Coleman holds the Daso Herb Chair in Gifted Studies at the University of Toledo. At present he is a professor in the Department of Early Childhood, Physical, and Special Education, teaching courses in teacher education, research methods, and gifted education, and he serves as editor of the *Journal for the Education of the Gifted*. Among his many professional activities, he is most proud of creating, with colleagues from three different fields, an innovative teacher preparation program based on the model of "teaching as a talent"; building the Summer Institute for Gifted Children in 1980 which has been "taken over" by the original students who attended it; writing several papers that have been accepted by his colleagues as meaningful contributions to his field; and continuing to be excited by his work.

Tracy L. Cross is the George and Frances Ball Distinguished Professor of Gifted Studies in Teachers College at Ball State University and the Executive Director of the Indiana Academy for Science, Mathematics, and Humanities. He is founder of BSU's Center for Gifted Studies and Talent Development, serves as editor of the *Roeper Review*, and is the former editor of the *Gifted Child Quarterly* and the *Journal of Secondary Gifted Education*. He writes a regular column on the social and emotional needs of gifted students for *Gifted Child Today* and is the past president of the Association for the Gifted (TAG) of the Council for Exceptional Children. He has authored two books, *Being Gifted in School: An Introduction to Development, Guidance, and Teaching* (with Laurence J. Coleman), and *On the Social and Emotional Lives of Gifted Children*. Dr. Cross's research has focused on the psychosocial and emotional development of gifted children and the relationship between research approach and knowledge construction.

John F. Feldhusen is Distinguished Professor Emeritus at Purdue University and Director Emeritus of the Purdue Gifted Education Resource Institute. He is a past president of the National Association for Gifted Children and of the Educational Psychology Division of the American Psychological Association.

David Henry Feldman is Professor, Eliot-Pearson Department of Child Development, Tufts University and Director of the Developmental Science Group, also at Tufts. He is a specialist on extreme cases of giftedness and creativity and his book on child prodigies, *Nature's Gambit*, won him the

Distinguished Scholar Award of the National Association for Gifted Children in 1988. A developmental psychologist by training, Professor Feldman has published books and articles on cognitive developmental theory, cognitive developmental transitions, and the development of expertise in addition to his work on creativity and giftedness.

Donna Y. Ford is a Professor of Education at the Ohio State University. Dr. Ford earned her Ph.D. in Urban Education, her M.Ed. in Counseling, and her bachelor's degree in Communications and Spanish, all from Cleveland State University, Cleveland, OH. Her research centers on four areas: recruiting and retaining diverse students in gifted education, gifted Black underachievers, multicultural curriculum, and social-emotional needs of gifted diverse students. She is the author of *Reversing Underachievement Among Gifted Black Students: Promising Practices and Programs* and *Multicultural Gifted Education* (with J. John Harris III).

Mary Anne Heng is an Assistant Professor in the Specialised Education Academic Group at the National Institute of Education (NIE), Nanyang Technological University, Singapore. A graduate of Teachers College, Columbia University, she completed her doctoral work with Professors James H. Borland and Herbert P. Ginsburg. At NIE, she is involved in teacher education at the graduate, undergraduate, and diploma levels and was twice awarded the Commendation for Excellence in Teaching. Her research interests include identifying and providing for the learning needs of precocious children and clinical interviewing as a means to understanding children's thinking.

Aimee Howley is Chair of the Educational Studies Department at Ohio University, where she divides her time between paperwork and complaining about paperwork and also coordinates and teaches in the Educational Administration program. She also provides line editing to doctoral students, who wish she wouldn't. Her most recent research considers the effects of educational policies and practices on schools (especially rural schools) and communities. Ongoing scholarship, especially with colleagues Craig Howley and Edwina Pendarvis, focuses on the role of intellect (and intellectual purpose) in U.S. schools.

Craig B. Howley currently directs the ERIC Clearinghouse on Rural Education and Small Schools for AEL, Inc. and co-directs the ACCLAIM Research Initiative at Ohio University. He studies the influence of school and district size on achievement, the relationship between rural education and community, and, more generally, the social and cultural circumstances of education. Craig and Aimee Howley farm 80 acres in Appalachian southeast Ohio, a vantage essential to their scholarship. The Howleys have three children and two grandchildren.

Susan K. Johnsen is an Associate Professor in the Department of Educational Psychology and the Associate Dean in the School of Education at Baylor University. Currently, she directs and teaches courses in the area of education of the gifted at the undergraduate and graduate levels. She is editor of *Gifted Child Today* and serves on the editorial boards of *Gifted Child Quarterly* and *Journal for Secondary Gifted Education*. She is the co-author of the *Independent Study Program* and three tests that are used in identifying gifted students: *Test of Nonverbal Intelligence* (TONI-3, *Screening Assessment for Gifted Students* (SAGES-2), and *Test of Mathematical Abilities for Gifted Students* (TOMAGS). She has published numerous articles and is a frequent presenter at state, national, and international conferences.

Margie K. Kitano serves as Associate Dean of the College of Education and Professor of Special Education at San Diego State University. She co-developed and works with a K–12 school-university collaborative graduate certificate and master's degree program in Developing Gifted Potential. The program combines current theory and research with best practices to support services to gifted students, with special attention to underrepresented populations. Her current research and publications focus on improving services to culturally and linguistically diverse learners.

Paula Olszewski-Kubilius is the Director of the Center for Talent Development at Northwestern University and an Associate Professor in the School of Education and Social Policy. She has worked at the center for over 18 years, during which time she has conducted research and published widely on issues of talent development, particularly the effects of accelerated educational programs on students and the needs of special populations of gifted children, including girls and minority children. Olszewski-Kubilius is active in national- and state-level advocacy organizations for gifted children. She has served as co-editor of the *Journal of Secondary Gifted Education* and on the editorial advisory board of the *Journal for the Education of the Gifted*, *Gifted Child International*, and the *Roeper Review*. She currently is the editor of *Gifted Child Quarterly*.

Edwina D. Pendarvis is a Professor in the Department of Special Education at Marshall University in Huntington, West Virginia, where she coordinates gifted education master's degree and certification programs. With Aimee and Craig Howley, she has co-authored three books and a number of articles on gifted education. Her current research focuses on gifted children in rural Appalachia.

Jonathan A. Plucker is Associate Professor of educational psychology and cognitive science at Indiana University. His research interests include creativity and intelligence, giftedness and talent development, and comprehensive school reform. He is especially interested in improving creativity assessment and enhancement, with an emphasis on problem-based learning.

Sally M. Reis is a Professor and Department Head in the Educational Psychology Department at the University of Connecticut, where she also serves as Principal Investigator of the National Research Center on the Gifted and Talented. She was a teacher for 15 years, 11 of which were spent working with gifted students. She has authored more than 130 articles, 9 books, 45 book chapters, and numerous monographs and technical reports. Her research interests are related to special populations of gifted and talented students, including students with learning disabilities, gifted females, and diverse groups of talented students. She serves on several editorial boards, including that of the *Gifted Child Quarterly*, and is the past president of the National Association for Gifted Children.

Mara Sapon-Shevin is Professor of Inclusive Education in the Teaching and Leadership Department at Syracuse University. A long-time peace and social justice activist, she teaches in the university's Inclusive Elementary and Special Education Teacher Education Program, which prepares teachers for inclusive, heterogeneous classrooms. She is past co-president of the International Association for the Study of Cooperation in Education, and she gives workshops on cooperative learning and cooperative games for the classrooms. Dr. Sapon-Shevin is actively involved in an antiracism project with high school and college students and is the co-author of a seven-session curriculum *ENDINJUSTICE: Eliminating Oppression, Building Allies*. The author of many articles and book chapters on cooperative learning, full inclusion, diversity education, and the politics of gifted education, she is the author of *Playing Favorites: Gifted Education and the Disruption of Community* and *Because We Can Change the World: A Practical Guide to Building Cooperative, Inclusive Classroom Communities*.

Rena F. Subotnik is Director of the Center for Gifted Education Policy at the American Psychological Association. Before she came to APA, and since 1986, Dr. Subotnik was a Professor of Education at Hunter College and research/curriculum consultant to Hunter's laboratory schools for gifted children. She is author of *Genius Revisited: High IQ Children Grown Up* (1993), and co-editor of *Beyond Terman: Contemporary Longitudinal Studies of Gift-edness and Talent* (with Karen Arnold), *Remarkable Women: Perspectives on Female Talent Development* (with Karen Arnold and Kathleen Noble), and the second edition of the *International Handbook of Research on Giftedness and Talent* (with Kurt Heller, Franz Monks, and Robert Sternberg).

Joyce VanTassel-Baska is the Jody and Layton Smith Professor of Education at the College of William and Mary in Virginia, where she has developed a graduate program and a research and development center in gifted education. Formerly she initiated and directed the Center for Talent Development at Northwestern University. She has worked as a consultant on gifted education in over 40 states and for key national groups, including the U.S. Department of Education, the National Association of Secondary School Principals, and the American Association of School Administrators. She is past president of the Association for the Gifted of the Council for Exceptional Children and a current member of the Board of Directors of the National Association of Gifted Children. Dr. VanTassel-Baska has published widely including five re-cent books: *Curriculum Planning and Instructional Design for Gifted Learn-ers* (2001), *Excellence in Educating the Gifted* (1998), *Developing Verbal Tal-ent* (1996) (with Dana Johnson and Linda Boyce), *Comprehensive Curriculum for Gifted Learners* (1995), and *Planning Effective Curriculum for the Gifted* (1992). She also serves as the editor of *Gifted and Talented International*.

Index

Gardner, Howard, 10, 13, 14, 19, 25, 32, 39, 54–58, 146, 155, 194, 202–203, 207, 208, 210–211, 220, 230
Gardner, John W., 52, 59, 147, 149, 150, 153, 157
Gaventa, J., 85
Gaviotas (Weisman), 84
Gay Science, The (Nietzsche), 105
Ge, F. J., 146, 152
Gelman, R., 209
General intelligence, 19–20, 24
Genius
    defining, 9
    view of creativity based on, 220
Gentry, M., 192
Geographical giftedness, 111
George, W. C., 115
Gersten, R., 164
Gerstl, C. K., 152
Getzels, J. W., 210
Giele, J. Z., 234–235
Gifted Child Quarterly, 13
Gifted education, 159–170. *See also* Talent development
    assessment in, 202–203
    critical perspective on, 128
    cultural diversity in, 143–158
    educational inequity and, 115–117, 133–135, 138–139
    equal opportunity in, 151
    without gifted children, 117–121
    limits of academic success and, 47–48
    minority student underrepresentation in, 157
    nature of, 128–129
    nonuniversal development approach and, 23–29
    ongoing problems in, 77–78
    paradigm shift in, 15, 121–124
    promotion of, 128–129
    questionable validity of construct, 113–115
    reexamining curriculum and, 196–200
    rural communities and, 86–88, 93–103
    situating in broader context, 135–142
    social inequity and, 115–117, 133–135, 138–139
    sociological perspective on, 160–170
    thesis-antithesis period in study of, 15
Giftedness
    challenging assumptions about, 130

defining, 9–10, 111–112, 133–134
as developmental, 15–16, 20–29
as evolutionary, 15–20
genesis of concept of, 110
gifted education movement and, 10–11
identifying, 34–36, 38–39, 40–41
IQ tests and, 22, 24, 78–79, 107, 148
maturity and, 154
questionable validity of construct, 107–113
talent development and, 36–38
taxonomy of, 78
Gifted underachievers, 190–193
Gifts
    defined, 26
    nature of, 21
    talents versus, 24–26
Gilmore, W. J., 81
Ginzburg, H. P., 53
Ginzburg, N., 58
Giorgi, A., 76, 79
Glaser, B., 68
Glaser, R., 209
Goddard, H. H., 109
Goldberg, M. D., 114, 160
Goldsmith, L. T., 15–17, 19, 23, 26, 27, 29, 235
Goleman, D., 20
Gonzalez, R., 168
Goodlad, J., 198–199
Gordon, E. W., 167
Gorman, M. E., 224
Gorski, V., 191, 192
Gould, Stephen J., 22, 95, 107, 109, 149–150
Gowan, J. C., 191
Grant, B., 58, 233
Grant, C. A., 89–90
Grantham, T. C., 154–155
Gray, J., 56, 124
Great Books programs, 129–130, 139
Grigorenko, E., 24
Gronlund, N. E., 201
Gross, M., 14, 20, 23–24
Grossman, S. R., 216–217, 220
Grounded theory, 68, 95–96
Grouping
    multi-age, 94, 101
    policy on, 182–183
Guba, E., 73–74
Gubbins, E. J., 191
Guilford, J. P., 10, 64, 216, 218